Hemingway, Cuba, and the Cuban Works

Hemingway, Cuba, and the Cuban Works

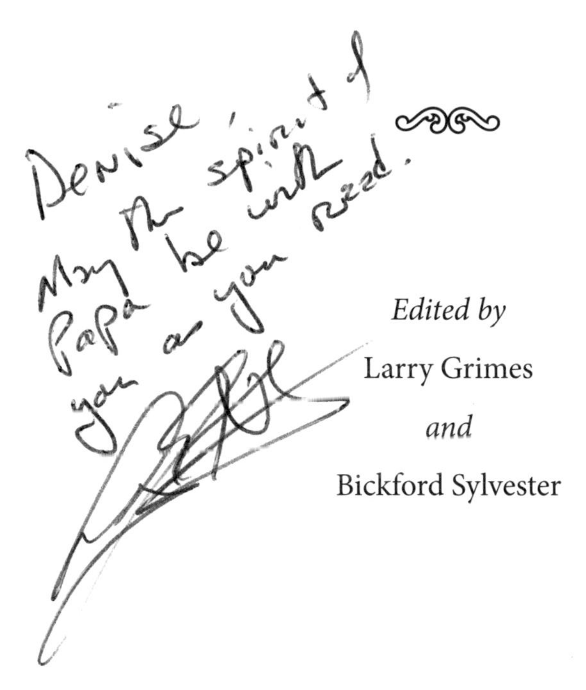

Edited by

Larry Grimes

and

Bickford Sylvester

The Kent State University Press

KENT, OHIO

Library of Congress Catalog Card Number 2013012599
ISBN- 978-1-60635-181-9
Manufactured in the United States of America

Every effort has been made to obtain permission to reproduce copyrighted material in this book.

A list of permissions acknowledgments appears on page ix.

LIBRARY OF CONGRESS CATALOGING-IN-PUBLICATION DATA
Hemingway, Cuba, and the Cuban works /
edited by Larry Grimes and Bickford Sylvester.
pages cm
Includes bibliographical references and index.
ISBN 978-1-60635-181-9 (hardcover) ∞
1. Hemingway, Ernest, 1899–1961—Knowledge—Cuba.
2. Cuba—In literature. I. Title.
PS3515.E37Z617917 2013
813'.52—dc23 2013012599

18 17 16 15 14 5 4 3 2 1

Contents

THE CUBAN WORKS

To Have and Have Not

The Old Man and the Sea

Islands in the Stream

SELECTED BIBLIOGRAPHIES

Permissions Acknowledgments

Every effort has been made to obtain permission to reproduce copyrighted material in this book.

Quotations from letters of Mary Hemingway in "Mary and Ernest: Too Close to See" by A. E. DeFazio appear courtesy of David Meeker.

"The Cuban Revolution" was published originally in Spanish in *Hemingway en Cuba* by Yuri Paporov and appears courtesy of Siglo XXI Editories, Mexico.

Quotations from letters by Ernest Hemingway to Leland Hayward (July 5, 1957; ©2003) and to Waldo Peirce (October 1928; ©2003) in "A Shared Palette: Hemingway and Winslow Homer, Painters of the Gulf Stream," by Charlene M. Murphy, appear courtesy of the Ernest Hemingway Foundation. Quotations in the same essay from a letter by Valerie Hemingway to the author (November 29, 2000) appear courtesy of Valerie Hemingway.

"Hemingway: His Impact in the Cuban Press Today" appears courtesy of Ned Quevedo.

"Hemingway: The Man Who Worked In and Enjoyed Cuba" appears courtesy of Gladys Rodriguez Ferrero.

"Hemingway, Parody or Pastiche?" was written in Spanish by Jorge Santos Caballero as "Hemingway, parody o pastiche?" The publisher and volume editors thank Jorge Santos Caballero for granting permission to include this essay. The English translation appears courtesy of Emma Archer.

"Hemingway's Impressionistic Islands" by James Nagel appears courtesy of the author.

Introduction

LARRY GRIMES

More than thirty years ago on a small "island in the stream" Hemingway scholars gathered to celebrate the opening of the Hemingway Collection at the John Fitzgerald Kennedy Library in Boston. There Michael Reynolds challenged the assembled with an essay, "Unexplored Territory: The Next Ten Years of Hemingway Studies," that has informed and shaped Hemingway research across the years. The agenda Reynolds set was ambitious and has served Hemingway scholars well. However, it had one serious omission—Hemingway's life and work during the Cuban years. Reynolds's references to Cuba are slight and perfunctory; he mentions the Brasch and Sigman inventory of books Hemingway collected during his Cuban years and notes that Hemingway brought copies of T. S. Eliot's poems and essays to Cuba. As for Hemingway's relations with other nations and cultures, Reynolds writes, "another obvious necessary study is Hemingway and Africa. As with Spain, his fascination and his study go beyond the obvious."[1] Reynolds does not call, however, for scholars to carefully investigate the "unexplored territory" that was Hemingway's life and work in Cuba. That was not deemed necessary. Hemingway studies have been slow to correct this omission from their agenda. To date, no scholarly book or collection of essays has been devoted to filling this gap.[2] These essays are offered as a first expedition into that "unexplored territory."

This book includes essays by scholars and journalists from both the United States and Cuba. In the first part, the emphasis is on Hemingway's place in Cuban history and culture, Cuban evaluations of the man and his work, and moments in Hemingway's life as an American in Cuba. These essays look directly at

Hemingway's Cuban experience from perspectives ranging from the academic to the journalistic, allowing different voices to speak and different tones to be heard. In the second part of the collection, scholars analyze specific works by Hemingway from a variety of literary critical perspectives. Their essays provide close and careful readings of certain of Hemingway's longer fictional works, specifically those sharing an explicit Cuban setting. For this reason, much of his posthumously published work from the Cuban years is excluded. The whole collection reminds us that for most of his life Hemingway's primary residence was on Cuban soil, where, as scholars have shown with regard to his European works, he absorbed and wrote from the culture, the place, around him. Taken together, therefore, these essays serve as prolegomena to serious scholarly work that lies ahead.

It is fitting to begin this collection with reflections from Gladys Rodriguez Ferrero, long-time director of the Hemingway Museum (1980–97) and point-person for all things Hemingway in Cuba. Her words capture nicely the deep affection Cubans hold for Hemingway. He is an iconic figure in Cuba, with a status no writer holds in the United States. Her exuberant comments may lean toward hagiography, but for those who have had an opportunity to walk the streets of Havana and Cojimar, they ring true. While she admits that Hemingway has his detractors (see, for example, the essay by Jorge Santos Caballero), she is quick to address the charges against him. She also thoughtfully considers why literary scholars in the United States have neglected Hemingway's Cuban years. She ends with a call to which there has been a positive response in recent years, a call for the Cuban people and the people of the United States to "join forces to preserve this patrimony for future generations."

As noted above, Caballero's essay exemplifies the approach of those Cuban literary-journalists with reservations about Hemingway's work. As Ned Quevedo Arnaiz demonstrates in his bibliography of critical response to Hemingway in Cuba, much of what is written about Hemingway there incorporates political and cultural evaluation into the assessment of Hemingway's literary merit. Caballero's essay is harsh in its criticism of Hemingway's presentation of the Cuban people and their revolutionary heritage. He charges Hemingway with misrepresenting revolutionary characters and with advocating an individualistic stance that denies the social solidarity of the Cuban people.

The essay by Yuri Paporov (with an introduction and comments by me) provides the Russian diplomat's view of Hemingway's relation to and appraisal of Fidel Castro and the Cuban Revolution. My remarks connect the Paporov selection with pertinent materials in the Hemingway Collection at the John Fitzgerald Kennedy Library. In short, Paporov paints a picture of Hemingway as a sympathetic supporter of the revolution. Reporting conversations and interviews with several Cubans who knew and were close to Hemingway during those years, Paporov suggests that Hemingway approved of Castro's movement and provided some funds and arms to Castro followers. He notes that Hemingway wanted to interview Castro and give him advice, and asserts that eventually Hemingway did meet with Castro advisers, proffering advice to them with regard to Castro's visit to the United Nations. He also records Hemingway's sympathetic comments about Cuba and its revolution when he returned from Spain to Havana in May 1959.

David Martens's interview with the now-elderly members of Las Estrellas de Gigi (Gigi's Stars, also known as Gigi's All-Stars) provides solid evidence that Hemingway was deeply involved in the community in which he lived, San Francisco de Paulo in Havana. The memories of these men are fresh, sharp, and affectionate some fifty years after the baseball games were played. Their attitude toward Hemingway does not seem to be that of peasants toward the lord of the manor but rather that of men recalling a patron from their youth. As one sees in Rene Villarreal's memoir, *Hemingway's Cuban Son*, these ball players found in Hemingway a mentor who gave them hope and opportunities that have lasted a lifetime.

Much yet needs to be learned and written about Hemingway and the women in his life during his Cuban years. We have included two essays on the topic: one looks at the turbulent relationship between Hemingway and his fourth wife, Mary Hemingway, as revealed in a series of letters; the other explores fact and myth surrounding his relationship with Jane Mason.

Al DeFazio's essay is woven around letters written by Mary Welsh Hemingway to Ernest from early in their marriage though that "dangerous summer" of 1959. The letters present the marriage in microcosm. Particularly telling is a long letter written in 1959. DeFazio contends that the letters help us understand failures in communication between Mary and Ernest that prevented her from acknowledging his serious health problems. Unable to understand the causes of his erratic behavior, Mary failed to recognize her husband's desperate condition. The letters, and DeFazio's commentary on them, help us to see a tragedy in the making.

William Deibler's essay on Hemingway and Jane Mason challenges the emphatic claim by Cuban writer Enrique Cirules that the two had "an intense and scandalous love affair" in 1934. Deibler presents information suggesting that Cirules's dates and biographical data cannot be trusted, and consequently he questions Cirules's assertions that Cubans saw Hemingway and Mason together everywhere. Deibler suggests, instead, that Cirules's thesis derives from a growing Hemingway myth in Cuba. To quote Deibler, "His legendary reputation as a lover, adventurer, sailor, fisherman, and hunter continued to grow and today, four decades after his death, it pervades the urban landscape." Deibler asserts that Cirules has based his claims on oral history rather than traditional academic research. To prove his point, Deibler cross-checks available facts against Cirules's claims about Hemingway's travel with Jane Mason in the Romano Archipelago. He also researches claims about Hemingway's submarine hunting, as reported by Cirules. His conclusion is that "Cuba is still largely an undiscovered country for Hemingway scholars."

The second part of the collection is composed of scholarly essays examining works from Hemingway's Cuban years that have specific Cuban settings. The first fiction to grow from Hemingway's Cuban experience are the short stories, "One Trip Across" and "The Tradesman's Return," first published in *Cosmopolitan,* and the novel that grew from them, *To Have and Have Not* (1936). The negative reviews of that novel have, perhaps, contributed to the devaluation of Hemingway's work from the Cuban years. The letter and essays included in the *To Have and Have Not* section will, we hope, renew scholarly interest in the novel and in those tumultuous Cuban years that produced it.

To ensure accuracy in his portrayal of recent revolutionary activities in *To Have and Have Not*—activities he was not on the ground in Havana to observe—Hemingway asked journalist Richard Armstrong to provide him with a summary of detailed newspaper accounts of the uprising. Hemingway had known Armstrong at least since 1933, when Armstrong had served as photographer for the Cadwalader marlin expedition. On August 27, 1936, Armstrong sent him a photograph (front plate to our section on *To Have and Have Not*) and a thirteen-page letter full of information. The Armstrong letter was subsumed into the text of the novel, sometimes almost verbatim, in the manner of Hemingway's earlier work with newspaper materials in *A Farewell to Arms.*

The long excerpt from *Cuba y Hemingway en el gran río azul* (*Cuba and Hemingway on the Great Blue River*), a book by Cuban scholar Mary Cruz (here translated by her daughter, Mary Delpino), provides ample evidence that a detailed knowledge of Cuban social, political, and economic history (a knowledge Hemingway certainly had) gives *To Have and Have Not* depth and resonance that U.S. critics have not seen. Cruz's approach to the work is that of critical realism (Marx), an approach most adept at foregrounding Hemingway's nuanced and insightful political analysis of "haves" and "have-nots." Cruz's book in its entirety makes important contributions to the study of Hemingway during the Cuban years. It is my hope that this selection will encourage the publication of an English translation of her book in the near future.

Scott McClintock's essay serves as a fine extension of the work of Mary Cruz. He acknowledges the importance of her Cuban perspective on Hemingway's novel, but suggests that "interculturalism studies" provide an integrative corrective to both American and Cuban national perspectives. McClintock places *To Have and Have Not* in the context of Cuban national literature (particularly Enrique Serpa's novel, *Contrabando*) and the interaction of American and Cuban history. The result of his careful scholarship is an intriguing look at literary influences on Hemingway and a fresh reading of the novel which shows that "the wrong kind of cross-cultural relationships lead equally to perfidy and disaster." McClintock concludes his essay with this important observation: "At home in two countries in the Americas, Hemingway is a vital figure for inter-American literary study, and, I would argue, one must adopt an inter-American framework to read his Cuban fiction well. He is a writer who, more than has generally been appreciated, teaches us that national literatures cannot be studied outside the context of their relationships with other national literatures."

Charlene Murphy's essay cautions us against a simple realist reading of Hemingway's fiction. He explored the Gulf Stream with a naturalist's eyes, but he also knew that truth came through the arrangement of facts by an artist's eye. Murphy demonstrates the profound effect of Winslow Homer's eye on Hemingway's perception of the Gulf Stream through a close reading of the text of *To Have and Have Not* and a careful, detailed comparison of that novel with Homer's "The Gulf Stream." Her essay also offers perceptive commentary on Homer's influence on *Islands in the Stream* and on the thematic concerns of Hemingway's fiction.

In the section devoted to *The Old Man and the Sea,* Alma DeRojas provides a history of the Virgin of Cobre and her place in Cuban culture. Readers of the essays by Grimes and Stoneback will find much useful background in DeRojas's essay.

Two essays on *The Old Man and the Sea* explore religious issues in the novel through specific Cuban ethnic lenses. In my essay, I examine Hemingway's deployment of characters with Afro-Cuban religious markers in two works, *To Have and Have Not* and "Nobody Ever Dies," to establish a baseline from which to read Afro-Cuban religious themes, images, and symbols in *The Old Man and the Sea.* Special attention is paid to the Lukumi orisha Oshun, who is also the Virgin of Cobre, the patron saint of Cuba. H. R. Stoneback takes Santiago's name (St. James) and this panethnicity (Cuban-Spanish Canary Islander) seriously. He establishes links between Santiago and the ancient religious tradition of the Islands of the Blessed, between Santiago and St. James, and between the Spanish mysteries of St. James and the Virgin of Cobre, finally placing the novel firmly in the company of pilgrimage narrative and concluding that *The Old Man and the Sea* is "a complex study of saintliness, not only in the way that it connects with the history and legend of a particular saint, but in its deconstruction (for want of a better word) of Santiago de Compostela, not for purposes of debunking and dismissal, but in order to reconstruct a version of the original, historical saint—anchored in time, immersed in nature, rooted in the bright particularity and dailiness of lived saintliness. That is to say, the old fisherman Santiago is Hemingway's version of Saint James the Fisherman grown old as a fisherman, not as an Apostle."

Yoichiro Miyamoto argues that the text of *The Old Man and the Sea* "functions as a semiotic site where exchanges occur between the colonizer and the colonized." His reading is political in nature, examining cold war tensions as they play out in the text and, more importantly, in the reading of the text. He presents us with a good introduction to Cuban readings of the novel as he contrasts those readings with U.S. commentary. He argues that for U.S. readers, Santiago is a mythological hero, while for Cuban readers he is a national hero. Miyamoto argues that the text both supports and undermines both sets of readings, ultimately providing "transactional space in which different social realities are negotiated."

Through a close reading of "The Undefeated," first published in 1925, Ann Putnam demonstrates that significant continuities of form and vision connect Hemingway's early writing with his later Cuban works, *The Old Man and the Sea* in particular. The close and careful reading she provides in support of her claim does much to counter notions that Hemingway's fiction during the Cuban years is inferior to that created in Paris during the twenties. A sense of tragedy, she argues, pervades these two works: "both Manuel and Santiago have stepped outside the clean, well-lighted place which marks the landscape of mastery and control, and in essence, have entered the 'terrain of the bull.'"

Kim Moreland and Lawrence Broer offer two markedly different readings of *Islands in the Stream.* For Moreland, *Islands* is a "depressing and enervating experience not redeemed by sympathy." Broer, on the other hand, thinks that Hudson (and also Santiago, whom he discusses at length) moves beyond despair and, nourished by an explicitly Cuban landscape, ends his life with a sense of fullness. Read together, these essays confirm Hemingway's capacity, even in his later unfinished, posthumous works, to write powerful, polysemous works. Moreland provides a post-Freudian reading of trauma issues in *Islands in the Stream.* Informed by current trauma theory, especially the work of Cathy Caruth and Judith Hermon, Moreland provides a close reading of the various "drowning incidents" in *Islands.* The result is deep insight into Hudson's complex psychology as artist and person, insights that Moreland extends at the end of her essay into the life of Hemingway as writer and man.

While Moreland focuses on constriction and numbing in *Islands,* Broer explores themes and figures of plenitude. Like Moreland, Broer is attentive to the text and reads it closely. His patient teasing out of these themes and tropes lends great credence to his claim that "central to Hudson's ironic and life-affirming approach to plentitude is not just his knowledge that for every 'bad' there is an off-setting 'good,' but that the good sometimes requires the bad as a regenerating force, and that the existence of the bad may sharpen sensitivity to the good in a way that intensifies one's appetite for experience, and certainly one's ability to make art." After reading these two essays, it would seem that Hemingway's *Islands in the Stream* is a two-hearted text.

Like Charlene Murphy's essay on *To Have and Have Not,* James Nagel's essay reminds us that Hemingway relied on art (aesthetics) and not just naturalistic description to present to the reader the "real thing." Nagel carefully rehearses the aesthetic of impressionism, its impact on imagism and polyphonic prose, and Hemingway's assimilation of that aesthetic. This complex aesthetic, Nagel maintains, remained part of Hemingway's artistic creed throughout his life, even in the "loose and baggy" posthumous work, *Islands in the Stream.* Nagel then presents several closely read passages in *Islands* that demonstrate clearly Hemingway's use of impressionist images and polyphonic prose in that novel. The result of this aesthetic, he asserts, is that "the ultimate tragedy at the end is the impending death of a man who so adores being alive, who has such a rich involvement in the simple things around him, things forever lost in Hemingway's impressionistic *Islands.*"

Joseph DeFalco's essay, like Ann Putnam's and James Nagel's, argues that Hemingway's later works are a continuation of the aesthetic and thematic concerns begun in the twenties. His essay argues that *Islands* is another of Hemingway's attempts to enter the ring with the great authors of literature. This time he takes on Homer's *Odyssey* (and, by extension, Joyce's *Ulysses*). DeFalco makes a very important point early in his essay. Unlike Joyce, who foregrounded Homer's work in *Ulysses,* Hemingway backgrounded it in *Islands.* Hemingway, I think, employed this backgrounding technique in many of his works, and perhaps more scholars should join DeFalco in searching out such backgrounded material in his work. DeFalco then reads the text of *Islands* with careful attention to parallels with *The Odyssey* and makes a strong case for a direct, though backgrounded, connection between these works.

To round out this exploration of Hemingway's life and work in Cuba, the book ends with two bibliographies that give an overview of the lively interest in and response to Hemingway and his works within Cuba itself. Kelli Larson provides a comprehensive annotated list of scholarly treatments of Hemingway's Cuban fiction. In his bibliography, Ned Quevedo Arnaiz broadens the focus to include not only Cuban publications about Hemingway's Cuban works but also ones examining Hemingway's life in Cuba, and also includes a list of Hemingway's works that have been published there—which is not yet all of them, "a fact," comments Quevedo, "to be regretted." Both bibliographies should be useful to scholars planning further forays into the neglected territory of Hemingway's Cuban fiction.

I end with special thanks to those who organized and participated in the First Hemingway International Colloquium held in Havana, Cuba, in July 1995. They opened the eyes of fans, scholars, and preservationists alike to the "undiscovered country" that is Hemingway's life and work during the Cuban years.

Notes

1. Michael Reynolds, "Unexplored Territory: The Next Ten Years of Hemingway Studies," *College Literature* 7 (Fall 1980): 198. Reynolds's reference (189–90) is to James D. Brasch and Joseph Sigman, *Hemingway's Library: A Composite Record* (New York: Garland Publishing, 1981). Throughout his essay Reynolds uses his wonderful title phrase "unexplored territory" to describe new research challenges facing Hemingway scholars. I have appropriated that phrase.

2. Bickford Sylvester pioneered the study of Hemingway and Cuba in his essay, "The Cuban Context of *The Old Man and the Sea*." In *The Cambridge Companion to Hemingway.* Edited by Scott Donaldson (Cambridge: Cambridge Univ. Press, 1996), 243–68. Michael Reynolds treats Hemingway's Cuban years in the fifth volume of his biography: *Hemingway: The Final Years* (New York: W. W. Norton and Co., 1999). He was not able to make the trip to Cuba, where he could have done the excellent literary detective work that marks his earlier volumes. Hilary Hemingway and Carlene Brennen published a narrative of Hemingway's life in Cuba that is wonderfully illustrated but lightly researched: *Hemingway in Cuba* (New York: Rugged Land, 2003). Two very useful memoirs have been published in the past decade: Walter Houck's essays in the *North Dakota Review,* "On the Gulf Stream on Board Hemingway's *Pilar,*" 65:3 (1998): 70–90, and "In 1949 Havana, Revolutionaries as Literary Inspiration," 70:4 1 (2003): 96–213; see also Rene Villarreal's memoir, *Hemingway's Cuban Son* (Kent, OH: Kent State Univ. Press, 2009). Paul Hendrikson's most original work, *Hemingway's Boat* (New York: Alfred A. Knopf, 2011), presents wonderful windows into Hemingway's life in Cuba. To our knowledge, only Larry Grimes and Philip Melling have published careful scholarly essays on Cuban influences in Hemingway's fiction (see works cited page in Grimes's essay).

Cuba

Hemingway

The Man Who Worked In and Enjoyed Cuba

GLADYS RODRIGUEZ FERRERO

No, here in Cuba Hemingway can never be considered as only a writer, even less as a man who did not know Cuba's geography and reality. Never. Hemingway is much more for Cubans. Hemingway has never been considered as a man of sterile actions, but as a man whose life and work were aimed at defending humanist morals and justice, aspects widely reflected in his literary and journalistic work as well as in his public and private life.

No, we need not be reminded of Hemingway's presence in Cuba by official decree. We do not conceive of Hemingway in that way. You can walk along the streets in Havana and ask anyone who Hemingway is. Although they may not have read any of his works, they will tell you something about the author. Our image of Hemingway is filled with anecdotes that contribute to the mystery, the myth, and the legend of this man.

Hemingway spent his years in Cuba primarily in two humble towns in Havana: Cojimar and San Francisco de Paula, both poverty-stricken places where the face of wanton hunger was common and where people fought daily for existence. In these places especially, people remember the absent "Mister Way," as we called him, with nostalgia.

If you go to Cojimar, you will find that the people of this small town by the sea know him well. They will show you his monument, the first in the world, erected by Boada, a Cuban sculptor, with bronze spare parts, pieces, and screws, all collected by the people. The monument is an homage to the writer, offered by the grateful Cuban people, who see themselves immortalized in literature in the figure of a fisherman.

In the streets of San Francisco de Paula, the humble people will offer many stories about "Mister Way," the American who lived at Vigía Farm. This tall, strong man walked the streets of the neighborhood, permitted the local children to play on his property, and sometimes attended mass in the church, in general behaving very differently from Frank Stinhaert, the other American who lived near by. The old people who were the children of that epoch remember Hemingway's occasional efforts to alleviate their daily problems and speak gratefully of Hemingway's helping hand, a quality well hidden in his iceberg.

Hemingway's contacts with Cuba began in 1928, when the writer settled in Key West and from there began to visit Cuba, among other places. Those contacts with Cuba became more and more frequent, until Hemingway decided to establish his residence there. From that time on, Hemingway's life began to change radically, especially in regard to his use of the environment and his portrayal of it in his writing. We see this in his hunting and fishing scenes: fur is replaced by feathers, the river by the deep blue sea. He bought the yacht *Pilar,* on which he learned to fish for marlin, soon becoming an expert.

In Cuba during the twentieth century, Hemingway had both his champions and his detractors, even among those who still love him. He made friends with some members of the Cuban intelligentsia: Enrique Serpa, Fernando G. Campoamor, Antonion Gattorno, Lino Novás Calvo. But other Cuban intellectuals were more critical. The famous Cuban novelist and poet José Lezama Lima, for example, thought that Hemingway's participation in the war and in big-game hunting in Africa was what had made him famous.

Members of Cuba's intelligentsia, like those everywhere, have used a variety of criteria, sensitivity to different issues, in forming their individual opinions of the American writer. Since they have been influenced to a greater or lesser degree by Hemingway, their subsequent responses to the man and his work can be contradictory, as the following comments by intellectuals roughly contemporary with Hemingway illustrate.

Nicolás Guillén, named Cuba's poet laureate in 1961, and Alejo Carpentier, winner of the Miguel de Cervantes Prize in 1977, met Hemingway in Paris and later during the Spanish Civil War. Carpentier recreated a passage of Hemingway's real life in his novel *La Consagración de la Primavera.* He even compared Hemingway with the Cuban journalist and writer Pablo de la Torriento Brau, who died in Spain during its civil war, considering that Pablo's style was similar to Hemingway's "brutal style." There are studies in Cuba related to both styles.

José Antonio Portuondo, renowned Cuban critic and essayist, criticized Hemingway's portrayal of revolutionaries, noting that Hemingway himself was very far from being one himself. In 1952, Portuondo stated that the American author "followed from Cuba, with anguished attention, the political process in the United States"—that is, the effect of the Red Scare on that process.

Other Cuban intellectuals differ over the purpose of Hemingway's fiction and its portrayal of Cuba and Cubans. Cuban writer Edmundo Desnoes, for example, considers *The Old Man and the Sea* to be an allegory of the human condition—the relationships of men and nature—more than a novel with a Cuban setting. Cuban movie director José Massip evaluates the novel's protagonist, Santiago, as characteristic neither of our identity, nor of the Cuban working class; however, he acknowledges *The Old Man and the Sea* (*OMS*) as one of Hemingway's best literary achievements. The poet Sidro Ramos, in contrast, contends that *The Old Man and the Sea* strongly reflects Hemingway's love for Cuba and its people. Novelist, critic, and essayist Mary Cruz also believes that Hemingway's appreciation for Cuba became a significant strand in his fiction, claiming that "after his first visits to Cuba, he wrote each time more accurately about Cuba and its people." While Hemingway's decision to establish himself in Cuba may have been guided by economic reasons and by Cuba's proximity to the Gulf Stream, Cruz argues that "the proximity to the humble people above all, allowed him to understand life and its fundamental questions better." Cuban essayist and novelist Enrique Cirules echoes Cruz's contention of the importance of Hemingway's contact with the realities of life in Cuba, stating that "the most impressive thing is . . . that the myth of Hemingway in Havana began not [at] the literary level but in his relationship with daily life, with the human beings."

The opinions of the current generation of Cuban intellectuals may contrast with those of Hemingway's contemporaries, but they still reflect his stature. In the dawn of the twenty-first century, Cuba's intelligentsia continue to feel the imprint of Hemingway, as symbolized by the "bronze god" erected in Cojimar. Compare the remarks of the earlier generations with this one from Senal Paz, author of the story upon which the famous movie *Fresa y Chocolate* is based. Pal affirms that

> for Cuban readers—and even more for writers—Hemingway is like measles, something you must go through at some point in your life. When this moment comes, you only want to read and know and talk about Hemingway, go to the Floridita and Cojimar and fish for marlins and write following the iceberg technique, using many "ands"; I had resisted myself to the measles because I thought of Hemingway as an arrogant American, and did not feel attracted by his writing or his world or the iceberg technique in which he put [in] one-eighth of the story and reader had to put [in] the other seven-eights.

> I thought it was [a] swindle. But finally, and since it had to happen living in this island, I was contaminated with the virus.

This comment explains the way in which this current generation of writers is interested in and understands Papa's *The Old Man and the Sea* and *Islands in the Stream* (*IS*). This is the way in which they end up reading most of his works, if sometimes reluctantly. And they feel strongly the weight and influence of his style and his theory about what one should write.

When I analyze such points of view, again and again I ask myself why Cuba has been so neglected by Hemingway biographers in discussions about the last twenty years of the writer's life. Cuba was so important to his life and his work. Cuba, and especially Finca Vigía, his house in suburban Havana, represented Hemingway's consolidation as a writer, his reaffirmation as a human being, and his identification with this people and its idiosyncrasies. Let us look at some samples of how Cuban elements are integrated into his work.

In addition to the many chronicles and articles—especially his fishing chronicles—in which he mentions Cuba, Hemingway also dedicated a great part of *The Green Hills of Africa* to Cuba. In *The Fifth Column,* the only play he ever wrote, he returns to a Cuban setting, while the story "Nobody Ever Dies" is filled with detail, well hidden in his iceberg, that recreates the Cuban environment. Three of Hemingway's novels, namely *To Have and Have Not* (*THHN*), *The Old Man and the Sea,* and *Islands in the Stream,* are intimately related to Cuba. They form a structural unity, reflecting different aspects of a single leitmotif: alone, a human being is worth nothing. The Cuban environment undergirds Hemingway's literary development.

In the Cuban works themselves, Hemingway intermingles fishermen and the population in general. From this fact we can see in his later works the prolific recreation of issues related to Cuban life before 1959.

Some question the depth and accuracy of Hemingway's understanding of Cuban reality. Was he not distanced, they ask, from the political environment of the thirties, forties, and fifties in Cuba? How did he get to know such political groups as ABC or Joven Cuba? We know, though, that in 1936 he asked his friend Dick Armstrong to collect newspaper testimonies and materials in order to take a closer look at Cuban reality and the violence of the Batista regime. Is it not that reality we find in his novel *To Have and Have Not?* His contact with the sociopolitical situation in Cuba at that time is clearly evident, here and elsewhere.

Many have spoken about Hemingway's superficiality when he puts into Santiago's mouth, in *The Old Man and the Sea,* allusions to the Big Leagues in baseball, when he speaks of DiMaggio or the Detroit Tigers. But in Cuba at that time, the media did broadcast daily information about baseball from the United States. Disregarding this fact would be like forgetting the presence of Cuban players in the Big Leagues in the United States before 1959, Cubans like Adolfo Luque, Orestes Minoso, Camilo Pascual, or Willy Miranda. Santiago's baseball allusions show that Hemingway knew the habits, customs, and preferences of the Cuban people.

Santiago is Cuban. His ethnicity—whether he was born in Cuba or the Canary Islands—is not important because both the ethnic heterogeneity of the Caribbean and the Spanish influence are strong in Cuba. Santiago embodies the fishermen of Cojimar, men like Manuel, Anselmo, Jorge, and Gregorio Fuentes. Santiago is the sum of all the fishermen who came from many parts of Cuba and many parts of the world to live, work, and die in Cojimar. The Russian critic Ivan Kashkin affirms that Hemingway's writing reflects his deep respect for the brave Cubans.

So did Hemingway disregard Cuban reality? Was he distanced? On what ethical basis can we measure Hemingway's moral behavior toward the Cuban reality? Only through his literary creation, we believe, which transcends without poses.

We remember, too, that when he was given the Nobel Prize in 1954, Hemingway agreed to give a press conference to Cuban journalists and refused to give one to the foreign press at that time. Why did he do that?

Many modern critics examine Hemingway's work in the context of other American writers while ignoring Cuban writers. We see studies, for example, that compare *The Old Man and the Sea* with works by Hawthorne, Jack London, and Melville, but fail to mention works by Cuban authors, published before Hemingway's, that deal with similar themes. In fact, Hemingway's Cuban works have many points of contact with those of some Cuban writers. In 1891, for example, Cuban novelist and journalist Ramón Meza published in the newspaper *La Habana Elegante* a story of a fisherman in his daily struggle for a living. Likewise in 1938, Enrique Serpa, journalist, novelist, short story writer, and Hemingway's friend, published his novel *Contrabando,* which won the National Award in Cuba; Hemingway's *To Have and Have Not* has many points of contact with this novel. Finally, what can we say about Carlos Montenegro's work *Hombres sin Mujer,* whose title coincides with the title given by Hemingway to a collection of his stories published in 1927 as *Men Without Women?*

Another Cuban writer with whom Hemingway had many connections is Lino Novás Calvo, who first translated *The Old Man and the Sea* into Spanish. Calvo was closely linked with the Cub, an intelligentsia during the thirties, forties, and fifties, as I said before. Calvo was especially linked with the writers of the group called Orígenes (1944–56), a name also given to a magazine on arts and literature published by a literary circle that gathered the best minds of those decades. This magazine received unpublished works of Cuban and foreign authors.

Both in Hemingway's work and in his own life—especially in his associations with Cuban artists and their works—we find evidence supporting his accurate knowledge of Cuba, our people, and our social and political situation over time.

The clouds begin to fade away as we clear up these questions about whether Hemingway was really detached from our reality and our intelligentsia. Was he just a migratory bird, as many have presented him? No, "Mister Way" is frozen in our memory, and we are warmly researching the places where he lived and worked to build our understanding of him as a live person.

Ernest Hemingway is one of the most famous and most widely read writers in Cuba. Although in Cuba the first place belongs to José Martí, the second, perhaps, belongs to Ernest Hemingway. His legend is already part of the Cuban culture. This giant of North American letters revolutionized literature in English. But it was in Cuba that the seed of his artistic métier germinated. It was in Cuba that he grew as a mature writer and perfected his style. It was in Cuba that he wrote *The Old Man and the Sea,* his best and most acclaimed novel.

While we can not divorce Hemingway's life and work from a part of the North American realistic school, we in Cuba find a symbolic and synthetic realism in the link between his life and work. He is one of his characters. He wrote about the terrible things in life, not about what could be done to change them. He believed only in what he could see. He wrote only about that which he knew very well. That is why he could write about the Cuban people and environment, immortalizing both in his art.

How, then, do we explain Cuba's neglect by Hemingway biographers, the ill feeling against the Cuban period of his creative life as a writer? Perhaps, as writer Norberto Fuentes has suggested—and here I agree with him—that neglect reflects possible American resentment that Hemingway preferred to live and write not in his native country, but in Cuba. However, we must make a reflection at this point. It is true that Hemingway found in Cuba things that made him decide to establish a permanent residence there. But, above all, Hemingway and his work are the patrimony of both the Cuban people and the people of the United States. His earthly belongings, the dearest ones, are found in both countries, and it is imperative that we join forces to preserve this patrimony for future generations.

Life is a long and wide road that narrows as we walk on it; Hemingway selected the road not taken, and this has made all the difference for posterity. And here in Cuba, he's still alive.

Hemingway, Parody or Pastiche?

JORGE SANTOS CABALLERO

TRANSLATED BY EMMA ARCHER

To my son
Men are about knowing their present;
things concerning the future could only be
managed by god, the very and absolute
owner of all lights.
—Constantine Cavafy

In his novel *To Have and Have Not,* the American writer Ernest Hemingway created his main character, Harry Morgan, on a restricted and limited model, something like a tough guy, full of pragmatism. But Morgan has other qualities, too. His charismatic behavior helps him cope with difficult or dangerous situations without ever having to work out a clear plan for proceeding in life. Rather, he reacts to the trouble of the moment, depending on his ability to influence and control events. This reactive and impulsive behavior excites him and makes him feel special, distinguished. He may even instigate trouble for the thrill of standing on thin ice, because it pleases him to do so, not because life has imposed such danger on him.

To Have and Have Not was written more than seventy years ago, and when you review its plot, you realize that the story is somehow denigrating, essentially negative about human life. The protagonist is neither influential nor compelling as he interacts with the other flat characters in the novel. This man, Harry Morgan, runs some risks, but he runs them because he wants to, not because he has to. He is a kind of bootlegger who is willing to do anything for money. He kills a Chinese man (someone who even provided him with substantial business) "just because," and he gets involved in an adventure with supposed Cuban revolutionaries until he finds his death.

Cuban readers of *To Have and Have Not* perceive a sort of offence to our identity when, on Harry's boat, a so-called revolutionary, the young idealist, talks about his murderous partner: "Roberto is bad. He is a good revolutionary but a bad man. He kills so much in the time of Machado he gets to like it. He thinks it is funny to kill. He kills in a good cause, of course. The best cause" (*THHN* 158; *TYNT* 134). And I ask myself, What kind of unity and cohesion does this group of supposedly revolutionary men have? Evidently, the young idealist regards one of his colleagues, Roberto, as despicable. It logically follows that Roberto is a chronic and *indiscriminate* killer, not a revolutionary. We cannot confuse the actions of killers like this with the actions of people who deserve the term *revolutionary* or *revolutionist,* as understood by Cubans. The Cuban people conceive of a revolutionary as one who may kill, but only in support of a principled cause—one who is a *discriminating* killer, killing only in the specific cause of solidarity in the class struggle.

Hemingway fails to distinguish between these two kinds of fighters when he has this young bank robber refer to Roberto as a "revolutionary." Clearly, from the boy's comments about Roberto, we must conclude that the robbers are members of ABC, an organization active in Cuba until Machado's overthrow in 1933. The ABC was anarchist in its activities and fascist in its thinking. Its members were Cubans who had, it is true, supported the anti-Machado fighters, but they were not themselves really fighting for Cuban independence. They had little or no base of ideological values and were embroiled in social and financial activities that indicate weak moral principles. They fought only for their own economic gain and political power. So Roberto's idealistic young partner is wrong to believe he and his group work with an organization that kills in "a good cause," simply because their violence sometimes supports good people. A revolutionary's main motivation must be dedication to the class struggle and the solidarity and freedom of the Cuban people. In this book, then, we see only "social fighters" who lack that essential commitment, a portrait that leaves readers of the book with a false, negative impression of Cuban revolutionaries.

Readers are also confused in a second way. Hemingway depicts these self-centered social fighters as acting on their own, committing their crimes, as I have said, without really being part of any decent organized moral authority. Yet true Cuban revolutionaries also *appear,* sometimes, to be acting independently, when their acts of violence are actually in the cause of solidarity in the class struggle. Therefore, the novel risks presenting all people who take justice into their own hands as criminals. And it is not fair for Cuban revolutionaries to be misrepresented in that way. To be historically accurate, as he was famous for being in his other works, Hemingway should have added information identifying the robbers as members of ABC in *To Have and Have Not.*

Hemingway's intentions in the novel may have been good. There is no evidence in the book of any subterfuge meant to criticize the Cuban people's revolutionary struggle. But by failing to differentiate between people devoted to that struggle and people representing mere passing trends and tendencies, Hemingway has committed an injustice. If Harry Morgan—being just an adventurer without principles—was to be shown meeting "pseudo-revolutionaries" in his last adventure, Hemingway should have specified that these bank robbers were members of ABC. If he had explained that connection in a fair and accurate way, he might well have faced their blazing guns afterward--rhetorical guns and maybe real guns—but his work would have been true and safe. Mary Cruz has explained something about this in her book *Cuba and Hemingway on the Great Blue River.*

I will admit that it is often worthwhile for a writer to change a historical fact in order to beautify it or to remove uninteresting details. It is also permissible to change time, or to use this or that stylistic device to express the author's point of view. However, to misrepresent ideological principles or distort well-defined facts assaults a people's dignity. Such misrepresentation constitutes an unbearable lack of respect for the culture being portrayed.

All my life, I have defended Hemingway's attitude toward his life and all his works. There is much evidence of my support. But everything changes with this novel, *To Have and Have Not.* When I read it most carefully, delving deeply into its plot, I conclude that writing it was the greatest blunder the God of Bronze of North American literature ever made.

One wonders if Hemingway was purposely imitating the retrogressive position of an uninformed North American tourist as an artistic device to illustrate the erroneous opinions that can be corrected to improve our situation. That would be one way of accounting favorably for Hemingway's having seemed to overlook important information. I believe that Mary Cruz perceptively arrived at this conclusion when she wrote: "Harry Morgan's is a distorted vision of Cuba and the Cuban situation, as it was then. And his view is still the vision of most North Americans" (154). Her statement supports my point of speculation, but it doesn't satisfy me. I must infer, as many people have, that Hemingway was still evolving his view as he learned more and more about Cuban life, and that he was relatively uninformed when he wrote this book. Still, everybody knows that Hemingway was not a boy when he was learning about Cuba, nor was he an emerging writer when he wrote *To Have and Have Not.* He had experienced the scenes of World War I, Paris, and the miseries of his own country in the Great Depression. So how can we finally explain his limited understanding of similar problems in Cuba?

When comparing Hemingway to other writers, we can see the way he reflected in his works his vivid experiences from real life. But in *To Have and Have Not,* he portrays inwardly violent characters, characters unworthy either of admiration or of being seen as parallels to any of his other protagonists. What really attracts the reader's attention in Hemingway's other literary works—his simple style, his daring statements, even his violence—all seems incapacitated, frozen, in this novel. As a result, we must agree with those who conclude that its protagonist, Harry Morgan, is not a memorable character; rather, he is an undesirable person.

Our history and the real revolutionaries of that time were quite different from those portrayed in *To Have and Have Not.* The honorably motivated freedom fighters were workers and students who fought idealistically for the sake of the country; they were not criminals or killers. If in Cuban society some bandits emerged at that time, they were bound to an older minority of people who had been affected by a corrupted system. We cannot deny that some such pseudo-revolutionaries were involved. But the ethical principles of a majority of the Cuban people were not shown in Hemingway's novel.

It is noteworthy that only when Harry Morgan is close to death are some characteristics of his innermost feelings revealed, even though they were supposedly hidden all his life. To be honest, though, it is difficult to discern whether his attitude in the last encounter on the boat comes from a wish for revenge after the killing of his friend Albert, from fear of being killed himself, or from an increased awareness of his subconscious emotions, as a result of his regret. Whatever the impetus, his behavior certainly corresponds to that of one who fears death, one who fears being killed or thrown into the sea, and is concerned with nothing but such fears.

For Harry Morgan, and then for Hemingway, Sartre's "nothing" had no meaning, but for us, the Cubans, that "nothing" was everything: it was the pseudo-republic that had been imposed on us; it was a frustrated revolution; it was a life full of uneasiness, miseries, and abandonment. For this country, therefore, no alternative was possible: either we would fight for our freedom or we would die living immorally rather than honorably. Thus, we may ask a question about this novel: what part of it is authentically Cuban?

Note

This essay is an abridged translation of the original.

Works Cited

Cruz, Mary. *Cuba y Hemingway en el gran río azul.* Havana: UNEAC, 1981.
Hemingway, Ernest. *Tener y no tener.* Barcelona: Editorial Edhasa, 1989.
———. *To Have and Have Not.* New York: Charles Scribner's Sons, 1937.

The Cuban Revolution

YURI PAPOROV

TRANSLATED BY KENETH KINNAMON

Introduction by Larry Grimes

When Keneth Kinnamon wrote about Yuri Paporov's book, Hemingway en Cuba, *in* The Hemingway Review *(117–20), he praised Paporov for his interviews with Hemingway's friends and associates in Cuba and noted the absence of such interviews in the standard biographies. Kinnamon hoped that Michael Reynolds would correct this oversight. He did not, although he did read and quote from Paporov, as does Carlos Fuentes in his book,* Hemingway in Cuba. *Fuentes, it must be said, did conduct interviews in Cuba, but by Kinnamon's count, Paporov interviewed sixty-three of Hemingway's Cuban friends and acquaintances (118), while Fuentes interviewed only forty-two. Paporov's archive of Cuban interviews and assessments of Hemingway's life and work should be available to all Hemingway scholars. Kinnamon's translation of a selection from Paporov for this volume will begin to make this work known.*

Paporov, a Russian cultural attaché to Mexico from 1953 through 1956,[1] *offers a pro-Castro, pro-revolutionary reading of Hemingway's life in Cuba. According to René Villarreal, Hemingway and Paporov never met; Paporov visited the Finca Vigía in 1963–64, after Hemingway's death, and conducted interviews in the 1960s.*[2] *His book was published in Russia in 1979.*[3]

NOTES TO THE INTRODUCTION

1. Information about Paporov's role in the expatriate life in Mexico can be found in Diane Anhalt, *A Gathering of Fugitives: American Political Expatriates in Mexico 1948–1965* (Santa Maria, CA: Archer Books, 2001).

2. Raul Villarreal, e-mail to the author, 8 Aug. 2008.

3. This chapter is taken from a Spanish translation of Paporov's book *Hemingway na kube.* Originally published in Moscow in 1979, it was expanded and revised by Jorge Portilla Livingston and Marti Soler and translated into Spanish by Armando Partida T. as *Hemingway en Cuba* in 1993. Our English translation is from that expanded Spanish edition (Mexico, D.F.: Siglo Veintiuno Editores, 1993).

* * *

That night when Juan took Dr. Monnier,[1] who had drunk too much, to the boat at Matanzas, Hemingway sat down to read the accumulated newspapers. All the dailies of February 15, 1957, emphasized the news that "homemade bombs continued to explode in the city, seriously endangering the lives of its inhabitants." Hemingway did not go to bed until he had read all the coverage from December 1956 and January 1957 relating to the landing in Oriente Province of a detachment of patriots headed by a former student leader, the young lawyer Fidel Castro. This unit had been formed for the struggle against the dictatorship of Fulgencio Batista by the political organization called the Movement of 26 July. Formed and trained in Mexico, this detachment, landing from the vessel *Granma,* was besieged and dispersed, but a small group, led by Castro, managed to hide out in the mountains of the Sierra Maestra.

From his first talk with José Luis,[2] Hemingway said that he was convinced that the actions of Castro in the mountains were directly linked with the explosions and sabotage occurring in Havana. Just after the Argentinian Manuel Fangio, a famous race-car driver, arrived in Cuba to participate in some extended races, for example, he was kidnapped by patriots to advertise that they existed and were on a war footing. In the Vedado neighborhood a house was mined, and when the police arrived, two more explosions went off. On E Street, house number 553, other police discovered a cache of arms on February 23 and arrested nine persons planning disturbances as the Carnival parade was ending. The next morning, a second deposit of arms was found in a house under construction on the corner of E Street and La Quinta. In an abandoned house in the El Porvenir neighborhood, police confiscated 2,000 cartridges, 150 grenades, and some homemade bombs. On the night of February 26–27, bombs were placed in twenty-eight private automobiles, and on the same day a fur store was set on fire. All of these were actions of the Movement of 26 July.

Informed that Batista himself would cut the ribbon of the new facilities of the El Cerro hunting club, Hemingway did not attend the opening. He didn't appear at the club until February 25, the last day of the international pigeon-shooting tournament, and then he didn't arrive alone, but in the company of Gary Cooper and his wife, who had arrived in Havana.

According to Rodrigo Diaz, former treasurer of El Cerro, Hemingway didn't like the new club. "With prudence, which he concealed, he came near, examined the place, frowned, and announced: 'Pretentious, but ordinary.' Then he pulled me aside. He was aware of my viewpoint, knew that I was an enemy of the dictatorship, for we had spoken about the country's political situation several times. 'What do you think: will what has begun in the mountains become serious?' In reply, I admit that I let my shoulders droop, but he immediately summed it up, as if he were recording on tape for history: 'I believe it! Those youngsters will put an end to this!'"

At this time it was very important for the Movement of 26 July to demonstrate to the public that most of the patriots who had taken up armed struggle against Batista were still in action. Under pressure of censorship, the press, radio, and television exerted themselves to downplay the political significance of the struggle under way, offering fake assurances that Fidel's group had been annihilated and that Fidel himself was dead.

The well-known North American journalist Herbert Matthews, principal correspondent for the *New York Times,* was invited to Havana and afterward secretly taken to the mountains, where he interviewed Castro. On his way back, Matthews went to the Finca Vigía to visit Hemingway, his colleague and companion during the Spanish Civil War. Hemingway had invited José Luis and Sinbad to dinner,[3] and Matthews arrived accompanied by a Cuban who, according to intelligence from the Spanish Communists, had collaborated with SIM, Batista's military intelligence police. Knowing from Hemingway that Matthews had interviewed Castro, José Luis warned Hemingway, who warned Matthews and then instructed René Villarreal [4] to get the collaborator drunk and at the end of the evening to drag him into the kitchen. When the four were alone, Matthews related what he had seen in the Sierra Maestra.

"The trip and the interview impressed Matthews," José Luis said as he pulled out from a folder on his desk two clippings from the *New York Times.* In the one dated March 1, 1957, appeared a photograph of Matthews and Castro: "To the journalist it seemed that a numerous detachment operated in the mountains, divided into groups receiving excellent military instruction and discipline. In reality in those days only Fidel and no more than twenty men were there. They knew how to do their duty."

"Castro is a man of strong will. He enjoys undeniable authority and power. This is serious, Ernest," Matthews said, "I wouldn't bet on Batista!" And to a question about Castro's philosophical platform, Matthews responded: "He studies

Descartes. He has broad general knowledge. He reads a lot. His point of view is very liberal. He is an *ortodoxo,* too far to the left."

I was already acquainted with the photograph José Luis showed me, in which Matthews is seated in a clearing in the forest with an enormous cigar in his hand, wearing an overcoat and a kepi. He is next to Fidel, who is smoking an equally large cigar. This photograph was published in response to a declaration by Cuba's minister of war, Gen. Santiago Verdeja, who asserted not only that Matthews's account of his interview of Castro, published in the *Times* on February 24, 1957, was the invention of an idle journalist, but that there was no uprising in the Sierra Maestra, and much less was Fidel Castro there.

The second clipping was an article from the same newspaper, also by Matthews. This article was written later, after mid-1958, when several Americans from the U.S. military base at Guantanamo were captured by a detachment of rebels led by Fidel's brother, Raul Castro. Here Matthews's tone is harsh, and he describes the rebels as revolutionary bandits.

"Ernest, who spoke of Matthews without the least respect, gave me the clippings and told me he was very quick and capable, but without a conscience and interested only in sensationalism that would make him money," José Luis said excitedly.

> Speaking of money, I remember something that happened that summer. I arrived at the Finca Vigia without letting him know I was coming and found him by the swimming pool lost in thought. "Are you bored?" I asked him, and he responded in a low voice: "No! A person gets bored only if he has nothing to talk to himself about, whereas I am speculating about how much you need this time." He gave me a blank check. We really needed funds for the special edition of our newspaper. I started to explain, but he cut me off. "It's not necessary! Never explain anything to me, Feo.[5] What for? For these young guys I do it with great pleasure."

Between him and me I need to explain something. We Spanish and Cuban Communists did not take seriously the undertaking in the mountains by *ortodoxos* of the left. We thought they could not rouse the masses and that their method of struggle against a strong military dictatorship was doomed to failure. Ernest did not agree with me, showing astonishment at our short-sightedness now that we "had friendly relations with Batista." He announced decisively that he was convinced that none of the known political parties could achieve anything, for they were under the close surveillance of the police and the F.B.I. He considered the platform of the 26 of July Movement very attractive. Since I didn't agree with him, Ernest kept himself somewhat reserved toward me concerning the fighting in the Sierra and the actions of clandestine groups of the 26 of July Movement in Havana and other Cuban cities until the final victory of Castro.

As a rather eloquent addition to the record that shows Hemingway's relation to the initial phase of the Cuban Revolution, I think that we should consider the testimony of Roberto Herrera; of Luis Gomez Vanguemert, editor of the daily *El Mundo;* of Sara Chemendez; and of Mario Cuchilán.

"Beginning in 1957," Roberto Herrera tells me,

> Papa frequented Nino's bar, El Hoyo, really just a hole in the wall compared to the bar across the street, but Papa never went to that one. After five in the afternoon, alone or with his new secretary Valery Smith, he sat in a corner. Sometimes he invited to his table someone who seemed interesting and started up a conversation about politics. Anyone under thirty who came in got free drinks. Nino said that he invited, but Papa paid and told Nino to keep quiet about it. There, in El Hoyo, Papa had previously interviewed Camilo Cientuegos, a boy from Cotorro with whom he sometimes played baseball. Camilo had worked as a clerk in a clothing store run by a Galician in Havana; now he was fighting in the mountains with Fidel. Toward the end of February 1958, Papa invited me to go with him one afternoon to Bellas Artes for the opening of an exposition of the work of the Cuban painter Mari Pepa Lamarque. He liked her engravings and charcoal and colored pencil drawings, especially the landscapes of Mexico and Spain. After the ceremony as everyone was leaving the salon vendors were outside with the evening newspapers shouting, "Victory en Pino del Liza, the army has liquidated the barbudos." The young boy running from one side to the other stuck a copy of *El País* under Papa's arm and held out his hand for the coins. Papa angrily threw the paper down and said in a loud voice, "All that is a lie! They won't be able to kill Castro! The patriots will triumph one way or another." Hearing these words, everyone near him moved aside, and Papa continued: "A hoax! Lies! Batista thinks that he can finish them off with a victory on paper! He's dreaming! All this is a lie!"

"I remember," Vanguemert says,

> one time during the opening of an exhibition at Bellas Artes when Hemingway was present. Among the people attending were some of Batista's bloodhounds. We saw them. At that time not a single thing escaped the vigilance of uniformed or secret police. Batista was feeling that the end was near, and his paranoid malaise was becoming violent. In the salon a rumor was spreading that a fierce battle had taken place in the mountains of the Sierra Maestra

and that Fidel Castro had been killed. Then Hemingway began to be irritated. "They are lies! The papers have sold out and will print anything, but they can't kill Fidel. The rebels will win one way or another!"

"We met in Cojimar"—the thin hands of Sara Chemendez are very restless.

> Everyone was eating and he was seated waiting for someone. He was drinking and writing. It was cold. Later he took out a piece of paper and began sketching me! He showed it to me and observed that I ought to have contact with art. At the time I was working as a model in the San Alejandro School of Fine Arts and lived in the San Francisco neighborhood on F Street between Carballo and the Bulevar. On that day I was with university students, and he invited us to visit him. We wanted to go, but we had a lot to do. Nevertheless, on 10 May 1956 police burned to the ground my little wooden house because students met there. I was left with nothing! Hemingway found out about it and sent René to help with money, and he let me go into his garden to eat fruit from the trees. Thanks to him and some painters I knew, I got together seven hundred pesos and had a new house built in two weeks. Once he had a bad stomach ache. I said to him, "Permit me to put my hand on you. You will feel better. I know how to do it." And he felt better. He knew that I was a friend of Camilo, who was now fighting in the mountains with Fidel, and he told me that I could use his grounds in any way I wished. "No one will come in here!" But he was wrong. They came in and killed his favorite dog.

"He had known me for a long time"—Mario Cuchilán squinted through half-closed eyes.

> In the forties we often ran into each other in the taverns at the port in the company of mutual friends. In 1957 and 1958, each time he saw me he hugged me and said, "Take care of yourself, take care of yourself, boy!" It was a big laugh to see how he awkwardly squeezed my face against his big belly saying, "Take care of yourself. Take care of yourself." We all had good intentions, but only acts have value. It was pleasing that a man like Hemingway shared my views and encouraged me; it meant that he considered my actions correct. But at the same time it frightened me. What did he know, and from what source? Through the barman (who helped us, though he had worked at the Floridita only a short time and did not know Hemingway well), I tried to pull from his tongue what he really thought of me, what he knew about my affairs. But nothing resulted. Hemingway replied that he did not know me personally, but only as a capable journalist.

"Mario, why do you think that you gain nothing with your verification?" I asked to this small man, half Chinese, and I was pleased when he said, "I could have occupied an important position, but I thought it necessary to eliminate the dictatorship that cost the lives of twenty thousand Cubans, the best of us. I didn't risk my life for a victory that would win me a good post."

"It seems to me, Mario," I said, "that showed you then in the best way how seriously he took your complementary activity. It immediately put an end to any further questioning."

"Yes, that's possible, but I didn't think of that at the time. I had to organize an ironclad alibi for El Curita (one of the directors of a group carrying out clandestine activities of the 26 July movement in Havana). He was under suspicion."

In August 1958, an act took place at the Finca Vigía that saddened Hemingway and caused him to reflect. It was night and everyone in the house was asleep when the butt of a gun began banging on the door. Rubbing his eyes, Hemingway went to open it to see what was happening. In the entrance he saw five soldiers, armed to the teeth, led by a sergeant. He asked if the owner of the Finca had not seen two peasants whom they were looking for and had to interrogate. They might be hiding in the house. While Hemingway was choosing exactly the right words so as not to provoke or irritate these people, drunk and armed, and explaining that he knew of no one and that there were no strangers in the house, his strong hunting dog Machacos rushed out of the kitchen, barking at the soldiers. Without even thinking about it, the sergeant fired his Thompson gun right through the dog's body. With an immense effort, Hemingway forced himself to stand still and not jump on the sergeant and try to strangle him with his bare hands, as he would have done under other circumstances. If he had done so, his destiny would have reunited him with his beloved Machacos. The soldiers withdrew, shouting their worst curses.

The next morning, Hemingway buried the dog with all possible honors, next to the pool by one side of the net of the tennis court, and put up a stone with an epitaph. He fired off one shot as a farewell and remained very depressed. Mary advised him to fly to New York as a distraction, but there he felt even worse. He returned to the Finca and took up a lifestyle even more withdrawn. He seldom went to the Floridita and almost never to sea. The rebels were winning one victory after another in the mountains. Infuriated, Batista's forces were shooting down people in the street at the least suspicion; the atmosphere was getting white hot. Winter had been cold, with storms and northers; summer was torrid and sultry.

For his part, Hemingway felt sharply the need to free himself from such tension through the tranquility and simplicity of nature. He decided to go to Sun Valley, to the mountains of the state in which he was so well known. His American friends Taylor Williams, Lloyd Arnold, El Chiquito Don Anderson, Doctor

Saviers, and Gary Cooper thought that he "had lost much of his old form." Coming to his small wooden rental house on the outskirts of Sun Valley, one after another of the people dear to him began to visit: Bronislaw Zelinsky, the Polish translator of his works; Aaron Hotchner; and Gary Cooper. Hemingway quickly recovered his physical and mental tone. Excursions of several hours to the mountain ridges with his shotgun, as well as use of a special gymnasium and the observance of a diet, permitted him by December to sit down to work on some chapters of his book on Paris. By then, the course of events in Cuba was accelerating, and Hemingway was listening to the radio to follow what was happening there. In the first third of December, he and Mary sent more than ten Christmas cards. Here is one of them, with a view of a green valley and snowy mountains: "Doctor Infiesta Vázquez, fourth street, house number 304. Best wishes and regards from the mountains of Idaho, Mary. Good luck and warm abrazos, Ernest."

At dawn on January 1, Batista, who with his servants had cleaned out $800 million from state coffers, loaded fifty suitcases stuffed with securities and flew on an army plane to Ciudad Trujillo to take refuge with his coreligionist of bloody business, the dictator of the Dominican Republic. At eight o'clock in the morning, in a dance hall in San Francisco de Paula,[6] a general staff for assistance to the detachments was set up. At noon, Castro's representatives arrived at the Finca to take possession of the arms that were there. René categorically refused to turn them over, stating that he could not do so without the consent of their owner, whom he promised to call by telephone: "I immediately asked a telephone operator to connect me with Sun Valley, and all day I sat by the telephone. The good thing was that the radio was constantly transmitting various interesting communiqués"—René pours some rum into a glass with ice and Coca-Cola.

> At seven-thirty that night Papa himself succeeded in getting through to us. He congratulated me and all Cubans on our victory. He was laughing, in high spirits, and we had the following conversation:
>
> "How is everything at the Finca?"
>
> "Everything is in order, Papa. They only wanted to take over the arms. In town a militia detachment has been formed."
>
> "And what did you do, René?"
>
> "I said I would call you."
>
> "Too bad. Now listen to me carefully, René. Give them anything they want to take. All the cartridges! Still more, if it's necessary, fill up the gasoline tanks of the cars and tell Juan to do what they want him to and to take care of the cars. If the house is needed because of its strategic position, let them use it. You yourself can maintain order. Understand?"

"Sure, Papa, I'll do as you say."

"Who were they, René?"

"You don't know them, but they commissioned Ismael, Luis Coto, Gallegos, and Bebo to form the staff. It turns out that in November they captured the sergeant that killed Machacos and hanged him at night to a lamp post in San Francisco. I wrote you about this."

"No, kid, I didn't get that letter. But it doesn't make any difference now. Do what I told you and call me if necessary."

Immediately I went down to town and looked up Ismael and Bebo to let them know Papa's decision. They told me that they needed the arms, the car, and the pickup for a few days until the barbudos entered Havana. I turned over ten shotguns and rifles, a pistol, and all the grounds. Quite soon Camilo with a detachment came through the streets of San Francisco on his way to Havana. Afterwards everything was returned without a single cartridge having been fired, and I thanked them. I let Papa know when he called in the middle of February, immediately after the burial of Colonel Williams. He cried. I cheered him up with the news that Dr. José Luis had received the post of military health officer of the rebel army, and in the meantime Jaime Bofill, whom Papa knows well, was appointed to the provisional government. Papa promised to see all this with his own eyes.

"Nevertheless, they didn't arrive until March," Roberto Herrera completes the story of those frenzied but happy days.

I received them at the Rancho Boyeros airport. Papa got off the plane in a joyous mood, and I learned right away that he knew a lot about what had been happening here. He told me right in the airport that he wanted to interview Dr. Castro so that he could give him some advice. After returning home, Papa began to watch television. Before then he couldn't endure it. He followed attentively the judicial processes, listened to the radio three times a day, and read all the newspapers. He especially enjoyed the interventions of Fidel. Toward the end of April they unmasked a fellow. He had lived the whole time in town, but he disappeared in January and after a month reappeared, but now with an olive-green uniform and sporting a beard. He had the rank of captain in the rebel forces. Then Papa said, "Monstruo, this always occurs in any revolution and frequently turns out to be the cause of its failure. You will see now how those who were shitting in their pants when others were shooting are now worming their way in displacing the ones who fought. This is one of the dangers in a revolution, Monstruo.[7] This is why I need to see Castro."

It is known that upon his return to the United States, Hemingway gave an interview to the North American journalist Emmet Watson, in which he made a precise and definitive declaration:

> The armed insurrection against Batista is the first revolution in Cuba that is necessary to consider as a real revolution. Castro's movement awakens great hopes. I believe in the cause of the Cuban people. Many changes of government have occurred in Cuba, but these were only changes of the guard. The first task of the recently arrived is to bring alongside the people. Some of those close to Batista were valuable and honest people, but the majority were thieves, sadists, and executioners. They tortured children, sometimes with such cruelty that they had to finish off their victims. The trials and just executions by Castro are indispensable. If the government does not sentence these people to the firing squad, they will be exterminated by avengers. The result would be an epidemic of vendettas in the cities and towns. What would happen to these people if they are pardoned? The people recognize the masters of evil and would make them pay sooner or later.
>
> Castro's movement owes its success to his promise to punish those guilty of villainy. . . .
>
> I pronounce myself in favor of Castro's revolution because the people support it. I believe in his cause.

In April, Hemingway insistently sought contact with Fidel Castro through José Luis Herrera, who recalls the episode:

> Ernest was especially insistent that an interview with Fidel be arranged when he learned that he was flying to New York to head the Cuban delegation in the General Assembly of the United Nations. "You should understand, Feo, that Fidel should know something about the politics, the politicians, and the idiosyncrasy of the American people. I can explain these to him. He should go with a plan for a triumph." Since Fidel was too busy to give an interview to him, he entrusted Vázquez Condela, associate editor of the daily newspaper *Revolución,* to go to Hemingway's house to interview him.
>
> It was late at night when I drove Vázquez in my car to La Vigia. He was afraid of traps and ambushes, for the times were tense. At night there were shots fired in the streets; in the mornings corpses would appear. Ernest received us with a pistol in his pocket.

Vázquez Condela himself relates what happened:

Without being completely sure that Hemingway really had something important to communicate to us, I went to San Francisco with the man calling himself "friend and doctor" of the writer, but no one on the paper knew him. But everything went off without any problem whatever, and my misgivings were pacified a hundred times over. During a visit of two unforgettable hours I got to know a personality such as is rarely born here on earth. It began with an agreeable disillusionment, if one can put it that way. I was expecting to see a proud man who had made his name immortal in world literature, for whom a talk with me would be of little importance, but as soon as I entered the house I felt that the host was generous, compassionate, agreeable, and unaffected, and that his only desire was to make me feel comfortable. The three of us began to talk.

Who and where?

"Hemingway, Doctor Herrera, and I. From time to time the author's wife would enter and leave the room quietly. We sat in soft armchairs in the living room. It was a veritable museum. Music was playing at a low volume: Beethoven, Bach, Ravel. It did not hinder conversation, but instead formed a marvelous background. We drank white Italian wine and chewed on nuts, but we spoke about important matters."

For example?

"You yourself can judge!" Vázquez Condela responded, and continued:

A citizen of the United States, the capitalist monster, the famous Hemingway, wanted Fidel to avoid the slips, traps, and provocations which he would inevitably encounter in the country where the press was beginning to show animosity and where some political circles were openly expressing antipathy to the Cuban Revolution. Hemingway spoke in detail about the situation in the United States, about the "weaknesses" in public opinion that Fidel could utilize in the interest of the Cuban Revolution, of the particularities of the press, the points of view characteristic of some of the newspapers and magazines. He then immediately touched on the issues that most irritated the powerful monopolies, such as the laws and changes adopted for the economic structure of Cuba, the periodical decrees against obvious traitors and criminals that were closely connected to the monopolies, declarations concerning the independence, sovereignty, and international policy of Cuba, and its desire not to submit itself any longer to the Department of State. You must agree that it turned out to be strange that Hemingway worried about Fidel's visit to the United States, and the subsequent triumph of our revolution. As he walked me out to the car he asked that I let his comrades know that he strongly shared their intentions and supported the actions of the Cuban Revolution.

"Ernest was really sad," added José Luis, "that René let him know too late that Fidel and Camilo were playing baseball at El Cerro stadium on 14 April after the international competition inaugurated by them. At first Ernest was going to take the car out of the garage, but then he realized that he would arrive too late. He complained that he had really wanted to see Fidel, who flew to New York the next day."

That summer of 1959, early in July when Hemingway was in Spain, during the height of the campaign in the United States known as "the bloody river," Fidel Castro appeared on the Cuban television program, *This Is Your Life.* To the inevitable question of those times, posed by a journalist—How do you explain the general executions that wound the sensibilities of many people in Latin America?—Castro responded with well-known and irrefutable arguments, and in conclusion said: "And now permit me to inform you of the opinion of the world-renowned writer Ernest Hemingway, who received the Nobel Prize only because all his work itself represents a defense of human rights. Listen: 'The executions in Cuba are an indispensable phenomenon. The delinquent military who were executed by the revolutionary government of Cuba received what they deserved.'" And he showed to journalists and television viewers a newspaper from Uruguay that printed the interview with Hemingway.

At the end of April, Hemingway and his wife traveled first from La Vigía to New York and then took the transatlantic liner *Constitution* to Spain, where the writer planned to follow all the performances of Dominguín and Ordoñez in order to write a book about them. But before he left, a comical event took place. An enterprising hat dealer known as the Haberdashery King, seeking to advertise the ties in his shop, sent one to Hemingway with a note: "Our products have a good reputation and are much in demand. We trust that you will voluntarily send me two dollars for this tie." Without thinking much about it, he answered immediately: "My books have a good reputation and are much in demand. I hope that you will voluntarily acquire my last short novel. It costs $2.85. So you owe me eighty cents. Greetings, Ernest Hemingway."

No one in La Vigía could remember the name of the store, but everyone remembers that November 4, 1959, when Hemingway returned from Spain to Cuba. I had the good luck of finding the correspondent of the press agency Prensa Latina. He turned out to be the Cuban poet Heberto Padilla, who had met Hemingway at the airport on his arrival and wrote the notice printed in all the dailies. Padilla met me in his office. Rolling aside a small table with a typewriter on it, he offered me a seat in a chair on whose large arm I sat down with a notebook.

"Two things took place that day," Padilla began,

in the city a rumor began to spread that Camilo Cienfuegos, who had disappeared, had been found, and in the airport Rancho Boyeros Hemingway's return to Cuba was awaited. As soon as the writer descended from the plane a compact circle of reporters and photographers surrounded him: "I feel very happy to be here again, because I consider myself just another Cuban," declared the North American writer Ernest Hemingway upon arriving from New York in Havana that night. "I have not believed any of the misinformation published abroad against Cuba. I sympathize with the Cuban government and with all of *our* difficulties," underlining the word *our.* Continuing he explained, "I don't want to be considered a Yankee."

"Tell me," I asked, "Did Hemingway fly back from Spain with his wife?"

Mary met him at the airport. Hemingway flew with the Spanish bullfighter Ordonez and his wife Carmen, the sister of Dominguín. A numerous group of people from San Francisco de Paula, where he lived, met Hemingway. One of the Americans asked him if he still maintained the declarations of support for the Cuban Revolution he had made at the beginning of the year; Hemingway corroborated them totally. For his part, Hemingway was interested in the fate of the disappeared Camilo Cienfuegos, the commander in chief of the rebel army, and after learning that there was no result, he declared: "I'm very sorry. On the entire trip I have been worried about this problem." Then they launched another deceptive question at Hemingway: What could he say about the note sent by the Department of State to the Cuban government concerning the latest happenings that had taken place on the island? He replied that he had not the slightest idea what the note said, but added that "in New York, which I just passed through on my return from Europe, no one knows anything about Cuba or about anything else that's happening in the world. There the only thing they're talking about is Van Doren and his scandalous television program of questions and answers."

"Did he say anything about intending to leave Cuba?" I asked.

What?—no, quite the contrary. No one had the least doubt that Hemingway was going back to his house, where he felt quite at home. He said that he wanted to make changes in his short novel [*sic*] *Death in the Afternoon,* based on material he had collected on his trip to Spain, and that Antonio Ordoñez had promised to help him. After clearing customs he fell into the hands of his friends and admirers from San Francisco, and I thought that they received him not as a public figure, but as a close and dear friend. Someone waved the Cuban flag and handed it to Hemingway as an emblem, I think, of his declarations concerning Cuba while he was abroad. The writer leaned over the railing and kissed the flag. The press photographers had not caught up to register the moment and began to ask Hemingway to repeat the gesture. He exclaimed, "I kissed it with all my heart, and not as an actor." Around him applause broke out. No less than twenty automobiles followed Hemingway's car. The next day all the Cuban dailies published the story of Hemingway's arrival, and many foreign press agencies transmitted it to their countries.

In the photographic archive of Prensa Latina I discovered a complete series of photographs taken when Hemingway's plane landed. A neighbor of the finca, David Hernandez, remembers Hemingway's arrival at San Francisco:

The streets were so completely full of people that the cars could not turn into the finca. Everyone was singing, dancing, laughing. I got out (René and I were in the second car) to see if they would let us get through. When I got near the Chrysler, Hemingway asked in a low voice, smoothing his hair: "Are they waiting for me like this?"

"No, Papa, it's more likely that it's because it's been announced that they have found Camilo," I said.

"Oh, that *is* really important. Great! Camilo is a real man. Anyway, I appreciate the reception in Rancho Boyeros. If it were for me, I don't know what we would do." Antonio Ordoñez and Carmen were guests at La Vigia for only five days. Hemingway wanted to show them the house he had bought by mail a year and a half earlier, in which neither he nor Mary had ever set foot. Miss Mary flew there to prepare the house for guests, and in the meantime Hemingway took Roberto with him, Ordoñez, and Carmen for the drive across several states. In seven days they traveled 4,038 miles.

Hemingway returned to Cuba at the end of January 1960. On February 8, Anastas I. Mikoyan visited La Vigía. Hemingway declared to him that for the first time there was a clean government in Cuba. On May 16, he met Fidel Castro. Before he awarded to the prime minister the trophies he won in the Ernest Hemingway Marlin Tournament, the writer and the revolutionary chief talked for more than half an hour, somewhat apart from others. The minister of communications, Jesús Montané, then subdirector of the Institute of Sport and Recreation, recalled the day over the muffled sound of the airplane motors as we flew to Santiago de Cuba:

> Fidel is passionate about nature and is a worthy sportsman. A fellow named Joe Cambria, a talent scout for the major leagues in the United States, saw Fidel pitch and declared that the prime minister could easily play for any club in the majors. He's also a passionate deep sea fisherman. When Fidel took first place in the Hemingway tournament, the writer celebrated it: "I congratulate you, comandante! On the other hand, you know, I have never had luck in competition. In general I don't have good luck!" The next day, after the closing of the tournament, a messenger arrived at La Vigia with a packet of photographs taken of the only time Hemingway and Castro met. Having selected one, he framed it and placed it on the table where he kept his most valued souvenirs.

On May 28, Hemingway put the last period after the 108,746 words of *The Dangerous Summer.* "Over a period of twenty-five days in June Papa called twelve times to El Pecoso.[8] He was worried and asked that an agreement be reached with the editors of *Life,*" René Villarreal recalls.

> The magazine had already paid Papa, according to the terms of the contract, for 25,000 words, but the work was now four times as long. At the end of June Hotchner flew to Havana. For the return flight Hemingway accompanied him to the airport, where posters were hanging—"Cuba Si, Yanquis No"—and Hotchner ventured to joke about it. When Hotchner's flight took off, Hemingway said that Americans, unless they are politicians, understand absolutely nothing about anything except business. That night, after dinner, Papa read in the dailies that President Eisenhower had ordered the suspension of technical aid to Cuba and had ordered that Cuba would be denied economic aid beginning 1 December. Papa insulted Eisenhower with his complete repertory. He said that he was a brainless politician and treacherous as well. This development showed again the true dictatorial face of the United States. Miss Mary did not agree with him, they argued, and they separated to sleep in different bedrooms.

When Hemingway arrived again in New York, it was natural that journalists attacked him. To all questions about the situation in Cuba, Hemingway had the same answer: In Cuba everything is fine! In Cuba everything is coming along in the right way.

NOTES TO THE ESSAY

1. Jean Monnier was the physician on the *Île de France,* the ship on which Hemingway returned from Europe early in 1957. Juan Pastor was Hemingway's chauffeur in Cuba.

2. José Luis Herrera Sotolongo was a Spanish Communist and chief medical officer of the Republican Army during the Spanish Civil War, who fled to Cuba after Franco's victory, along with his younger brother Roberto. The Herrera brothers were among Hemingway's closest friends during his Cuban years. José Luis served as his personal physician and Roberto as his secretary.

3. Sinbad was the nickname of Juan Duñabeitía, another Spanish exile serving as captain of a Cuban vessel.

4. Villarreal was Hemingway's house servant at La Finca Vigía.

5. Feo ("Ugly") was Hemingway's nickname for the elder Herrera brother, José Luis.

6. San Francisco de Paula is the town adjacent to La Finca Vigía.

7. Monstruo ("Monster") was Hemingway's nickname for Roberto Herrera.

8. El Pecoso ("Freckle Face") was Hemingway's nickname for Aaron Hotchner.

COMMENTS: THE CUBAN REVOLUTION

To understand Hemingway's relation to revolutions in general, and to Cuba's revolution in particular, both his life and his writing need careful study. Little has been written, for instance, about his involvement in a plot to overthrow Rafael Trujillo, dictator of the Dominican Republic from 1942 to 1952. Paporov provides a chapter on that incident. Paporov, however, strays from his interview notes, or so it seems when we asked René Villarreal to respond to quotes attributed to Paporov. Commenting on Paporov's account of a visit by U.S. newspaperman Herbert Matthews to Hemingway, Villarreal recalls the visit as taking place on a Wednesday, since the Herrera brothers visited that day as usual. He does not, however, recall, as Paporov states, that Matthews and Hemingway spoke privately in Papa's workroom after dinner or that Papa instructed him to get anyone drunk or that he dragged anyone into the kitchen—although he does note (in an e-mail to Larry Grimes dated July 6, 2008) that other people often did get drunk in Hemingway's company, because it was difficult to keep up with Hemingway when he was drinking. Similarly, with regard to Paporov's account of his meeting with Sara Chemendez and her story, Villarreal (in the same e-mail) says he does not remember the woman, the burning of her house, or giving her money. René Villarreal conferred by phone with his twin brother, Luis, on this matter and Luis also recalled nothing about the woman or the burnt home. As for the request for arms and ammunition from the Finca described by Paporov, Villarreal says, "most of it occurred as it is told." However, Villarreal does make some significant corrections to Paporov's account, asserting that no sergeant was hanged from a lamp post in San Francisco de Paula and that the men who killed Machakos were not from the village.

Villarreal's corrections should be kept in mind as one reads Paporov. So, too, should this line from the end of John Ford's classic western, The Man Who Shot Liberty Valance: *"When the legend becomes fact, print the legend." Hemingway's Cuban legend is a most powerful and little studied phenomenon. Hemingway's celebrity in Cuba approaches that of José Martí, Che Guevara, and Castro himself. As a bookend to John Raeburn's examination of Hemingway's American celebrity,* Fame Became of Him, *a scholarly study of the Hemingway legend in Cuba is needed.*

We had hoped to supplement the Paporov essay with a reproduction of notes that Hemingway made in April 1959 to help brief Castro as he prepared for a visit to the United States; these briefing notes, filed under Cuba, are held in the Hemingway Collection of the John F. Kennedy Presidential Library in Boston (hereafter JFK). However, permission to reproduce was denied. Nevertheless, scholars need to be made familiar with the general content of this four-page, 165-word document. In it, Hemingway poses general questions he thinks Castro must be prepared to answer, focusing on cold war tensions concerning Communist influence, and advises Castro to make assurances that Cuba is now a safe place. Hemingway also warns Castro that he is likely to face some hostility. Stating that Castro should expect to be "heckled" and noting that the heckling may be orchestrated, "vicious," and unjustified (Hemingway, sheet 1 of briefing notes, Hemingway Collection, JFK), he stresses the need for Castro to control his emotions and stay calm. He speculates that certain adversarial news publications and agencies (he names names) will ask "trick" questions (Hemingway, sheet 2 of briefing notes, Hemingway Collection, JFK)).

Additional sheets of handwritten notes in the Cuba file at the Kennedy Library demonstrate that Hemingway had a detailed knowledge of the Cuban Revolution and of Cuban politics. On one sheet, he cites the number of deaths at specific sites and names individuals detrimental to the revolutionary cause. On another handwritten sheet he reflects on the likelihood and consequences of the seizure of private property, concluding that such a seizure was unlikely, while conceding that if it did occur he might lose his house. Accompanying these handwritten notes is a typed summary of Hemingway's relation to the Cuban revolution, in which he states that the matter was "very complicated," and that while he "always believed [sic] in [the revolution's] necessity," he took no part in Cuban politics (Ernest Hemingway, undated statement typed by JAH, Cuba file, Hemingway Collection, JFK). Hemingway's relation to Cuba and its politics may be as complicated as the Revolution itself. Cuban responses to both the man and the literature, as selections from Caballero, Cruz and Fuentes demonstrate, cannot be separated from the politics of the Revolution. Future biographers need to explore the matter carefully and in great detail.

Works Cited

Kinnamon, Keneth. Review of *Hemingway en Cuba* by Yuri Paporov. Translated by Armando Partida; revised translation by Jorge Portilla Livingston and Marti Soler. *The Hemingway Review* 16.1 (Fall 1996): 117–20.

An Interview with Gigi's All-Stars

at Ernest Hemingway's Finca Vigía, San Francisco de Paula, Cuba, July 6, 2004

DAVID B. MARTENS

What follows is the transcript of a recorded 2004 panel discussion led by American journalist David Martens with Cuban men who, as boys, played baseball with Ernest Hemingway's son Gregory, nicknamed Gigi. Gladys Rodriguez Ferrero, then director of the Finca, Hemingway's home that is now a public museum, made the introductions. Questions came later from Scott Schwarr, who helped organize the trip for the American travelers; Carmen Fournier Cusa, a Cuban Hemingway scholar, and other unidentified Cuban and American audience members.

Gladys Rodriguez Ferrero: In 1997, David Martens interviewed Neftalí Pernas, who participated in the Hemingway colloquium that year. Among the many memories they discussed, Pernas told David his recollections of submarine hunting during World War II; Neftalí had lived in Guanabo, which was one of the places where they used to dock their boats. In 2003, Martens brought a tape of that interview to the annual colloquium, where he made a presentation with the interview. Since Pernas had passed away, Martens also gave a copy of the tape to Pernas's relatives.

After the 2003 colloquium ended, Martens interviewed Alberto Ramos Enríquez, known as Fico, who had been a member of the staff of the Finca Vigía—a cook—as well as earlier being a member of Gigi's All-Stars (or Gigi's Stars), the baseball team for his sons and local boys that Hemingway organized in the 1940s. This team (whose original name in Spanish was Las Estrellas de Gigi) was—as far as I know, and I've done some research on this—the first young baseball team, baseball team with children, in the whole municipality. Then later, in the 1950s, we had the Las Estrellas de Camilo (Camilo's Stars). I'm not a specialist in sports, but anyway, we are treading around there.

The following account presents a later interview with Fico and other members of Gigi's Stars. We wanted to talk with these other members of the baseball team, the boys; we wanted them to be here today also. We have Fico; Humberto Hernandez (known as Berto); and Oscar Blas Fernandez (whom the boys called Cayuco, to which Hemingway added Jonronero, or "the home-runner," because he hit the ball so hard that he was the only one who could make home runs). So here we have the boys of a long time ago, dear friends of today.

David B. Martens: *Gracias, gracias.* I begin by saying thank you to Fico, because Fico brought me back. Last year, as Gladys mentioned, at the end of the conference, one of my friends here at the Finca said, "David, would you like to interview Fico? He was Hemingway's cook." So I met with Fico poolside, and we spent a little better than an hour chatting, and he was telling me the stories of his life here in the Finca, and I will tell you a few of the stories he told me.

But the real reason we are here is for the reunion of Gigi's All-Stars. And after I tell you a bit of Fico's story, I'm going to ask them to tell us their stories of life here at the Finca, and their experiences with Gigi and the All-Stars, and their relationships with Hemingway. So I'd like you all to be thinking of what questions you would like to ask of Gigi's All-Stars. Because we're going to open it up later on, and let you ask the questions that you'd like to know.

Alberto Ramos Enríquez, now seventy-two, was nine years old when he went to work at the Finca in 1940. Fico told me that Hemingway talked to his father about his opening the main gate to the property, and afterwards he went to the main house to run errands, sweep the terrace, feed the cats and ducks, and he would occasionally go to the post office for mail in the morning.

Gigi and Patrick came here, and because Hemingway was such a fan of baseball, he made a small baseball field; I'm not quite sure where it was on the grounds, where the boys used to play baseball. That was in about 1941 or 1942, and, according to Fico, Hemingway was the pitcher.

Fico worked in the main house providing service, his family lived in town, and when he was young, he used to stay at the Finca. He said, "We were like a big family, not treated as servants. We were treated like his children." So Fico worked at the Finca from about age nine to age eighteen.

As time passed, Hemingway married Mary, about 1946–47. She knew about how things went in the kitchen. The cooks were from Haiti or China. Ramón was the last cook. He was Chinese, and he died here, and they had a funeral and a wake here.

Alberto "Fico" Ramos Enriquez: The wake was close to the place where most of the Chinese community in Chinatown was—Sonja Street. He died here. And then he was taken to the funeral home, over there.

David B. Martens: After the Chinese cook died, Mary said, "Fico, you will be our next cook."

"How can I be cook?" Fico said.

"Don't worry, I will teach you," Mary said.

Fico had been a helper in the kitchen prior to that, so Mary looked to Fico to become the next cook. And there were many special people that came to dinner here, the ambassador, United States ambassador to Cuba, many artists, Gary Cooper, Adriana, athletes.

There was a hunting club nearby, where they would go to shoot pigeons, and next to that hunting club there was a baseball field. They would go by car, and Gigi and Hemingway would be shooting the pigeons while they played baseball. And Gigi was a very good shot. The baseball team was composed of boys in the neighborhood. Why don't we start with the home-run hitter, and have him tell how he first came to be on the baseball team?

Oscar Blas "Cayuco Jonronero" Fernandez: I met Papa for the first time by the entrance gate when he came here to see the Finca. There was a group of kids playing around; we used to meet or gather at the Villarreal family's house, and then from there we went to play around in the fincas or wherever we could. It's important for you to know that the children who lived on Vigía Street didn't have a place to play; we couldn't play anywhere, so we had to run around and find a place around the fincas to play.

So that day, when we saw a car stop by the gate, we were just on our way to one of the fincas and we stopped, came back to see who it was. Also, we were very shy at the beginning, because we had been taught not to try to talk to elders or older people, out of respect. So when Hemingway saw we were just shy and didn't want to go to him, he called and said, "Come on, come on, children. Come on to me."

He greeted all the children, shaking hands, and started asking questions. Among the questions he asked was if there were more children like us, like our age. We told him that yes, there are more children, but they are playing around somewhere. Those of us who lived on the same street pointed and said who lived there—"I live here, I live there," and so on. He asked us if we knew how to play baseball. We told him we did, but we didn't have any gloves or bats or balls or anything with which to play.

He asked us, "Where are you going?"

And I said, and we said, "Well, we are going to find a place in one of the fincas to play." He then asked if we used to play here at the Finca. And we answered, "No, the owner of the Finca doesn't let us come into the Finca to play or to eat fruit." I noticed that every time we answered his questions he smiled, as if he liked or as if he was expecting what we were saying.

Then, when he was about to leave, he said, "When I buy the Finca, I will let the children come in to play and to eat fruit, but no throwing stones at the trees."

So after some time we were called to meet his children for the first time. So that day he introduced Gigi and Patrick, and we all told them our names and our nicknames. I told him my name was Blas, but everybody called me Cayuco. Everybody called me Cayuco, and that was it.

After we knew and we talked for a while, the butler in the house brought baseball gear, bats and gloves and everything. So then we all went to the lawn near the gate, and we played the first baseball game. And as Fico told you, he divided us into two teams and Papa always was the pitcher. That's how we played our first baseball game. Then we were not called Gigi's All Stars. We were just "Hemingway's Baseball Team."

After some time and several games, one day Papa called us asking what our sizes were, because he had ordered some baseball suits for us. Then we asked him, "What will be the name of the team?" And Joseito told him of the idea of calling the baseball team Gigi's All-Stars. So that's how we got our baseball uniforms, and the first time we played with uniforms and everything was in the baseball field near a place, near the hunter's club called Campo de Armada. And almost every week Papa took us to play baseball with the kids around. That's how we came to be Gigi's All-Stars. That's what, all I remember, everything. I was ten years old, and I'm seventy-four today, and that's what I remember.

Alberto "Fico" Ramos Enriquez: I want to explain how, being older, they came and were part of the baseball team. Because around the neighborhood on Vigía Street, most of the children were younger. The point is that twice, when he took us to the hunters' club to play baseball while they were shooting, the other children who played baseball with us were older and taller boys. So that's how we had to call for older people and taller people to play baseball in the team. That's how they came and started, belonged to Gigi's All-Stars, to sort of reinforce the team.

Blas "Cayuco Jonronero" Fernandez: I just wanted to say how we started calling me Cayuco Jonronero. The point is that Hemingway used to pitch and usually nobody could hit the ball, or if you made a hit it was a small fly or something not big. But one day when he was pitching I made a hit, and made a home run. So he came to me and said, "Very good," congratulating me. And he said, "You are a very good baseball player, you are 'Cayuco Jonronero,'" because I had made the first run and the first home run ever. So then everybody started calling me Cayuco Jonronero.

Humberto "Berto" Hernandez: The point is that every time someone tells the story, there are several versions of the story. I want to clarify this, because even though we are related, I have a somewhat different story than that of Blas. I met Hemingway, or Papa, as we used to call him, in two different ways, one as Blas has just told us and the other way as I am going to tell you.

Though we were all children, some were older and some were younger, as both Fico and Blas just said. One day, Saturday—we used to have our own team, but we were older than Fico and Blas. So one day, on Saturday, we went house by house trying to collect money to buy a baseball. So we had very little money, because what people could give was a penny or two, and we had practically no money to buy a baseball. Someone said, "Why don't we go and ask Mister _______ for money," and he was a millionaire who lived on the neighboring finca, in the back of Finca Vigía, and he was the owner of the streetcars in Havana, Cienfuegos, and Santiago de Cuba.

We tried to access Mister _______, but he had a gatekeeper, so we told him what we wanted. It seems that he asked Mister _______, but they just put the dogs on us, so we had to run away. Someone said, "Why don't we go to see this American guy, this new neighbor, now living in Mister _______'s finca?" We came up the drive and came to the veranda and the housekeeper talked to us.

She asked, "What do you want?"

We said, "We want to see the American guy"—we didn't even know his name—"because we want to ask him for money so that we can play baseball tomorrow."

Then Papa came. He said, "What do you want?"

We said, "We want to ask you for money to buy a baseball."

So then he said, "Why didn't you go to see the guy on the other finca, the Primo?"

"Because he put the dogs on us," we said.

So he said, "How much do you want?"

We said, "Whatever you can give us." We showed him the cap, and he could see that we had just a few pennies.

So then he said, "If I give you twenty pesos, twenty bucks, how many balls can you buy?"

Young members of Gigi's All-Stars. Ernest Hemingway Collection, John F. Kennedy Presidential Library and Museum, Boston.

I was sort of the boss of the team and I said, "Well, a ball cost two fifty, so if you give me twenty bucks I can buy eight balls, so that we have a ball for eight Sundays."

So that's why I told you before that the story has two versions. But it's not a contradiction.

Then he said, "Why don't you come here and play baseball with my children?" Patrick and Gigi were there. He said, "We have gloves, we have bats, we have balls, we have everything."

I just said, "When can we come?"

"Tomorrow?"

And then I said, "Well, not tomorrow, because we have our own games, but on Monday we will come. On Monday we will be here." It was the summer vacation, so we were off school. And I said, "Well, we have to tell our parents that we are coming here." Because at those times you couldn't just go out of your house and disappear. You had to tell your parents. We had to ask for our parents' permission.

On the next Monday we came, and there was Gigi and Patrick and Hemingway and the rest of the boys who, even though they were younger, . . . came here before and played baseball. That's how the Gigi's All-Stars began.

Joseito Rodriguez: I have not much to say because I played not for long. I came to be a part of the team and to reinforce the team. I never played here, but we were taken several times; I played several times at Campo de Armada. I never played baseball, but I used to come here and play sometimes with the rest of the children, and sometimes to collect money.

Humberto "Berto" Hernandez: He was just a backup. He recruited.

David B. Martens: Anything else you want to say before we open up to questions? What do you want to ask Gigi's All-Stars?

Scott Schwarr: How was the baseball field laid out? Was home plate by the front gate, facing towards the house?

Alberto "Fico" Ramos Enriquez: Coming up the drive on the left, and home was facing to the gate, and there were only three bases, home and two bases.

Scott Schwarr: Home was at the gate?

Alberto "Fico" Ramos Enriquez: By the gate, towards the gate.

Humberto "Berto" Hernandez: Three bases; remember, they were very young. Nine, ten years old.

Alberto "Fico" Ramos Enriquez: Home, first base, and second base.

Humberto "Berto" Hernandez: Papa used to pitch, but not very hard. He was a big, strong man and we were just little kids.

Audience member: Hemingway bought each boy a uniform, a flannel uniform with stripes with a number in the back. The cap had a blue star, and they were the first children to ever wear a baseball uniform in the whole municipality. He wore number nine, because he asked for it. He told Papa that he wanted a nine on his uniform.

Audience member: Where did they come from? Who made them? How did they get them?

Audience member: Three famous stores had an atelier. But they don't know exactly.

Audience member: This is for the cook: Did Hemingway eat the fish that he caught, the animals that he shot, and also serve them to his guests? Did he like wild game?

Alberto "Fico" Ramos Enriquez: Yes, he did. Usually when they were shooting pigeons they never ate that. Just the breast maybe. And then the fish, when they were fishing three or four days, they brought the fish. The fish was to be kept wrapped in special paper, cut to pieces, and then they wrote the date, the day . . . the date, and they kept the fish in freezers that were under Mary's room, in the basement. And yes, they did eat the fish and serve them to the guests. And something I want to add is that whenever they came and brought fish, René and Fico—the maid usually gave fish to the staff people.

Gladys Rodriguez Ferrero: Dr. José Luís Herrera Sotolongo, who was his personal doctor, used to say that Hemingway liked to know the date when he had caught the fish, because he liked telling his guests the story about how he had caught the fish (he made up the story), and they had to keep records of the dates so that they used the oldest fish. And they had to take the fish out maybe two days before, because it was like a rock. Frozen like a rock.

Jose Rodriguez and Blas Fernandez. Supplied by David Martens.

Alberto "Fico" Ramos Enriquez: They used to go to the hunters' club on Wednesdays and Sundays. And the pigeons they brought they gave away to Fico, to the Villarreal brothers, and Blas, all the children. Baseball players.

The day before, Miss Mary used to tell us what they wanted for the meals for the next day. So, usually, vegetables a lot, and not as much seasoning as we use in Cuba, salad, mashed potatoes, any kind of greens.

Audience member, Cuban woman: Cubans used to eat large portions of fruit. She remembered Miss Mary ordered the fruit to be cut into smaller pieces, into smaller portions, and, for example, turtle soup, but Fico said that turtle soup, usually they used hen soup.

Alberto "Fico" Ramos Enriquez: The pieces of avocado were smaller than we Cubans used to eat. And strawberries they brought in small boxes, and they ate the strawberries with cream. We had—the staff had—meals in the pantry, and Gigi *did* like the Cuban seasoning and he used to go a lot to eat with us.

Carmen Fournier Cusa: First of all, to thank David for bringing this living memory to the context of the conference. And thank these people here, who have become our dear friends. First of all, for their faithfulness to the truth, and in second place, because of their discretion towards Hemingway's private life. Because in my research, I am trying to, always trying to find out what happened, how his personal life was, what happened with his women. For example, I know, and Fico will say if it's true or not, that the first day Adriana Ivancich came to the house, she was coming with her mother, and Fico carried her huge suitcases into the house. And many times I've asked him . . . *pushed* him, about it, asking, "Fico, what happened? Did you see them? Where did you see them? By the pool?"

And he said, "I saw nothing."

Alberto "Fico" Ramos Enriquez: When Adriana Ivancich came, the day she arrived, Hemingway was out of Cuba, he was abroad; there was no one in the house, no maid, just René Villarreal and me. I carried her suitcases, and then all of a sudden she took a huge dress with fancy laces and everything, embroidery. And she gave it to me to iron. Very daring as he is, René took it, opened the ironing board, took the iron, turned the iron on, and he started ironing. But he burned part of the dress. He had to take the dress, running, to the Villarreal, to the mother of the Villarreal brothers, and she was, in the end—she was repairing and had to iron the dress. And that night he took it back.

David B. Martens: We are out of time, but let me just say that it is a high honor and a great privilege to be up here with the "boys." And I appreciate the fact that we've studied Hemingway's work, but these men have told us a bit about Hemingway the man. And I'd like to close on a personal note. All of us are here today because we have one thing in common: our passion for kindness and understanding. It's *far* stronger than our passion for politics. And for us Americans, our temporary president makes it hard for us to get here. But we come. We have friends here. Thank you.

Blas "Cayuco Jonronero" Fernandez: We want to thank our friend Carmen here, because her words have been timely said. And we want to thank her for what she said to us. We think that we should exactly maintain that discretion towards who was for us like a father. The memories we have from the times we lived here and the times we shared with Hemingway . . . mean a great deal for us. Hemingway was our second father, for all of us.

Mary and Ernest

Too Close to See

ALBERT J. DEFAZIO III

There's a wonderful moment in Salinger's *Catcher in the Rye* when Holden and Phoebe are alone in the pitch darkness of her bedroom, their mother having just kissed her good night, oblivious of her son's presence. After Mrs. Caulfield leaves, Holden tries to locate Phoebe, the adoring younger sister whose willingness to sacrifice her Christmas dough, to forego her role as Benedict Arnold in the Christmas Pageant, and to loyally follow her wayward brother "out west," teaches him about unconditional love and inevitable change. It being pitch black and all, Holden cannot find Phoebe until she speaks and he realizes that she has been right next to him all along. Sometimes our very nearness to a thing blinds us to it.

This irony seems to have visited Mary Hemingway: the thing that was too plainly visible to see was her husband's failing health. She was not alone in her oblivion, for the alluring rewards of genius are so attractive that they often steal our gaze: think on Hemingway's Nobel Prize, his cosmopolitan experience, and his incalculable impact on English prose. The toll of genius is less appealing: consider Hemingway's alcoholism, his mercurial personality, and his unquiet domestic life. Mary Welsh was the last of Hemingway's wives to attempt to balance her husband's Janus-faced genius, and she tells that tale in *How It Was*. Rife with detail, what became her autobiography was initially conceived as an aid for her husband: she imagined that one day he would turn to her for the names and places and minutiae—the things and their sequences—that often characterize his prose. Hemingway never drew upon this resource, so a decade and a half after his death, Mary reshaped her diaries and supplemented them with passages from their correspondence.

The Hemingways' correspondence included more than the letters that they posted to one another; it also included formal notes that they exchanged about serious matters. Theirs was an acrimonious relationship, and even on their wedding day their sniping was enough to unsettle friends. Chief causes of Mary's discontent included her husband's inconsistent attention, his propensity to strut before other women (Jigee Viertel, Adriana Ivancich, the Wakumba native Debba, and Valerie Danby-Smith), and his absorption in his writing. Another source of strife—one that would grow increasingly troublesome as years passed—was money management. In the undated letter that follows,[1] Mary balances apology and explanation for having upset Ernest regarding finances. Internal evidence—a reference to "generously permitted me . . . this year" and another to items that they would be sending to Martha Gellhorn—suggest that the letter was written during their first year of marriage, but in her memoir, *How It Was,* Mary includes a lament from June 1945—prior to their marriage on March 13, 1946—that seems to echo its tone: "In spite of visiting children and the challenges of a whole new range of skills to learn, I sometimes sank into depressions of spirit, no deeper than gullies; I was probably longing for the concomitants of my old life. Instead of independence and my personally earned income, I was dependent on Ernest in all decisions about our living as well as economically. I didn't like my income appearing haphazardly as gifts. Economic slavery, I thought. . . . I had been an entity; now I was an appendage" (162).

Having long been used to running her own life and finances, Mary chafed against Ernest's "executive technique" at the Finca:

> Dearest Mountain—I always said we would never have disputes about money and meant it, knowing how truly generous you are and knowing that by itself, it has always been the least of my troubles. And I'm terribly sorry about this dispute and want very much to be forgiven for what sounded like big injustice, but truly truly not intended as such.
>
> You were also hurt last night by my speaking of margins of spendable dough because you got from it the inference that I thought you weren't earning enough. Darling, as we both know, you earn massively and impressively, according to my old standards or any other standards.
>
> And what I was trying, so unsuccessfully, to say is that wealth, as I feel wealthy or not, has little to do with massive or impressive dough (though no dame who likes luxury as much as me would deny that it's often very nice thing to have). But wealth, I think, is a state of mind—though it may sound like hotair nonsense to you. It's like the security I used to feel in my topfloor flat in London, where the roof was papiermache and you could crumble away

the bricks with your fingernails. I think wealth is freedom from fear of being broke, freedom from the irritation of feeling pinched, and from the need to apologize for small gaieties to oneself or dependents or partners. But I don't ask you to accept this idea which is sort of unorthodox. But I want to keep it myself, if I can, because it keeps me peaceful, or contributes thereto.

It's not your fault at all—as I failed to say clearly enough—or maybe at all, that I have got the pinched feeling a couple of times (not when we thought we were broke) from checking details of household expenditure. I am beginning to understand that your larger menage requires a different executive technique that my small ones did. And I will learn your system of bookkeeping, and will try to do it more efficiently and better than I have. Also, I will not forget that, even when I am wishing I could spend the time on something else, it is one of the few things of our life that is not lovely and pleasant to do. Darling I apologize for saying this so badly before that you thought I was accusing you of cupidity. No possible accusation could be less justified, and I didn't mean it that way, or to hurt you.

Maybe, if you would consider last night's discussion in the light of the fact that since before I got out of college I've earned my own dough, paid hospital bills and other emergencies, lent to Dad and my friends, generally made dough dispositions and managed to save as well as to live without worrying about it, it would be easier for you to understand my meaning, and that I was not at all critical of your general procedure.

About me and dough, for the record, this is my permanent attitude: 1. I am tremendously greedy and constantly concerned for security for my parents, that they may have moderate comforts and no worry about money as long as they live. 2. I love to compete with Les Girls in pretty clothes and decor, and you have generously permitted me to do so with ease and satisfaction this year. (And of course I like to do it on a basis of ingenuity and grace as well as pure dough.) 3. This is the first time in my adult life that I have been "a dependent" and not unnaturally, there are odd, *rare* moments when it feels funny. But the only actual security I ever had was a job and small or medium savings, and I risked them both more than once. So for myself, ie. not you or us or the children, about security I do not give a damn.

About the current riches, I think it would be nice if you could, under special expenses or some other department, earmark some of the money for the piano, a mechanical lawnmower (when they are available) and houselinen—towels, sheets, pillowcases and napkins—which can substitute for those we will be sending to Martha.

About the cheque, darling, you have given me many gifts and I have loved and enjoyed every one of them and been so happy spending and using them. This one is especially generous in heart as well as dough, coming now. But I have no use for it, don't want it and couldn't take it, and will only be unhappy if you press it on me. False pride, probably, I don't know. But thank you very much and very sincerely, just the same.

Yours,
Mary

The Hemingways must have reached an understanding about household finances, because they successfully endured a lengthy campaign of home renovations and additions. Nevertheless, their years together remained turbulent: damaging plane crashes, disappearing friends, and failing health were constant visitors. Their nadir was probably the dangerous summer of 1959, spent following the mano a mano between Antonio Ordóñez, son of Cayetano Ordóñez (the prototype for Pedro Romero in *The Sun Also Rises*), and Luis Miguel Dominguín, whose sister, Carmen, was Antonio's wife. Ernest began traveling with Ordóñez beginning in late May and continued through August. It was exhausting. It also immersed Hemingway in an environment where he was a man among men—something akin to his wartime experience. Such an environment did not encourage his awareness of domestic responsibilities or familial obligations. Further complicating things, Spain contributed an attractive eighteen-year-old woman to Hemingway's cuadrilla, Valerie Danby-Smith. Mary had seen this before: in Venice, it was Adriana Ivancich; in Africa it was Debba, the Wakamba native. In Spain, the Hemingways' marriage and Ernest's health suffered.

Preoccupied with work and friends, Ernest had diminishing time and less patience for Mary's needs. Not even the spectacular birthday party that she threw for him restored her place in his affections. In *How It Was,* Mary recalls that although Ernest "had written me a couple of sweet notes," she found that "I seemed to have become inaudible to him" (475). When she did speak up, asking in one instance for water, she "set off a torrent of harangue" and was accused of being "just like my mother, or his mother, who drove his father to suicide" (475). The tirade lasted until 4 A.M. (475). Following this, Mary observed, "where I had been inaudible to my husband, I now seemed also to be invisible, a worthless quality in a wife, I thought" (476). Tired of being a "ghost wife" (476) and knowing that both the Finca and the house that they had recently purchased from Robert Topping in Ketchum, Idaho, would require extensive preparations before the arrival of Antonio and Carmen at summer's end, Mary chose to return to Cuba in advance of Ernest, crossing the Atlantic, by jet for the first time, on October 4, 1959. Their separation prompted an exchange of letters, as well as unsent drafts by Ernest.

The Cuba to which Mary returned, which had been Batista's when the Hemingways had departed, now belonged to Castro; once home at the Finca Vigía, she gathered her thoughts and, judging from the specificity of her missives, may well have consulted her journals before writing her husband. Two of the following letters address the condition of the Finca; the third letter explains why Mary intends to leave Ernest. She and other biographers have published excerpts and paraphrases of her letters, written in October 1959. In reply, Ernest sent a pair of letters and a cable, the upshot of which has made its way into biographies, but he also drafted replies that he apparently did not send, for Mary makes no mention of them. A paraphrase of these unsent replies follows.

Thursday, Oct. 8—Savoy-Hilton hotel
N.Y. [date in MH's? hand, "1959"]

Dear Ernest—Situation report:

As we suspected, [Robert] Topping [from whom the Hemingways purchased the house in Ketchum] removed from the house this summer everything except the furniture listed in the inventory Chuck [Atkinson, a friend from Ketchum] sent us—sheets, towels, kitchen utensils, china, glassware, etc. When I talked to him on the phone, he said Topping's wife's father had come up from Hailey and removed the stuff. "He claimed they were all personal effects," Chuck said in a rather helpless tone. Since there seems to be nothing sound I can do about the thievery on my own initiative from here, I have done nothing about that.

But Chuck said he could get us such stuff as sheets and pillowcases and towels at wholesale prices, so I got a letter off to him yesterday suggesting quantities and sizes of an initial order, so that that part of the furnishing will be on hand when you are ready to move in. I also ordered from Maison Glass:

A small quantity of kitchen crockery—baking dishes etc.—to be sent out out there, and

A small quantity of food—breasts of chicken in glass, smoked trout paste, etc.—to be sent to Cuba.

I have also bought this typewriter—German made, called Olympia—portable but very solid ($119) all steel parts chrome-covered against rust, with a hard case of some new composition—and will have it shipped to Ketchum before I leave here.

The guns are with Mr. Arent at Abercrombie's—to be cleaned and held there until you write him to send them to Ketchum, also a cold-weather hunting jacket for the use of Carmen [Ordóñez] or other females. Also a pair of hunting boots for ditto. Abercrombie's have better ones than we could find last year in Ketchum.

This afternoon I will buy and send out a set of the double-walled plastic glasses for drinks and some kitchen knives, which we can't find out there.

Some of the luggage I am shipping to Ketchum, some to Chicago, and taking the rest back to Cuba. Have plane booked for Saturday, the 10th, have wired René [Villarreal, the majordomo of the Finca (M. Hemingway 186)] asking for Juan [the chauffeur (154)] to come to airport. Will try there to organize the Finca for entertaining Antonio and Carmen and will there await suggestions for further procedure from you.

The flight from Paris was my first physical contact with our great new world of scientific accomplishment—amazing, wonderful, and somehow on the outer edges of reality. I kept remembering the Nevile Shute book about the pilot taking the British scientist and his daughter along the same route with their stops in Greenland and all the mysticism about ancient cultures. Didn't know it in advance, but this flight stopped in Iceland for refueling—we had all just finished reading the N.Y. morning papers brought that night from the U.S. Even coming off the huge almost-silent smooth-moving ndege [bird], one felt how remote and strange that big brown island was, floating in it[s] acqueous northern light.

They refuel so quickly, and we were up to 33, 000 feet again in minutes, me having a drink with Mr. Hayes and his wife—both very pleasant. Lunch—good gray fresh caviar, hoards of other things and wonderful rare roast beef and a fine Beaujolais. The blue-eyed gentleman who was my seat-mate turned out to be Simon Elwes, the British portrait painter, coming over to paint society women here and the King ranch woman. He is gay and amusing, told me a lot about the King ranch which they run in the manner of an eighteenth century kingdom. His son, who married the heiress in Cuba and got into the papers, is doing fine in London and Elwes says the girl is very sweet and also intelligent.

About the time they came along with the roast beef on its trolley—as at Simpson's in London—the pilot said to look down through the clouds on the right of the aircraft and we'd see Greenland—sure enough, there it was, with dark outlines and glaciers on top. "The temperature on the outside of the aircraft is 54 degrees below zero," said the pilot over the loudspeaker. We could see plenty of iceburgs too, through gaps in the clouds. All the way, we had a fairyland landscape below us—an immense, sunny snowscape, with hills and canyons and occasionally a little pond, calm and blue-gray—the ocean, six miles beneath us. We were having luncheon coffee when we passed over Gander, and we were trailing out of the plane at Idlewild [New York], after a stop in Boston, exactly 12 hours, Paris time, after I got out of bed at the Ritz that morning. How I wish you could do this flight instead of the boat. It is a really new and wonderful experience, especially coming the northern route.

I have seen Hotch [A. E. Hotchner, companion and collaborator for adaptations], George Brown [longtime friend and sometime boxing trainer of Ernest (M. Hemingway 247)] and Georgette here. Hotch wonders if you will do the short recording about which he wrote you for the T.V. *Killers*. He sweetly took me to see the Ethel Merman show, Gypsy, of Leland [Hayward, Broadway producer (M. Hemingway 295)]—show worthless—but advice Hotch gave me very good. George and Georgette took me to dinner last night at Le Veau Dort—both in fine shape. Otherwize nobody but have talked on the phone to Harvey Breit [of the *New York Times*] who hopes to see you when you get here. Called Slim—not in—and by some strange mix-up, Pam Churchill got a message. She and Leland are only waiting for his divorce in order to marry. She has sold her Paris flat. Talked to Connie on the phone—she is being operated on tomorrow for cancer of the breast—I'll call her Saturday morning before I leave.

The letter you asked me to write you about our personal relations, I find very difficult to do. Too clogged up with emotions and loneliness and heartbreak. The essence of it is that all evidence, as I see it, shows that you have no further use for me in your life. I am therefore beginning to arrange my removal from it, and hope to establish a new life for myself. I have not mentioned this to anyone except Hotch, who will not tell anyone.

I am sorry you did the thing about the ring, which makes me feel like an extortionist [Ernest had presented Mary with a large ring in Madrid (Reynolds 332)].

Love and devotion, just the same as always, and good luck to you and to all La Consula—Mary

Dear B.B. [Bernard Berenson, art critic, recently deceased]—I hope they have fine pictures in Heaven.

[From margin of first page of letter:] Checked with James Cochran—West Palm Beach Terminal Co—They can ship stuff from Cuba—set it off overland.

The dangerous summer had put Ernest and Mary out of touch: he had become absorbed with his writing, with Alfred Rice's costly errors on previous tax returns, and with his station in Antonio's cuadrilla; she, having grown weary of her husband's callous treatment of her, had distanced herself from his problems as well. They had both been away from their beloved Finca for nearly a year, and neither of them could guess how or where the revolution in Cuba would leave them. Ernest's drinking, in conjunction with the pharmacological stew he had been taking (which should have precluded alcohol) and the stress of bringing *A Moveable Feast* to a conclusion and of finding some shape for the *Life* article, bore on him. The resulting ire he mercilessly directed at Mary. And abroad, Mary had no retreat. At home, she might have greeted her husband's irritability with delicacies at the table or with her deft management of the Finca and its raft of servants. In Spain, their hosts, the Davises, usurped her role as mistress of the manor. In Cuba, she had learned to focus her imagination and energies toward the end of pleasing her husband; in Spain, she found herself little more than a passenger, practically a hanger-on. And she despised it.

In response to Mary's missive of 8 October, announcing her intention of removing herself from his life, Ernest reminded her by letter that he had helped her when she was in trouble and complained about his head and neck and about Rice's $51,000 error. He also insisted that they discuss this problem face to face before she left (Reynolds 333). Just as Ernest seems to have been oblivious of the impact of his behavior toward Mary, she, too, was missing an important message: he was in trouble; his head was in bad shape. Something was wrong. In retrospect, Mary and others came to view Ernest's erratic behavior as an outward sign of his inward troubles, but as she typed her lengthy reports on the Finca and her feelings toward Ernest, she clearly viewed his treatment of her as a meanness of spirit and not as a manifestation of illness.

Monday night, Oct. 19th, 1959

THIS IS THE FINCA AND CUBA SITUATION REPORT

There is such a lot to tell you, I'll put it into departments as much as I can.

WELFARE OF FRIENDS: Everybody better than I anticipated. Mayito [Menocal, wealthy Cuban friend (Reynolds 266)], little (big) Mayito and Pedro came to lunch Sat., are surviving economically—they sold practically all the land, retaining the rice and sugar mills, got $2 [million] instead of the $1,800,000 Mayito pere expected—the govt. bond deal in which they have faith. Generally they have much more faith, and are more cheerful, than I'd expected—so is almost everybody I've so far talked to—fatalistic, but with a hopeful shrug rather than a shudder. They say Elicio [Arguelles, who, along with Mayito, Ernest described as "my best friends in this country" (M. Hemingway 411)] has had everything confiscated except a couple of houses in town—it was he who decided not to renew his lease of the Fronton—their son's father-in-law (we saw wedding) was pal of [Fulgencio] Batista altos, so son and wife are in U.S. Raul exiled. They are in favor of many of present govt. ministers. Will envite Elicio for when he can come.

José Luis [Herrera, formerly chief surgeon for the 12th International Brigade in Spain; friend and doctor to Hemingway in Cuba (M. Hemingway 153–54)] still working, part time, at Lab., and every night giving Red Cross lectures to all sorts of group. Was in charge of the 8 first aid stations for the 26 July rally—half-million guajiros [peasants] in Havana—all, so far, for no dough. In good health, cheerful, sweet as ever.

Roberto [Herrera, brother of José Luis, and Ernest's "sometime odd-job helper" (M. Hemingway 180)]—transferred from Sears store—no stoves left to sell—to work warehouse, salary cut from average $300, with commissions, to $140—violently pro-revolution, happy to make any sacrifices necessary now, brimming with hope and confidence. I arrived with $80 and some U.S. dollars—Roberto said, "Best thing you can do with them is give them to govt." Almost no American currency in circulation now—BRING IN ENOUGH TO GET YOU OUT AGAIN—unless current travel convention brings it in.

[Dr.] Cucu [Kohly, Ernest's friend and fellow fisherman (M. Hemingway 157)] came to lunch, put cars back on active insurance, admired Fidel [Castro] etc. etc. for ideals etc. He is in good health and spirits, inclined to make speeches rather than to converse. Friendly and pleasant.

Gregorio's [Fuentes, mate on the *Pilar* (M. Hemingway 157)] two sons-in-law, the army one and another one, out of jobs, also the relative who used to drive him here. G. in good health still not touching drink, taking some injections for strength—may be getting poor-health complex, maybe not. Had provided no fish whatsoever for house, apparently worried about family finances. More below.

Lee Samuels [friend of the Hemingways (M. Hemingway 307)] well recovered from stomach-cutting—cheerful. Some parts of business wobbly, but he's fatalistic too. Freddy [Samuels, son of Lee and Cecile (M. Hemingway 308)] suddenly got married last Sat. night in N.Y., and Lee and Ceil went up for it. He'll be back soon, or is back. Says of three top banker friends he knows, one—Bill Heagney—undecided about future, one confident, one unconfident.

(Interruption: Roberto just arrived, says Feo is coming—I hadn't realized the date was fijo [fixed]—must get some food.)

11 P.M. They have just left. I rustled up spaghetti with sauce from the deepfreeze, salad, etc. Feo impatient with Red Cross—"can't eat ideals." Otherwize pleasant—lots of talk about Almeria, Murcia—that part, where Roberto was during the war.

All Finca people okay—Rene has kept house beautifully. Lola [Richards, housemaid (M. Hemingway 451)] nice as usual. She has passport, in case you want to take or send her to Ketchum for winter months. Pichillo [the head gardener (M. Hemingway 451)], Ana [the laundress (M. Hemingway 451)], Mundo—others, all smiling. I hired, for this temporado only, Marta, the village girl we had here a couple weeks last spring—she understands job is temporary, will be necessary to help with Casita [possibly *caseta,* "little house"] and general work when A. [Antonio] and C. [Carmen] arrive.
SITUATION AT FINCA: Except for this typewriter, the electric wiring, and the big water pump, every machine here was either not functioning at all, or mal-functioning when I arrived. Tampoco Pilar. Juan met me at airport with Chrysler—starting home, couldn't get lights to function. Said it was "Bobina" [coil]. Next morning I asked him to get new bobina, check and clean all electric wiring, clean filter etc. etc.—Mufflers and tubes full of holes. Got new ones—Cucu checked old ones with me—agreed it needed new ones. It has now had a general overhaul, greasing, oil change—sounds okay. Plymouth not functioning. Went to town in it, motor stopped, couldn't get it started again. It is now getting overhaul, battery check, new bobina, etc. Pisacora [local dialect for "station wagon"] doesn't function—battery gone—need new echapa [one of the exterior parts of the car]—will do that after Plymouth.

Pool pump was not functioning—called Schmidt who took *motor* to town for cleaning—found family of dead rats inside. Pump itself making racket—shaft alignment all wrong and shaft ground away. Schmidt agreed to deduct the $125 we lent him two years ago from present repair costs, and guarantees to have pool properly functioning by Nov. 1. Is removing rocks, gravel and sand from filter tanks, for washing with hydrochloric acid—necessary he insists after 10 years of use—and returning them. He showed me the sand, clotted with chloro from the pool.

Disk-changer in living room not making records fall, not moving its arm from rack to record. Took it to repair place Lee Samuels recommended. Will go check on it tomorrow.

Little "deans of S. Florida" radio not functioning. Got new batteries.

No batteries in new "All Transistor" Zenith radio—will get.

Latest kitchen stove—we bought from Roberto at Sears—only semi-functioning. Wiring dirty and rusted. Got Roberto to call pal in repair-dept. All fixed now, and only cost 3.50.

Called Gregorio, suggested we go fishing in *Pilar.* He said, better *Tin Kid* [the launch]. *Pilar* not in good condition. I invited him to come chat here at house. Turns out *Pilar* hasn't been up on the ways for a cleaning of her bottom in seven months—since before we were here last April. G. went into long discourse on the importance of ripping the canvas off the decks, relaying new canvas, etc., but, remembering that you usually have her hull scraped and repainted three times a year, I urged him to get a turno [turn] at the varadero [dry dock], and to call me up about it. No call, so I called him today. He still hasn't got a turno, but hopes to get one this week. I had you[r] letter with checks, for which many thanks, saying "Please see for Christ's sake has boat ready for when Antonio comes." So I told him you said it was urgent, and he agreed to do all possible. Will check on this—it usually takes a week of cleaning, painting etc. to put her in good shape after the varadero.

Could you let me know when Antonio is coming, and, if you have news, whether or not Carmen is also coming. We're working close to deadline on everything.

Have had bomberos [firefighters] come and replace liquid in the fire-extinguishers.

Have Cecilio [Finca's carpenter (M. Hemingway 451)] replace window panes broken in Casita by Guanabacoa explosion last year, also repaint some furniture in Castia, also repaint front gate, which weatherbeaten and dirty, also replace couple tablas [possibly "floorboards"] in bottom of Casita and a couple broken screens in Biblioteca [library]. No big jobs, just sprucing up.

Found comejen [insects] in big library table—am attacking with Flit bombs.

Rain every day since I got here. Hurricane Judith passed close and we got heavy rains. Got home, having been stalled in Plymouth in storm, found rain dripping through roof of my room like sieve—bed, desk etc. wet—but bed not yet soaked as before. Action by all hands, and we got bed moved and saved—now, after two days, mattress appears dry.

[Inserted atop p. 3] Am sending in big envelop Hotch's story (Hotchner 10–11, 24, 26) of you and teen-agers in Hailey—both of you very good, I think.

René had thought that part of roof okay—but dripping was in same part where Ceiba bough crashed through when you were here and my mother had died. René went up next morning between showers, spread plastic cement over all the holes he could find and dripping slowly subsided except near front edge. Have been working in library. No torrential storms since then, just fine rains and showers—so don't know how much roof will resist.

In living room, the place where the plaster fell and has been patched, has not been painted. It still drips inside from some hole where there is an elbow of the top canal leading into the pipe which fills the reservoir on the front terrace. I think I can get the village taller [repair shop] to come and solder a new piece of zinc to the old one and stop up the hole. Mayito knows a roof-repair man who is an expert in our kind of asbestos-cement repair, and I have asked him—if he can find the man—to ask him to come and look. Although living room ceiling patch is not pretty, think it better not to repaint until we have assurance of no more leaking. If you want it painted, please let me know.

We were full out of Finca writing paper—have ordered more.

Lee lent René $170 to pay exorbitant water bill. René filed protest and they promised to send inspector, check meter, gave him receipt for the money and promised either to return it or to apply it as credit for future water bills. Lee also paid insurance premiums. He came out the morning after I arrived and I wanted to write him a check, but he insisted on waiting to deal with you. With the extra check you sent me, and the one to René for running X's, I can handle car and pool and other repair and also repay Lee. Let me know if you want me to insist on this.

Mr. Zia warned me that when present stocks of liquor are sold, new imports will be double in price. So I ordered case of Pinch Bottle, also case of gin, brought home bottle of White Horse, not yet used up.

You asked a reminder of what you could bring with you on boat. Only 3 things.

1. My American Express Credit card, if it arrived.
2. Small box of Dupont Cigarette Lighter gas refills.
3. Vuitton bottle bag, which they will deliver to Ritz hotel and is paid for by Credit card.

A present for René, if you wish to make one. I brought something for Lola, Anna and René's wife.

Cristobal Colon, the sybarite, is fine, lazy, loving and willing to have me share breakfast, lunch and dinner with him. Ambrose fine, Strangey fine and loving as ever. Misouri, orange kitty and other cats in good shape. Dogs noisy but okay. Finca green and lush with all the rain, trees, bushes and vines burgeoning, first planting of vege seeds already in la huerta [garden], if not washed away.

I'm sorry your neck is so bad and hope you can rest on the boat and make it better. In spite of all the problems, I find it lovely being here at home again among the friendly, familiar faces and things—swam 40 round trips in the pool 2 days before the repairing started. Fascinating and happy too, the atmosphere of Cuba (in contrast to what I had expected from reading the outside press)—everybody so *proud* of the government's honesty, so proud of the little boxes on the streets where citizens may write and put a complaint against a policeman who has been rude, so proud of their new home-building program, so proud of Fidel's tree-planting which is everywhere visible—a happy thing to live among confidence and hope—and I hope so very much they will not be disappointed.

Greetings from and welcome to the new Cuba—

THIS IS THE PERSONAL LETTER

The reason I feel I must move out of your life is that I cannot, physically or in my nerves or in my reason, stand up to [the] neglect you have showed me from San Isidro onwards right up until the morning I left Paris, combined with your frequent barrages of disparagement, cruel and unjust abuse and criticism. And also your leaving me with no hope for the future.

Item about neglect: You spoke to me only with irritation and annoyance after I got the nose and throat infection—pharyngitis—never said a word of sympathy.

Item: When I broke my toe on the river beyond Aoiz, you raised on your elbow and said courteously, "I'm sorry you broke your toe." (I have heard you mention many times how painful a broken toe can be and I was very careful at no time to complain about it.) But you showed no concern about sending me any food or drink while you dined out, nor did you ever help me dig out something edible from the remains of the picnics.

Item: Most hurtful of all as the summer waxed and waned, your compliments and attentions and interest and kisses for many girls and women, nothing for me. Nothing spontaneous towards me on your part, not even on the night of your birthday party. Nothing unless I, longing for some sign of affection, pushed myself up to you and asked. Whereupon you would give me a summary peck, thinking of other things or people.

Item: Our last night in Paris, after Charlie's big dinner party and you charming with all the people, you went to bed, briefly criticized my excess clothes and went to sleep. No "Good night." You knew we were about to be separated for four or five weeks, longer than we ever have been before. But no offer of a good-night kiss, no touch of hands.

All this very different from our ride back to Masindi after the second crash. Different from your coming into my room after a chop suey lunch years ago, peering around and saying, "I'm looking for an acolade—to give to you."

Item about hostility: Many many mornings when you were at La Consula, if I went to ask you a simple question about plans, programs or whatever, your face took on a look of irritation and impatience and you would say, "I haven't got time. I have to go shit now. I have to go swim now." If you did talk to me it was with resentment and hostility, giving me the wounding impression that I was intruding into prohibited reserves where, unlike other friends and admirers, I had no right to enter. Except for the night at the parador on the way to Ronda after Murcia, you didn't talk to me at all, all summer. Once at Pamplona at the bulls you sweetly said, "Nice to be with my kitten" but when Polly Peabody came to join us you turned your back to me and spoke exclusively with her.

Item about abuse: In Pamplona, when you woke me out of a deep sleep to massage the cramp in your leg and I could not do it immediately, my muscles being relaxed from sleep—a well-known phenomenon—you criticized and excoriated me for days thereafter.

Item: In Valencia, I having arrived late for the bar session but a full hour before it was take-off time for dinner, I told you and it was true that both Annie [Davis] and Teddy-Jo [Paulson] had arrived five to ten minutes after I had. You said, "You are the biggest liar I have ever known." It seems improbable that a man should make such a strong statement about such a minor issue to a woman he professes he love.

Item: Arriving in Madrid at 2 A.M., you ordered take-off at 9:30—if I correctly recall the hour—and said you wanted me to buy you a bottle of Listorine in the morning. Exhausted, and having planned my morning minute by minute in order to be ready precisely on time—not then knowing that nobody else would be ready and that the set hour was fiction at least for that day—I said I didn't know if I would have time to get the Listorine. As it turned out, I had plenty of time, since I *was* ready on time, we left an hour later, and I got the Listorine and told you so. But for nights thereafter you bawled me out and criticized and nagged me for having said, at 2 A.M. I wasn't sure I'd have time to do your errand.

Very different from here in Cuba when I brought the hot lunches in the *Tin Kid* to you and Elicio, fishing, and was hauled aboard and hugged by you, even though you were very busy paying attention to steering and fishing and cameramen. Very different from our hard work and personal friendship and harmony and affection and fun at Cabo Blanco, even though you were terribly busy running that show and I was busy helping you.

Item about no hope for the future: As we were driving north from Merida toward Caceras, after the hideous night at Ronda, you said, unequivocally, simply—"I will go shooting with Nietz Gray whenever I wish." You and Bill [Davis] in the front of the Ford, Valery [Danby-Smith], sick, and I in the back. This leaves me with nothing but hurt and isolation and work to look forward to in Idaho this winter. Therefore, if I go there at all, to put the house in some kind of working order, I will not stay.

Item: You have this summer grown into the habit of giving orders. Not requests or suggestions. Very few "will you's" or "pleases." If not to everyone—Antonio, Carmen—certainly, consistently, to me. I was born in a country which, at least politically, is free; and, except on *Pilar* or other small boats, I will not submit for the rest of my life to being ordered about, if I can stay out of prison camps.

Item: You have appeared to be happy, delighted and contented with the events of the whole summer, with your way of living—the cuadrilla [group] existence, the immense eating tables, me seeing you dimly in the distance, with your personal manners, and with your attitude toward me (you chuckled when you said the thing about shooting with Nietz), unremittingly callous and hurtful and, I must admit, new in your nature. But you obviously enjoyed it so much that it appears most unlikely that you will wish to change or will change.

Very different from our holidays at Parajaiso with the gaiety and excitement of fishing the reefs and the tranquillity and affection of the evenings and nights.

Summing up: In the four months since May, you kindly lunched with me alone, once, in the Hotel Suecia and were pleasant and sympathetic and friendly. In Paris, after a couple of unjust accusations on the way there, you spent half an hour with me, alone together, at the Jeu de Palme looking happily at the pictures. That is not enough, for me, to counterbalance all the hurt.

Your letters, including the one which has just come from La Consula, have been consistently kind and affectionate, observing the principles I have so often heard you expound to other men who were having wife-trouble. Your behavior toward me has been consistently in contrast, except for the two occasions I just mentioned.

For the last couple of months you have preached, "Think of others. Don't think of yourself." A very good rule, and you may never have noticed that for years and years I have placed ahead of all other considerations your work, your welfare, your health, your comfort, your Finca, your food, the entertainment of your friends, and lots of times of you and you have found me sometimes amusing. Except for the ice cream, which Annie insisted upon ordering and which was a total failure, I organized and produced, single-handed, your birthday party this year which everyone acclaimed as a spectacular success. It was intended to be a tribute to you. (You never thanked me.) I have written you poems, tributes to you, and made you songs, tributes to you. So why do you feel it necessary to tell me to think of others.

It did not seem to me that you yourself were following your preaching. At Cuenca, reputed to be a town well worth seeing and photographing, there was daylight after the bulls for sightseeing, but you insisted upon everyone's sitting drinking in the hotel with Einaudi and a Spanish publisher who was not your publisher. You insisted by threatening to go into such bad humor that, for my part, I gave up the sightseeing in order to preserve the peace.

On the way from Salamanca to Madrid you kept asking Bill the rhetorical question, "You know where we're going to eat tonight? "You know where we'll go tonight?" There was no room in your mind left for the consideration of others.

The business of the ring: I mentioned changing it several times after you first decided to go to Spain. Also I mentioned the pretty lighter Rupert [Bellville; English friend and traveling companion (M. Hemingway 327)] gave me. I know you heard me at least one of the times because you responded, in light manner, to my saying something about "turning it in for the next size larger." But in Paris, as all summer, you were too busy with your own affairs to devote ten minutes to a project of mine. What I wanted was not a ring or a pin, but a symbol of your regard for me. An object, without the regard or the affection, means nothing. Nov 7—His Saint Day, said pin was "a drop in the bucket."

Slim once wrote you, years ago—perhaps you had been complaining to her about me—"But she gives you so much and so generously. In case you had not noticed, I am happy doing any amount of work, giving forethought, making plans, carrying out programs, praising and goading people to get things done, paying attention to the detail, if I earn approval, and, in this case, affection and respect from The Boss. More than monetary compensation, I value friendship and solidarity and affection. But I doubt that you now wish to or could provide me with that sort of compensation for the work I do, am now doing, for you.

You will see in the other letter what we are doing here to make the place pleasant for Antonio and Carmen and you and whoever else you may have invited. I will stay to help entertain them here, if you wish me to; and when you get here we shall decide together whether or not I go out to Idaho, briefly to get things started there.

My plan is to establish a tiny flat in New York and get started earning my living as a journalist or free-lance writer or whatever you want to call it, since it is the trade I know best after housekeeping. I do not like New York at all, but Hotch points out, and he is right, you have to be there or near there to keep contact with editors and people who buy stories. I talked with a young man from *Sports Illustrated* and with Carl Brandt, and I now hear from Brandt that *Sports Illustrated* wants two of the four stories I discussed with them. A smaller one for a woman's magazine I hope to send off tomorrow—cooking.

No one in New York including Ben Finney, whom I ran into at the Savoy-Hilton (formerly Plaza) imagines that it is anything but the "difficulties" of the situation in Cuba which cause "us" to look for a pied-a-terre in N.Y. I explained to Brandt and *S.I.* that since we would be living less here and I doing less fishing, gardening, and entertaining here, I expected to have more time for writing pieces. No one but Hotch and Lee Samuels has been informed of my plans. (There are no big difficulties here in Cuba, at least now—Cuba likes its revolution—but N.Y. doesn't know that.) I haven't rented an apartment there yet, nor shipped anything up there.

It is sort of comic, me, now old and beat-up reviving an ancient "career" especially in New York, that loneliest of all towns. But I will take the loneli ness and somehow support it, in preference to your discuidado [discussing] and scarification.

I am sorry this letter has gone on so long and hope you will excuse it. You would doubtless have edited my thoughts differently than I have; but I don't have you here for advice, and anyhow I have to start learning to get along without you. I did that all summer, unwillingly, and protesting. No more.

I wish you health, true love, prosperity and a pleasant voyage, fun in New York, and will try to arrange a pleasant homecoming for you.

Love and devotion
as ever, Mary

In reply, Ernest wrote a cable, most of which Mary reproduces in her memoir. It thanks her for her letters and her "tremendous work" at the Finca; it notes that Antonio has been in touch with her and relates his flight information. It addresses some of the domestic details: Ernest will pay Lee Samuels for the water bill upon his arrival; he had already paid Gregorio and given him direction regarding the *Pilar.* As for Mary's decision to remove herself from his life, he claims to respect her views but to disagree profoundly with her conclusions. He closes with "still love you" to which Mary replies in her memoir "let's see a bit of evidence" (477).

Ernest's initial response to Mary's complaints was much less circumspect. He apparently began drafting a rebuttal, undated fragments of which survive. In one note, he seems to be recalling Mary's half of previous conversations: she wants to enjoy herself and not be a drudge but will not venture out alone as if she were a divorcee; she's impatient with his complaints and tells him to act like a man; she's tired of hearing about his work and his problems and will scream if he persists. A second fragment picks up in mid-sentence on page 3 and relates an anecdote from Ernest's point of view in which he explains condescendingly that a man needs more rest in twenty-four hours than the five and a half hours that the sleeping pill provide. Ernest's version concludes with his being told to shut up and leave Mary's room. The caustic tone of these fragments lends credence to Mary's laments about her husband's treatment of her, for these notes seem to be a continuation of the bitter conflicts that engaged the two over the summer. While he did not share these fragments with Mary, he did include a comment in *The Dangerous Summer* about the difficulty of maintaining domestic tranquility while following the bullfights: “Pamplona is no place to bring your wife. The odds are all in favor of her getting ill, hurt or wounded or at least jostled and wine squirted over her, or of losing her; maybe all three” (135).

On October 27, Hemingway boarded the *Liberté*, bound for New York. After a stopover, during which he delivered his Paris memoirs to Scribners and visited the apartment that Mary had decided to rent, he arrived in Cuba on November 4, bearing a $4,000 platinum and diamond pin for his angry wife (Reynolds 335). The pin wasn't the “bit of evidence” that Mary sought. As Hemingway explained to Hotchner in a letter dated November 8, 1959, “Not thanked for pin. Was clearly told, as I should have known, she did not want pin. If got pin own fault. Don't tell her about difficulties” (DeFazio 273).

Mary was clearly angry enough to tell her husband by letter that she was making plans to leave him, and she had gone so far as to rent an apartment and contemplate how she might make her own living. But despite the litany of ills that she recalls and her stated intention to leave, Mary's actions seem designed to illustrate that she was an essential element of the Hemingway house and that, without her, it would literally fall down around Ernest's head. Her situation report covering her first few days back at the Finca occupies three pages; her personal letter, covering a year's worth of personal grievances, covers only two and a half. Was she poised to leave him? Hotchner, who spent time in Spain with the Hemingways and had visited with Mary in New York upon her return, wrote Hemingway on October 27, 1959, that he shouldn't take Mary's decision seriously and assured him that “you're in control” (DeFazio 272).

Actually, as Mary's situation report illustrates, she enjoyed abundant “control” at the Finca. When Ernest departed Spain, he would be leaving behind his generous hosts, the Davises, and the adoring cuadrilla that gathered for meals and listened to his stories. Once home, he would soon be reminded that Mary was his durable domestic partner, a status that she earned and enjoyed, and one that came at a dear price: she had, after all, traded independence and a career in journalism for it.

Just as there was no drama to provide a convenient conclusion to the mano a mano between Antonio and Luis Miguel, so too was there no crisp resolution to this conflict between the Hemingways. Antonio and Carmen enjoyed two weeks with the Hemingways in Cuba, but as soon as they arrived in Idaho (November 19), they were called away on family business. Mary fell while duck hunting and shattered her elbow (November 27); Ernest, she felt, behaved as if she had purposefully done so in order to thwart his work. This, of course, was ridiculous. And so was Ernest's claim, in early January, that the FBI was reviewing his account at that local bank. When Mary heard this, she suggested,

"Maybe you're tired, honey" (M. Hemingway 481). That she was not seized instantly by the fear that he was losing his mental balance indicates how slow she was to acknowledge her husband's illness.

Thinking that the Finca would be more conducive to his writing, the Hemingways returned to Cuba in mid-January and were joined in early February by Valerie Danby-Smith, who would serve as secretary. Mary's elbow precluded her typing, and Valerie's presence might lift Ernest's spirits and help him to bring *The Dangerous Summer* to conclusion. In the spring, Mary relinquished the idea of leaving Ernest: "For seven months I had been considering some manner by which, with the least trauma for each of us, I could retire from what seemed to me his new style of living. But I shelved the idea. He seemed to have so many grave problems confronting him that I could not increase them. Again he was addressing me as 'My dear kittner'" (M. Hemingway 485).

Convinced that he must fly back to Spain to check facts in his manuscript, Ernest made arrangements to rent an apartment in New York. Mary, anticipating that Ernest might be planning to leave Valerie with her in New York in his absence, campaigned to find some new occupation for the young woman. In a carefully worded note that emphasizes the financial burden of accommodating Valerie, Mary makes clear that everyone's best interests would be served if Valerie moved on with her own life.

July 13th, 1960

Honey—in the midst of all our other preoccupations, I feel we must think a bit about Valery and what would be good for her, and I wanted you to have this for when you pull out that drawer. In writing not to be pretentious but because it will be quicker than talking it, if there should be diversions from the subject.

The other evening when you had gone to bed early, I re-suggested to her the idea of taking some courses at Columbia this fall, to augment her education (I'd mentioned this briefly some earlier time, in the pool, I think). She was not interested. She said she had had fun so far and "got by" without more than her convent education and that she did not think that education would make you happy. (I mean, could make one happy.)

She said that what she would like most to do is press agentry for the Dublin theater, but she did not think that theater or writing courses, completed at Columbia, would help her to that end. They had told her in Dublin, the thing to do was "write." But although she has a highly developed critical sense about other people's writing, she frequently mentions how terribly difficult it is for her to write letters to her friends.

If you decide to leave us both in New York together, until you return, we will get on amiably I feel sure, and Val will doubtless learn something about New York, for what it is worth to her. (I would naturally prefer to invite Tilly [Arnold, a friend from Sun Valley], who, if she could come, would much more appreciate the trip and would be an adult and stimulating companion. But I understand your financial problems, and don't want to increase them.)

In considerations of talking Val out to Ketchum this fall, perhaps you should include an estimate of how much use you will make of her as a secretary, and the costs of equipping her for life out there and paying her room in the town. Since her proclivities are toward the bar-theater-party life of Dublin, it would seem uselessly extravagant to spend much on teaching her to shoot. Also, if you need a secretary there, there is that long-legged, tennis-playing girl, Peggy something, who they say is very good and very efficient. Or maybe Miss Till would like to do something like that, for the extra income. We must remember that except for shop clerks and bus boys, the people of her (Val's) age are away at college during the fall and she would have little chance of companionship among her own age group.

If we cannot get Lola out west to help in the house and kitchen as we did last year, I think we cannot consider Val as a possible substitute, since cooking and housekeeping are not at all her cup of tea.

I know that unsolicited consejos [advice] are doubly unwelcome—so please excuse all of this.

X X X—M.

Hemingway's response to Mary's unwelcome suggestions regarding Valerie can be read in his actions. He did bring Valerie to New York and put her up in a hotel before departing for Spain. In his subsequent letters from Spain to Mary, he complained of nervousness and feared a complete breakdown; could Mary send Valerie to help him? Despite the litany of reasons that Mary had offered in mid-July for extricating Valerie from their lives, she sent the young woman to Ernest in late August. But when he returned home, in early October, Mary accompanied him in heading to Ketchum; Valerie remained in New York. Unfortunately, she had reentered the country on an expired visa, providing Ernest with another reason to fear the FBI.

Mary's note articulating the financial, social, and personal reasons for leaving Valerie behind may have served to separate Valerie from Ernest, but it did not isolate the two. On October 25, he sent Valerie a check for $1,500 for living expenses and tuition at Columbia. As Michael Reynolds has discovered, Valerie was not enrolled at Columbia, but, given Mary's repeated suggestions that she take courses there, Ernest invented the "tuition" as a way of getting money to Valerie under auspices of which Mary could hardly disapprove. He also arranged with Valerie to correspond henceforth through George Saviers so that Mary would know nothing of their letters or financial arrangements (Reynolds 348). Mary apparently never learned of the ruse. But she was not alone in being fooled by the wily writer of fiction: in his final months he duped his doctors, too.

This correspondence very nearly spans the entire relationship between Mary and Ernest, and it serves as a microcosm for many of their most important issues. In the mid-1940s, Mary bemoaned her lack of financial independence; in March 1961, Mary and Ernest engaged in a "full-scale emotional explosion" when she refused to surrender her checkbook for his examination (Reynolds 353). Hemingway's inattention to Mary and his preening before younger women was a perpetual source of conflict in their marriage. But the most telling document is the "personal letter," because it reveals how Mary could have been so close to Ernest for so long but still failed to acknowledge his health problems: angered by his poor treatment of her, something that she admits is "new in your nature," she would not see the potential causes for his erratic behavior. Ironically, during his final trip to Spain, he seemed to recognize his own desperate condition, writing Mary "I wish you were here to look after me and help me out and keep me from cracking up" (qtd. in M. Hemingway 490). About this, Mary could only write, "I failed totally to evaluate the importance of these successive warning signals" (M. Hemingway 490–91), despite the fact that they had been right there all along.

Note

1. Mary's letters are typed and signed and include a few handwritten insertions and corrections. I have retained her spelling and reproduced her corrections. Unless otherwise noted, the annotations have been drawn from Mary's memoir.

Works Cited

DeFazio, Albert J., III, ed. *Dear Papa, Dear Hotch: The Correspondence of Ernest Hemingway and A. E. Hotchner.* Columbia, MO: Univ. of Missouri Press, 2005.

Hemingway, Ernest. *The Dangerous Summer.* New York: Scribner, 1985.

Hemingway, Mary Welsh. *How It Was.* New York: Knopf, 1976.

Hotchner, A. E. "Ernest Hemingway Talks to American Youth." *New York Herald Tribune* 18 Oct. 1959, This Week sec.

Reynolds, Michael. *Hemingway: The Final Years.* New York: W. W. Norton, 1999.

The Fishing Was Good Too

Cuban Writer Claims Torrid Love Affair with Jane Mason Drew Hemingway to Havana

WILLIAM E. DEIBLER

While many North American scholars still debate whether Ernest Hemingway and Jane Kendall Mason were lovers, Cuban writer Enrique Cirules has no doubts. In his book *Ernest Hemingway in the Romano Archipelago*, he asserts unequivocally that the two had "an intense and scandalous love affair" (23) that was gossiped about across the island.

In his book, published in Cuba in 1999, Cirules claims that the ultimate purpose of Hemingway's many visits to Havana in the 1930s was not to fish for marlin, but "to see the radiant Jane Mason" (21). Not only were they often seen carousing together in Havana's fabled night spots and at the Masons' home on the banks of the Jaimanitas River, he asserts, but they also carried on their affair at sea, first aboard a friend's yacht and later on Hemingway's boat, the *Pilar.*

When Hemingway and Mason spent four months together in 1934, "everything rapidly became scandal," Cirules writes (40). They cruised the northern coast of Cuba aboard the *Pilar*, literally shacking up for several days in a fishing hut at Punta Ganado.

Particularly intriguing is Cirules's assertion that "in the days of World War II" (58–59) Hemingway spent two days in a hotel in San Fernando de Nuevitas—the Cuban writer's hometown—with a beautiful and mysterious blonde. As described, the tryst is strikingly similar to the fictional meeting between Thomas Hudson and his first wife in Hemingway's posthumous novel *Islands in the Stream.*

Cirules writes that by all indications Hemingway met Jane Mason when she was barely twenty years old, during the writer's second visit to Havana in April 1929. "Beginning in 1929 Hemingway was constantly on the Cuban coast," Cirules writes, and "in the company of Jane Mason he developed an almost excessive liking for the splendors of Havana" (22). He asserts that the two engaged in "an intense and scandalous love affair" (23) that lasted until 1936.

Between fishing trips in the morning, attending the horse races and jai alai games in the evening, and eating, drinking and "some womanizing" (20) at night, Cirules writes, Hemingway revised the galley proofs of *Death in the Afternoon* in his fifth-floor room in the Ambos Mundos Hotel on Obispo Street. The 1929 date he gives is clearly wrong, however. Hemingway did not begin writing *Death in the Afternoon* until 1930 and didn't finish it until 1932.

There are other problems with this account, too. In fact, Hemingway and his second wife, Pauline Pfeiffer, sailed for France in April 1929 and did not return to the United States until mid-December of that year. Moreover, all of the biographical sources state that Hemingway and Pauline met Jane Mason and her husband, wealthy American businessman Grant Mason, not in 1929, but in 1931, sailing for New York aboard the *Île de France*. The events that Cirules erroneously states took place in 1929 actually occurred in April and May 1932, when Hemingway and his Key West friend, Joe Russell, visited Cuba aboard Russell's charter boat, the *Anita*, to fish for marlin in the Gulf Stream. That trip, originally planned for ten days, stretched out for two months.

The erroneous date might be overlooked as a simple mistake if it were an isolated incident, but Cirules's book is riddled with similar errors. He claims, for example, that Hemingway spent all of 1939 in Havana, "locked away, cloistered" (31) in his room at the Ambos Mundos, writing the first draft of *For Whom the Bell Tolls*, when actually, Hemingway was in Havana for only five months that year, April through August, during which time he worked on the novel and he and Martha Gellhorn rented and moved into the Finca Vigía, which he later purchased. Hemingway's travels that year are well documented. He was in New York and Key West from January to March, and traveled in September to Wyoming and eventually to Sun Valley, Idaho, where he remained until mid-December.

Problematic, too, is Cirules's claim that Hemingway and Mason spent four months together in 1934 sailing the northern coast of Cuba aboard the *Pilar*. The implication is that they were alone on a long, romantic cruise. Hemingway did spend nearly four months on his newly acquired cruiser that year, marlin fishing off Cuba, but he and Jane Mason were far from alone. Jane and her husband Grant were occasionally on board the *Pilar*. But so, at various times, were Pauline and a host of others, including Arnold Samuelson, a young literary apprentice; Sidney Franklin, the American bullfighter; Antonio Gattorno, a Cuban painter; scientists Charles Cadwalader and Henry W. Fowler; Dick Armstrong, an American reporter; and several crew members. It would have been difficult for Hemingway and Mason to carry on an intimate affair surrounded by such a varied and shifting audience.

So the reader is faced with a dilemma: If basic facts such as dates and biographical data can't be trusted, how credible are Cirules's assertions that Cubans saw Hemingway and Mason together everywhere, in the most unusual places, and that their torrid love affair was widely known and a topic of gossip across the island? Compounding the problem is the nearly total absence of evidence to document reported events that may or may not have occurred.

The most likely explanation is that Cirules has compiled a collection of tales about Hemingway that are based on oral history rather than traditional academic research. Words like "strange," "mysterious," and "secret" appear over and over again in his prose. The stories illustrate that Hemingway has become an almost mythical figure to Cubans and an important part of Cuba's folklore. Whether true or not, it is apparent that the stories that were told to Cirules by friends, neighbors, and relatives, many of whom claim to have known Hemingway, have become local legends.

The Hemingway myth began in Havana and in its early stages had little to do with literature, Cirules writes, but rather with Hemingway's involvement in everyday life and his relations with the people of the Cuban capital. His legendary reputation as a lover, adventurer, sailor, fisherman, and hunter continued to grow, and today, four decades after his death, it pervades the urban landscape. The myth has become so strong, Cirules maintains, that "anybody who roams through the streets of Havana today, if he is white, tall, strong, broad shouldered, if he has a beard and wears a sun visor, may be surprised by being mistaken for Hemingway" (26). Most biographers have focused their attention almost exclusively on Hemingway's life in Havana, except for his submarine-hunting activities in the Gulf Stream during World War II. Cirules has added a new and previously unreported dimension to Hemingway's Cuban experience by recounting stories about the writer that he claims have circulated for years in out-of-the-way areas of the island.

According to Cirules, references to sailing expeditions by Hemingway, sometimes accompanied by Jane Mason, to the Romano Archipelago—part of a chain of more than 400 keys and islands stretching 248 miles eastward along Cuba's northern coast—date from 1930. By 1933, "everyone in the area knew—be they turtle hunters, fishermen, or adventurers who made raids on the Romano Archipelago—of an American who was making expeditions to the remote, unknown areas of those islands" (36), although everyone thought Hemingway was just an adventurer, not a famous writer (35).

Cirules, who was born and grew up in the village of San Fernando de Nuevitas, recounts stories that were told to him by friends, neighbors, and relatives recalling what they claimed were their vivid memories of Hemingway's frequent visits to the region over the years. A hunter known as Caciano, who sailed all over the area in a broken-down schooner, was one of the first persons to make contact with Hemingway in the early years, Cirules writes. On board his boat was a horse that Caciano rode around town, and which he claimed was the same horse Hemingway had ridden for several days all over Cayo Romano while Caciano followed along on foot. On another occasion, Caciano said that he and Hemingway had covered every part of Cayo Romano—Hemingway with a twelve-gauge shotgun, Caciano with a huge blunderbuss—looking for something to shoot.

Agustín el Tuerto ("One-Eyed Agustín"), who operated a tavern near the pier of San Fernando de Nuevitas, recalled Jane Mason being there with Hemingway. "That woman, what she brought to this pier was uneasiness," he told Cirules. "She undressed at dawn. She spent all morning stretched out on the deck of the yacht, in her excessive love of sunbathing. With that beauty, in this cove, everything became scandal, until the American owner of the yacht decided to leave" (40).

Fishermen and turtle hunters recalled seeing Hemingway anchor his boat in several other coves in the region. He and his companion left the boat at Punta Ganado, they said, and went ashore to spend several days in a hut of the sort used for salting fish—a hut without walls, with a roof made of palm leaves, surrounded by coconut trees. They said they remembered "how that girl walked around every afternoon collecting flowers, shells, sea urchins, while the owner of the yacht went hunting with a shotgun" (40).

"Everything seemed very strange," Cirules writes, "but that is how it was in the memory of the turtle hunters and in the recollection of Agustín" (40).

Agustín, who claimed that he had known "that American" since 1930, recalled that Hemingway was almost always upset, frequently in a very bad mood, and often "with a strong will to drink" (63). He went to Agustín's tavern as soon as he docked, and approached the counter, barefoot, shirtless, and wearing an old cap, and asked for a bottle of Matusalén. The tavern owner recalled that on one or two occasions Hemingway stayed at the Miramar Hotel, a popular gathering place for poets and "illustrious travelers" (64–65) passing through the town. He said the finest parties in the region were held in the hotel's salon.

The tavern owner also remembered frequent arguments between Hemingway and a Galician named José, a man who always showed his bad side. "Whether because of their drinking or because of the bad weather in the Channel, when the American and José got together they began to argue about anything and everything: politics, or the way a certain woman walked," Agustín said. "They argued about the arts and stratagems of fishing and, above all, about struggles with sharks" (64).

The story of Hemingway's "very special visit" with a beautiful and mysterious blonde sometime "in the days of World War II" (58) was recounted by La Colombiana, a woman who once operated a seaside inn at San Fernando de Nuevitas.

Cirules writes that her once-elegant inn, built of oak, cedar, and mahogany, had a large salon and bar and thirty spacious rooms with polished floors and great windows that opened on the ocean. "The place had great charm," Cirules writes. "It also had a touch of mystery because of those celebrated parties that La Colombiana used to hold in the years of the World War and because the establishment was visited on various occasions by the writer Hemingway" (57).

Cirules writes that La Colombiana was reluctant at first to talk about Hemingway, telling him that she was not in the habit of talking about her clients. But after several visits, she began to discuss her memories of the writer's visits to her inn. She claimed that Hemingway and Jane Mason had stayed there for two days in 1934 before boarding the train for Camagüey.

"Hemingway always gave the impression of being a solitary sailor, dressed like a sailor," she said, "like on the first occasion when he came into the port to get drunk in Agustín's tavern. Although there were, of course, many other occasions. Some years later he made a very special visit. He approached the counter of the inn and requested the best room, with wide windows, facing the sea breeze" (58).

La Colombiana said that Hemingway had waited endlessly that night but the woman did not appear until early the next day. She said the "tall woman, blonde, splendid, with a very pretty face and large breasts," was a movie star (58). That description could fit Jane Mason, or Martha Gellhorn, to whom Hemingway was then married, or the movie star Marlene Dietrich.

The innkeeper may have been reluctant to talk about her clients, but she apparently was not above prying into their affairs. She told Cirules that she had asked one of her employees to question the woman's chauffeur to see what he could find out. The driver said he had picked up the woman at dawn at the airport in Camagüey after she had arrived on "one of those special flights" (59)—presumably military transports that arrived daily in the war years en route to American air bases in Panama.

Hemingway and the woman stayed in his room for two days, according to La Colombiana. He requested rum and ice, and on several occasions he also asked for clean sheets and pillowcases. She said Hemingway ordered plenty of food in the morning and the evening and more rum and bottles of wine, and she recalled that after the first day he had opened the windows to let in the sea breeze.

The couple left the room the second night to dine at the nearby El Gato Negro restaurant, "the most exquisite place of all the region" (59), which Hemingway was said to have frequented many times over the years. The restaurant's Canary Islander chef took great pains to prepare oysters, paella, and lobsters "in a mysterious way" (60) that pleased Hemingway and drew him back again and again.

Later, fishermen and turtle hunters in the town said they always remembered Hemingway from the time they saw the woman apparently arguing with him on the hotel terrace, before her car arrived the next morning. "Then she left the terrace quickly and got into the car without saying goodbye," Cirules writes, "while Hemingway went to the bar, paid the bill leaving a good tip, headed toward the pier to untie his yacht, and disappeared quickly" (63).

Cirules does not date his interviews with La Colombiana, so it can't be determined if he was told the story before or after the publication of *Islands in the Stream* in 1970. It is possible, of course, that the story of the mysterious encounter is a local legend that grew out of rumors about a scene in the novel in which Thomas Hudson has a similar meeting with his first wife. (Later, Cirules refers to the scene in the novel in which Hudson "experiences the pleasant yet unfortunate joy of watching the most beautiful woman in the world" [98] enter the Floridita.) But if the meeting described by La Colombiana actually occurred, it is equally possible that it could have been Hemingway's inspiration for the fictional meeting in the novel.

The meeting in *Islands in the Stream* takes place in Havana, not in Nuevitas. Hudson's ex-wife, a movie star who is traveling with a USO unit, arrives unexpectedly from Camagüey in a chauffeur-driven car. After a warm greeting in the Floridita, where Hudson has been drinking all day, they go to his finca, where they make love and the ex-wife learns of the death of their oldest son, Tom, a pilot in the British air force. They quarrel briefly over the causes of the breakup of their marriage, and the bittersweet reunion ends when Hudson is called away to return to duty as a submarine hunter.

Hudson's ex-wife appears to be a composite based on several women in Hemingway's life. There are glimpses of Hadley in the ex-wife's memories of skiing in the Alps with their young son in the early days of their marriage. The fact that she is an actress traveling with a USO troupe suggests Marlene Dietrich, a movie star and longtime friend of Hemingway, who traveled extensively to entertain servicemen during the war. The ex-wife is married to an indifferent husband, which is suggestive of Jane Mason. And, like Martha Gellhorn, Hudson's ex-wife is a rival as well as a lover.

While the Cuban innkeeper's physical description of the mystery woman fits either Jane Mason or Martha Gellhorn, based on circumstantial evidence at least, a strong argument can be made in favor of Gellhorn.

If Jane Mason had been seen often with Hemingway in the region during the 1930s, as claimed by the tavern-owner Agustín and others, it is likely that someone would have recognized her just a few years later. In fact, La Colombiana probably could have recognized Mason, since she claimed that Hemingway and Mason had stayed at her inn for two days in 1934. By all accounts, including Cirules's, Hemingway ended his affair with Mason in 1936, after which they saw little of each other. Moreover, Mason and her husband had moved from Havana to Washington in the late 1930s. She divorced Grant Mason in 1939, married John Hamilton, chairman of the Republican National Committee, and became active in Washington's social and political life during the war years. Two more marriages would follow.

In 1942, the second year of the war, and the year Hemingway began submarine-hunting patrols in the *Pilar,* Martha Gellhorn was eager to get to Europe to cover the fighting and was trying to persuade Hemingway to do the same. Women were not permitted to go to combat zones, however, so Gellhorn instead set out on a three-month island-hopping tour of the Caribbean to gather material for a series of articles for *Collier's* magazine. Ironically, although Gellhorn disparaged Hemingway's submarine-hunting activities, she planned to report on Nazi U-boat activity in the region. She failed in this, though, never spotting a submarine during her extensive travels.

It is conceivable that Gellhorn, a determined and enterprising reporter, could have managed to secure a flight on a military aircraft from Haiti or Puerto Rico to rendezvous with Hemingway for a few days in Nuevitas. It is also conceivable that the innkeeper, who presumably had never before seen Gellhorn, could have mistakenly concluded that the attractive blond journalist was a movie star.

Finally, the mystery woman's stormy departure from the inn after apparently arguing with Hemingway would be consistent with the tensions that existed between Gellhorn and her husband at the time. Not only was she angry about Hemingway's counterespionage activities in Havana and his sub-hunting patrols on the Gulf Stream, but she also was having great difficulty finishing a novel. Although Gellhorn continued to profess her love for Hemingway in letters written when they were apart, they quarreled often and with increasing intensity when they were together. Above all, Gellhorn wanted to be covering the war at the front, and she could not understand Hemingway's reluctance to join her. For his part, Hemingway resented Gellhorn's long absences from their home. Given the volatile mixture of conflicting emotions that were at work, it is possible that they planned a brief romantic encounter in Nuevitas that began well but ended badly.

All of this is speculation, of course, that probably can't be proved or disproved without further research. This story, like many others in Cirules's book, begs for hard evidence to support it. Such evidence would be difficult to obtain, however. Neither Agustín's tavern nor La Colombiana's inn exists today, and Cirules's text does not make clear if the erstwhile proprietors are still alive.

Cirules also writes of a meeting, not mentioned in any of the standard biographies, that he claims took place in Camagüey in 1940 between Hemingway and the German writer Gustav Regler. A wealthy Cuban friend, Mayito Menocal, had invited Hemingway to spend several weeks at his sugar plantation in

Camagüey, three hundred miles east of Havana, to rest after he finished writing *For Whom the Bell Tolls.* While there, Hemingway began to work on a preface for Regler's autobiographical novel of the Spanish Civil War, *The Great Crusade.* Curiously, after stating that Hemingway had been invited to Menocal's estate, and without explaining the need for secrecy, Cirules adds that Hemingway had carried the novel with him "on a secret trip to Camagüey."

Hemingway greatly admired Regler, whom he had met when the militant German communist was the political commissar in the 12th International Brigade in Spain. Hemingway had helped secure Regler's release from a French internment camp after the war.

"In those days when Hemingway was staying in the Menocals' house, Regler appeared at the Camagüey airport," Cirules writes. "He arrived on a flight that landed at an airport that was converted into an American air base as soon as the World War broke out." Cirules also claims that Hemingway earlier had made a brief trip to Mexico, where Regler lived for several years as an exile from Nazi Germany, and "one must assume that his contact with the German novelist was very intense on that occasion" (47). No dates are given for these meetings, and there is no indication as to what the two discussed.

According to Cirules, Hemingway had taken Regler's manuscript with him to Camagüey after the German writer had asked him to review the text and make recommendations, but it was not foreseen that Hemingway would go beyond a simple reading and begin to work on a prologue. "To everybody's surprise," Cirules writes, "months later, *The Great Crusade* appeared with a prologue by Ernest Hemingway, dated 1940 at Camagüey" (48).

The last three chapters of the book concern Hemingway's World War II submarine-hunting expeditions—which Cirules declares were "the most unusual adventures that any writer had undertaken in the twentieth century" (69)—and their relevance to the fictional accounts of Thomas Hudson's sub-chasing operations in *Islands in the Stream.* In discussing the "At Sea" section of the novel, Cirules sometimes blurs the distinction between fact and fiction, using the names Hemingway and Hudson interchangeably and putting Hudson in command of the *Pilar.*

Between May 1942 and the end of 1943, Cirules writes, Hemingway returned again and again in the *Pilar* to sail the beautiful, wild Cuban coast from Cayo Francés to the bay of San Fernando de Nuevitas. He claims that Hemingway stayed occasionally for several months in locations that he had favored since he had first visited them with Jane Mason a decade earlier. Although German U-boats were prowling the waters, Cirules quotes the tavern owner, Agustín, as saying it was "all like a big party" for Hemingway (75), who was never bothered by anxious moments or surprises.

Cirules contends that *Islands in the Stream* is Hemingway's most autobiographical novel, claiming that in its pages he not only brings to life the real men who manned the *Pilar* but also reconstructs the coastline of the Romano Archipelago—its beaches, shallows, channels, shoals, swamps, and confusing keys—with unerring accuracy. "One can sail along the Romano Archipelago as though the novel were a veritable nautical chart" (104), Cirules writes.

"In this extensive novel there is only one event about which the informed reader can ask himself a disturbing question," Cirules asserts. "Where did the writer get the story of a German submarine that was damaged and got lost on the Bahama Bank near San Fernando de Nuevitas? Where did he get the inspiration to write about some submariners that Thomas Hudson began to chase after the Germans conducted a massacre on a key and commandeered two turtle boats?" (105).

Cirules erroneously claims that U.S. World War II records "report the sinking of only two submarines" (105), one sunk by the Cuban subchaser CS-13 on the reefs near Cayo Mégano Chico, west of the Camaguey archipelago, and the other sunk off the coast of Brazil. Actually, as many as thirty German U-boats were sunk off the East Coast, in the Gulf of Mexico, and near Cuba, together with eight in the Caribbean.

Neither of these U-boat sinkings could have been Hemingway's inspiration for the fictional account in the "At Sea" section of *Islands,* Cirules argues, because details of both were widely reported by the press of the day. "It is impossible that [Hemingway] would have been inspired by a well-known event to write *Islands in the Stream,*" he writes. "It made no sense to write a novel about a story that had already been heard around the world, a story in which one could not even remotely allow for the possibility of the Germans' reaching the Bahama Bank" (105).

This is not a convincing argument. It is naïve to maintain that newspaper reports of a sub sinking, even if widespread, would have deterred Hemingway from using details of the event as the basis for a fictional retelling. From the beginning, Hemingway demonstrated an uncanny ability to construct completely believable fictional accounts of widely reported events that he had not witnessed. There is probably no better example of his finding inspiration in a well-known event than his dramatic account, in *A Farewell to Arms,* of the retreat of the Italian army at Caporetto in World War I. Hemingway was a high-school student when the retreat occurred in 1917, but his account in the 1929 novel was so powerful, so realistic, that many readers believed that he had been a participant.

Cirules maintains that the submarine that Thomas Hudson and his crew pursue in *Islands* was not a fictional invention, but was based on an actual U-boat that was sunk at Camagüey sometime in 1943. Moreover, he claims that proof for what he calls "the Third Submarine" can be found in Hemingway's novel. Hemingway "assures the existence of a third submarine," Cirules writes, when Thomas Hudson and his crew discover that the German survivors of a sunken U-boat have murdered nine civilians and escaped in two stolen turtle boats. Hudson, trying to determine where the sub went down, concludes "they must be [survivors of] the one Camagüey claimed" (106).

The story of the sinking of a third submarine by a Cuban freighter, the *Dominous,* near Nuevitas is a rumor that is "fixed in memory, in myth, in the legend of the region," Cirules writes, although he obviously accepts it as fact. There was no official report of the battle, he claims, because it was silenced, "perhaps because people wondered how it was possible for a merchant ship to sink a submarine so near the coast of Camagüey" (106). How, indeed?

The U-boat sinking was never confirmed, Cirules writes, but sailors and fishermen from the area said they saw the freighter enter the port the day after the battle with its bulkhead and command bridge pierced by artillery fire. They also said a large oil slick, canned goods, and other debris could be seen in the water. Turtle hunters and mariners of the region, Cirules claims, "assure that the submarine was sunk at a depth of almost 1,000 meters" (106).

Cirules also asserts that the officers and crew of the *Dominous* described what had happened during the night when they came ashore the following day: As the freighter approached the mouth of the channel, the captain, aware that there were submarines in the area, ordered the engines stopped. A U-boat already had begun tracking the ship by sonar, however, and when it lost contact its commander decided to surface. In the meantime, a dense fog had set in, so that when the sub surfaced it found itself almost at the bow of the freighter. While the U-boat maneuvered to dive again, it opened fire with its deck guns, piercing the freighter's bow and command bridge. The artillery officer in charge of the freighter's bow, ducking bullets, ran up a stairway and fired a three-inch cannon at the half-submerged sub.

There is a problem with this account, however. If the submarine was maneuvering to submerge, crewmen would not have been on deck firing at the freighter; the deck would have been cleared in preparation to dive. Certainly a U-boat that was half-submerged, as Cirules states that the freighter's artillery officer claimed, could not have been firing at the merchant ship.

Celebrations of the victory erupted everywhere, Cirules writes, but the main one was organized at the home of his relatives, the Cruz family, where revelers, including the freighter's officers and crew, partied for three days. The second night, he continues, a lieutenant and four members of the rural police force arrived and ordered the revelers to stop talking about "ships and submarines"

(109). Local officials had planned a festival, but they canceled it when they received the order to be silent.

That is the real story, Cirules asserts, the unknown story of "the submarine that was damaged but which was able to pass through the Great Bahama Channel, to settle on one of the sand banks close to Maternillos lighthouse." This, however, contradicts his earlier claim that there were assurances that the sub was sunk at a depth of almost one thousand meters. It was, he concludes, "a good story for the writer Hemingway" (112).

A good story, perhaps, but one that should be viewed with a great deal of skepticism. "Neither the air base of Camagüey, nor the hydroplanes in the bay at Nuevitas, nor the warships, nor the subchasers that operated in the area gave the incident any importance" (112), Cirules writes, undoubtedly for good reason. There is no discernable reason why officials would have kept secret the sinking of a U-boat.

In the end, this reader came away from Cirules's book with many more questions than answers. This ambiguity, though, is probably the book's greatest value. If nothing else, Cirules has shown that there is a great deal more to be learned about Hemingway's life in Cuba. What has been written so far may be only the tip of the biographical iceberg.

Cirules's stories, whether rumors, folklore, or fantasy, show that irrespective of his stature as an artist, Hemingway holds a unique and enduring place in Cuban culture. They also demonstrate that Cuba is still largely an undiscovered country for Hemingway scholars. Unfortunately, it is likely to remain so until scholars are permitted to spend enough time there to explore regions far beyond the well-traveled Hemingway Trail in Havana. Fortunately, there are encouraging signs that such opportunities might soon be possible.

Note

Hemingway en la cayerila de Romano was published in 1999 in Havana by the Union of Writers and Artists of Cuba. This review was based on an English translation, *Ernest Hemingway in the Romano Archipelago*, by Douglas Edward LaPrade, a Hemingway scholar who has attended several Hemingway conferences in Cuba, where he met Enrique Cirules.

Works Cited

Cirules, Enrique. *Ernest Hemingway in the Romano Archipelago* [*Hemingway en la cayerila de Romano*]. Translated from the Spanish by Douglas Edward LaPrade. Havana: Ediciones Unión, 1999.

The Cuban Works

To Have and Have Not

Photograph sent to Ernest Hemingway by Richard Armstrong of two dead men lying on a dirt road. It was inscribed "Pupille f.16 diaphragm 22 bright sun. Being gentlemen obnoxious to the govt." and stamped "Agfa-Brovira." Ernest Hemingway Collection, John F. Kennedy Presidential Library and Museum, Boston.

The State of Things in Cuba

A Letter to Hemingway

RICHARD ARMSTRONG

Introduction
Larry Grimes

To insure accuracy in his portrayal of the more recent revolutionary activities he wanted to include in *To Have and Have Not,* Hemingway asked journalist Richard Armstrong to provide him with a summary of detailed newspaper accounts of the uprising. Hemingway had known Armstrong since at least 1933, when Armstrong had served as photographer for the Cadwalader marlin expedition. On August 27, 1936, Armstrong sent Hemingway a photograph (reproduced here) and a thirteen-page letter full of information. Hemingway subsumed the information in Armstrong's letter into the text of the novel, sometimes almost verbatim, in the manner of his earlier work with newspaper materials in *A Farewell to Arms*. In the manuscript of the novel, this material was included in what Hemingway designated, in his one-page outline of the novel, as "the Story of the Dynamite trip and its capture."[1]

That important Cuban material was deleted from the manuscript of To Have and Have Not as Hemingway edited it for publication.[2] Scenes from the revolution were cut, together with a very important reflection on the nature and purpose of terrorism by Tommy Bradley, a central character, that justifies terrorism as a part of revolutionary activity. It begins with the observation that when people live in a state of absolute tyranny, there is no noise. Freedom of speech is denied. Protest is throttled. According to Bradley, in the silence that tyranny creates one must use dynamite, dynamite that kills. Bodies must be found. The revolutionaries are not seeking approval. Such violence is not to be liked, but in a revolution it is necessary because it creates "the uneasiness that come[s] before conscience." The reflection, referring to the necessity of dynamite and, the need for undeniable noise, affirms the nature and purpose of terrorism and concludes with words that point toward For Whom the Bell Tolls: "The victory grows in the soil of defeat . . . There is no hope in terrorism. It is a noise you make when you are hopeless. . . . But the dynamite for the bridges is for when we fight again. And that is all I live for now."[3]

Notes

1. Ernest Hemingway, Outline of *To Have and Have Not,* Hemingway Collection, John Fitzgerald Kennedy Library, Boston, MA (hereafter, JFK).
2. Ernest Hemingway, Item 212, Hemingway Collection, JFK.
3. Ibid., Pt. 5 of 5: 162.

Works Cited

Hemingway, Ernest. Item 212. Hemingway Collection, JFK.
———. Outline of *To Have and Have Not.* Hemingway Collection, JFK.
Reynolds, Michael S. *Hemingway's First War: The Making of a Farewell to Arms.* Princeton, NJ: Princeton Univ. Press, 1976.

Following pages: The source of the scanned letter is TLS Dick, 27 August 1936, 7pp. Ernest Hemingway Personal Papers, Incoming Correspondence, Armstrong, Richard. John F. Kennedy Presidential Library.

August 27,1936

Dear Ernest,

Here I am just one month after your letter from Key West with more excuses than a Cuban hotel keeper, the principal one being that I was on beam ends for the first ten days with two sets of visiting friends from the states after which I acquired, of all god damned things, an attack of rhumatism in the left arm that made it impossible to lift it above the waist line, let alone use the mill. There remain twinges but it is definitely better and I am back on the range.

So--first:

The Communist party in Cuba today is an amorphous group, divided, I have heard on emphatic but not particularly reliable authority, into some 22 different groups.

Tho largest group of reds, I'm told, are the members of the CONC (confederacion obrero nacional cubana) of which the notorious Cesar Vilar was the general secretary and boss. However the CNOC is not communistic--it is just that the majority of the members are communists and apparently are the backbone of the red movement in the island.

Then it shades down to the Young Communist's league which takes in everything the rest of the party doesn't.

Members of the Joven Cuba have told me that the Communists definitely are NOT a part of the United Revolutionary front which was organized in Mexico against the regime of Batista. They say the Communists, and I have confirmed it, are willing to join in the coming Constitutional Assembly scheduled within the next six months, if they are recognized as a party. Communists of course, do not exist here as a legal party. They have been suppressed. The CNOC also was suppressed by government decree.

Leader Cesar Vilar was arrested last year and jailed on charges of plotting the assassination of Caffery and Batista. At the time he was picked up, he was a fugitive, being charged with subversive acticities.

Six Communists were pinched the other day and among the papers found on them were plans for Communist protests in New York for the release of Vilar. Vilar was released early this month under the amnesty law for political prisoners approved by Congress which effected the release of about 150 out of 1,500 prisoners--figures inexact and unavailable presently.

But he was repinched as he walked out on other charges. The anti-administrationers are sore as hell over the ineffectual amnesty which leaves most of their imprisoned members in jail.

At the outside, it is estimated by army authorities, there have never been more than 5,000 members of the Communist party in Cuba and they estimate that not more than a tenth of these were really active --

You remember, you wanted a description of the police station--the Jefatura at Monserrate and Empedrado. The building has had a third story added and is slightly flatironed shape conforming with the contours of the streets. Inside the patio is paved with concrete, pentagonally shaped and has an anormous royal palm growing out of a patch of ground retained with a small circular wall of comcrete.

The main entrance is the motor driveway on the Monserrate street side which is a tunnel effect through the building into the patio where white walls are broken with a shoulder high fringe of figured tiles.

But prisoners, usually, are taken in through a small door to the left of the motor entrance which opens into a high-ceilinged but relatively small room. At the right as you enter is a heavy wooden rail covered with some sortb of dark stain and through the heavy swinging gate is a slightly elevated, darkly stained typical police sergeants desk behind which sit the sergeant on duty and a clerk to take records.

Another door in the room opens directly into the patio and at the imm right is a stairway going to the offices above. Go around the stairway and continuing to the right for a few feet, you come to a bare cell furnished only with a long wooden bench. This is on the ground floor and is the first stopping point before they are taken somewhere on the upper floor for questioning. The main entrances is at the apex of the "flat iron"at the junction of Empredrado and Monserrate which leads into an always guarded ante-room, beyond which at the left is a marble winding stairway to the upstairs while beyond the anteroom can bee seen offices mmhhm encaged in bars halfway to the ceiling like an old fashioned loan-shark office.

Chief Pedraza's office is in a remote corner of the third floor and damned hard to get into. I haven't been there--always talked to him in some other part of the building.

Now for the story of the Mesa killings as I heard thhmmm it.

Antonio Mesa, 58, and his three sons, Alberto, Antonio jr, and Jose, were arrested April 6 of this year in a round up of members of Joven Cuba suspected of such subversive activities as organizing the "insurrectional army". They were pinched in Guanabacoa.

On the morning of April 7 the body of the old man and his three mmmmnm mmmmn sons, all bullet-ridden, were found on the side of the Havana-Guanabacoa road.

The official story is they asked to get out of the haula to take a piss and then attempted to flee. Okay.

The story that seeped down through y e grapevine is that the four of them were lined up and the old man told to talk. He had nothing to say. They shot him. Then they asked Alberto. Also silent, and they shot him. In turn they shot Anotnio and Jose, all of whom had nothing to say about their activities or associates. Then they were eft on the side of the road for the sunrise and buzzards.

4

Another group of Guanabacoa killings starting April 24th grew out of the Mesa slaughter. Around midnight an open Buick loaded with deconocidos swept down mm the main street of Guanabacoa and as it nearly Maximo Gomez and Pepe Antonio streets, in front of El Morro cafe, they unloaded a salvo at Sub Lieutenant of Police Ramon Peña and plugged him 13 times. He returned the fire and punctured tires, then collapsed. Died the next day at 3:30 p.m.

After shooting Pena they ripped on down the street and let loose on a cop, Patrocinto Andacia, and blasted him. Andacia returned the fire, fainted, and died within the hour.

During the shooting a mullato, unindentified, coatless, about 25, was kille in a manner unexplained.

Early in the morning of April 25 police found the black Buick which had a Santiago de Cuba license of the alquila classification. In the back seat they found a sawed-off shot gun, a revolver, a white cap and a white c coat.

When daylight came on the morning os April 25th, the bodies of two youngsters, brothers, Juan and Adolfo Cuervo Galan, were found with the customary punctures lying in the graveyard of Guanabacoa. Police "revealed" they had been detained for questioning and attempted to flee.

--The next night the Pilar arrived in Havana harbor.

Two nights later--April 28, two charred bodies were found in a burned automobile on the side of the highway near Santiago de las Vegas and the car was identified through its chapa as belonging to Octavio Seigle. The bodies later were definitely identified as those of Octavio and of an inoffensive little mug by the name of Agustin Martinez Dominguez. The car was found about 9 p.m. I learned through grape vine that a representative of the army went to members of the family and protested vigorously that the army had nothing to do with it.

5

There may be some truth inx it for the smoke included countless tales of Octavio, broke, coming into sudden affluence. He had a botella with the government which brought him around $250 a month--it developed, which from the stand point of his Autentico party, which he was a member, would brand him as a traitor.

Autentico he was, without a doubt, although he told me aemphatically a few weeks before his death that he was to hell out of politics and forever. He said it like that. His English was so good he could speak it as rottenly as I.

On the other hand, he was known to have had a sweet list of names filched from the Palace during Grau's time, which revealed who was on the secret pay roll of Machado. Stories bubble through the slime to the surface that the list furnished him an excellent living and that mayhap someone tired of disgorging. Though the method was crude, lots of people are content with his passing.

The army acted so damned naive in the matter I have a hunch that, for once, they were innocent. I DONT KNOW, however. I know that his brother, a druggist, and Dr. Finlay, former secpub health under Grau, his fatherinlaw, were staging an investigation and were supposed to have learned who did it, but if they did they have kept discreetly silent for I questioned both of them.

The automobile was backed off the road with its hood pointing toward the highway. The bodies were found in the back seat. I was told by Autentico grapevine the wrists and ankles and fingers, although charred, revealed signs of torture. I don't know. Nearby was found an empty gallon tin can, used first for olive oil but could conveniently, have been a container for the gasoline that burned the automobile.

Before I drown in my tears over the pasing of Octaviom let me go into a little early history. Octavio was the first political exile from the Machado tyrrany.

Octavio was one of the finest automotive engineers in Cuba. During good y
he was agent in Cuba for the R. Royce. He sold Machado a nice one for
$15,000. The chauffeur was driving it home one day and the motor conked.
Chauffeur looked inside and behold, the 15 G RR had an old motor.
Seigle was called in to explain and is reported to have explained that
"it made no difference" since the motor was guaranteed for life and
that he had put the old motor in while he was doing som additional
tuning on the new one. He rapired the old motor and Machado was satisfie
for a while. But it seems in the meantime Seigle had sold Machado's
motor to another person and he was in a hell of a fix. He was was told
repeatedly by Machado's agents to bring that new motor and hep kept promi
until the time when Machado gave him until the next day to bring the
motor or be on a boat. Octavio caught the boat--the first political exile
O.Kay pal, I don't guarantee it.

I am digging out the Guiteras story from my own files and will send it alo
tomorrow as I believe I had a better story of that than anyone else and
what I can't find in the cables, I'll remember.

--

Papers? Pais' file was burned when the paper was sacked. Mundo wasn't
publishing most of the time. I went to Diario and the Havana Post and lef
orders for Aug. 9, 10, 11, 12, 13, 14, 15, Sept. 28, 29 (Mella and
massacre), Oct. 2, 3 (National) Nov. 8 and 9 (Atares) of 1933;
June 17,18 (ABC Massacre) 1934 and went back twice before I come sick
and the shiftless bastards either didn't have them or hadn't bothered.
I am going to get around some today and try them again. American editions
simply aren't available here unless they are in the files of Phillips,
of the New York Times, who is in Los Angeles on a six weeks vacation.

7

I should be able to get Havana Posts on the March 1935 strike but The Post accounts usually are not worhh a shit, they are so afraid of offending some damned sub lieutenant of the latrine detail.
But I'll have to go through their bound files on that as I can't remember dates of events, things were so drawn out.
I rememner Mar. 13 all right for that was the night they shot up my apartment and raided it and Mar. 14 was a bad day because I got drunk and made the mistake of broadcasting how I'd like to have a lot of the nigger bastards called Cubans in Key West. I'd hate to be inducted into the Sioux tribe because they'd probably title me, "Chief Big-Megaphone-Up-The-Ass."

As I come out of the fog I get an idea/ I'm airmailing today to the circ depts of the New York Times and Tribune about the forgoing dates and if they are available, I'll have them sent you from New York.
I only hope, Ernest, this will not be too late. I'm sorry as hell about the delay but one-handed typing was impossible and the other fist is just getting into the swing.
You'll hear from me again tomorrow, now that I have the rag out. On Guiteras.
Jane is fine, Our Youngster, Phyllis, will be here today week to start school. Very best to Mrs. and the fmily. Let me hear from you if you have any ideas I have missed. The last Cosmopolitan has gone into the Armstrong collection. Was surprised to see "Snows of Kilimanjaro" in Esquire. Reminded me the old yarn about the Duchess on her bridal night, when approaching orgasm, remarked twas "much too good for the common people." However, heard a helluva lot of favorable comment from Esquire readers and sfars could determine, none of them muffed the point. I still think its the grandest yarn I ever read, bettern the superb One Trip Across even, and that's traveling. Hasta Manana. Cordially

Selection from "It is hard for you to tell,"

Chapter Three of Cuba y Hemingway en el gran río azul *(*Cuba and Hemingway on the Great Blue River*)*

MARY CRUZ

TRANSLATED BY MARY DELPINO

In the art of literature, an image is not fixed on paper in the same way as a sculpture is set in stone or a painting on canvas, or even music on a score. The fictional world that the reader perceives is reconstructed in his imagination, bit by bit, from written clues, much like a jigsaw puzzle is put together as each piece is found and added.

The frequent gaps or the seemingly random order in which information is supplied, as well as the subjective distension and contraction of time, are not fortuitous. They are technical devices deliberately employed to achieve certain effects aimed at a specific objective. When those effects are achieved and that goal is reached, the work has surpassed the threshold of the ordinary to become something elevated: art. That is why, in my opinion, *To Have and Have Not* (*THHN*) is a work of art.

What appears to be a clash between form and content is resolved through a single all-encompassing meaning. Hemingway himself was not satisfied with the result (Lidskii 282). Nevertheless, after reading the three stories that make up the novel—"One Trip Across," and "The Tradesman's Return" (previously published separately), and the one that gives this novel its title—the reader has a complete and coherent view of the protagonist's psychology and life, but still can't expel from his mouth the bad taste of a sick society in a chaotic world that victimizes the main character. The reader has witnessed the painful process of a man's awakening consciousness. He has participated in an unforgettable experience.

The novel must be considered a structural unit and not the mere sum of its parts. The conflict between the *haves* and the *have-nots* is already set forth in the title, not surprising for those of us who, like Hemingway, know Cervantes.

In chapter 20 in the second part of *Don Quixote de la Mancha,* Sancho Panza says to his master: "There are only two lineages in the world . . . the haves and the have-nots" (Cervantes 705). In Hemingway's novel, that conflict gradually grows in definition and clarity, building to its culmination in a powerful picture of the moral bankruptcy of many of those who have all.

The length of each part matches the size of its geographic setting: Cuba, Key West, and the mainland United States (which in the novel represents the oppressive social order). In the second and third parts, the reader is transported on an imaginary journey from the Gulf of Mexico to Key West; then from Key West to the mainland.

All three stories offer a proportionally compressed reproduction of reality. Figuratively speaking, the third story is an inverted, magnified reflection of the first story, much like the reflection of an image on the retina or a photographic lens, but reversed.

The "healthy animal" that is Hemingway's main character does not "suddenly" become "vaguely political" (Atkins 46). The story describes the process through which his ignorance is replaced by knowledge as circumstances force this common man to face in real life the dilemmas that philosophers solve in their chambers.

It would seem irrelevant to analyze each story separately. However, the slight, albeit significant changes made to each in transforming it into a component of a larger work, as well as the significance that each part takes on within the structure of the whole, not only allow but demand both separate and general analytical approaches.

"One Trip Across"

Written in 1933—a time of intense revolutionary activity in Cuba—"One Trip Across" was published by *Cosmopolitan* in April 1934 with ostentatious title and by-line, plus illustrations. The timing of the publication deserves special attention.

It is worthwhile to recall some history. Precisely on August 7, 1933, while he was waiting to board the ship that would take him to Europe on the first leg of a trip to Africa, Hemingway had witnessed one of the most horrendous massacres perpetrated by the henchmen of the tyranny that was strangling the island.

Later, while he was on the high seas, he would learn that Dictator Gerardo Machado had been overthrown while Benjamin Sumner Wells, Washington's envoy to Havana, used all sorts of trickery to prevent the inauguration of a progressive government on the island. For a brief period, the people were victorious. But reactionary forces were too powerful, and Cuba fell once again under the control of successive puppet governments propped up by the United States administration.

At the time the story was published in *Cosmopolitan,* however, the people's victory was still a reality. All of this explains the editor's offensive and misleading introductory remarks: "Along the coast of Cuba, land of violence, a giant marlin rises to the bait of a deep-sea fisher—and starts a train of events that makes of this short novel perhaps the most gripping tale yet to come from the author of "A Farewell to Arms" (Hemingway, "One Trip Across" 20). This introduction offensively dismisses Cuba as a "land of violence" without clarifying the nature and causes of that violence and misrepresents the thrust of Hemingway's tale as merely a "gripping" adventure story. While unspecified violence and adventure are undoubtedly interesting, the editor's emphasis on them misdirects readers as they enter the story. These elements are certainly less important to the story than the brutal deaths of three young Cuban men who were fighting against a tyrannical government or the murder of a human trafficker.[1]

What is Cuban in this story? I could answer briefly: a few places, some foods and beverages, certain characters, and specific events that portray a moment in Cuba's history and politics—a sort of backdrop created with brushstrokes of local color. But is that all?

The story begins with an impressionistic description of a spot near the Havana docks at sunrise. Since it is written in the first person, the narrator lends the reader his vision so that the reader can view it as if with his own eyes. The eyes move from the San Francisco dock, across the square with its fountain, to identify the surrounding buildings. Only the café, La Perla, is singled out and mentioned by name. The café's full name is identical to that of the dock and the plaza. Cinematic objectivity gives way to remembrance when the narrator recalls the ice-wagons that have not yet made their rounds of the bars, an effective device to signal the early hour.

Next, Hemingway gives us another view of the city, this time from a sea vantage, suggested solely by naming landmark buildings: beyond the Morro Castle, the National Hotel and the Capitol, the tallest structures in the Havana skyline at the time.

The narrator, whom the reader already knows as the story's main character, sails out of the harbor aboard his fishing boat, chartered to a wealthy client. They leave behind the hatcheries anchored in front of the Cabaña fortress and some skiffs by the Morro, heading into the Gulf Stream. The water is purple and full of eddies. They are about to catch a marlin with purple fins and a striped body; later, another huge black one. These details are included in a sequence that takes place in the afternoon.

At sundown, Hemingway again presents a postcard view of Havana: the Morro lighthouse, its beam cut short by the glare of the city; the dome of the Capitol, still visible. Later, in the story the narrator passes the lights of Rincón Baracoa, Bacuranao, and, finally, Cojímar, but only Bacuranao is described. Here, the narrator zooms in like a camera ready for a close-up, but the lens is a human eye that has not actually approached the object hidden in shadows; behind the eye, the mind remembers and supplies the details: "Bacuranao is a cove where there used to be a big dock for loading sand. There is a little river that comes in when the rains open the bar across the mouth. The northerners, in the winter, pile the sand up and close it. They used to go in with schooners and load guavas from the brook, and there used to be a town" (Hemingway, *THHN* 49).[2] A hurricane swept the town away, though, and now nothing is left but a single shack, built out of debris from the ones the hurricane had destroyed.

The smell of sea grapes and the sweet aroma of the warm underbrush float out to the boat. It is late at night. The narrator cannot see the things that he describes or names, but they are there. Closer now, the reader sees—through the eyes of his host—a cheap Chinese restaurant where you can eat well for forty cents, and La Perla café, where a generous serving of black beans, beef, and potatoes, plus an Hatuey beer, cost only a quarter.

These details are absolutely accurate. Although they are only external—mere color, so to speak—they are indicators of an economic reality. The description does not portray the whole situation, but the "landscape" cannot be considered a superfluous element.

As soon as the first Cuban characters are introduced—no matter how seemingly insignificant—the true dimension of the setting becomes evident. The beggar drinking at the fountain and the out-of-work men sleeping against the buildings are more than brushstrokes of local color. They convey the poverty that existed in the underdeveloped and neocolonized country that was Cuba at that time.

Probably not everyone who reads the novel becomes aware of the significance of these two subtle elements built into the story's setting. But the author knows what he has planted in the reader's subconscious, and he has done so with the skill of a marksman.

When the main character runs into three young Cubans toward the beginning of the story, the rhythm accelerates, interest sharpens. The author gives no definitions or analyses. He brings the scene into focus, takes a snapshot, and records what his character sees and hears. These three young Cubans represent one side of a certain struggle.

Two other Cuban characters represent the opposite side of the same struggle. One of them is black and carries a Thompson submachine gun; the other—most likely white—wears a chauffeur's duster and holds a sawed-off shotgun. They approach the scene in a closed car and open fire on the three young men, who are also armed and courageously fight back. But they fall, riddled with bullets. The scene is one of the clearest examples of Hemingway's mastery of accurate description of detail with an economy of expressive means.

The blood splattered on the walls and the sidewalk is not local color; nor is the horse-drawn Tropical brewery wagon, behind which the last of the three Cubans standing takes cover as he shoots the man wearing the duster with his Lugar, mere decoration. These are realistic details carefully chosen for an aesthetic purpose.

The characters mentioned above are not the only Cubans in the story. There is a cunning, somber, black—very black—man who wears a string of blue Santería[3] beads under his shirt, dark sunglasses, and an old straw hat. This man is an expert at baiting fishing hooks and charges one peso a day to procure and prepare bait. But what he most enjoys doing on board is sleeping and reading the newspaper. He apparently has no sympathy for any of the three Americans aboard the fishing boat (Harry Morgan, the owner; Eddy, the first mate; or Johnson, the wealthy client). There is a young man who rows, but he appears only once in the story. There are two Cubans who threaten Harry and some Galicians who, being an integral part of the island's ethnic makeup, must also be considered Cuban characters. These are the men who drink, eat, and play dominoes at La Perla, and the ones who built the shack at Bacuranao, where they spend their Sundays. There is also a waiter at the café who never speaks.

In addition to the Cubans, there is Frankie, of undecided origin, who is deaf, drinks a lot, and always smiles. He appears deceptively stupid, but his expressive shortcomings might be the result of poor schooling, or might be a defense mechanism. There is also a little Spaniard who acts as a messenger in one of the scenes.

The remaining characters are American (Eddy, Mr. Johnson, and Donovan, the customs officer) or Chinese (Mr. Sing and his twelve Chinese men). But this inventory of elements is not illuminating unless we understand how they are integrated into the whole work. In order to do so, we must look closely at the reciprocal relationships of all the elements—characters, plot, and setting—used by Hemingway to construct his story.

Hemingway's fable is the story of how Harry—a tough guy, a hardened man who rents out his services and his boat to sports fishermen—is tricked out of his earnings by a wealthy client, and, to make up his loss, takes on an illegal commission which he dislikes but which will solve his financial problems. Thus reduced to its basics, the story shows no apparent connection whatsoever between the topic and the Cuban elements mentioned above, nor is there any indication that these are the elements that can best tell this particular story. But are they really superfluous? Are they simply exotic embellishment?

No storyteller merely tells a story. However interesting, the adventure alone, the mere sequence of events, is not enough to produce a work of art. To become a work of art, the story must be held together by a configuring thread of causes and effects that conveys an all-encompassing message. Every writer aims to say something through his stories. In order to do so, he must carefully select the materials that best convey that message, incorporating them in the construction of each character, event, and setting. He must also choose the composition and wording that best express his message. Some writers pursue this process without being fully aware that they are doing so, but that does not make it any less important.

The overall meaning of "One Trip Across," which in my opinion is conscious and intentional on Hemingway's part, is that any individual attempt at rebellion against the social order is doomed. Its small victories are mere illusion and always won at a high price. This particular novelette presents the rebellion of a penniless American against a society in which he cannot adequately provide for himself and his family while remaining an honest man. However, individual rebellion requires a collective framework to be calibrated in its full dimension. That framework is provided by a project of much broader proportions: not a rebellion, but a revolution. The revolution in this story is the one Cuba was waging against the tyranny of dictator Gerardo Machado and the interference by the U.S. government.

History is a good teacher. When the United States intervened—with well-known intentions and toward the very end—in the war that Cuba had been waging for three decades to obtain its independence from Spain, it robbed the Cuban people of its victory. The island became the first victim of U.S. interventionism, for the Cuban government became "a veritable management office for US monopolies" (Pino-Santos 298). No wonder that the first three decades of that century were marked by deeply rooted popular discontent.

The influence of the October Revolution in Russia and the spread of bourgeois democratic and liberal ideas contributed to the emergence of the 1923–35 revolutionary process, in which the leading organizations were the First Cuban Communist Party, the Confederación Nacional Obrera (National Labor Confederation), the Directorio Estudiantil (Students' Leadership Body), the Ala Izquierda Estudiantil (Students' Left Wing), and, later, the Joven Cuba (Young Cuba):

> The duel between the Cuban people and Gerardo Machado began in 1925 and ended on August 12, 1933, with the overthrow and flight of the dictator. During those years the merciless repression by Machado, far from intimidating and

> forcing the people to give up, only broadened and intensified their opposition. . . . The people, on the offensive since 1923, were forced to retreat under the furious blows Machado had dealt them since 1925. From 1927 onwards, the people gradually regained the offensive, fought bitter battles and paid a high price in blood, self-denial, sacrifice and courage until they gained a victory, which would go "down the drain." (Tabares 209)[4]

This is the revolution with which Hemingway brings his character face to face. Why precisely *this* revolution? Because Hemingway works with first-hand materials. Because his surroundings offer him the theme and the substance that he needs to tell his story. Because he forms a critical opinion about what is happening in the world around him. The Cuban situation of the period—the abuse, the Machado regime-ordered assassinations, and the violent revolutionary opposition to it all—underscores the brutal setting in which Harry Morgan struggles, even while Morgan's American world both impinges on and agitates the Cuban world. The U.S.-imposed Platt Amendment to the Cuban constitution of 1901, by virtue of which the United States reserved the right to intervene directly in Cuba, remained in force until 1934.

The situation was extremely complex. The moral laxity shown in "One Trip Across," precisely embodied in the main character, is a result of the economic crisis that began in 1929. The United States' prohibition of alcohol, still in force at the time the story takes place, had caused and was causing the exact opposite of its intended effect. It offered opportunities to those who broke the law while leaving the honest man in a "kind of spiritual anarchy," confronted with the upheaval of all the values supposedly respected by society.

Even if they wanted to earn an honest living, the poor were caught between ill-paid jobs and a meager government subsidy, which drove them to walk a fine line between legality and illegality, morality and immorality (or amorality). At times, Harry behaves like any two-bit crook, while at others he seems to adhere to the moral principles of a good man. I believe his character to embody these contradictions, being typical of the American scene at the time, more particularly, typical of Key West.

At the time the story unfolds, Key West was still "Cuban." Ownership of Florida and its adjacent keys had been turned over to Britain many years before, and later became part of the United States. But Key West's most outstanding feature was its Cuban character, resulting from a population heavily Cuban either by birth or descent. Although Key West was no longer known mainly for that warmth, understanding, and support for Cuban independence that José

Martí found there, the rigid boundary between the races that was elsewhere typical of American society had not yet been drawn there.

Key West's prevailing atmosphere in those days was one of poverty and corruption. Gambling and prostitution were its main "industries," and both were mostly owned by Cubans. Well-off Cubans and Cuban Americans, whatever the origins of their wealth, dominated the scene, including politics. Even the police force was mostly of Cuban origin. The natives of the Florida Keys, known as Conchs, were at the bottom of the social ladder. In addition, as McLendon notes, the 125 miles that separated Key West from the mainland afforded a freedom that was almost equivalent to independence.[5]

Closer to Cuba—not only geographically, as we have mentioned—Key West at that time was a distorted reflection of the Cuban reality. That reflection is what Harry—in all likelihood not a Conch but a mainlander—takes in.

Harry is an outsider both in Key West and in Havana. Before settling in Key West and taking up bootlegging, he was a police officer in Miami, a background that probably has served him well in his new occupation. However, he is not much higher on Key West's social ladder than the Conchs. He is not among the wealthy, but rather one of the lowly poor. He refuses, however, to suffer the insecurities that poverty imposes. In naming this character "Harry," Hemingway may have been thinking of its close homophone, *hairy,* suggested by the Spanish expression *hombre de pelo en pecho* ("a man with hair on his chest," strong, brave, virile). Harry wants to play the game of the powerful, emulating their practices to enjoy their security and well-being. Now owning an asset he can use as a source of income—the boat, probably bought with dirty money—he intends to avoid unnecessary risks by once again becoming a law-abiding citizen.

The action begins when Harry enters La Perla café with Eddy, the drunk. The three young Cuban revolutionaries are already there. The narrator gives identifying details without explicitly saying who they are. This fact has given rise to misinterpretation, from believing them to be just members of one gang at war with another gang to believing that the fighting that follows is nothing but a clash between two factions of the whole anti-Machado movement (Desnoes 43).

The mistake is the reader's, not the author's. Hemingway has described the three young men so accurately as anti-Machado revolutionary students that when the two assailants appear, there is no question that they are the dictator's henchmen.

The three young men are well dressed but wear no hats; they speak English well. Their clothing and diction are typical of educated Cuban middle-class university students, most likely from the Directorio Estudiantil, the student organization that, together with blue-collar workers, led the movement against the Machado regime. The fact that they are not wearing hats is significant: ever since Cubans had gone hatless in a show of solidarity with a hat makers' strike, the gesture had come to signal defiance, especially among young people (Augier 1980).[6] At times, innocent pedestrians were even detained merely for not wearing hats.

As the story unfolds, the political involvement of the three young men is confirmed when one of them tells Harry that later on it would be to his advantage to have helped them because things were going to change. Harry replies, "I don't care who is president here" (*THHN* 4). This scene also implies that Harry has a shady reputation, when Pancho—the only one of the three young men named—accuses him of smuggling Chinese immigrants.

Harry has said that he will not carry on his boat anything that can talk, and the Cuban takes offense: "Do you think we're *lenguas largas* [snitches]?" (*THHN* 4). Harry then lists cargo that "can't talk," such as sacked liquor and demijohns. The Cuban retorts, "Can Chinamen talk?" (5).

At the time, the smuggling of illegal immigrants into the United States, especially from Asia, was as common as rum-running.[7] With no chance of legally entering the United States, where they hoped to improve their lives, many poor Chinese—and others—sought out human traffickers, who would defraud them.[8]

Smuggling was a lucrative but extremely dangerous business, especially if dealing in human cargo. Transporting Cubans was less risky because they, like other Latin Americans, had "free" access to the United States as long as a legal resident guaranteed that the newcomer would not become a public burden.

Harry's reply is the expression of a firm decision made earlier. It is the same answer he had given them in another conversation outside the scope of the story. Harry himself mentions it: "it's just like I told you last night" (*THHN* 5). Normally, Harry would tend to respond differently to a request like this. When Harry says, "I'm all for you" (4), he is not just being polite. Harry's sympathy for the revolutionaries can be traced back to that of the author himself, who had already expressed his hope that Cubans would manage to rid themselves of this ruthless tyrant, Machado (Baker 245).

But Harry is single-mindedly pursuing his one goal. He is unwilling to jeopardize the hard-earned safety that he feels he has achieved with his business of renting out his boat to wealthy clients. Moreover, he doesn't seem to realize the danger that the three young men really face, and even if he does, he is more intent on what he believes to be his duty to his family: keeping safe, staying out of trouble, and trying to earn honest money from Mr. Johnson.

It may be somewhat far-fetched to interpret Harry's refusal and its dire consequences as a commentary from Hemingway on his country's policy toward

Cuba. What *can* be affirmed without straying from the semantic framework of the text is that the whole scene, including the shootout in which the three young men are killed by the hired guns, is a crucial moment in Harry's life. Thus, it is likewise crucial to the whole novelette. The cold-blooded objectivity with which the scene is described does not detract from its extreme, acute intensity. This is the way in which the author points to the significance that this scene will take on as events unfold.

When Harry later discusses the state of affairs with his client, the calm that he had shown the three young Cubans has turned into concern. The shootout and the deaths of the three Cubans, which he could have averted, weigh heavily on his conscience. Harry's remorse does not surface in his mind or in the text, but it gradually transforms certainty into distrust—a muted fear that finally emerges in talk about money and in the irritability that he tries to hide from Mr. Johnson.

Mr. Johnson turns out to be a despicable crook, but Harry is not surprised, only disgusted, when Johnson slips away without paying him. To Harry, this flight is a confirmation of the fears that he tried to ignore. It is never clear whether Johnson is a powerful industrialist, a banker, or a gangster. It makes no difference. His dishonesty contrasts with Harry's scrupulous behavior, with his code of honor. The differences between the two characters are evident from the very moment of Johnson's first appearance in the story. The contrast between the wealthy client and the penniless boatman is extraordinarily effective: although neither is a model of virtue, their similarities do not detract from their fundamental differences. One is an expert swindler; the other is a down-and-out nobody. One defrauds others deftly; the other, no matter how hard he tries, always ends up a loser.

The whole episode of Harry's interaction with Mr. Johnson is technically and thematically complete. The leitmotif is loss: first, the loss of the marlin that bite but get away, then the loss of the fishing gear because of Johnson's carelessness. The loss of honestly earned money is magnified by its contrast with the earlier losses and thereby takes on greater significance for both the character and the entire story's message.

While the story is an undeniably interesting and coherent narrative unit, it is also, as discussed above, an intrinsic structural part of "One Trip Across," where it serves the same purpose as might a psychological profile in any other story. When Hemingway describes in minute detail his characters' experiences while fishing, he is not showing off his expertise as a sportsman; Harry's skill as a seaman, his abstinence from drinking while on the job, his scrupulous fulfillment of his side of the bargain are all insights into his character. Harry's "ethics," his reticent masculinity, his self-control in the face of overwhelming emotion all prepare the reader for what is to come.

The second interview at La Perla, so much like the first in appearance—and even in content and consequences—is different because of Harry's reply. His potential client provides another point of contrast. This time he is not dealing with young revolutionaries offering him money to help them avoid falling into the hands of the government's henchmen but with Mr. Sing, a Chinese man who speaks with a British accent, dresses smartly, and behaves like an English gentleman but also proves to be a ruthless businessman. Harry's circumstances this time are also different. Cheated by Mr. Johnson, broke, and with no way of providing for his family throughout the summer when business is slow, Harry lets Frankie, an old acquaintance from the docks, set up the meeting.

Frankie is a true and loyal friend. The clues are obvious: he is frank, open, sincere. Although his hearing impairment isolates him from the world, Frankie is open and engaged with Harry; his goodwill is genuine. In his eyes, Harry is a hero, not the antihero that the reader knows. Besides the three young revolutionaries, Frankie is the only selfless character in the whole story. Never is there any mention of payment for his services in setting up the deal. Although Frankie probably gets something out of it from Mr. Sing, and by the "code of honor" that Frankie and Harry share, it never occurs to Frankie to ask for payment, nor Harry to offer it. Significantly, based on his faulty English and Harry's comment that he doesn't understand English well, it can be assumed that Frankie is Cuban.

The irony lies in the fact that the deal set up by this true friend, while possibly affording Harry his only chance to recover from the setback of Mr. Johnson's swindle, is quite shady and dangerous. Thus, Hemingway reveals the truth behind "freedom of choice." The destitute might quickly reach the point at which they opt for the only remaining way to survive: to ignore moral and legal social conventions and instead to steal, cheat, and even kill. The less fortunate also have a smaller chance of getting away with such actions than those with greater resources. Harry does not think about these things, but the story definitely points the reader to these conclusions.

Dramatic tension rises. The shootout at the very beginning between the revolutionaries and the goons seems to cast a shadow over the rest of the story. Harry describes both the boarding of the Chinese "passengers," whom he has promised to drop off at a small key, and the subsequent events with absolute callousness and skin-crawling disregard for the basic ethical values that mankind has developed through the ages. His preparations reveal his intentions: Mr. Sing's murder is premeditated. Yet Harry seems to be following an irrational impulse to fend off future threats to his safety, an impulse that numbs his already weakened sense of compassion. The closing phrase in this scene, when he breaks the Chinese man's neck with his bare hands, is in my opinion one of the most chilling Hemingway ever made any of his characters utter, with the deliberate objective of jolting the reader: "And don't think you can't hear it crack" (*THHN* 54). This statement reveals how dehumanized a person can become as a result of circumstances. It also lets the reader know that this is the first time that Harry has killed, at least in this way. The statement carries a sort of unsuspected wonder, almost an epiphany.

It is likely that when Harry was a member of the Miami police force, he used a Smith and Wesson or other firearms similar to the ones he carries on board his boat. Given that likelihood, the method of Mr. Sing's murder would be something new, yet similar to, and as impersonal as, deaths Harry may have caused earlier in his life. If so, the reader is entitled to infer that the cold blood with which Harry kills to prevent Mr. Sing from reporting him stems from Harry's background, a reflex conditioned by the practice of killing on behalf of society. It is well known that during the postwar period gang violence escalated alarmingly throughout the United States, strengthening during the Great Depression.

I do not believe, as does Carlos Baker (211), that Johnson's betrayal is the catalyst for Harry's eventual failure. From a sociological point of view, his downfall is fatally predetermined by a situation that he—one man—cannot change. Psychologically, the device that artistically justifies the negative outcome is his refusal to help the Cuban revolutionaries and the deadly consequences of that decision. That is how the author seems to put it: the fishing expedition has failed, the money owed to Harry fails to materialize, and an arrangement intended to solve Harry's financial problems—the deal with Mr. Sing—quickly becomes Harry's moral undoing, ending in theft and murder. The sum of these elements produces that peculiar effect of tragedy so frequently seen in Hemingway's work. There are no deities here, no higher power; that role is filled by a society that severely limits the options of the underprivileged. There is also an error of judgment on the part of the protagonist, as in the Greek *hubris*.

Harry is not a member of the working class. He works for a living, but he has no class awareness. His individualism is typical of the society he lives in, and he never sees the need to change it. This is, in fact, his most serious flaw.

Harry is not a positive figure. He is not a hero. Like many of Hemingway's main characters, Harry is an antihero, or better still, as Young puts it, a nonhero, a "hero of the code" or a *hero with a code.*[9] He is a man who wants to live and let live but finds himself pitted against a society that corners him. In his own way, he has a sense of honor.

Through Harry, Hemingway illustrates his theory of retribution, of inevitable payment, which, from various angles, appears frequently in the author's works and is especially clear in *The Sun Also Rises* (*SAR*), where references to money become symbolic. Everything has a price and nothing comes free, although not necessarily in terms of money, as Scott Donaldson assumes when literally interpreting the words "to get your money's worth" and "the world was [is] a good place to buy in" (*SAR* 152). Even when taken out of context, the concepts of "money" and "buy" in these two phrases are used metaphorically, which is not to say that at some point they cannot be read in their literal meaning.

Nothing is free, indeed, and everything certainly must be paid for. Mr. Johnson's deceit is the price that Harry pays for his gullibility on the one hand, and his refusal to help the revolutionaries on the other. Life, Hemingway seems to be saying, is a peculiar chain of events. Thus, what Mr. Johnson does to Harry is paid for by Mr. Sing at the highest possible price—his life. However, the justice that Harry takes into his own hands, his taking of what he is owed, could be seen as morally evened out by his saving the Chinese illegals, whom, according to the deal, he is supposed to drop off on some key with no chance of being rescued. In fact, though, Harry's act of "kindness" toward the Chinese illegals is an act of deception since they had paid for passage to the United States and Harry takes them back to Cuba.

With an irony so characteristic of Hemingway, the facts are connected and contrasted. The bareness with which they are exposed makes them, at first sight, seem innocent. Hemingway manages to momentarily freeze the reader's sensibilities, to paralyze the reader's judgment long enough for him to witness, without flinching, the most horrendous abomination. I believe this to be one of the most effective forms of condemnation used in critical realism: the reader's reaction is not any weaker for the slight delay.

Harry has no scruples. He will stop at nothing—even stealing and killing—to regain financial security; still less will he stop when his personal safety is at stake. He wanted no witnesses to his cargo or to his crime, and there, on the boat, is Eddy the drunk.

Eddy the drunk, who has seen everything and even contributed to its happening, has no clue of the decision his captain has been "forced" to make. As Harry ponders his dilemma, we can see the significance of Eddy's name. Throughout the text the word *eddy* is used in its literal meaning as a small countercurrent, a whirlpool. To me, the name describes the character not only as a drunk but also as a small-caliber opponent.

In the end, purely by chance, Harry does not kill Eddy. Silently suspecting that his mate may betray him, Harry tells Eddy that he will be making the return trip alone. Later, the customs officer adds Eddy's name to the departure documents, at the drunk's request. Harry discovers the inclusion when he is about to eliminate the only person whose betrayal he fears (since the Cuban who saw him from Mr. Sing's boat does not even know what Harry looks like). Harry feels genuinely relieved, not for being unable to kill Eddy, but for not having to explain Eddy's disappearance on arrival in Key West.

This relief is expressed in the repetition of certain words and phrases that seem to symbolize steps approaching a revelation. Emotions and thoughts are restrained, bound, barely perceived by the mind as we see in these words: "That was luck for me all right. I could have said he fell overboard" (*THHN* 63).

It bears repetition: Hemingway's writings follow the iceberg principle. "One Trip Across" is a perfect example of how what we see is merely a small portion of what lies hidden below the surface. The text refers to and is supported by a subtext; together, both suggest and imply a broader context. The omissions that the method requires are justified by the vantage point that has been chosen.

The first person—both literally and grammatically—that the reader meets is Harry, a man of action who thinks only when necessary. He does not ponder or try to interpret what he observes. He functions like a well-oiled machine, reacting to internal and external stimuli, a task for which he is aptly equipped. To others, he is inscrutable, and this inscrutability creates a barrier that obstructs communication, an effect intended by the author.

The narrator starts out as merely one of many individuals who make up a certain indefinite *us.* This amorphous group includes Eddy the drunk, who we slowly realize is one of the individuals into which Harry's generic "foe" fragments. The story addresses a *you* who knows this *us,* this group from which the narrator speaks in a language typical of those sharing his social condition. The reader's role is to listen in on a conversation that he is not a part of. The narrator and his listener live on the same social level and share similar experiences, a fact made evident from the very beginning: "You know what it's like in Havana at sunrise . . ." (*THHN* 3).

Although in his own way Harry resists, his ideology is molded by the values of the ruling class—as is frequently the case. Thus, he uses the word *bums* to refer to the homeless—expressing contempt for them in terms used by the socially dominant to mask their distaste for an unsavory reality whose root causes are best ignored—while still seeming to believe that these out-of-work men are not completely marginalized. In his mind, the individual must make his own way in this hostile world where he has been told that opportunities are equally available to everyone.

Between author and reader there are two refractions, two takes on the facts: one being the narrator's and the other being the imaginary listener's. This arrangement is necessary in order to objectify the subjectivity of the first person. The story and its reception are oblique. It would be wrong to mistake the role of the listener for that of the reader. Nothing prevents the reader from taking on the role of listener if he so decides, but the reader must remember the characterization that this role entails. If forgotten, offense might be taken, as it was by Philip Young (Cowley 793) when Harry, not feeling good after beating Eddy, declares, "You know how you feel after you hit a drunk" (*THHN* 38).[10]

This is not Hemingway speaking to his reader but Harry, in character, speaking to a listener as fictional as he is, who must be recognized as an implicit character. Several decades ago, Andrei Platonov stated that Hemingway's style is "highly sophisticated and can be explained by its sense of measure." This is especially evident in "One Trip Across." Each element has been carefully selected, and its incorporation into the whole leaves no gaps and creates no overlaps. Every piece of information needed is present to work the magic of art and create the suggested world in the reader's imagination. If something seems superfluous, the text must be revisited; the reader is missing something.

In this novelette, the full integration of form and content is evident in its thematic, compositional, and linguistic aspects. All the motifs and symbols are suggested by the theme, and they are, for the most part, Cuban. The simple mention of a name, repeated, transforms it into a symbol: Bacuranao, for example. Others, having allegorical origins, take on a new and mysterious poetic quality, like the café, La Perla, which is not fictional and therefore carries greater evocative value. The many variations on one of Harry's most recurring refrains—*some Eddy, some Mr. Johnson, some Mr. Sing, some nigger*—constitute a formula that starts out as the character's way of expressing slight disdain, but later takes on various affective nuances. It is never used in reference to the Cuban revolutionaries. In their characterization, however, the expression "good looking" followed closely by "fine young men" (*THHN* 6) is intensified in such a way that the phrase no longer describes only their appearance but also traits and qualities that the narrator links to their social and financial standing, but which the reader can interpret more accurately.

The few words used in Spanish—besides geographic names—are marginally significant, contributing mainly to the atmosphere. The setting—limited in the text to parts of Havana seen from the sea or from the Plaza de San Francisco and the waters along the northern coast of Cuba—is all Cuban, and is described just as it was in 1933 and as it remained, with few changes, for years. When Harry mentions a *Chink place,* for example, we know without a doubt that he is referring to one of the cheap Chinese restaurants so common in Cuba back then. When he speaks of the hotel in which his client, Mr. Johnson, was staying, there is no question that he means the Ambos Mundos, which Hemingway himself used to frequent.

All the devices used by Hemingway are a function of the single artistic purpose of telling the story in the best possible way, and that way, the most fitting, requires the presence of the Cuban element. Not only must the Cuban element be present, but it must be contrasted with other elements. The fact that Hemingway uses elements with such real connotations creates a different correlation of forces between what appears to be secondary and what seems significant, to such an extent that, in the end, the roles are reversed. What at first comes across as subordinate takes on the greater importance in the total meaning.

In brief, the Cuban elements in "One Trip Across" are without a doubt part of the atmosphere, but, more importantly, they constitute a code-complex of organic elements that construct the message of the whole work: individual acts of defiance against unscrupulous haves—doomed because of their separate, isolated nature—must coalesce into collective action against the social order, whose effects, unpredicted, only time will tell.

Notes

This is an excerpt from *Cuba y Hemingway en el gran río azul* (Cuba and Hemingway on the Great Blue River) by Mary Cruz (Havana: Ediciones Union, 1981). Although an English translation exists, Mary Cruz does not recognize that translation. Her daughter, Mary Delpino, has generously and carefully translated for us this selection from chapter 3, "'It is hard for you to tell': An Essay on *To Have and Have Not,*" of her mother's book. It is hoped that this selection, which discusses only the first part of *To Have and Have Not,* will encourage the translation into English of the whole of Mary Cruz's book. It contains factual information about Hemingway's Cuba not readily available to American readers, together with a well-articulated Marxist critique of his works.

1. The disjuncture between the editorial lead and the actual story is glaring and disturbing, especially when read against the background material supplied to Hemingway by Richard Armstrong in his letter of 27 August 1936, included in this anthology. Hemingway was not writing a mere adventure story and the violence that concerned him was realistic and not romantic. The photo from the Armstrong folder at the John F. Kennedy Library, placed in this anthology just before the letter, speaks to the reality of the violence Hemingway is depicting.

2. All references to the text of *To Have and Have Not* will be to the Scribner's edition of 1965 and abbreviated as *THHN.*

3. Forced to adopt the beliefs of their masters, African slaves used this syncretic religion to disguise the fact that they continued their indigenous religious practices. *Santeria* necklaces were steeped in holy water. The first one, received by the neophyte, is *Obatala's*—Immaculate Conception—white. The blue-beaded necklace is *Yemaya's*—Virgen de Regla. The previous information was contributed by folklore researchers at the Social Sciences Institute of the Cuban Academy of Sciences. Hemingway uses the

word *voodoo*, not *Santeria*. It is quite likely that he was unaware of the difference; on the other hand, he may have sacrificed accuracy for the sake of understanding, since the former term is more generally known in reference to Haiti. Professor Grimes's essay in this volume extends the observations about Hemingway's use of Afro-Cuban religion first noted here by Mary Cruz.

4. The ironic use of the popular figure of speech serves here to lay bare the grief that Cubans felt at the failure of the uprisings. The expression was taken from Raul Roa in *La Revolucion del 30 se fue a bolina* (Havana: Ediciones Huracan, 1969).

5. James McLendon's study, *Papa: Hemingway in Key West, 1928–1940*, has helped me to better understand Key West in the 1930s, and although his approach and mine are completely different, he is less caustic in his commentary on Cuba than most critics.

6. Information supplied by Dr. Angel Augier, deputy director of the Institute of Literature and Linguistics, Cuban Academy of Sciences, and vice president of the Cuban Union of Writers and Artists. When very young, Augier participated in the anti-Machado movement.

7. The U.S. immigration quota was one-sixth of 1% of the country's population in 1920. From that portion, less than 20% corresponded to the whole of Asia. The Chinese were not even included in that quota until 1943, when the 1862 Special Chinese Exclusion Act was repealed.

8. In his novel, *Contrabando* (1938), Enrique Serpa deals with the very same issue. Scott McClintock's essay in this volume explores this literary connection at length.

9. Young here develops the theory, which was so well received by Hemingway's critics. It is interesting to note that Young seems to have drawn from Kashkeen not only his hero and code theory, but also that of the single hero under various names, starting with Nick Adams. It should be noted that the English translation of Kaskeen's essay came out two years before Young's Ph.D. dissertation and that Young is not the only critic who has found inspiration in Kashkeen.

10. It is rather odd that twenty years later, Young should entertain the idea of resorting to his fists (Cowley 793).

Works Cited

Arrowitz, Alfred G., and Peter Hamill. *Ernest Hemingway: The Life and Death of a Man.* New York: Lancer Books, 1961.

Atkins, John. *The Art of Ernest Hemingway: His Work and Personality.* New York: Roy Publishers, 1953.

Augier, Angel. *Nicholás Guillén: Obra poética* (edición crítica). Havana: Unión de Escritores y Artistas de Cuba, 1971.

Baker, Carlos. *Ernest Hemingway: A Life Story.* New York: Scribner, 1969.

——. *Hemingway: The Writer as Artist.* Princeton, NJ: Princeton Univ. Press, 1952.

Cervantes, Miguel de. *Don Quijote de la Mancha: Edición del IV centenario.* Real Academia Española, 2004.

Cowley, Malcolm. "Nightmare and Ritual in Hemingway." *The Portable Hemingway.* New York: Viking Press, 1945.

Desnoes, Edmundo. "Lo español en Hemingway." *Lunes de Revolución* 118 (1961):14–15.

Donaldson, Scott. "Hemingway's Morality of Compensation." *American Literature* 43.3 (Nov. 1971): 399–420.

Hemingway, Ernest. "One Trip Across." *Cosmopolitan* Apr. 1934: 20–23, 108–22.

——. *The Sun Also Rises* (*SAR*). New York: Charles Scribner's Sons, 1929.

——. *To Have and Have Not* (*THHN*). 1934; New York: Charles Scribner's Sons, 1965.

Lidskii, Y. Y. *Ernest Hemingway's Creative Works.* Kiev: Naukova Dumka, 1973.

McLendon, James. *Papa: Hemingway in Key West, 1928–1940.* New York: Popular Library, 1972.

Pino-Santos, Oscar. *Historia de Cuba: Aspectos fundamentales.* Havana: Editora del Consejo Nacional de Universidades, 1964.

Platonov, Andrei. "On to Meet the People." *Literaturni Kritik* 11 (1938): 158–71.

Roa, Raul. *La Revolucion del 30 se fue a bolina.* Havana: Ediciones Huracan, 1969.

Tabares del Real, José A. *La revolución del 30: sus dos últimos años.* Havana: N.p., 1973.

Young, Philip. *Ernest Hemingway.* Minneapolis, MN: Univ. of Minnesota Press, 1963. University of Minnesota Pamphlets on American Writers, No. 1.

The "Matter of Being Expatriots"

Hemingway, Cuba, and Inter-American Literary Study

SCOTT O. MCCLINTOCK

As a comparatist specializing in U.S.–Latin American relations in literature and culture, I view Ernest Hemingway's greater-than-two-decade association with Cuba as one of the most compelling cases for inter-American study. Hemingway's affiliation with Cuba supervenes in the experience of the Paris exile as the acme of the high modernism memorialized in Hemingway's *A Moveable Feast,* which Hemingway began in the fall of 1957 at the Finca Vigía in Cuba, twinning the Cuban and inter-American context of expatriation with European relations. In a piece written from Cuba and published in *Look* magazine the previous fall, in September 1956, Hemingway called the Finca Vigía and Cuba his home, a place to which he and Mary would always return, one not yet "overrun" like Spain, Africa, or "the places in Wyoming, Montana and Idaho that I loved" ("Situation Report" 471).

Ironically, a few paragraphs later in the same article, Havana appears inescapably "overrun" in Hemingway's list of the plethora of "compatriots" inhabiting the city during the prerevolutionary period:

> All you have to do to see your compatriots is to get into the car after work and go into the Floridita bar in Havana. There are people from all of the states and from many places where you have lived. There are also Navy ships in, cruise ships, Customs and Immigration agents you have known for years, gamblers who are opening up or have just closed or are doing well or badly, embassy characters, aspirant writers, firmly or poorly established writers, senators on the town, the physicians and surgeons who come for conventions, Lions, Elks, Moose, Shriners, American Legion members, Knights of Columbus,

> beauty contest winners, characters who have gotten into a little trouble and pass a note in by the doorman, characters who get killed next week, characters who will be killed next year, the F.B.I., the former F.B.I., occasionally your bank manager and two other guys, not to mention your Cuban friends. ("Situation Report" 475)

After defending himself from criticism of his expatriate status in Cuba by noting his regular attendance at "wars in which my country participates" and his payment of federal taxes, Hemingway pretends to confuse the spelling of the word *expatriate,* first writing "There is the matter of being expatriots," and later seeming to correct his spelling error by commenting, "I looked up the spelling" ("Situation Report" 474).[1] At home in Cuba from 1932 (when he began commuting between Key West and Cuba) to 1960, Hemingway is an unavoidable figure for inter American study. More than this, his Cuban fiction challenges his readers to adopt a point of view similar to his own inter-American outlook.

In 1980, speaking at a Hemingway conference on Thompson Island in Boston Bay that would herald not only the launching of the Hemingway Society and the renaming of *Hemingway Notes,* the flagship Hemingway journal, as *The Hemingway Review* but also, more broadly, the professionalization of Hemingway studies, Michael Reynolds observed that in the "Hemingway terrain" there was "much unexplored territory yet to be mapped," referring to "that future" research and scholarship as an "act of the imagination" (Reynolds, "Unexplored Territory" 189). In his 1980 address, Reynolds forecast many of the directions Hemingway study would take not only over the next decade but over the next two and a half decades. Among these directions for future research, he indicated specifically the study of Hemingway's correspondence (just then becoming available) and of Hemingway's literary relations with other authors; pointed out the underutilization of archival materials and urged scholars to "[b]ring back all the data" (191); recognized the problems of textual study that his own *Hemingway's Reading* (published that year) would begin to address; and noted the need for a true, critical literary biography of Hemingway—a mention that turned out to be the advance notice of his own five-volume biographical project. While acknowledging that Hemingway's early years had already been extensively covered by previous biographies, notably Baker's, Reynolds asserted that the Key West period and the decade of the 1930s (the focus of this paper), which was Hemingway's "most productive . . . and his most stable," had always been given "short shrift" (194), an observation the truth of which has not changed very much, even today. In terms of my own interest here, Reynolds's admonition, "Do not believe that *To Have and Have Not* is as bad as some have said" (194), continues to resonate.

In his 1980 address, Reynolds also looked at the future of Hemingway studies in terms of the context of his novels. He intimated the interest Hemingway's "African book" would exert for future scholars, and correctly stated that "[w]e still do not have the final word on Hemingway's relationship with Spain" (197). Given his own interest in the influence of Hemingway's reading on his writing, Reynolds emphasized the importance of inventorying the books Hemingway took with him when he relocated from Key West to Cuba in 1940, and acknowledged the significant advance represented by the Brasch and Sigman bibliography of Hemingway's library,[2] the first to incorporate the holdings at the Finca Vigía. Yet in his inventory of the imagined future of Hemingway studies, Reynolds overlooked the importance of Cuba, as context and influence on Hemingway's writing. The papers in this volume represent a response to this neglect. And I would argue that to truly appreciate the Cuban context and influence on Hemingway, future study of this topic must be comparative in method and inter-American in perspective. Hemingway's life and writing must not be treated as the center of a solar system around which the Cuban context revolves, as mere background or periphery; instead, the mutual, reciprocal influence of this context on Hemingway, and the relationship between Hemingway's presence on the island and its literary culture, must be examined in a dynamic, interactive way.

In the decades since Reynolds's 1980 address, several scholarly studies, memoirs, and popular media productions have been produced, works that have begun to map the territory of Hemingway's relationship with Cuba. Arnold Samuelson's memoir, *With Hemingway: A Year in Key West and Cuba,* appeared in 1984, the same year as Norberto Fuentes's biography of Hemingway, which incorporated oral histories and interviews with Cubans who knew him. The documentary "Hemingway in Cuba," mainly comprising interviews with North American Hemingway scholars and biographers, was released in 1996. It provides a good sense of how North American scholarship, at least, was starting to account for the "unexplored territory" of the Cuban context of Hemingway's life and work in 1995 and 1997, the period around the two joint meetings of the Hemingway Society and the Cuban International Hemingway Colloquium, held in Cuba. In 1999, Cuban author Enrique Cirules published his *Ernest Hemingway in the Romano Archipelago,* an oral history based on interviews with various individuals in the Romano Key, whose stories about Hemingway were ones that Cirules had grown up hearing. "Hemingway's Cuba," another documentary video produced in the United Kingdom, appeared in 2000, and a television documentary with the same title, hosted by Mariel Hemingway, appeared in 2005. Hemingway's niece, Hilary, visited Cuba in 2002 with a group of American scholars, who were granted access to archives at the Finca for the first time in many years, resulting in the richly illustrated *Hemingway in Cuba,* in 2008. Not only does the book contain a wealth of photographs, excerpts from correspondence, and a profusion of other documentary material, but Hilary Hemingway also interviewed many Cuban Hemingway scholars and archivists, making her book one of the few published in North America to reflect this Cuban scholarship, before the present volume. In 2004, she also produced a television documentary based on this trip for public television.

Still more works brought in specific aspects of the Cuban context. In a 2006 essay, Philip Melling analyzed Afro-Cuban religion and cultural imperialism in *The Old Man and the Sea.* Mark Ott's 2008 study of the stylistic influence on Hemingway's literary writing of Hemingway's "Anita" log, chronicling his fishing voyages between Key West and Cuba in the 1930s, is based on the kind of archival research that carried out Reynolds's exhortation to "bring in all the data." René Villarreal's memoir, *Hemingway's Cuban Son, Reflections on the Writer by His Longtime Majordomo,* although originally written in the early 1970s, had to be reconstructed from memory and oral interviews by Villareal's son after Villareal moved to the United States, before being published in 2009. That same year saw publication of Terry Mort's fascinating study of Hemingway's U-boat patrols on the *Pilar* in the 1940s, incorporating research at U.S. Navy archives in addition to research in more traditional Hemingway collections; it literally mapped the "unknown territory" of Hemingway's exploration of the keys off Cuba's northern coast, since it is full of maps. After all the controversy over whether Hemingway had an affair in Cuba with Jane Mason, Andrew Feldman explored Hemingway's alleged relationship with a Cuban mistress, Leopoldina Rodríguez, in a 2011 article. Finally, Paul Hendrickson's wonderful biography of Hemingway, centering on his boat, the *Pilar,* appeared in 2012. All of these media documentaries and studies have brought us much new "data" about Hemingway's years, and life, in Cuba. But none of them utilize the type of comparative, inter-American approach that brings this Cuban context out of the "background" and explores Hemingway's relationship to Cuba in a true interactive study, as I propose to do in this paper.

Studying Hemingway from an inter-American perspective can naturally be approached from a variety of angles. We could inquire into Cuban themes and materials in Hemingway's work, as did many papers at the Hemingway Colloquia in Havana in 1995 and 1997.[3] The most comprehensive study of this sort must be *Cuba y Hemingway en el gran río azul* (*Cuba and Hemingway on the Great Blue River*), by Cuban novelist Mary Cruz. We might concern ourselves with biographical connections, hoping to supplement what we know from some of the standard biographies about Hemingway's relations with Cuba.[4]

Mary Hemingway's *How It Was* and Norberto Fuentes's *Hemingway in Cuba* offer greater detail about Hemingway's years in Cuba than the standard biographies, and James McLendon's *Hemingway in Key West* provides a lot of valuable insight into the decade of the thirties, when Hemingway shuttled between Key West and Cuba before buying a permanent home at the Finca Vigía in 1940.[5]

Another possible inter-American approach might be to investigate Hemingway's reading about Cuba or his reading of Cuban writers to see if there is any pattern, or to discover if any of this reading influenced his literary writing about Cuba. We know that Hemingway subscribed to the review *La Habana* and that he owned biographies of the Cuban guerilla chief Caoba and of San Cristóbal de la Habana. He also owned a book by or about Cuban independence leader José Martí, a book about pirates published in Cuba, and a general history of Cuba, while his library at Finca Vigía contains books on Cuban botany and agriculture, on fishing and hunting in Cuba, and on Cuba's natural history as well as its social and political history.

As for Cuban writers, Hemingway knew many personally, according to Fuentes—including Alejo Carpentier, Nicolás Guillén, Fernando Campoamor (a friendship that lasted the twenty years of Hemingway's residence in Cuba), and Lisandro Otero—and owned books by many more, including Victor Agostini, Eduardo Benet y Castellón, José Antonio Fernández de Castro, Miguel Angel Macau, Jorge Mañach, Fernando Ortiz, Regino Pedroso, Félix Pita Rodríguez, Juan Manuel Planas y Sainz, Alberto Riera y Gómez, Ezequiel Vieta, Alejo Carpentier, and Enrique Serpa.[6] (Of these, Hemingway owned the most books by Serpa, whose writing parallels Hemingway's in a fashion I'll discuss in greater detail below.)

In "The Cuban Context in *The Old Man and the Sea*," Bickford Sylvester expressed what I think is the most promising avenue for inter-American study of Hemingway, reading Hemingway in terms of interculturalism, observing that we need to read Hemingway "with . . . attention to topical and historical specificity" (263), because Hemingway "requires his readers around the world to notice the specific cultural context of his narrative and familiarize themselves with that context in order to follow . . . the plot" (243). Focusing on Hemingway's first Cuban novel, *To Have and Have Not* (*THHN*), published in 1937, I will demonstrate that the novel's superficially banal plot is actually more complex than it seems: we need to carefully read details of both the Cuban and American contexts to correctly date the action of its three parts. Gaps in the narrative of one part can be filled in by information provided in another, but this requires us to supplement American cultural knowledge with Cuban cultural knowledge, and vice versa. Following Hemingway's plot involves us, as Sylvester suggests, in an intercultural reading experience that enhances our understanding; a purely monocultural reading denies us some of this meaning.

Two Portraits of the Same Subject: Ernest Hemingway and Enrique Serpa

The interculturalism of *To Have and Have Not* involves us in the second kind of comparison-across-the-Americas I will discuss in this paper—what I will call intrinsic comparison, in which cross-country affiliations are internal to the work itself. But first, I want to demonstrate an extrinsic type of comparison by sketching some parallels between Hemingway's *To Have and Have Not* and *Contrabando* [Contraband], a contemporary novel by Cuban writer Enrique Serpa.[7] Although Serpa's book was published in 1938, one year after Hemingway's novel, it was written during the exact period that Hemingway began work on material that would be published together as *To Have and Have Not.*[8] Extrinsic comparisons would include cross-country affiliations between authors and texts of the kind suggested by Hemingway's and Serpa's contemporaneous literary portraiture of prerevolutionary Cuba.

Mary Cruz discusses connections between these two novels in light of differences in their techniques of realism.[9] Serpa is not mentioned in any of the standard biographies of Hemingway, but, given the strong correlations between the two novels, it would be fascinating to learn more about the relationship, if any, between these two writers. Serpa dedicated a collection of stories to Hemingway, writing, "To Ernest Hemingway, a great writer, complete man, perfect friend, with admiration and affection."[10] Did Serpa really know Hemingway, as his dedication implies? Hemingway's text involves us in questions whose answers cannot be found within a single national perspective or within the research resources of a single country, whether the United States or Cuba.

Their two novels, written nearly simultaneously, make Hemingway and Serpa among the first to take the historical period of the dictatorship of Gerardo Machado y Morales (1871–1939), president of Cuba from 1925 to 1933, as a setting for works of fiction.[11] Democratically elected Cuba's president in 1925, Machado became an authoritarian and corrupt leader who maintained his office through rigged elections and repression of his opposition. Part 1 of *To Have and Have Not* takes place during Machado's reign; parts 2 and 3 are set after the general strike and revolution of 1933 that overthrew him, forcing him into exile in Miami. *Contrabando* (*CB*) is set during Machado's tenure and alludes to events leading up to the revolution of 1933, but concludes before it begins.

Both novels contrast the social conditions and values of Cuba's "haves" with those of its "have nots," depicting the underworld of Havana and the Florida Keys, inhabited by fishermen, foreign sailors, prostitutes, bums, and smugglers counterpointed with tourists oblivious to these social conditions.

Besides overlapping chronological and physical settings, *To Have and Have Not* and *Contrabando* employ similar modernistic narrative techniques. The narrator of *Contrabando,* known only as El Almirante (the Admiral) in the novel, is a petit bourgeois, whose fortunes during the global economic depression of the 1920s (which affected both the United States and Cuba) have declined to the point that he uses his pleasure yacht, *La Buena Ventura,* to smuggle alcohol from Cuba to the United States. The novel's action centers on the conflict between the middle-class morality of the protagonist/narrator and the values of the criminal underworld and underclass of smuggling. Like *To Have and Have Not, Contrabando* juxtaposes two Havanas. One is frequented by Cubans of the narrator's class and North American tourists learning to drink the newly invented martini in nightclubs and casinos; the other is inhabited by fishermen struggling to earn enough to feed their families, by prostitutes, and by smugglers, both Cuban and American. Unlike *To Have and Have Not,* however, in which only the first part of the novel is narrated from the viewpoint of its protagonist, Harry Morgan, *Contrabando* is narratively unified by its first-person point of view.

One might conclude that the different narrative viewpoints and discontinuous perspectives of *To Have and Have Not* make it more modernistic, despite the features of realism it shares with *Contrabando.* Structurally, *To Have and Have Not* is more of a collage than *Contrabando,* which is more unified in terms of both narrative perspective and action. All the action of *Contrabando* takes place in the few weeks surrounding the protagonist's inaugural smuggling voyage, probably around 1927. Although the three parts of *To Have and Have Not,* "Spring," "Fall," and "Winter," suggest a similar unity of action within a single year, I will endeavor to show that this apparent unity may represent a narrative trap laid by Hemingway for the monocultural reader, taking advantage of our tendency to fill in narrative gaps (such as the gap in the progression of the annual seasons here) with our unifying assumptions.

Both novels contain lengthy interior monologues influenced by James Joyce. In *Contrabando,* the first such passage occurs in chapter 3, in which El Almirante and an acquaintance, Cornua, discuss the prospect of smuggling alcohol to the United States, while knocking back highball after highball themselves. Briefer interior monologues follow in the ensuing two chapters, in which the narrator worries about acquiring a sexually transmitted disease from his night of bleary intercourse following the conversation with Cornua in the bar. In chapter 18, the conflict between El Almirante's middle-class values and those of the desperate underclass of sailors and smugglers is presented through another lengthy interior monologue, in which the narrator struggles with the bleak, fatalistic morality of Ricardo Scot, a sailor hired on for the smuggling trip planned by the Admiral and Cornua.

Harry Morgan likewise has two interior monologues in the third part of *To Have and Have Not.* The first, which forms the whole of chapter 10, presents Harry's planning of the trip he has contracted for with the crooked Key West lawyer Robert Simmons (Bee Lips) to transport four Cuban revolutionaries, who have robbed a local bank, from Key West to Cuba. The second forms the conclusion of chapter 18, in which Harry lies dying on the deck of his boat after being fatally wounded by one of the four Cubans in a shootout on the Gulf Stream (a scene replicated later in *Islands in the Stream,* when Thomas Hudson dies from wounds resulting from a gun battle with German U-Boat commandos). Finally, the novel concludes (except for a panoramic scene of Key West) with a long interior monologue by Harry's forty-five-year-old wife, Marie, a monologue almost certainly modeled on Molly Bloom's soliloquy in Joyce's *Ulysses.* If the conventional wisdom that Joycean internal monologue creates an interior world distanced from the external environment is true, Hemingway's and Serpa's uses of the technique differ both from Joyce's and each other's. Hemingway's interior monologues, rather, reduce the distance between characters and events, rendering the immediacy of events through the inner experience of them by actors. In *Contrabando,* in contrast, Serpa employs the interior monologue somewhat differently, to externalize the moral conflicts and contradictions within the novel's protagonist.

Both novels incorporate commercial fishing as a plot element ancillary to their central plots involving smuggling activities. The two days presented in chapter 1 of *To Have and Have Not* begin with three Cubans approaching Harry Morgan, seeking to charter his boat to escape some kind of political trouble with the Machado government. Harry turns down their offer, only to become an unwilling witness to their assassination by government agents, after which he keeps an appointment with his client, an ill-behaved tourist named Johnson, for the last day of their second week of deep-sea fishing. The chapter details the fishing expedition in a vein similar to the sportfishing articles Hemingway was writing during this period.[12] The attitude toward big-game fishing that Hemingway expresses both in this passage and in his sportfishing articles suggests he regarded it much as he did bullfighting or hunting—as one of the few experiences remaining in modern life allowing humanity to reveal greatness or nobility, values that Morgan represents here in contrast to the casual disposition of the tourist, Johnson. If *To Have and Have Not* is tragic in its construction (the three-part narrative structure, for example), Johnson's double-crossing of Morgan could constitute a peripety that begins Morgan's fall from at least potential nobility of character to the base, criminal underworld of smuggling to which he now resorts, unable to continue his charter-fishing enterprise without his tackle or money to replace it.

Like Morgan, the narrator of *Contrabando* uses his boat, *La Buena Ventura,* for charter fishing before the passage of Prohibition in the United States, when its captain, Cornua, suggests to him switching from fishing to smuggling alcohol. Early in the novel, the narrator describes his reading of sportfishing journalism, notably the writing of Zane Grey and Ernest Hemingway. "When I learned Zane Grey was the champion amateur fisherman of the United States, I bought six of his books and put them next to my nautical and oceanographical books," he says (*CB* 42; my translation).[13] The narrator adds, "Later I was to find out that another writer was accustomed to come during the summer to Cuban waters, fishing for sharks, named Ernest Hemingway" (42; my translation).[14] The narrator tells of his desire to own a few books by this writer who shared a taste for fishing with Grey and himself, but adds that, having failed to find any of Hemingway's books, he contented himself with a couple of photographs of Hemingway from a newspaper. When anyone asked him about these pictures of Hemingway on his wall, he would say that Hemingway "was a millionaire friend of mine" (42; my translation).[15]

In light of Serpa's dedication to Hemingway of his 1951 short-story collection, this passage leads one to wonder if the friendship with Hemingway Serpa claims in the dedication was real, or, like that of the narrator of his earlier novel, a wish for association with a writer known through publicity and reputation. In any case, participating in commercial sportfishing in the Gulf Stream and writing nonfiction articles about it become highly intertextual—and intercultural—activities for readers in both Cuba and America. Writing from the contact zone of the Gulf Stream tends inevitably to reveal inter-American characteristics.

In *Contrabando,* a story told by crew members of the Admiral's yacht, *La Buena Ventura,* not only shows similarities between the social values of the Cuban fishermen taking tourists on sportfishing trips in Serpa's novel and of Hemingway's Harry Morgan but also reveals the local culture of anonymous fisherman's tales on which both Serpa and Hemingway drew in their literary portrayal of Cuba between the wars. The story contrasts the values of the bourgeois tourist fishermen like Johnson with those of Cubans whose livelihood and sense of personal dignity depend on deep-water fishing:

> One day an American from Shell, who was an aficionado of fishing, saw an elefante and told Cobian that a museum would pay three thousand pesos for

> a fish like that. Imagine that—three thousand pesos! They spent around three hundred getting ready. Well, finally everything was ready and they went out looking for the animal, and spotted it. It was something to strike fear in your heart, let me tell you! After cutting the motor, Cobian approached it using the oars, and zoom! Gave it the harpoon. The fish started stirring up the water like a waterspout and dove into it, who knows where! Three hours later it came up four nautical miles off Santa Cruz. Cobian is a macho, no one argues with that, and he wanted to stick another harpoon in it. But the American wouldn't let him. Finally, when he saw Cobian was going to do it anyway, he took out a gun and told him, "Don't touch it again, or I'll kill you." There wasn't anything to do but wait. And meanwhile, the struggle had been long and there was a big wound from the harpoon in the fish. Three days later it appeared in the bay of Matanzas, completely eaten by sharks. (*CB* 235–36; my translation)[16]

The story satirizes wealthy Americans, contrasting the economic status and values of the haves and have-nots, of the big-game fishing tourists and those they employ, in much the same way as *To Have and Have Not* does. The story's conclusion derides the expenditure of so much money for a fish ultimately consumed by sharks, and this last detail, of course, bears some resemblance to Hemingway's later story of a Cuban fisherman whose prodigious catch is finally devoured by sharks.

Besides their common subject matter of big-game fishing and tourism, numerous affinities in the character types found in these novels suggest that they are, in Mary Cruz's expression, two portraits of the era's Gulf Stream culture, a meeting place of the United States and Latin America. Both novels, for example, include characters who exposit communist ideas: Nelson Jacks in *To Have and Have Not* and Pepe el Catalan in *Contrabando.* Likewise, Harry Morgan (*THHN*) and Cornua (*CB*) exemplify the Hemingwayan ideal of the man of action, individualistic and indifferent to political ideology. The physical descriptions of both characters convey the traits of power and action. Morgan is presented as tall, with wide shoulders and narrow hips, moving "like some kind of animal" (*THHN* 128), while Cornua is drawn as tall and slender ("de elevada estatura" and "magro de carne"), with a prizefighter's fists, and like Morgan is compared to an animal: his walk "suggests a cat's elasticity" ("Sugería, al andar, la elasticidad de los gatos") (*CB* 52).

Morgan possibly resembles even more closely *Contrabando*'s Mr. Bourton, an American who helps arrange the alcohol-smuggling expedition of *La Buena Ventura.* He is similarly described as possessing a vigorous, animal strength. With a broad mouth, a large, bulldog's nose, and blond hair slightly bleached from the sun, he resembles the description of Morgan as "blond, with sunburned hair, his face with the broad Mongol cheekbones, and the narrow eyes, the nose broken at the ridge, the wide mouth and the round jaw" (*THHN* 128).

The allusion to Morgan's "Mongol cheekbones" in the above passage is particularly noteworthy in light of yet another similarity between the two novels: their parallel incidents involving the smuggling of Chinese immigrants. Chapters 2 and 3 in the first part of *To Have and Have Not* recount Morgan's first illegal activity after being cheated by Johnson out of his tackle and charter fee for the fishing trip, when a "smooth looking" Chinese scofflaw named Mr. Sing hires him to transport twelve Chinese men from Cuba to Tortugas, where Sing has falsely promised them another boat will pick them up. Instead of getting rid of the twelve men as Sing suggests, Morgan takes the commission, kills Sing, and returns the men to Cuba. Two similar incidents are related in *Contrabando.* The first involves *La Joven Princesa,* "a boat dedicated to smuggling people, carrying Chinese to the North. Once . . . it was discovered that the crew had stabbed to death four Chinese in the middle of the Gulf, saying it was because they couldn't put them on the American coast and the Chinese had demanded their money back" (103–4; my translation).[17] In the second incident, Ricardo Scot tells of a ruse he observed while crewing on a boat, in which, as in *To Have and Have Not,* twelve Chinese being smuggled to Tampa were hidden when the boat was boarded. He goes on to tell his fellow crew members that smuggling immigrants is easier than smuggling alcohol, because all you have to do is take them out on the water for a couple of days, return them to a different part of the Cuban coast while telling them they are in America, and take their money (*CB* 241–42).

Cuba had imported Chinese slaves as well as Africans during much of its colonial history, and after slavery was abolished there in 1871, it continued to be a point of illegal entry for Chinese immigrants to the United States (Mandel 168). *To Have and Have Not* and *Contrabando* depict this traffic in exploited Chinese immigrants in strikingly parallel incidents. Both Hemingway and Serpa, writing their novels in the same period, probably drew from the local cultural pool of fishermen's stories in creating these incidents.

Cross-Country Affiliations in To Have and Have Not

Our appreciation of the detail of Hemingway's local knowledge of the Cuban materials he uses in *To Have and Have Not* is increased by the kind of extrinsic, cross-country comparison of authors and texts I have profiled in Hemingway and Serpa. But, as I noted earlier, transnational links are also internal to the novel itself, and this kind of inter-American comparison will be the focus of the remainder of the paper. Despite the surface simplicity of its plot, I think I can show that the timeline of *To Have and Have Not* is more complex than it initially appears, although this becomes evident only when the reader supplements the cultural context of U.S. history with Cuba's, and vice versa, in order to date the novel's three parts.

Besides passages of fine stylistic analysis, Mary Cruz's study of Hemingway's relations with the Gulf Stream offers a bounty of the kind of historically specific details of the Cuban context in Hemingway's fiction that Sylvester speaks of. Most valuable for the present purpose are particulars that allow us to more accurately date specific episodes within *To Have and Have Not* and, in the process, to glean the intercultural nature of the local knowledge on which Hemingway based his Cuban fiction. For Cruz, *To Have and Have Not* is a work of critical realism that portrays the contemporary historical and social circumstances on both the American and Cuban sides of the Gulf of Mexico.[18] It reflects the economic realities of the 1929 stock market crash, the Great Depression, and dry laws and Prohibition, while the personal challenges facing its protagonist, Harry Morgan, reflect the economic conflicts between legal and illegal, moral and immoral ways of earning a living. The Cuban context of *To Have and Have Not* includes the revolutionary process against Machado and against the neocolonialism symbolized by the Platt Amendment, which gave the United States broad powers in the administration of the Cuban government.

Hemingway's compositional principle of omission—that what is left out of a narrative can affect a reader as much as what is directly presented—here produces a text in which details that are included function as signposts, pointing to what is left out in the narrative's gaps. The apparent simplicity of Hemingway's writing is belied by the demand it places on the reader to pay very close attention to details. An unwary or hasty reading will tend to bridge these gaps with generalizing assumptions, assumptions that may result from ignorance (perhaps especially cultural ignorance) or may be the product of ideology. This risk, and the careful attention needed to avoid it, can be illustrated by Hemingway's depiction of a range of revolutionaries in *To Have and Have Not.*

Cruz presents a compelling case that the three men who approach Morgan at the beginning of the novel are anti-Machado revolutionaries, who are assassinated by Machado's agents, rather than mere rival gangsters in a shootout, as some critics suggest. Though Morgan refuses their request to charter his boat, he describes them as "nice looking fellows" and expresses regret at having to turn them down, reflecting that he "would have liked to have done them the favor" (*THHN* 3). In the short, descriptive paragraph in which, frustrated in their failed negotiation with Morgan, the men leave, it is the details that allow Cruz to more accurately identify them: "They were good-looking young fellows, wore good clothes; none of them wore hats, and they looked like they had plenty of money. They talked plenty of money, anyway, and they spoke the kind of English Cubans with money speak" (6). Cruz points out that the men's lack of hats is significant; during that period, going hatless was a highly visible protest common among youth, especially university students, to express solidarity with a strike by hatmakers. According to Cruz, other descriptive details identify the three as left-wing students (a group that helped lead the anti-Machado revolution at that time; Cruz 122). Also characteristic of the Machado period in Cuba was the rise of leftist organizations, including the Cuban Communist Party, the National Confederation of Workers, the Directory, the Student Left Wing, and Young Cuba. These details, following Cruz, place the action in the novel's part 1 definitively before the fall of Machado in August 1933.

The second group of revolutionaries who wish to charter Morgan's boat, introduced in part 3, are more explicitly identified as such, and in a Hemingway novel, this very clarity, in contrast to the oblique identification of the first three revolutionaries, should possibly serve to put the reader on notice. This second group comprises Roberto, a pathological killer; Emilio, an apparently well-intentioned young militant; and two unnamed men, clients of the lawyer Robert Simmons (Bee Lips). A reader lacking historical knowledge about this period in Cuba might well lump this second group of revolutionaries together with the first one, as Morgan himself does when he thinks after listening to Emilio expound the goals of his group, "What the hell do I care about his revolution. . . . The hell with his revolution." The Cubans, he reflects, are all the same: "They all double cross each other. They sell each other out. They get what they deserve" (*THHN* 168). But, according to Cruz, these are not the same kind of revolutionaries as the young students in the novel's first part.

Emilio begins his exposition of his group's ideology by claiming, "We are the only true revolutionary party" in Cuba (*THHN* 166), thereby signaling to the alert reader the possibility of differences among the various Cuban political parties calling themselves "revolutionary" during this time. Cruz suggests that Emilio's reference to the "only true revolutionary party" might allude to the Authentic Cuban Revolutionary Party (Partido Revolucionario Cubano, Auténtico, named after the party of Cuban independence leader José Martí), a loose coalition of people with differing political ideologies. But she thinks it is more likely that Hemingway had in mind the ABC, a terrorist organization modeled on Mussolini's Blackshirts, which advocated armed struggle against the post-Machado Mendieta government backed by Batista. It is significant that the

Cuban Communist Party rejected armed struggle and terrorism, and Emilio tells Harry, "We are not communists" (166). The benevolent sounding goals Emilio describes to Harry, Cruz observes, were part of the official platform of the ABC and were shared by a number of organizations to the left and right, but it was right-wing groups like the ABC that espoused terrorism as a means to topple the government. "I regret the necessity for the present phase very much," Emilio tells Harry, "I hate terrorism. I also feel badly about the methods for raising the necessary money" (167)—that is, robbing banks.

The four Cuban revolutionaries of part 3 may be a composite of any number of right-wing groups, Cruz admits, and Cubans themselves could be confused by the proliferation of parties and cells with important ideological and tactical differences that were, nonetheless, difficult to distinguish from one another (Cruz 157–60). If Cruz is right, it may be that the novel dramatizes Harry's ideological confusion, his groping toward but never quite reaching a political perspective. Harry's political confusion tragically leads to his fatal mistake, agreeing to charter his boat to the wrong group of revolutionaries.

The historical material and analysis Cruz presents helps readers of *To Have and Have Not* to gain a more accurate and detailed picture of Cuba during the period, and may prevent us from making the same mistake as the novel's protagonist in failing to differentiate among revolutionary groups, a mistake, incidentally, that Cruz doubts Hemingway made. Besides such allusions to the activity of political organizations like the ABC during the political chaos that followed Machado's ouster, several historical references in part 3 allow us to date it after the fall of Machado in 1933.

Describing social conditions in Cuba to Harry, Emilio remarks, "Now they have a military reserve with every kind of crook, bully and informer of the old days of Machado in it" (*THHN* 167). Earlier, discussing the brutality of Roberto, Emilio tells Harry, "He is a good revolutionary but a bad man. He kills so much in the time of Machado he gets to like it" (158). Earlier still, when Harry discusses with Albert Tracy (who will later be shot and killed by Roberto) the trip he has agreed to make from Key West to Cuba, Tracy asks him if it is common for people to hire boats to get to Cuba. Harry responds, "Sure. All the time since the revolution" (95).

At this point, we can confidently say that part 1 of *To Have and Have Not* must occur before the August 1933 revolution that deposed Machado, and part 3 must take place after it. This is still consistent with the action of the novel all taking place during the single year of 1933, however. Part 1 could describe events in the spring of 1933, and part 3, those in the winter of the same year. We can positively identify the chronological setting of parts 1 and 3, then, by specific historical references to the Cuban context of the novel's plot. The gap in the novel's three seasons, summer, could be an example of Hemingway's technique of omission, but at any rate we are left with the unified action of one year.

I do not believe that the time sequence is this continuous, however, an assertion supported by references to U.S. history in the novel that supplement its references to Cuban history already discussed. Of such references to events in the United States, the critical missing piece of the puzzle I have presented so far is the repeal of Prohibition.

In part 2, subtitled "Fall," the action begins after Morgan and his friend Wesley have been shot by a Cuban water patrol during a rum-running trip. "Why they run liquor now?" Wesley asks Morgan. "Prohibition's over" (*THHN* 70). Morgan doesn't answer the question. In a brief internal monologue later, Harry asks himself why the patrol boat picked that time to enforce the agreement between Cuba and the United States against importing alcohol. "How was I to know they'd shoot at us in Mariel after we could go and come there open for six months," Harry wonders (86).

The 21st Amendment to the U.S. Constitution repealed Prohibition, the 18th Amendment, which had been adopted in 1919. The answer to Wesley's question might be that while the 21st Amendment deleted provisions in the 18th Amendment l banning the manufacture, sale, or transportation of alcohol within the United States, it retained the ban on importing alcohol into the United States from abroad. At any rate, the 21st Amendment was ratified on December 5, 1933. Thus the events described in the novel's second part, subtitled "Fall," could not have taken place until the following fall, in 1934, while Harry's remark that they had been able to come and go openly for the past six months probably refers to the six months after ratification of the 21st Amendment, which likewise would place the action of part 2 in fall 1934, rather than fall 1933. Such timing also explains what Harry has been doing in the gap between parts 1 and 2: running rum from Cuba to the United States.

Perhaps Hemingway is having a little game with his reader's expectations, dating the three parts of *To Have and Have Not* in such a way that we are tempted to assume the continuity of a single year in the time sequence, when in fact the gap between parts 1 and 2 is greater than it appears to be. What is significant about this, if I'm right, is that only by alternating between U.S. and Cuban frames of historical reference do we see the length of the gap between parts 1 and 2. We must become "expatriot" readers, abandoning the perspective of a single national frame of reference in order to accurately read Hemingway's intercultural text.

If I am right that the novel's plot and structure force us to become cross-cultural readers, it may be that Hemingway is pointing us to the solution to

Morgan's problem: his fatal error in misjudging different groups of Cuban revolutionaries is a failure of cultural understanding. In fact, the scene that opens the novel, where Harry refuses to help the young revolutionaries escape their political trouble, dramatizes the tragic consequences of such misunderstandings between Americans and Cubans. One of the three men, Pancho, misunderstands Harry, thinking Harry is accusing the men of being "lenguas largas," stool pigeons, and becomes angry with Harry (*THHN* 4). Harry doesn't know enough about the political situation in Cuba to understand the difference between this group of revolutionaries and the one he later agrees to transport from the American side of the Gulf to Cuba ("Listen," Harry says, "I don't care who is President here" [4].)

To Have and Have Not is centrally concerned with the problem of achieving the right cultural relationships. These cannot be defined simply along national lines, as the design of part 1, with its triple set of characters betrayed by their own compatriots, vividly illustrates. Morgan is betrayed by Johnson. The Chinese immigrants are betrayed by Mr.Sing. And the young Cuban revolutionaries, it is implied, have been betrayed by a "lengua larga," an informer. On the other hand, the wrong kind of cross-cultural relationships lead equally to perfidy and disaster, such as that Morgan experiences in part 3 of the novel with the second group of revolutionaries.

At home in two countries in the Americas, Hemingway is a vital figure for inter-American literary study, and I would argue that to read his Cuban fiction well, one must adopt an inter-American framework. He is a writer who, more than has generally been appreciated, teaches us that national literatures cannot be studied outside the context of their relationships with other national literatures. *To Have and Have Not* has the potential to illuminate for us the tragic consequences of misunderstandings between countries lying on both sides of the Gulf. Its construction guides Hemingway's readers to an inter-American perspective that may lead us away from the inevitability of the tragic plot engendered by cultural misperception.

Notes

1. Jeffrey Herlihy's study, *In Paris or Paname: Hemingway's Expatriate Nationalism,* is the most theoretically sophisticated analysis I know of that concerns multicultural themes and "foreignness" as a literary device in Hemingway's fiction. Although it takes a quite different tack than my own inter-American approach in this paper, I would like to endorse Herlihy's felicitous phrase, "expatriate nationalism" to describe a similar cultural problematic of Hemingway's status as an "ex-patriot" North American writer in Cuba.

2. James Brasch was one of the first North American Hemingway scholars to recognize the significance of Cuba (and Spain) as "unexplored" territories in Hemingway studies, not only by supplementing the Hanneman bibliography by doing research on Hemingway's library in Cuba, but also in his other research, such as his publication of translated interviews with José Luis Herrera Sotolongo about Hemingway in Spain and Cuba. A critical response by Aden Hayes to this interview material was published, along with Brasch's reply, in *The Journal of Modern Literature,* in 1987. Aside from its rather pointless linguistic pedantry, Hayes' response illustrates a certain "positivistic" faith in the reliability of printed documents, and distrust of oral history and testimony, that seems common among North American scholars. The idea that a written document (a letter from Hemingway to his son, Patrick) should be taken just as much at "face value" by Hayes as he accused Brasch of taking Sotolongo's recollection of views Hemingway expressed verbally to Sotolongo, about his attitude toward the Cuban Revolution, shows the historical positivism of the culture of North American scholarship, and its inability to understand the documentary genre of testimony that is common in Cuba. Further, there is no reason to suppose that Hemingway's expression of political views regarding the Cuban Revolution should be coherent or consistent. Hemingway was hardly a systematic political philosopher. The idea that a single piece of written correspondence (or even two, if the vague quote in Hemingway's letter to Buck Lanham is added to the scales) should be taken as a more definitive expression of Hemingway's attitude toward the Revolution than multiple statements Hemingway made verbally to Cuban friends and to journalists, seems fallacious and, in Hayes's case, evidently biased.

3. For one participant's view, see Gerald Locklin, *Hemingway Colloquium: The Poet Goes to Cuba* (Palm Springs, CA: Event Horizon Press, 1999).

4. See, for example, Carlos Baker, *Ernest Hemingway: A Life Story* (New York: Scribner's, 1969); A. E. Hotchener, *Papa Hemingway* (New York: Random House, 1966); Kenneth Lynn, *Hemingway* (New York: Fawcett Columbine, 1987); James Mellow, *Hemingway: A Life Without Consequences* (Boston: Houghton Mifflin, 1992); Stuart McIver, *Hemingway's Key West* (Sarasota, FL: Pineapple Press, 1993); Jeffrey Meyers, *Hemingway: A Biography* (New York: Harper & Row, 1985); and Earl Rovit, *Ernest Hemingway,* Twayne's United States Authors Series, no. 41 (New York: Twayne, 1963).

5. Arnold Samuelson, *With Hemingway: A Year in Key West and Cuba* (New York: Random House, 1984), and, more popularly, David Schaefer, *Sailing to Hemingway's Cuba* (Dobbs Ferry, NY: Sheridan House, 2001), recreate Hemingway's discovery of Cuba in the 1930s. Michael Reynolds's *Hemingway: The 1930s* (New York: W. W. Norton, 1997), part of a definitive, five-volume biography of the writer, should also be mentioned. Recollections of Hemingway in Cuba are included in the memoirs of John Parker, a former secretary of the Cuban Claims Association and fellow expatriate (with an *a*), who called Cuba home in the prerevolutionary period (*We Remember Cuba* [Sarasota, FL: Golden Quill, 1993]). Cuban writer Enrique Cirules's *Conversación con el último norteamericano* [Conversation with the Last North American] (Havana: Editorial Letras Cubanas, 1988) is a testimonial of the last surviving member of the Gloria City colony of North Americans in Cuba (a relic of American annexational policy and itself a fascinating study of Cuban-American relations); this account contains tantalizing details about

Hemingway's excursions into the area during the 1930s not found in any of the available English-language biographies of Hemingway, pointing to the rich lode of fresh material on Hemingway in Cuba that Cuban writers and scholars bring to the table.

6. On Hemingway's reading of Cuban authors and imprints, I have consulted James Brasch and Joseph Sigman, *Hemingway's Library: A Composite Record* (New York: Garland, 1981) and Michael Reynolds's *Hemingway's Reading, 1910–1940: An Inventory* (Princeton, N.J.: Princeton Univ. Press, 1981). For identification of Cuban authors, I have consulted the Instituto de Literatura y Linguistica de la Academia de Ciencias de Cuba, *Diccionario de la Literatura Cubana,* 2 vols. (Havana: Editorial Letras Cubanas, 1980–84). Like Serpa, some of these writers, such as Jose Fernandez de Castro and Jorge Manach, were members of the influential Grupo Minorista that protested the governments of Zayas and Machado during the 1920s and 1930s. Manach was a founding member of the ABC, a terrorist organization I will refer to later. Interestingly, the 1920 novel by Planas y Sainz that Hemingway owned, *La corriente de Golfo* [*The Gulf Stream*], was the first Cuban science fiction novel, inspired by Jules Verne.

7. Mary Cruz writes, of the connection between *To Have and Have Not* and Serpa's *Contrabando* (Havana: Alvarez-Pita, 1938), that "Algunos hechos y algunos personajes coinciden, como pueden coincidir dos retratos del mismo objeto" ("such is the coincidence of some incidents and characters that they could be two portraits of the same subject"; 155).

8. The first Harry Morgan story, "One Trip Across," initially appeared in *Cosmopolitan* in 1934; the second story featuring this character, "The Tradesman's Return," came out in 1936; in 1937, following a suggestion by Arnold Gingrich, Hemingway published both stories, together with a third, untitled Harry Morgan story, as the novel *To Have and Have Not.*

9. Hemingway, says Cruz, employs the realism of Turgenev, while Serpa's is more like that of Zola (154–55).

10. See Serpa's dedication to his *Noche de Fiesta* [*Festival Night*] (Havana: Editorial Selecta, 1951). The Spanish says, "A Ernest Hemingway, gran escritor, hombre pleno, amigo cabal, con admiración y afecto."

11. *Papaíto Mayari,* by Cuban novelist Miguel de Marcos Suárez (Havana: Editorial Lex, 1947), also deals with this era of Cuban history. I am indebted to Jorge Santos Caballero for this reference.

12. There are many similarities between the marlin-fishing techniques Hemingway describes in "The Great Blue River," for instance, and the fishing scene in *THHN:* in both, for example, flying fish are described as a "good sign" that marlin are present. Hemingway's first published writing about Cuba was a fishing article, "Marlin Off the Moro: A Cuban Letter" (*Esquire* Autumn 1933); other deep-sea fishing articles of the decade include "Out in the Stream: A Cuban Letter" (*Esquire* Autumn 1934), "On Being Shot Again: A Gulf Stream Letter" (*Esquire*, June 1935), "Monologue to the Maestro: A High Seas Letter" (*Esquire* Oct. 1935), "On the Blue Water: A Gulf Stream Letter" (*Esquire* Apr. 1936), and "There She Breaches! Or, Moby Dick Off the Moro" (*Esquire* May 1936). Allen Josephs has argued that bullfighting or toreo, was central to Hemingway's "Spanish sensibility" (221–42), and he remarks at one point that Spain and Cuba were

"much the same for Hemingway" (222). I would add that big-game fishing in the Gulf is key to Hemingway's understanding of Cuba, just as Josephs suggests toreo is for his appreciation of Spain. Hemingway actually makes the comparison I'm suggesting here explicitly in "The Great Blue River," when he writes that his mate, Gregorio Fuentes, "is playing him [the marlin] as a bullfighter might play a bull" (408).

13. In the original Spanish, "[A]l saber que Zane Grey era el campeón de los pescadores amateurs de los Estados Unidos, compré seis libros suyos y lose pusé a enmohecer junto a los volúmenes de nautical y oceanografia." Hemingway himself owned several books on big-game fishing by Zane Grey and regarded his own sportfishing writing as being in competition with Grey's.

14. In the original Spanish, "Más tarde hube de saber que otro escritor solía venir a pescar agujas, durante el verano, en aguas cubanas. Se llamaba Hemingway, Ernest Hemingway."

15. In the original Spanish, "[Y]o le informaba que era un millionario amigo mio."

16. In the original Spanish, "Un día un americano de la Shell, que era aficionado a la pesca, lo vió ye le dijo a Cobian que un museo daba tres mil pesos por un elefante como aquél. Figurense, tres mil pesos! . . . Se gastaron como trescientos pesos en los preparativos . . . Bueno, pues al fin lo tuvieron to' preparao y salieron a buscar el animal . . . y lo vimos. Era una cosa que metía mieo, cuando yo se lo digo! Cobian, después de parar el motor de la lancha, se le acerco poco a poco, a remos, y zuayaba! Le mando el arpón. Pa' que fue eso! El elefante formó un remolino que parecía una tromba y con la misma se zambulló, que sé yo hasta donde! . . . El elefante vino a salir tres horas despues como a cuatro millas mar a fuera de Santa Cruz . . . Cobian que es un machito y eso nadie se lo pue' discutir, quiso acercarse pa' clavarle otro arpón. Pero el americano estaba cagao y no quiso de ninguna manera . . . Por último, viendo que Cobian se empeñaba en arponearlo otra vez, sacó un revolver y le dijo: 'No toca mas; si tu toca, yo te mata.' No hubo mas remedio que esperar. Y mientras tanto, como la lucha había sido larga y se l'habia abierto la heria el elefante largo el arpón. Despues apareció, a los tres días, en la bahia de Matanzas, to' comió por los tiburones" (235–36). The species of fish Serpa refers to here is a mystery; its identification occasioned much discussion among Cubans in the audience when I presented a version of this paper at the Second International Hemingway Colloquium in Havana in 1997, and gave me much trouble in the translation. I finally opted to leave it untranslated here.

17. "Era una lanche que estaba dedicada al contrabando de gente, llevando chinos al Norte. Y una vez . . . se descubrió que la tripulación había matao a puñala's a cuatro chinos, en medio del Golfo, dicen que porque no pudieron neterlos en la costa americana y los chinos pues reclamaban su dinero" (*CB* 103–4).

18. For the Marxist concept of "critical realism" that informs Cruz's discussion, see Georg Lukacs, *The Meaning of Contemporary Realism* (London: Merlin, 1979).

Works Cited

Baker, Carlos. *Ernest Hemingway: A Life Story.* New York: Scribner's, 1969.

Brasch, James. "Brasch's Reply." *Journal of Modern Literature* 14.1 (Summer 1987): 149–51.

———. "Hemingway's Doctor: José Luis Herrera Sotolongo Remembers Ernest Hemingway." *Journal of Modern Literature* 13.2 (July 1986): 185–210.

Brasch, James and Joseph Sigman, eds. *Hemingway's Library: A Composite Record.* New York: Garland, 1981.

Cirules, Enrique. *Conversacion con el ultimo norteamericano* [Conversation with the Last North American]. Havana: Editorial Letras Cubanas, 1988.

———. *Ernest Hemingway in the Romano Archipelago.* Havana, Cuba: Ediciones Union (Union de Escritores y Artistas de Cuba), 1999.

Cruz, Mary. *Cuba y Hemingway en el gran río azul* [Cuba and Hemingway on the Great Blue River]. Havana: Union de Escritores y Artistas de Cuba, 1981.

Feldman, Andrew. "Leopoldina Rodríguez: Hemingway's Cuban Lover?" *The Hemingway Review* 31.1 (Fall 2011): 62–78.

Fuentes, Norberto. *Hemingway in Cuba.* Secaucus, NJ: L. Stuart, 1984.

Hayes, Aden. "Comments on James Brasch's 'José Luis Herrera Sotolongo Remembers Ernest Hemingway,' *Journal of Modern Literature*, XIII: 2." *Journal of Modern Literature* 14.1 (Summer 1987): 147–49.

Hemingway, Ernest. "The Great Blue River." 1949. In *By-Line Ernest Hemingway: Selected Articles and Dispatches of Four Decades.* Edited by William White. New York: Charles Scribner's Sons, 1967. 403–16.

———. "Marlin Off the Moro: A Cuban Letter." *Esquire* Autumn 1933: 8–9, 39, 97.

———. "Monologue to the Maestro: A High Seas Letter." *Esquire* Oct. 1935: 24, 213–20.

———. "On Being Shot Again: A Gulf Stream Letter." *Esquire* June 1935: 25, 156.

———. "On the Blue Water: A Gulf Stream Letter." *Esquire* Apr. 1936: 31, 184–85.

———. "Out in the Stream: A Cuban Letter." *Esquire* Aug. 1934: 19,156,158.

———. "A Situation Report." 1956. In *By-Line Ernest Hemingway: Selected Articles and Dispatches of Four Decades.* Edited by William White. New York: Charles Scribner's Sons, 1967. 470–78.

———. "There She Breaches! Or, Moby Dick Off the Moro." *Esquire* May 1936: 35, 203–5.

———. *To Have and Have Not.* New York: Charles Scribner's Sons, 1937.

Hemingway, Hilary and Carleen Brennan. *Hemingway in Cuba.* New York: Rugged Land, 2005.

Hemingway, Mary. *How It Was.* New York: Knopf, 1976.

"Hemingway's Cuba." Dir. William Knight and Mark Ubsdell. Ironhill Pictures, 2000. Documentary film.

"Hemingway's Cuba." Dir. Stephen Crisman. Crisman Films, 2005. Television documentary.

"Hemingway in Cuba." Kultur International Films, 1996. Documentary film.

"Hemingway in Cuba." Prod. Hilary Hemingway. WGCU, Florida Gulf Coast University, 2004. Television documentary.

Hendrickson, Paul. *Hemingway's Boat: Everything He Loved in Life, and Lost.* New York: Vintage, 2012.

Herlihy, Jeffrey. *In Paris or Paname: Hemingway's Expatriate Nationalism.* Amsterdam, NY: Rodopi, 2011.

Hotchener, A. E. *Papa Hemingway.* New York: Random House, 1966.

Instituto de Literatura y Linguistica de la Academia de Ciencias de Cuba. *Diccionario de la Literatura Cubana,* 2 vols. Havana: Editorial Letras Cubanas, 1980–84.

Josephs, Allen. "Hemingway's Spanish Sensibility," In *The Cambridge Companion to Ernest Hemingway.* Edited by Scott Donaldson. Cambridge, UK: Cambridge Univ. Press, 1996. 221–42.

Locklin, Gerald. *Hemingway Colloquium: The Poet Goes to Cuba.* Palm Springs: Event Horizon Press, 1999.

Lukacs, Georg. *The Meaning of Contemporary Realism.* London: Merlin, 1979.

Lynn, Kenneth. *Hemingway.* New York: Fawcett Columbine, 1987.

Mandel, Miriam. *Reading Hemingway: The Facts in the Fictions.* Metuchen, NJ: Scarecrow Press, 1995.

McIver, Stuart. *Hemingway's Key West.* Sarasota, FL: Pineapple, 1993.

McLendon, James. *Papa: Hemingway in Key West.* Miami, FL: E. A. Seemann, 1972.

Melling, Phillip. "Cultural Imperialism, Afro-Cuban Religion, and Santiago's Failure in *The Old Man and the Sea.*" *The Hemingway Review* 26.1 (Fall 2006), 6–24.

Mellow, James. *Hemingway: A Life Without Consequences.* Boston: Houghton Mifflin, 1992.

Mort, Terry. *The Hemingway Patrols: Ernest Hemingway and His Hunt for the U-boats.* New York: Scribner, 2009

Myers, Jeffrey. *Hemingway: A Biography.* New York: Harper & Row, 1985.

Ott, Mark. *A Sea of Change: Ernest Hemingway and the Gulf Stream.* Kent, OH: Kent State Univ. Press, 2008.

Parker, John. *We Remember Cuba.* Sarasota, FL: Golden Quill, 1993.

Reynolds, Michael. *Hemingway: The 1930s.* New York: W. W. Norton, 1997.

——. *Hemingway's Reading, 1910–1940: An Inventory.* Princeton, NJ: Princeton Univ. Press, 1981.

——. "Unexplored Territory: The Next Ten Years of Hemingway Studies." *College Literature* 7.3 (Fall 1980): 189–201.

Rovit, Earl. *Ernest Hemingway.* Twayne's United States Authors series, no. 41. New York: Twayne, 1963.

Samuelson, Arnold. *With Hemingway: A Year in Key West and Cuba.* New York: Random House, 1984.

Schaefer, David. *Sailing to Hemingway's Cuba.* Dobb's Ferry, NY: Sheridan House, 2001.

Serpa, Enrique. *Contrabando* [Contraband]. Havana: Alvarez-Pita, 1938.

——. *Noche de Fiesta* [Festival Night]. Havana: Editorial Selecta, 1951.

Suarez, Miguel de Marcos. *Papaito Mayari.* Havana: Editorial Lex, 1947.

Sylvester, Bickford. "The Cuban Context in *The Old Man and the Sea.*" In *The Cambridge Companion to Ernest Hemingway.* Edited by Scott Donaldson. Cambridge, UK: Cambridge Univ. Press, 1996. 243–68.

Villarreal, René, and Raul Villarreal. *Hemingway's Cuban Son, Reflections on the Writer by His Longtime Majordomo.* Kent, OH: Kent State Univ. Press, 2009.

A Shared Palette

Hemingway and Winslow Homer, Painters of the Gulf Stream

CHARLENE M. MURPHY

In an October 1928 letter to his good friend Waldo Peirce, Hemingway complained about an exhibition he had seen at the Art Institute of Chicago: except for two works by Peirce himself, the show was worthless. However, Hemingway then wrote about his intense response to the Winslow Homer paintings on display: "But by Christ they have some Winslow Homers that give me the same feeling I get from the Monsters or a faena de Belmonte." Hemingway was profoundly moved by the Homer canvases, as moved as he was by the giant fish of the Gulf Stream or the bullfighter he described in *Death in the Afternoon* (*DIA*) as possessing godlike attributes (*DIA* 213).

In a 1993 article, "Hemingway, Winslow Homer, and *Islands in the Stream*" (76–85), I asserted that the influence of Winslow Homer's painting stayed with Hemingway a long time and that Forbes Watson's 1942 book *Winslow Homer* (which according to Brasch and Sigman is in the library at the Finca Vigía [390]), appeared to be a source from which Hemingway drew in composing *Islands in the Stream* (*IS*). The paintings of the character Thomas Hudson in that novel are similar to several of the Homer pieces reproduced in Watson, and, as I will presently show, much descriptive and thematic detail in *Islands* parallels that of certain Homer works reproduced in Watson's book.

Further investigation suggests that there is still more to be said about Homer's influence on Hemingway, not only with regard to *Islands in the Stream* and *The Old Man and the Sea* (*OMS*), but also the composition of *To Have and Have Not* (*THHN*), published in 1937.

In the years between Hemingway's almost religious response to the Homer watercolors at the Art Institute and his writing of *To Have and Have Not,* he made several trips to New York City (Baker 198, 208, 210, 223, 236–37, 239, 258, 280, 299). In fact, in that same October 1928 letter to Waldo Peirce cited above, Hemingway indicates that he will be leaving Chicago soon and staying in New York until November 17, after spending a few days elsewhere along the way. Given his intense feeling for Homer's work, it seems highly likely that he would have wanted to see additional Homer paintings at the Metropolitan Museum of Art. Thus, he could have seen the celebrated Gulf Stream oil (Spassky et al. 482–90),[1] as well as numerous watercolors with tropical subjects. The 1899 oil entitled "The Gulf Stream" (of much greater complexity than the 1889 watercolor of the same title in the collection of the Art Institute of Chicago) depicts a doomed black sailor on a wrecked boat, stoically averting his gaze from the menace of an approaching waterspout and circling sharks.

Patrick Hemingway, who pleased his father with his interest in and talent for painting,[2] recently told me that he had always thought his father's description of the blood in the water in *To Have and Have Not* was very suggestive of that in Homer's Gulf Stream oil painting.[3] If we look closely at the painting in relation to the novel (and the manuscripts), we can appreciate this insight.

Although in Homer's oil painting the blood is in the water, rather than in the boat, there two streaks of bright red on the outside of the boat, horizontal slashes near the waterline, contrast sharply with the white hull.[4] In writing *To Have and Have Not,* Hemingway seemed to be working toward a similar contrast and feeling. In both cases, the white hull of the boat appears in stark contrast to the dark blue water and the touches of blood red. Analysis of manuscript #204 suggests that Hemingway had such an image in mind as he wrote and revised. He originally began to write a sentence about "two dark streaks" on the hull of the boat that Morgan borrowed from Freddy Wallace.[5] This is then changed to "something dark" dripping from the splintered holes.[6] And, instead of streaking the boat, this "something dark" hangs in "ropey lines" in contrast to the boat's new white paint.[7]

These changes are retained in the published version of the novel (*THHN* 178). Although there are no sharks encircling the boat as there are in Homer's Gulf Stream oil, plenty of small fish are feeding on the dripping blood. In addition to the smaller fish, "Two gray sucker fish" "pulled away the ropey, carmine clots and threads that trailed in the water" (179). In manuscript #208, Hemingway focuses on the description of Harry Morgan's dry, cracked lips. The sentence about the bloody mark on the towel appears to be an insertion in the manuscript.[8] As we read the passages concerning Harry Morgan's death in the published novel, we may be struck by all the reminders of a violent, bloody canvas.[9]

Other sections of the manuscripts for *To Have and Have Not* (as well as the published novel) are very suggestive of the blues and greens of Homer's watercolors. In manuscript #204, when the launch carrying the dying Harry Morgan returns to port, Hemingway carefully describes the color of the water while also reminding us of the "green and white of the launch" itself. There is an insertion emphasizing the white paint of the boat. This is followed by a description of the water. At first the water is a "bright green." This is then changed to a "clear green."[10] A few pages later, Hemingway first writes that Mrs. Tracy fell into the "dark water." He then changes it to the "green water."[11] The exact color of the water is obviously important to him here. Perhaps he was learning from Homer's paintings how to observe and describe the tropical waters. Certainly, one comes away from Homer's watercolors of the tropics with a strong sense of color, a powerful visual memory of green/turquoise seas set off by touches of white.

In his interview by George Plimpton in the *Paris Review,* after saying that he had learned "as much from painters about how to write as from writers" (Plimpton 27), Hemingway remarked that the people on his list (writers and painters) "were a part of learning to see, to hear, to think, to feel and not feel, and to write" (29). Though Homer was not on the list (which Hemingway indicated was far from complete), surely, when beginning to write descriptions of tropical waters in *To Have and Have Not,* Hemingway turned to the painter that he loved so well, a painter known for his mastery of the subject. And Hemingway's later novel, *Islands in the Stream,* suggests that Homer continued to influence Hemingway's "paintings" of the sea and his portrayal of the painter, Thomas Hudson.[12]

In his essay in his 1942 book on Winslow Homer, a copy of which Hemingway owned, Forbes Watson claims that Homer "stands alone" in his mastery of the seascape (19–20). Commenting on Homer's later watercolors, Watson writes, "For intensity, direct and powerful statement, luminosity and trenchant economy of means, they are unsurpassed" (21). In the final chapter of Hemingway's *Islands,* as the wounded Thomas Hudson thinks about the painting he will do after the war if he can just "hold hard to life" and "make one more real play," he tells himself, "You can paint the sea better than anyone now" (*IS* 464).

The "Cuba" section of *Islands* reveals Thomas Hudson's acute observation of the varying color of sea water. During a conversation with Honest Lil, Hudson thinks of the sea as he looks at his frozen daiquiri. The clear part of the drink is almost exactly the same color as "when you were in shallow water over marl bottom" (276). Then he wishes "they had a drink the color of sea water when you have a depth of eight hundred fathoms and there is a dead calm with the sun straight up and down and the sea full of plankton" (276). As Lil makes herself another highball, Hudson is reminded of freshwater and "the Firehole River before it joins the Gibbon to become the Madison. If you put a little more whiskey into it you could make it the color of a stream that comes out of a cedar swamp to flow into the Bear River" (277). Thus Hudson/Hemingway tells us that the painter/writer must observe the water very carefully to portray it "the way it was," and that he has himself studied successfully.

In a letter to Leland Hayward written 5 July 1957 about a new script for the film of *The Old Man and the Sea,* Hemingway expresses his concern with modifications to his carefully composed seascapes. Cuts have been made, altering the script that had been worked out with Hemingway earlier, and he is distressed: "What makes it a little different is that I cut when I am writing and what is left in all is [*sic*] inter-related to make the magic. When you get someone cutting out things that seem perfectly easy to remove you find that the effect made is now missing. . . . Unless the cutter is as good a cutter as the writer is a writer you will find the magic is gone." As an example, Hemingway specifies, "In the cut to the fish striking eliminating the dark depths of the ocean, the color of the plankton, the clouds over the land and the strange light the sun made in the water . . . you lose validity enormously. . . . You have left out the mystery of the ocean."

Perhaps the correspondences between descriptions in Hemingway's novels and Homer's paintings tell us something about how Hemingway wrote. I think there is even more to be learned here, particularly insights into thematic issues. Immediately after Hudson's comparison of the color of the stream that flows into the Bear River with a stronger highball, he tells Lil the story of how, when he was young, he nearly drowned under the logs from the sawmill on the Bear River. Hudson explains that there were so many logs "they were almost solid across the river" (*IS* 278).

There are two reproductions of Homer's logging watercolors in Watson's book (101), the same book that apparently was the source for the Hudson paintings mentioned early on in *Islands.* Another logging watercolor is in the collection that Hemingway would have seen in 1928 at the Art Institute of Chicago (Art Institute of Chicago 164).

American art expert Helen Cooper explains that in Homer's day, the lumbering industry was destroying large areas of Adirondack wilderness. Log jams were common as "the great number of floating logs" were sent downstream from the mills (188). Homer's logging watercolors are part of a group of paintings that portray his concern "with the rape of the land" (187).[13]

Does Homer's concern with the destruction of nature in these paintings somehow relate thematically to Thomas Hudson's growing sensitivity toward nature, as his mission in the final section of the novel draws him closer toward his death? I have elsewhere suggested such connections between other Homer paintings and the "At Sea" section of *Islands* ("Influence and Tribute" 80–81). But Hemingway's indebtedness to Homer goes deeper than their shared ecological foreboding,[14] and I want to turn now to an important thematic correspondence between Homer's Gulf Stream oil and the three novels that Hemingway set wholly or partially in Cuba: *To Have and Have Not* and the later works composed when Hemingway returned to Cuba after World War II, *The Old Man and the Sea* and *Islands in the Stream.*

Homer scholar Nicolai Cikovsky Jr. believes that Homer's Gulf Stream oil is "not melodramatically about death and dying, but more profoundly . . . about death and destiny" (138). Homer's sailor, indeed, seems resigned to his fate, gazing into the distance with detachment rather than looking at the water, the spout, or the sharks. In the final chapter of *Islands,* Thomas Hudson thinks about medical treatment for his wound and then muses, "Don't worry about it boy. . . . All your life is just pointed toward it" (464). In *To Have and Have Not,* the dying Harry Morgan thinks how he might have chosen a safer line of work, but then realizes, "Hell, I couldn't run no filling station" (175). In *The Old Man and the Sea,* Santiago, as well, stoically accepts his pain and great loss, and as more sharks close in, he flexes his bloody hands "so they would take the pain now" (107). All three men "take it" as the novels end. Alone, and with his body broken, Santiago in *Old Man* carries home the heavy mast; as Bickford Sylvester has so cogently demonstrated, his death is imminent ("Informed Illusion" 473–77). Alone but for four corpses, Harry Morgan believes that the "sloshing sound" of gasoline is "in his own belly" (*THHN* 180). Numb from the cold, he realizes "there was nothing to do about the cold but take it" (181). As for Hudson in *Islands,* although he is not alone, he too "takes it" on a deck slippery from his own blood, as he thinks that "the engines came through the deck and into him" (466). Hemingway's protagonists, early and late, show the same resignation to the inevitability of material defeat displayed by Homer's sailor.

Indeed, upon occasion Hemingway portrayed his early characters' transcendence of material concern by using precisely the iconographical device Homer employs in his Gulf Stream oil painting. Homer's sailor looks detachedly into the distance, pointedly away from the approaching waterspout, away from the circling sharks the storm will deliver him to, and away from the viewer—in the direction the wrecked hull is drifting, toward a realm beyond these earthly inevitabilities. His posture conveys more than his weakness and his need to hold his precarious position on the tilting deck. It reflects, at the same time, the composed resignation centrally indicated by his gaze. And at the end of Hemingway's short story "In Another Country" (written in 1926), the major looks away from his observers, from his ruined hand, and from the useless therapeutic paraphernalia to which he had temporarily committed himself, staring fixedly out of the window into another country of the mind (210). He "has resigned himself, as have the three heavily decorated soldiers, the 'hunting hawks' with 'detached' eyes, who have faced death enough times to 'see' beyond the inevitability of material defeat" (Sylvester, "Sexual Impasse" 183). We remember, as well, Ole Anderson of Hemingway's "The Killers" (written in 1925–26), who looks away as Nick warns him of approaching death, and maintains his abstract gaze at the wall of his room (221).

If Hemingway saw "The Gulf Stream" oil just a few years after writing "The Killers" and "In Another Country," the painting must have appealed to him instantly, because Homer portrays exactly the stance toward adversity that Hemingway had just been portraying and affirming.[15] This early recognition of a kindred spirit could logically then be seen as a partial source of the sea scenes of *To Have and Have Not* as well as in the extended sea episodes of *Islands* and *The Old Man and the Sea.*

Literally, there is much blood "on the canvas" near the conclusion of all three novels. Literally, of course, Santiago also contends with sharks. Metaphorically, the sharks around the boat of the lone sailor in Homer's painting may suggest both the hardscrabble life of Harry Morgan and the blows life has dealt Thomas Hudson, especially the deaths of his sons.

Nicolai Cikovsky Jr. believes that Homer's Gulf Stream oil intentionally invokes the "Youth" and "Manhood" paintings in Thomas Cole's series, "The Voyage of Life." Cikovsky believes this allusion "makes clear that Homer's painting, too, is an allegory of life, in which the derelict boat with its helpless passenger is borne to its fate through the perils of existence by the inexorable . . . flow of that 'river in the ocean,' the Gulf Stream" (140). Similarly, Hemingway's characters endure their destiny, sharing with Homer's figure a similar journey across the complex and mysterious canvas of life.

Notes

1. The catalog *American Paintings in the Metropolitan Museum of Art 2,* by Natalie Spassky et al., indicates that Homer's Gulf Stream oil, which came to the museum in 1906, was also exhibited at the Museum of Modern Art in New York in 1932–33, 1934, and 1943–44. In addition, the Whitney Museum of American Art in New York hosted another exhibit, the "Winslow Homer Centenary Exhibition," in 1936–37 (Spassky et al. 490). According to Carlos Baker, Hemingway made a business trip to New York City in January 1937 (299).

2. See letters from Ernest Hemingway to Mary Hemingway, 20 Mar. and 30 Mar. 1945, Hemingway Collection, John Fitzgerald Kennedy Library, Boston, MA (hereafter cited as JFK).

3. In April 1995, at the John F. Kennedy Library, Patrick Hemingway told me that my

earlier observations on Hemingway's indebtedness to Homer ("Influence and Tribute" 76–85) were "right on the button" and that his father "loved Winslow Homer."

4. Spassky et al. indicate that the red streaks on the hull attracted much attention when the painting was exhibited in 1906. The *New York Press,* for instance, "singled out the 'note of brilliant red' on the sloop as 'a masterly stroke that kept a crowd of artists before the canvas all day long . . . in open admiration of Homer's genius for color'" (485–86).

5. Ernest Hemingway, Item 204, 154, Hemingway Collection, JFK.

6. Ibid., 155.

7. Ibid.

8. Ernest Hemingway, Item 208, 6, Hemingway Collection, JFK.

9. Spassky et al., *American Paintings in the Metropolitan Museum of Art 2,* provide information that suggests another interesting connection between Homer's oil painting and the boat carrying Harry Morgan back to Key West. In the painting, the name on the stern of the sloop is *Ann Key West* "although the studies for the 'Gulf Stream' were made in the West Indies" (486). In the published novel, Hemingway writes about the *Queen Conch* that "her name and home port, Key West, Fla., were painted in black across her stern" (178).

10. Ernest Hemingway, Item 204, 379, Hemingway Collection, JFK.

11. Ibid., 384.

12. In a letter to the author dated 29 Nov. 2000, Valerie Hemingway responded to three articles I had sent her: a draft of "A Shared Palette," "Hemingway's Gentle Hunters," and "Influence and Tribute." She wrote "I reread the articles last night and echo Patrick's comment that you've got it right. I think you have hit the essence of Hemingway's intrigue with Homer and pinpointed the influence of his paintings on Hemingway's writing. . . . Ernest talked about Homer around the dinner table and on the *Pilar,* he gave me the Watson book to look through, he encouraged me to see the paintings at the Met as soon as we arrived in New York. . . . I just know of his affection and admiration of Homer's work, and of his desire to evoke in his writing the emotion he felt when he studied and enjoyed certain painters and Homer was among them."

13. I believe that the titles of these paintings—"Hudson River," "Hudson River, Logging," and "The Rapids, Hudson River"—may have suggested to Hemingway the name he gave the painter in *Islands in the Stream.* However, the name Thomas Hudson may contain multiple allusions. In *Reading Hemingway: The Facts in the Fictions,* Miriam B. Mandel notes that Thomas Hudson was the name of an English portrait-painter in the eighteenth century (400).

14. See Charlene M. Murphy, "Hemingway's Gentle Hunters: Contradiction or Duality?" (400) for a detailed analysis of their shared ecological concern. I also make it clear, both in that article and here, that Hemingway, of course, had personally witnessed scenes of forest destruction as well as many other subjects of Homer's paintings.

15. I am indebted to Bickford Sylvester for suggesting a "transcendent gaze" in the sailor's depiction and parallels in the early stories, "The Killers" and "In Another Country."

Works Cited

Art Institute of Chicago. *A Guide to the Paintings in the Permanent Collection.* Chicago: Art Institute, 1925.

Baker, Carlos. *Ernest Hemingway: A Life Story.* New York: Scribner's, 1969.

Brasch, James D., and Joseph Sigman. *Hemingway's Library: A Composite Record.* New York: Garland, 1981.

Cikovsky, Nicolai, Jr. "Homer Around 1900." In *Winslow Homer: A Symposium.* Studies in the History of Art 26. Edited by Nicolai Cikovsky Jr. Washington, DC: National Gallery of Art, 1990.

Cooper, Helen A. *Winslow Homer Watercolors.* Washington, DC: National Gallery of Art, 1986.

Hemingway, Ernest. *Death in the Afternoon.* New York: Charles Scribner's Sons, 1932

——. "In Another Country." In *The Complete Short Stories of Ernest Hemingway.* New York: Charles Scribner's Sons, 1987.

——. *Islands in the Stream.* New York: Charles Scribner's Sons, 1970.

——. Item 204: 154, 155, 379, 384. Manuscript. Hemingway Collection, John Fitzgerald Kennedy Library, Boston, MA (hereafter, JFK).

——. Item 208: 6. Manuscript. Hemingway Collection, JFK.

——. "The Killers." In *The Complete Short Stories of Ernest Hemingway.* New York: Charles Scribner's Sons, 1987.

——. Letter to Leland Hayward, 5 July 1957. Hemingway Collection, JFK.

——. Letters to Mary Hemingway, 20 Mar. and 30 Mar. 1945. Hemingway Collection, JFK.

——. Letter to Waldo Peirce, Oct. 1928. Collection of Waldo Peirce materials 1907–70, Special Collections, Miller Library, Colby College, Waterville, ME.

——. *To Have and Have Not.* New York: Scribner's, 1937.

Hemingway, Valerie. Letter to the author. 29 Nov. 2000.

Mandel, Miriam B. *Reading Hemingway: The Facts in the Fictions.* Metuchen, NJ: Scarecrow Press, 1995.

Murphy, Charlene M. "Hemingway, Winslow Homer, and *Islands in the Stream:* Influence and Tribute." *The Hemingway Review* 13.1 (1993): 76–85.

——. "Hemingway's Gentle Hunters: Contradiction or Duality?" In *Hemingway and the Natural World.* Edited by Robert E. Fleming. Moscow, ID: Univ. of Idaho Press, 1999.

Plimpton, George. "An Interview with Ernest Hemingway." In *Hemingway and His Critics: An International Anthology.* Edited by Carlos Baker. New York: Hill and Wang, 1961.

Spassky, Natalie, et al. *American Paintings in the Metropolitan Museum of Art 2.* New York: Metropolitan Museum of Art, 1985.

Sylvester, Bickford. "The Sexual Impasse to Romantic Order in Hemingway's Fiction." In *Hemingway: Up in Michigan Perspectives.* Edited by. Frederic J. Svoboda and Joseph J. Waldmeir. East Lansing, MI: Michigan State Univ. Press, 1995.

——. "'They Went Through This Fiction Every Day': Informed Illusion in *The Old Man and the Sea.*" *Modern Fiction Studies* 12.4 (Winter 1966): 473–77.

Watson, Forbes. *Winslow Homer.* New York: Crown, 1942.

The Old Man and the Sea

"I am not religious, . . . But . . ."

The Virgin of El Cobre and Cuban Catholicism a mi propia manera

ALMA DEROJAS

"I am not religious," says Santiago in *The Old Man and the Sea.* "But I will say ten Our Fathers and ten Hail Marys that I should catch this fish, and I promise to make a pilgrimage to the Virgin of Cobre if I catch him. That is a promise" (71). For nearly four centuries Cubans have made similar promises to La Virgen de la Caridad del Cobre (the Virgin of Charity in Cobre), a statue of the Virgin Mary enshrined in the town of El Cobre, near Santiago, Cuba. The Virgin is the Catholic patroness of the island, but her significance transcends the realm of religion. As a symbol of national identity, she has appealed to diverse sectors of Cuban society for four centuries.

So how did a Catholic virgin become one of the most powerful and enduring national symbols of a relatively secular country? The answer partially lies in the popular image of her as La Caridad: surrounded by angels, she is often depicted as watching over three fishermen who look up to her for guidance through a storm. In this sense she is viewed as a maternal figure, who comforts and guides her children through the difficulties of daily life. Yet in popular Cuban songs of the nineteenth century, La Caridad is also portrayed as the Virgen Mambisa, leading the *mambises* (Cuban fighters on the battlefields of the independence wars) with machete in hand. As these contrasting images reveal, the most significant aspect of the Virgin's wide appeal is her fluidity as a symbol, her ability to meet the various needs of devotees who believe in her in their own individual fashions––*a mi propia manera* (in my own way), as each of them would say.

This essay explores why Cubans who are Catholic are able to place their faith in the Virgin in so many different ways. After exploring the historical origins of La Caridad's myth, I analyze her ability, as a symbol, to meet the varied spiritual,

Two Cuban fishermen pulling a fish aboard a small boat, c. 1934. Ernest Hemingway Collection, John F. Kennedy Presidential Library and Museum, Boston.

political, economic, and social needs of all her devotees, examining the *cobreros* (the people of El Cobre) in the eighteenth century, the *mambises* of the nineteenth-century independence wars, and the followers of the Afro-Cuban religion Santería. I conclude by considering the personal observations of contemporary pilgrims to the Virgin's shrine, who continue to journey to El Cobre to express their gratitude for La Caridad's intervention. Regardless of race, class, or religious background, devotees believe that the spiritual mother of Cuba will watch over her children as she has done for centuries, whether guiding them through a storm, supporting them in achieving political independence from Spain, or simply helping them, like Hemingway's Santiago, to catch a big fish.

"Yo soy la Virgen de la Caridad"

The myth of La Virgen de la Caridad originated in the copper mining village of El Cobre, founded by Spain in 1599 on the eastern tip of the island. By 1608 the village consisted of 215 African and Creole slaves, one of whom, Juan Moreno, went on to play a crucial role in the consolidation of the myth. In approximately 1612, Moreno accompanied two Indian brothers named Rodrigo and Juan de Hoyos in a small boat to collect salt in the Bay of Nipe, where they encountered a wooden statue of the Virgin Mary floating on the sea. On the base of the statue was the following inscription: "Yo soy la Virgen de la Caridad" ["I am the Virgin of Charity"]. The Indians then transported the statue to El Cobre, where it was eventually placed in its own shrine.

Taught to venerate Mary as the Mother of God by the Spaniards, natives of El Cobre quickly felt a connection with the Virgin of Charity, whom they associated with Atabey, the Taíno (Indian) goddess of lakes and rivers. Soon after the statue's discovery, devotees of La Virgen began to report miracles associated with her presence in the community, miracles that sealed the myth's survival among subsequent generations. The expansion of the myth is thus largely the result of the central role played by the slaves of El Cobre, who claimed the Virgin as their personal protector. According to Juan Moreno's 1687 account of the Virgin's apparition, she personally chose the site of her shrine, and consequently the *cobreros* believed that she had thereby chosen to protect the community of

Photograph of Cuban fishermen fishing, probably taken by Ernest Hemingway in 1934 and inscribed "Mako shark caught by commercial fishermen." Ernest Hemingway Collection, John F. Kennedy Presidential Library and Museum, Boston.

Photograph of the *Pilar* in Cuba. Ernest Hemingway Collection, John F. Kennedy Presidential Library and Museum, Boston.

El Cobre itself. Because of the Virgin's reputation as the protectress of this mining community, the *cobreros* began to regard themselves as her chosen people, an identity that encouraged them to believe in their rights and that unified the community in its political struggle for liberation from Spain.

The role of the Virgin of Charity in the negotiation of their freedom by the royal slaves of El Cobre is a story often ignored by both modern Cuban devotees and scholars, yet the account reveals intriguing insights into the historical power of the Virgin's symbolism. The story of the royal slaves begins in 1670, when Spain confiscated the mines of El Cobre from a private contractor; the 271 slaves of the mines thus suddenly became slaves of the king. The community was virtually free from government control for the next hundred years, until the mines were once again privatized in 1780. In reaction to the reprivatization of the mines, the *cobreros* wrote a document protesting their loss of rights, relying heavily on their privileged association with the Virgin of Cobre.

Despite the reprivatization orders of 1780, the royal slaves of El Cobre remained convinced that they were not slaves, because they had enjoyed freedoms for over a century, including the right to own property. Faith in the Virgin

Photograph of Cuban fishermen fishing: "The sail was patched with flour sacks. . . ." *The Old Man and the Sea,* 9. Ernest Hemingway Collection, John F. Kennedy Presidential Library and Museum, Boston.

played a prominent part in their argument, and also helped to keep the community united in its struggle. The *cobreros'* political negotiations culminated in the request for collective freedom. This was finally granted in a royal edict signed on April 7, 1800, and—appropriately—read from the steps of the Virgin's shrine. Although restrictions remained even after formal freedom was granted, notably forced labor obligations, the *cobreros'* achievement is nevertheless truly extraordinary in the historical context of Cuban slavery. Although La Virgen de la Caridad may not have been a necessary factor in these achievements, her power as a tool of unity in the *cobreros'* struggle for freedom cannot be denied.

Few remember the local context in which the Virgin's cult emerged. As María Elena Díaz observes, "there is . . . little memory among Cubans today of the remarkable historical community in which the Virgin of Charity's legend and tradition first flourished" (329). Yet while the origins of the cult may now be forgotten, it is crucial to remember that devotion to La Caridad first developed among this unique community before spreading throughout Cuba over the following century.

La Virgen Mambisa

Belief in the Virgin gained popularity in the nineteenth century because of the legend of the *cobreros'* struggle. As more and more pilgrims visited the shrine in El Cobre, the cult slowly spread throughout Cuba. At the same time, the desire for a *Cuba libre,* a Cuba free from the political domination of Spain, began to intensify. This was certainly so among the *criollos,* Cubans citizens descended from the early Spanish settlers. As *criollos* throughout the island assumed belief in the Virgin, she came to embody the goal of liberation. No longer merely a symbol of El Cobre, La Caridad symbolized the dream of a free Cuba.

The desire for a Cuba free from the control of Spain ultimately led, in 1868, to la Guerra de los Diez Años, the first Cuban war of independence. According to Olga Portuondo Zúñiga, the Virgin played a crucial role in this first armed struggle for freedom because she "served as a catalyst for unity among all Cubans" (226; my translation). Once again, as in El Cobre, Cubans appropriated the Virgin as a political tool of unity in order to achieve the goal of liberty. It is important to keep in mind that the hierarchy of the Catholic Church in Cuba did not share this popular view of the Virgin, largely because the Church continued to support Spanish control of Cuba. Despite this lack of official support by the Church, however, the revolutionaries immediately began to appropriate La Virgen as the symbol of their cause. As I have noted, she now became known as La Virgen Mambisa, in reference to the *mambises,* the Cuban rebels. Her association with the Cuban desire for liberty is reflected in a *copla* (folksong) common on the battlefields during the first independence war:

Virgen de la Caridad,
Patrona de los cubanos,
Con el machete en la mano
Pedimos la libertad.
Virgin of Charity,
Patroness of Cubans,
With machete in hand,
We ask for liberty. (My translation)

The potential of the Virgin to serve as a tool of unity among Cubans is evident in the actions of Carlos Manuel de Céspedes, the leader of the independence movement, who visited her sanctuary in 1868 with his *mambises.* At the shrine, Céspedes and his troops gave a patriotic tribute to the Virgin, an act of devotion that clearly was more than sacred, for "it was a political gesture of the Father of the

Homeland that recognized devotion to the Virgin as a powerful means of union among Cubans" (Portuondo Zúñiga 226; my translation). Although the first war of independence did not result in a *Cuba libre*, principles of patriotism remained embedded in the cult of La Virgen for the next several decades, until the second, and final, war of independence broke out in 1895. In this war, the *mambises* again associated the Virgin with their cause; members of the Liberation Army, including leaders such as Antonio Maceo, often carried medals of their protectress into combat. Wives and mothers of the *mambises* likewise frequently prayed novenas to La Virgen to protect their husbands and sons on the battlefields.

By the time Cuba finally achieved independence from Spain in 1898, the Virgin of Charity "had become the rebel Virgin, the patriot Virgin, the national Virgin" (Tweed 23). The actions of General Calixto García, the chief of the Cuban army in Oriente, clearly demonstrate the importance of the Virgin's role in the war. In gratitude for her help in securing the independence of the island, García and his troops celebrated a Mass at the Virgin's shrine on her feast day, September 8, 1898. At this Mass, in a gesture of thanksgiving known as la Declaración Mambisa de la Independencia del Pueblo Cubano (the Mambises' Declaration of Cuban Independence), the *mambises* formally acknowledged that she had accompanied them throughout the most difficult moments of battle. In the same sense that she had enabled the royal slaves of El Cobre to articulate their identity, she now enabled Cubans throughout the island, of all races and classes, to affirm their status as an independent and unified nation. No longer merely a symbol of El Cobre, La Caridad had become a symbol of Cuban national identity, a reflection of the desire of the island to achieve independence. The Virgin's power to unify is thus evident in the coming together of diverse sectors, bonded by their common belief in the national mother.

By the turn of the century, La Virgen de la Caridad was thus inseparable from the national identity of Cuba. This led to a growing desire among Cubans to declare her the official patroness of the island, a movement that was appropriately led by the veterans of the independence wars. In 1915, a group of 2,000 *mambises* traveled to El Cobre for a reunion in which they once again expressed their gratitude for La Caridad's role in their victory. More importantly, they wrote a letter to the Vatican requesting that the Virgin of Charity be declared the official patroness of Cuba, a title conferred on May 10, 1916, by Pope Benedict XV.

Thus the regional protectress of El Cobre had now officially become the patroness of all Cuba, a Catholic symbol of national identity that had unified the island in its struggles for independence. A closer examination of La Caridad's symbolism, however, reveals that Cuban society at the time was neither devoutly Catholic nor completely unified.

Virgin of Charity/Goddess of Love

For many Cubans who fought on the battlefields of the nineteenth-century independence wars, the Virgen Mambisa was not a Catholic virgin but a Yoruba goddess. According to the Afro-Cuban religion Santería, a syncretic blend of Catholicism and African myth, the Virgin of Charity is Ochún, the Yoruba goddess of love, rivers, and fertility. A central factor of the Virgin of Charity's appeal to diverse sectors of Cuban society is indeed her association with Ochún, whose story begins several centuries ago among the Yoruba people of present-day Nigeria, where she was revered as the goddess of the river that today bears her name.

Ochún became one of the most powerful goddesses in the Yoruba pantheon of orishas, intermediary divinities who govern the forces of the universe and give spiritual strength. As the most powerful female deity of the Yoruba pantheon, Ochún accompanied her enslaved children across the sea during the transatlantic slave trade. During a series of African civil wars at the beginning of the nineteenth century, thousands of Yoruba people were enslaved and sent to Brazil, Cuba, and elsewhere in the Americas in order to meet the insatiable labor demands of the sugar mills. During these years, more than 400,000 slaves were brought to Cuba, most from the west coast of Africa.

Often forced to convert to Catholicism, Yoruba slaves gradually adapted the Catholic worldview to suit their needs. They appropriated and transformed the religion within their own universe by creating a new religion called Santería, "the way of the saints," a name derived from the fact that devotions to the orishas were often carried out beneath the images of the saints. As this tradition emerged, each African orisha came to be identified with a particular Catholic saint. Ochún, for example, was understandably associated with La Virgen de la Caridad—another powerful female deity who emerged from the water to guide her spiritual children.

Although the association between a Catholic virgin and a flirtatious goddess of love may seem an anomaly, the relationship makes sense when the maternal symbolism of both is taken into consideration. In Caridad, the Yoruba encountered a compassionate mother who loves and protects her spiritual children, in the same sense that Ochún guides her devotees. While the Virgin of Charity may initially have been merely a mask to conceal the worship of Ochún from slave owners, her significance among the Yoruba in Cuba gradually transcended this role of concealment as they realized the genuine spiritual power of the Virgin.

The complexity of the Caridad/Ochún relationship is based on the deities' simultaneous similarities and differences. At the same time that Ochún is visually represented by the Virgin of Charity, the Yoruba goddess retains her distinct personality. As Joseph Murphy writes in "Yeyé Cachita: Ochún in a Cuban Mirror," the two religious symbols "are both the same and not the same. . . . Ochún both is and is not La Caridad" (94). While some devotees believe there is no difference between Ochún and the Virgin, others maintain that the deities are distinct. However one interprets the syncretic relationship, the fact remains that the fluidity of La Caridad's symbolism—its ability to signify a Catholic virgin and a Yoruba goddess simultaneously—is a significant factor of her popularity.

Just as Ochún herself is multidimensional, so too is her power, thereby enabling the goddess to meet the basic needs of her various and abundant devotees. To her children, Ochún offers health, wealth, love, and happiness, but she brings these gifts in certain ways that must be followed in order to receive her blessings. Rituals are thus a crucial component of her devotion. Through ritual divination, devotees acquire knowledge of their destiny and specific models of action in order to attain it. Many of the rituals focus on specific problems of the devotee. Because most of Ochún's children are poor, the problems are usually practical, involving money, health, or love. In this respect, Santería is a practical religion that enables its practitioners to deal with life's daily struggles.

In the minds of many white Cuban Catholics at the turn of the twentieth century, however, Santería was simply witchcraft. According to Catholic orthodoxy, devotees of Santería are confused practitioners of an "impure" religion. Since Santería's emergence in the mid-nineteenth century, a social environment of racial prejudice and oppression has required secrecy among its practitioners. Although slavery was officially abolished in 1886, racial tension remained. Thus while the Virgin of Charity appeared to unify Cubans at the beginning of the republic, a closer examination of her symbolic significance reveals the underlying racial tensions of the times. Cuba's white elite associated Santería with superstition, criminality, and laziness; until 1940, in fact, its practice was a punishable crime. Yet despite the attempts of Catholic officials to purify Cuba religiously, about one out of every four Catholics there (according to a 1954 study commissioned by the Cuban Catholic Church) occasionally consulted *santeros* (priests of Santería; De la Torre 56).

Thus although the tenets of Santería will always be theologically challenged by Catholic orthodoxy, its influence on Cuban identity cannot be ignored. While the religion originated among African slaves on the island, its flexibility and practicality appealed to Cubans of all ethnic groups throughout the twentieth century, as the 1954 study demonstrates. In light of Santería's influence on Cuban culture, an understanding of Ochún's significance is necessary for a full understanding of her Catholic counterpart, La Caridad, in popular Cuban Catholicism. As Jorge and Isabel Castellanos maintain in *Cultura afrocubana,* pilgrims to the Virgin of Charity's shrine in El Cobre can be divided into three groups: orthodox Catholics who come to venerate the Virgin, strict practitioners of

Santería who come to worship the goddess Ochún, and those who oscillate between the two (268). Since this third group represents the majority, it cannot be ignored in any ethnographical analysis of devotion to La Virgen de la Caridad. Although these pilgrims do not embrace the rules of Catholic orthodoxy, they do profess an intense belief in the power of the Virgin/Ochún. Thus in order to comprehend the spiritual significance of the Virgin of Cobre, one must understand the following phrase, already referred to above: *a mi propia manera* (in my own way). For this is truly the basis of popular Cuban Catholicism.

A mi propia manera

Although the Catholic figure of La Caridad had indeed become a symbol of national identity by the end of the nineteenth century, this does not necessarily imply that Cuba is, or ever was, a devoutly Catholic country. As Lisandro Pérez observes, "the Church never had as profound an impact on Cuba as it had on the rest of the Spanish colonies of the New World" (147). As a social institution, the Catholic Church in Cuba has been historically weak. Unlike bishops in the ecclesiastical hierarchies of most Latin American countries, Cuba's bishops have never possessed significant political power. This institutional weakness has been accompanied by a "relative lack of religiosity" in Cuban society, often characterized by its secularism (Pérez 148).

Pérez attributes Cuba's secularism and the Church's weakness to five factors: the role of Havana as a port city; the organization and operation of the Church in Cuba; the sugar revolution and the secularization of the mill; the importance of non-Catholic religions; and the Church's stance as an enemy of Cuban independence. The roots of Cuba's secularism can be traced, at least in part, to the cosmopolitan character of Havana, a busy port city that in the seventeenth century contained more than half of the island's population. Havana's "unquestionably secular character" permeated Cuban society, a significant factor in shaping the island's relatively weak Catholic faith (Pérez 150). Throughout the colonial era and into the twentieth century, the Cuban arm of the Church itself contributed to the country's secularism by providing it with too few clergy and concentrating its priests in the cities. In fact, as Pérez points out, the Church's presence in rural areas was "virtually nonexistent" (151). Although the majority of the rural population considered itself Catholic, the people's relationship with the Church was often limited to baptism.

Also contributing to the weakness of the Church was the sugar revolution, which began in the late eighteenth century and gave rise to a new elite class with secular values. Furthermore, the sugar revolution dramatically increased the number of African slaves in Cuba, and their religious beliefs gradually fused with Catholic practices. The proliferation of Afro-Cuban faiths in the nineteenth century is thus another factor in the institutional weakness of Cuba's Catholic Church. Although clerics did attempt to evangelize the slaves, the Church failed to obliterate their African religious beliefs. Yet despite the significant impact of Afro-Cuban religions, Pérez writes, a greater threat to the Catholic Church was posed by the growth of Protestantism during the nineteenth and twentieth centuries (154).

A final factor in the historical weakness of the Cuban Catholic Church was its support of Spain and defense of the status quo. With a hierarchy consisting mainly of Spanish priests who understandably supported the continuation of their homeland's rule, the Church was widely perceived as an enemy of Cuban independence and of the island's rebel fighters during the nineteenth century independence wars.

This brief overview of the history of religion in Cuba clearly reveals that the island has never been a devoutly Catholic country. According to a study conducted by a Catholic student organization in 1954, 73% of Cubans claimed to be Roman Catholics, yet only 24% of Catholics regularly attended Mass (Pérez 156). In rural areas, the percentage of those claiming to be Catholics dropped to 52%. Nevertheless, the survey indicates that, despite their lack of regular participation, most Cubans generally considered themselves to be Catholic in their "own way," an attitude that persists to this day. For many Catholic Cubans, this "own way" was limited to devotion to La Caridad/Ochún, to occasional consultations with *santeros* and to an annual pilgrimage to the Virgin's shrine in El Cobre.

Despite the institutional absence of the Church in rural areas in prerevolutionary Cuba, La Caridad's popularity remained strong, for a Catholic's veneration of the Virgin requires neither a priest nor a church building. Yet many Cuban Catholics felt the need to visit La Caridad's shrine personally, to fulfill a traditional promise to the Virgin to do so. This tradition continues to this day. For devotees, the shrine in El Cobre thus serves as the spiritual heart of the island. Eager to express their gratitude, pilgrims come by the thousands, confident that the spiritual Mother of Cuba will continue to answer their prayers, as she has done for nearly four centuries. "*Y si vas al Cobre . . .*" ("And if you go to El Cobre . . .") runs Rafael Cueto's popular song, "Veneración,"

Y si vas al Cobre,
Quiero que me traigas
Una virgencita de la Caridad,

Yo no quiero flores,
Yo no quiero estampas,
Lo que quiero es Virgen de la Caridad.
And if you go to El Cobre,
I want you to bring me
A little Virgin of Charity,
I don't want flowers,
I don't want holy cards,
What I want is the Virgin of Charity. (My translation)

Amidst the majestic Sierra Maestra Mountains in the town of El Cobre is the shrine of La Virgen de la Caridad. The cream-colored church rises dramatically against the breathtaking backdrop, a beautiful sight for those Cubans from around the island who make the journey to see La Caridad in person. Although most enter the sanctuary on foot, some climb the dozens of steep stairs to the entrance on their knees, fulfilling a vow they have made to the Virgin. Upon entering the church, the pilgrims are greeted by a sign with the following prayer: "Holy Virgin of Charity, Mother of all Cubans, I give you thanks for enabling me to arrive at your sanctuary to venerate you with all my heart . . . Upon humbling myself before your image, may my love of God and my brothers grow, and may peace and joy abide in me." Pilgrims then ascend the stairs to the Virgin's sanctuary above the altar. Devotees often fill the pews in front of the statue, sitting in silence and praying to the Virgin, who is dressed in an elaborately-decorated, gold-encrusted satin gown. Many bring flowers to offer La Caridad, everything from a single carnation or sunflower to elaborate bouquets.

Below the sanctuary is the Room of Miracles. Near the entrance to the room sits a glass display case, filled with objects left behind by grateful devotees: athletic medals, trophies, uniforms, coins, t-shirts, and caps, as well as notes of thanks. Inside the Room of Miracles the faithful can light a candle and leave behind a personal object or note of gratitude to the Virgin; many from past years are still on display:

"I give thanks to the Virgin of Charity for having played well in the championship basketball game of 2002. As I promised, here is my uniform."
"I leave you my trophies so you continue giving me victories in life and to thank you for your help."
"Many thanks for giving me the strength to win these prizes. With faith in you I will win more."
"To the Virgin of Charity of El Cobre, mother of all Cubans, I leave in your sanctuary your image so you give health to my family and so you help my

> daughter in her studies. Thanks for always hearing my prayers, don't forget your children, give us health and open the path to Cubans."

While this last writer left behind a statue of the Virgin, other devotees have left behind an assortment of objects, including rosaries, locks of hair, potpourri, baby clothes, watches, bracelets, and a wedding cake decoration. Ernest Hemingway even left behind his 1954 Nobel Prize, which has since been removed and placed in a more secure location.

While in Cuba to conduct research for my master's thesis on the cultural and spiritual significance of the Virgin of Charity, I spent several days in December 2003 interviewing pilgrims to the shrine. As Herminia, a black woman who volunteers at the shrine, told me, El Cobre is "the heart of Cuba" for those who believe in the Virgin. Or, as a deacon from the archdiocese of Santiago told me a few days later, the shrine is "the most magnetic place on the island. Like a magnet, it attracts Cubans from all parts." Although the majority of devotees I interviewed at the shrine were from El Cobre or nearby Santiago, a significant percentage comes from other parts of the island, despite the difficulties of transportation. Of my twenty-five interviewees, five were from other cities, including Havana, Matanzas, Pinar del Río, Camagüey, and Guantánamo. Alicia, for example, is a thirty-six-year-old black woman from Matanzas: "I came with a group of people from Matanzas by bus," she said. "This is truly an opportunity of a lifetime to see the Virgin in person." Sol, a twenty-seven-year-old black woman, traveled to El Cobre from Pinar del Río, at the other end of the island. "This is my third time here," said Sol. "I come every few years because I need to see her."

The shrine attracts many traditional Cuban Catholics who consider themselves Catholic in their "own way." Miguel, for example, goes to Mass once in a while, but, he admits, "I am not a good Catholic. I don't like to follow the rules." Alberto likewise confesses that "I may not be a proper Catholic. I don't go to Mass like I should, but I pray to the Virgin. I am Catholic in my own way." Visits to the Virgin's shrine thus enable such Catholics to maintain a spiritual connection without following the traditional rules of the Catholic Church, such as weekly Mass attendance. Rosa, for example, visits the shrine every month, yet she laughed when I asked her how often she goes to Mass. That day Rosa brought her five-year-old granddaughter to celebrate her birthday. "We wanted her to meet the Virgin for the first time," said Rosa.

As I have mentioned above, many who are Catholics "in my own way" continue to identify the Virgin of Charity with the Yoruba goddess Ochún. Patricia, for example, a black woman in her thirties, tells me that she considers herself a Catholic daughter of Ochún. "Of course Ochún is part of my faith. Look at the color of my skin." Like many Cubans, Patricia may not be an orthodox

Catholic, yet she is welcome at the shrine. No matter whether a Cuban believes in the Virgin of Charity, Ochún, or both, no one is turned away. As one of the volunteers told me, "The Church is the mother of all. The doors are always open here. Of course we see *santeros* dressed in white, but we don't turn them away. We hope and pray that they convert to the Virgin, but that is not a realistic goal for everyone."

Whether they come to venerate the Virgin of Charity, Ochún, or both, the majority of pilgrims to the shrine are motivated by immediate and practical needs. They come to pray for sick children, to give thanks for healthy babies, and to ask for help in the daily struggles of life. As Herminia told me in El Cobre, "We must endure daily the problems with our system. In Cuba there are some who live well, some live okay, but most are barely surviving. That is why we need the Virgin." In times of great difficulty, faithful Cubans often turn to the Virgin for the inner strength they need to face their problems. In the words of Patricia, the Virgin is "like a crutch, a means of support, for those who need it. She listens to all our problems and gives us the strength we need to continue on." Thankful for La Caridad's assistance with various problems in the past, the faithful often go to her shrine to express their profound gratitude, especially for the birth of healthy babies. For example, Celia, a twenty-two-year-old black woman from Santiago, came to El Cobre with her newborn son. In Celia's words, "About a year ago, I had a stillborn child. I made a promise to the Virgin that I would come here if I had a healthy baby. And here I am."

Health concerns are another frequent reason for visits to the Virgin's shrine, as should be expected in a country severely lacking in medicine and medical supplies. Pilar, an unemployed black woman, has a twelve-year-old daughter suffering the effects of malnutrition. Pilar comes to the shrine from Santiago once a week to pray to the Virgin. "I am going through some hard times right now. My daughter is sick, she needs better nutrition. She is very sick, and I need the Virgin's help." Omara, a seventy-three-year-old white woman, is equally concerned about the health of her family: "I came to pray for the health of my son, to give thanks for the birth of my great-granddaughter, and to pray for my grandson's operation. All of this is happening at the same time, so my head is a little crazy. But I have a lot of faith, and when I pray to the Virgin, I immediately feel better. She is like my mother, always listening and helping me. She gives me hope that things will be better."

Omara's words reveal the most significant factor in the Virgin's wide appeal to Cubans: her maternal nature. A maternal figure who offers her children solace and guidance in surmounting the obstacles of daily life, the Virgin of Charity is simultaneously viewed by many Cubans as both the Mother of God and the Mother of Cuba. When asked what the Virgin symbolizes to them, about half of my interviewees immediately offered a theological interpretation of La Caridad as the Mother of Christ or the Mother of God. Others offered a cultural interpretation, seeing her as the Mother of all Cubans or the Patroness of Cuba. In the words of Herminia, the volunteer in El Cobre: "To say 'Cuba' is to say 'the Virgin of Charity.'" Or as Jorge, a sixty-year-old white man from Santiago, told me: "To me she symbolizes the combination of human history and the mystery of God. . . . Like the flag, the national anthem, the *mariposa* [Cuba's national flower], the *tambor* [a drum used in Cuban music], and tobacco, rum, and the guitar, the Virgin is a symbol of our *patria* [cultural heritage]. And even more than that, she symbolizes the faith that Cubans have in the progress of our lives." Whether she is viewed as the Mother of God or as Cuba itself, the fact remains that her symbol, or image, is maternal. In the words of Victor, a twenty-nine-year-old black man from El Cobre, "She is an example of how to be a mother. That is the most beautiful thing about her, even for those who don't have faith."

Victor raises an interesting point about the symbolic power of the Virgin: many Cubans who do not profess faith in God do express faith in La Caridad. Victor considers himself to be a Rastafarian, yet he prays to the Virgin every day. According to Felicia, a sixty-two-year-old *mulata* who volunteers at the shrine, this phenomenon is common: "People come here with different ideologies, but here there is a sense of unity because everyone respects the Virgin. Some even come without faith, but even they experience something, an interior change. No one leaves the same as they entered." The fact that "faithless" Cubans have faith in La Caridad reveals that her symbolic power transcends the realm of the Catholic Church. For these Cubans, the Virgin is not the Mother of God, but a maternal figure who guides her children through the struggles of life.

As both a maternal figure and a symbol of the *patria,* then, La Caridad appeals to Cubans of all types: orthodox Catholics and adherents of Santería, atheists and those who are Catholics in their own way. The Virgin's appeal (nearly universal except among the growing number of Protestants) is reflected in the words of Vilma, a fifty-three-year-old *mulata:* "I am Catholic, but in my own way. I don't go to Mass every week, but I have a lot of faith in the Virgin. At least once a month, I dress all in yellow and go to El Cobre with my children. They are not religious, but even they like to go there because it makes them feel better, asking her for help. There are many people like that here, people who don't practice a religion, who say they don't have faith, but they do have faith in the Virgin. When they see her, they are moved. They know that she will help them."

The extent of the Virgin's appeal is revealed in an anecdote told me by Father José Conrado, pastor of Santa Teresita Parish in Santiago: "When I was in college, one day a professor, a known atheist, told me, 'I don't believe in God, but no one should mess with the Virgin of Charity.'" In this sense, Father Conrado agrees that La Caridad is a symbol of *cubanía,* a fact that alone would explain her wide following among Cubans of all ideologies. Yet during our interview, he stressed to me that "she is also something more. She transcends identity." In other words, there are two fundamental ways to interpret La Caridad's symbolic significance. One can choose to view her as a symbol of *cubanía* that transcends the realm of religion, or as a spiritual symbol that transcends the realm of national identity. Of course, such a binary opposition is too simplistic an interpretation, for one can simultaneously believe that La Caridad is both the Mother of God and the Mother of Cubans, both a Catholic virgin and a Yoruba goddess, both the Mother of Christ and the wife of Changó, god of thunder and lightening, a multidimensional father of the sky in the Yoruba pantheon. It is precisely this flexibility of La Caridad's symbolism that explains her enduring popularity.

As a national symbol of the island, then, the Virgin connects Cubans to their historical struggles for independence and incarnates the complexity of Cuban identity. As the spiritual mother of Cuba, the Virgin has watched over her children for centuries, whether guiding them through personal crises, leading them on the path to a free Cuba, or helping them catch the big one. Although the big one may sometimes get away, the pilgrimages of gratitude to El Cobre will certainly continue. After all, Santiago's promise to make a pilgrimage reflects more than the desire to catch an outsized fish; it reveals the ability of an enduring yet fluid symbol of *cubanía* to unify the diverse constituents of the island's society. More than sixty years after Hemingway wrote *The Old Man and the Sea,* the pilgrimages to El Cobre and the prayers to the Virgin of Charity continue, as they have for centuries. Like Santiago, most Cubans are not--and never have been--orthodox Catholics. Yet devotees of the Virgin of Charity will continue to find in their spiritual mother a sense of solace, guidance, and hope that one day the streak of bad luck will end.

Works Cited

Castellanos, Jorge, and Isabel Castellanos. *Cultura afrocubana.* Vols. 3 and 4. Miami, FL: Ediciones Universal, 1994.

Díaz, María Elena. *The Virgin, the King, and the Royal Slaves of El Cobre: Negotiating Freedom in Colonial Cuba, 1670–1780.* Palo Alto, CA: Stanford Univ. Press, 2000.

Hemingway, Ernest. *The Old Man and the Sea.* New York: Charles Scribner's Sons, 1952.

La Torre, Miguel de. *The Quest for the Cuban Christ: A Historical Search.* Gainesville, FL: Univ. Press of Florida, 2002.

Murphy, Joseph M. "Yéyé Cachita: Ochún in a Cuban Mirror." *Osún Across the Waters: A Yoruba Goddess in Africa and the Americas.* Eds. Joseph Murphy and Mei-Mei Sanford. Bloomington, IN: Indiana Univ. Press, 2001. 87–101.

Pérez, Lisandro. "The Catholic Church in Cuba: A Weak Institution." *Puerto Rican and Cuban Catholics in the US, 1900–1965.* Edited by Jay Dolan and Jaime Vidal. Notre Dame, IN: Univ. of Notre Dame Press, 1994. 147–57.

Portuondo Zúñiga, Olga. *La Virgen de la Caridad del Cobre: Símbolo de cubanía* [*The Virgin of Charity in Cobre: Symbol of Cubanía*]. Santiago de Cuba: Editorial Oriente, 1995.

Tweed, Thomas. *Our Lady of the Exile: Diasporic Religion at a Cuban Catholic Shrine in Miami.* New York: Oxford Univ. Press, 1997.

Hemingway's Religious Odyssey

The Afro-Cuban Connection in Two Stories and The Old Man and the Sea

LARRY GRIMES

In the summer of 1995, as I toured Hemingway's home, I saw in the upper right quadrant of the desk in his study off the little bedroom at the Finca Vigía a curious cluster of articles: a card printed with "The Prayer of St. Ignatius," a small carved African mask, and an ashtray containing lucky stones and curative buckeyes. Later, this "accidental altar" would call to my mind the larger, more elaborate altars maintained by practitioners of the Afro-Cuban religions.[1] Such faiths evolved in Cuba before the end of slavery, as the African religions of Yoruba and Kongo slaves evolved to express themselves through the hagiography and ritual of the Catholic Church. The Afro-Cuban connection settled more firmly in my mind when my Afro-Cuban guide through the Finca Vigía in the village of San Francisco de Paula, Hemingway specialist Joaquín Bernado Gómez Borrego, pointed from the desk to an African antelope skin visible under Hemingway's typewriter in the little bedroom. There, he told me, Hemingway would stand on the skin as he wrote, to absorb special powers. Bernado also pointed out a walking stick of wood from Africa said to have healing properties. Life in the Finca was regulated, at least in part it seemed, by the spirit that pulses through Afro-Cuban religions in the Caribbean.[2]

Hemingway first incorporates Afro-Cuban religion into his fiction in two short stories from the 1930s set in Cuba. The first, "One Trip Across," initially appeared in *Cosmopolitan* in April 1934 and later was subsumed, with only minor revisions, as part 1 of Hemingway's 1937 novel *To Have and Have Not*. The second story, "Nobody Ever Dies," appeared in *Cosmopolitan* in March 1939. Hemingway brings in Afro-Cuban religion by including a similar minor character (perhaps the same one) in both stories: a black man with blue Voodoo beads.[3] Appearing first in "One Trip Across," this Afro-Cuban religious devotee literally launches the story: "Just then this nigger we had getting bait comes down the dock and I told Eddy to get ready to cast her off" (385). "Just then" and "cast off," both action markers, accompany the entrance of a man who is described as "a real black nigger, smart and gloomy, with blue voodoo beads around his neck under his shirt, and an old straw hat" (385). Upon his arrival, the fishing expedition begins. With his departure, it ends, and like his entrance, his exit is emphatic. Hemingway writes: "The nigger gets his ball of twine he used for tying baits and his dark glasses, puts on his straw hat and goes without saying good-by. He was a nigger that never thought much of any of us" (391). Between his entrance and exit, Harry Morgan says, "I gave the nigger the wheel" (386), and he is at the wheel when the boat passes the Morro on its way back to the dock. Although the man with the voodoo beads is outside and above the action during most of the fishing expedition, as Harry says to Johnson, "He's necessary" (385).

To understand just how "necessary," matters of race and ethnicity must be addressed directly. First, I think it important to neutralize the term *nigger* and move the discussion beyond charges of racism against Hemingway. The word, as used in this story, seems precise and loaded with powerful, positive meaning. Henry Louis Gates Jr. begins a groundbreaking essay with this epigram: "Signification is the nigger's occupation" (Gates 285). So it is in "One Trip Across," and to understand the necessity, the significance, and the signification of this black man in the story, he must be placed in his ethnoreligious context. Gates's examination of the type to which Hemingway's character belongs links him with a spirit Gates terms "the trickster figure in Yoruba mythology, Esu-Elegbara in Nigeria, Legba among the Fon of Dahomey, whose New World figurations—[include] . . . Echu-Elegua in Cuba" (286). The primary function of this type, which Gates embodies in the African American folk character of the Signifying Monkey, is to mediate meaning. "The ironic reversal of a received racist image of the black as simianlike, the Signifying Monkey," Gates notes, " . . . is our trope for repetition and revision, indeed, is our trope for chiasmus itself, repeating and simultaneously reversing in one deft, discursive act" (286). The Signifying Monkey signifies, subverts, comments, and inverts through rhetorical language, gesture, and act. Always he signifies with style. Hemingway presents his character, whom I will call his "Signifying Bead-man," purely as rhetorical gesture, as pure style.

He stands cool and above the fray in his blue voodoo beads, straw hat, and dark glasses. Given no name, he exists only metonymically: as an extension of his body, as race, as color. He is "real black." "He's necessary." He signifies. That is to say, he confronts the events around him and calls out their meaning. He is the interpretive sign that discharges meaning from the incident. He can do this because he has the capacity (opening and closing the gates on this episode, as he does) to walk, magiclike, in and out of a have-and-have-not economy that brings white people to financial and moral ruin. Unlike Harry, who loses his tackle and almost three weeks' wages to Mr. Johnson, the Signifying Bead-man gets paid his dollar, plus tip. Unlike Mr. Johnson, he performs his job well and rips off no one. Unlike Eddy, he is no rummy. He stands above and outside the white world and its materialistic economy and signifies. Harry gets the point, economic, political, moral, and spirtual, and notes, "He was a nigger that never thought much of any of us" (Hemingway, "One Trip Across" 23). The Signifying Bead-man stands guard at the crossroads of meaning in "One Trip Across."

Nor is this the Signifying Bead-man's only appearance in Hemingway's fiction of the 1930s. As I said, he next appears in the wonderful and much-neglected Cuban short story, "Nobody Ever Dies." Early in the story Hemingway introduces "a Negro in a narrow-brimmed flat-topped straw hat and a gray alpaca coat and black trousers" (470). This Negro is an informer who turns a young revolutionist, Enrique, and his lover, Maria, over to the Cuban authorities. It is not until near the end of the story that the black man's identity as the Signifying Bead-man is revealed. As Maria lies hidden in tall weeds, while police move toward her "like beaters in a rabbit drive" (479), the Negro is described in considerable detail: "He wore a flat-topped, narrow-brimmed straw hat and an alpaca coat. Under his shirt he wore a string of blue voodoo beads. He was standing quietly watching the light working" (479).

The searchlights and the "rabbit drive" work. The police apprehend Maria. As they take her toward the police car, she appears hysterical and begins to scream out intercessory prayers to her brother, killed in Spain, and to her lover, recently slaughtered there behind her in the weeds. The following dialogue ensues:

> "It's the sister of Vincente Irtube," said the lieutenant. "She should be useful."
> "She's been questioned before," said another.
> "Never seriously."
> "No," she said. "No. No." She cried aloud, "Help me Vincente! Help me, help me, Enrique!"
> "They're dead," said someone. "They won't help you. Don't be silly."
> "Yes," she said. "They will help me. It is the dead that will help me. Oh, yes, yes, yes! It is our dead that will help me." (480)

Screaming "Everyone is helping me now," Maria is placed into the backseat of a police car. Her confidence certainly makes sense in an Afro-Cuban religious community, especially among those who practice Palo Monte.[4]

Sitting there, Hemingway writes, she "seemed now to have a strange confidence. It was the same confidence another girl her age had felt a little more than five hundred years before in the market place of a town called Rouen" (480). With this reference to Jeanne d' Arc, I think, Hemingway carefully merges Catholic and Afro-Cuban religions and begins a prose incantation that culminates in the powerful, palpable presence of the living-dead—a new *orisha,* Saint Joan—vibrant in the body of Maria. In the final pages of this little tragedy Hemingway does indeed double Maria with Jeanne d' Arc.

But this is not a simple doubling. Hemingway has not, as most assume, given us a modern-day Catholic saint's legend. He has not, as many have charged, weakened the story by a facile resort to gratuitious symbolism. Rather, he has presented Maria's transfiguration in the light of a vision apart from Joan's, a vision that Hemingway has artfully conjured from Afro-Cuban materials.

To determine the significance of this living-dead girl who sits "very straight with her face shining in the arc light" (480), Hemingway again leaves his story in the hands of the Signifying Bead-man. This time we read, "The Negro was frightened and he put his fingers all the way around the string of blue voodoo beads and held them tight. But they could not help his fear because he was up against older magic now" (481).

What the Signifying Bead-man recognizes—something the white lieutenant passes off as "crazy"—is that the girl is possessed. In the language of Afro-Cuban religion, the *aché,*[5] the power, of a great and powerful ancestor has "mounted" her. In the moment of the possession, the incarnation, that ancient power (*aché*) presents itself. That's what the Signifying Bead-man apprehends as he grabs for his beads. Miguel Barnet describes the relation of the possessed to a powerful ancestor this way: "These divinized ancestors did not die a natural death, understood in Yoruba as the abandonment of the body by breath. Possessors of a very potent *aché* and exceptional powers, they underwent a metamorphosis in a moment of emotional crisis provoked by wrath or other violent emotion. What was material in them disappeared, burned by that passion, and only the *aché* remained—power in pure state of energy" (82).

Barnet concludes by noting that the *aché* of these *orichas,* or divine ancestors, can become perceptible to humans only through possession. At the end of "Nobody Ever Dies," through the eyes of the Signifying Bead-man, we witness, I repeat, a possession that signifies the emergence of a new *oricha.* In the character of Maria, at least through the eyes of the Signifying Bead-man, St. Jeanne enters the pantheon of Afro-Cuban deities, something indeed to raise up fear and awe: through his eyes we behold the oldest magic of all, the sudden manifestation, the apotheosis, of the divine.

. . .

Although it would be more than a decade before Hemingway published another major story set in Cuba, we must not forget that he took up permanent residence there in 1940. Recently, in correspondence with René Villarreal, Hemingway's majordomo at the Finca, and Villarreal's son Raul, I learned that both the Lukumi/Santería and Palo Monte religions were widely practiced in Hemingway's village of San Francico de Paula.[6] Both René and Raul are followers of Palo Monte. The Villarreals confirm Hemingway's interest in Cuban folklore and his deep involvement in the lives of the ordinary Cubans—the Finca Vigía staff, the villagers around the Finca, the fishermen at Cojimar, and working-class people at cockfights. As H. R. Stoneback reminds us often, Hemingway was a great student of place.[7] He always got to know the territory. From the 1930s forward, Hemingway's territory included Cuba: its people, its culture, and its Great Blue River.

The Villarreals provided three examples of Hemingway's interest in and knowledge of Afro-Cuban religion: first, Hemingway's adoration and fierce defense of the giant Ceiba tree in his yard (sacred in Lukumi/Santéria and Palo Monte); second, Hemingway's acceptance of Rene's gift of a thunder rock—a rock belonging to Siete Rayo (Palo Monte) or Shango (Lukumi/Santería)—to be carried for good luck; and, third, Hemingway's arrangement for his chauffeur, Juan, to take the matador Luis Miguel Dominguin to visit a Babalao in Guanabacoa.[8] Finally, it should be noted that René is a high priest in Palo Monte who has passed the *fundamento* ("core") to his son Raul.

By the time Hemingway wrote the final draft of *The Old Man and the Sea,* his understanding of Afro-Cuban religion had deepened and he was able to incorporate specific symbols and cosmology from those religions into his novella.[9] In the creole tradition of Cuban religion and culture, these Afro-Cuban elements do not erase or displace Christian myth and symbol; they coexist alongside them, adding new religious dimensions to them. Creolized religion fit well into Hemingway's ongoing religious odyssey. Since in the 1930s he was disillusioned with institutional Catholicism and fascinated by Africa, his encounters with Afro-Christian culture in Cuba must have excited his imagination, providing him with new ways to think about the old religions.

After the appearance of the man with voodoo beads in the two short stories, there is no direct reference to Afro-Cuban religions in Hemingway's fiction until *The Old Man and the Sea* where, early in the telling, he calls attention to a picture of the Virgin of Charity in Cobre (La Virgen de la Caridad del Cobre) hanging on a wall in Santiago's shack (16). Direct though this Afro-Cuban reference is to Cuban eyes, it is probably obscure to most non-Cuban readers. In Cuba, the Virgin of Cobre has a double identity. She is Mary, Mother of God, and Ochún, African goddess of rivers, among the most venerated and most powerful of the old African *orishas.* Both of her faces are visible in the novel, although my concern in this essay is to foreground her presence as Ochún.

If one accepts, as I do, the calendar presented by Hurley and Sylvester for the narrative, Hemingway revealed the picture of the Virgin to his readers on September 12 (Sylvester 247–48). Since September 12 is the Lukumi/Santería Feast Day for the Virgin of Cobre (as distinct from the September 8 Feast Day celebrated among Cuban Catholics), it seems that Ochún's face shines brightest in the picture. September 12 is also the date for the pilgrimage to her shrine in Santiago, a pilgrimage the character Santiago explicitly acknowledges and promises to make if he catches the fish (*OMS* 65).

For Cuban readers, the picture of the Virgin of Cobre has specific content. She is painted as a mulatto and she is placed above the image of a skiff manned by three fishermen (two Taino Indians and a young slave).[10] According to tradition, these fishermen found her in about 1612, when she appeared as a statue floating in the water near their boat, calming a stormy sea. That statue is enshrined in Santiago, Cuba, bringing *orisha* and the old man together linguistically in the word *Santiago.* There is a light trace of that traditional picture in the opening lines of *The Old Man and the Sea:* "He was an old man who fished alone in a skiff in the Gulf Stream . . ." (11).

Although Santiago no longer displays a picture of his wife, this old fisherman still displays a picture of the *orisha* Ochún, goddess of all rivers, including the Great Blue River, the Gulf Stream, where the old man will catch his big fish. Pictures of Ochún are commonplace on Lukumi/Santéria altars,[11] and, while Santiago may not, as he asserts, be religious [read, "Catholic"] (64), he may practice Afro-Cuban religions that can speak the language of Catholicism and display its symbols, even as they also evoke the power of ancient African *orishas.* Santiago's "Our Fathers" and "Hail Marys," and the color picture of the Sacred Heart of Jesus, may be presented with an Afro-Cuban twist. Looking through Afro-Cuban eyes, Santéria scholar Joseph Murphy reminds us that, "the *orishas* are capable of appearing to ordinary Catholics as pallid white saints, and to *santeros* as the invisible forces of ashé" (*African Spirits* 40). From an Afro-Cuban perspective, the absence of his wife's photo on the wall and the remains of her presence in the pictures of the Virgin of Cobre and the Sacred Heart of Jesus, alte(a)r Santiago's loss and emptiness. These relics (re)call and (re)present the *aché* (power) of the water *orishas* whose blessings would bring him fish. He needs to once again come under, and be possessed by, the spell and power (*aché*) of the feminine. His own resources (for example, his fishing skills), which are many and of which he is proud, will not suffice.[12] To restore his luck, he will need the powers represented by "the relics" (a word carefully chosen for its religious weight) of his wife.

Keeping Ochún, the painting, the feast day, and the pilgrimage in mind, I turn to Santiago's thoughts about *la mar:* "He always thought of the sea as *la mar* which is what people call her in Spanish when they love her. . . . Some of the fishermen, those who used buoys as floats for their lines and had motorboats . . . spoke of her as *el mar* which is masculine. They spoke of her as a contestant or a place or even an enemy. But the old man always thought of her as feminine and as something that gave or withheld great favors, and if she did wild things it was because she could not help them" (*OMS* 30).

Susan Beegel's reading of this paragraph is fresh and strong. Naming the sea as a major character in a powerful and tragic love story and identifying *la mar* with the Eternal Feminine, she locates the numinous dimension of the story in the mythologies of Christianity and Ancient Mediterranean cultures.[13] Although it catches much that is generally true about *la mar,* such an identification of *la mar* with the generalized force of the Eternal Feminine misses the particular, the Cuban, the specific names of feminine power: Ochún and her sister, Yemaya (Beegle 131–56).

With regard to Ochún, Lukumi priest and scholar Miguel "Willie" Ramos (here quoted in Castellanos 40) has this to say: "She is very kind, but can become vindictive and rancorous when she encounters opposition. It is precisely because of this irrational and stubborn character that she is considered the most fragile and feared *orisha* in Afro-Cuban lore. When she cries, she does so out of joy; when she laughs, she does so out of anger. When offended, she will ignore the offender, acting as if nothing has occurred. At some future date, when her offender has probably forgotten the occurrence, she remembers an old debt and claims immediate payment. The lady wants it and she wants it now!"

Ochún's similarities to Santiago's *la mar* are obvious. In a religious sense, as Joseph Murphy observes, she represents "the holy mystery of water that comes from nowhere to give life and to take it away" ("Yéyé Cachita" 97). Associated with the waters of life, she also is the "patroness of love, money, and yellow metals; [she] rules sex and marriage" (Brandon 77). This makes her particularly important to Santiago, whose nearly empty shack reflects the horrible luck that has befallen his life. He has lost his wife (marriage, sex, happiness), and for more than eighty days he has been unable to catch a fish. He is emotionally and financially at a loss. He is man who needs to know again, if only as spirit, the power of sex, marriage, and money.

Santiago consistently uses the language of luck as he reflects on his loss. According to a count made by a group of my students, the concept of luck receives comment and attention on seventeen separate pages, from the beginning reference to *salao* through this exchange between Manolin and Santiago, two pages from the end of the book, where Santigo says, "No. I am not lucky. I am not lucky anymore" (*OMS* 125).

Santiago's bad luck, his great loss, is gendered feminine. He has lost his lover/wife/marriage. And luck (Fortuna), itself, as Frank Sinatra reminds us, is a lady. About her, Santiago thinks "luck is a thing that come in many forms and who can recognize her. I would take some though in any form and pay what they asked" (*OMS* 117). Given the prominence of luck as plot device and theme, it is little wonder that Hemingway embeds powerful allusions to Afro-Cuban religions into the novel, since they are concerned with control of one's environment, with luck—good and bad—and how one makes it good.

Ochún is present in the novel as the force that can bring balance to Santiago's life and restore his luck. After she is introduced in the picture of the Virgin, her presence is extended into the novel through the use of her color—the most obvious identification of an *orisha.* Ochún's ritual color is yellow in all its hues,[14] a prominent color in the novella. Santiago's rice is yellow, the ever-present Sargasso weed is yellow, the African beach and the lions of his dreams are yellow (golden/tawny). The color yellow/gold appears on twelve separate pages in this short novel (*OMS* 16, 24, 31, 35, 36, 38, 54, 72, 81, 98, 106, 108), and at least once appears as many as three times on a single page (72). It is implicitly present (through references to elements already identified as yellow/gold, such as the lions and the seaweed) on another eight pages. In a most telling reference to Ochún, Hemingway allows the full erotic power of this water *orischa* to surface in the text. "Just before dark," he writes, "as they passed a great island of Sargasso weed that heaved and swung in the light sea *as though the ocean was making love with something under a yellow blanket,* his small line was taken by a dolphin" (72; my emphasis). Hemingway's simile dramatizes Ochún's powerful presence, which floats in the Gulf Stream current, changing Santiago's luck.

His agon at sea is a pilgrimage toward balance and harmony—conditions associated with and obtained through Ochún. From Santiago's thrust of the skiff against the ocean, to the rise of the mast to his shoulder, to his long and triumphant arm-wrestle with the Negro from Cienfuegos, to his many comments about the fishing tricks he knows, Hemingway's depiction of his protagonist places in the foreground the old man's masculinity. Hemingway also underscores Santiago's lack: the fact that he is a man without women, a man living outside the power of the feminine, having lost both wife and good fortune. In Afro-Cuban religion, particularly in the cosmogony of Cuban Palo Monte, the old man's life is out of balance. To be out of balance is indeed *salao*—the very worst of bad luck. Only the *aché* of an *orisha* can restore balance to Santiago's life and bring him good luck. Ochún's feminine presence (the picture, her Feast

Day, her pilgrimage day, her manifest colors) combines with Santiago's masculine gifts (such as his considerable skill as fisherman) to produce the balance, the luck, needed to attract, catch and secure the marlin.

The language used to describe the catch suggests that Santiago succeeds in landing the fish because of his superior skill as a fisherman (masculine) and because he is able to keep his head clear, something that he accomplishes through the power (*aché*) of Ochún. Mentioned at length on several occasions (77, 85, 87, 92, 99, 101), the necessity for a clear head is declared directly in these lines: "All I must do is keep my head clear. The hands have done their work and we sail well" (99). Certainly such lines can be read against the old man's physical exhaustion, his experiences of dizziness. However, in the world of Afro-Cuban religion the references ring differently:

> The 'head' or '*orí*' is a spiritual faculty within the physical head of every individual. It preexists the physical body, choosing the destiny of an earthly life. At death *orí* is disengaged from the body and moves on to other destinies. The *camino de santo* is a path of development of an individual *orí,* bringing the capacities of this spiritual dimension of the human psyche to guide the whole person . . . *Most misfortune in life is attributed to a failure of people to listen to their orís. They do not keep their heads clear and cool,* and so lose touch with the fundamental insight that is their guide. (Murphy, *Working the Spirit* 90; my emphasis)

A clear head comes about as one's *orisha* draws the individual ever deeper into the invisible meaning and power of the visible world. The *camino de santo* is the spiritual path of the *orí,* the head, to work out its destiny *en santo,* in the way of the individual's patron *orisha* (Murphy, *Working the Spirit* 91). Read from this Afro-Cuban perspective, Santiago's attempts to keep a cool head (*orí*) are moments when his masculine skills are joined to the feminine *camino* of his patron *orisha,* Ochún. Then he possesses (and is possessed by) the fullness and balance needed to meet his destiny, to catch and secure the fish.

To a reader with basic knowledge of Palo Monte cosmogony and cosmograms, Hemingway's detailed description of Santiago's struggle to bring in the great fish provides confirmation that Ochún's *aché* returns to the old man during the struggle. Hemingway's carefully chosen words graft the old man's experience to a simple diagram of harmonic life, a design that appears often in Palo Monte ritual and in contemporary Cuban art influenced by Afro-Cuban religion:[15]

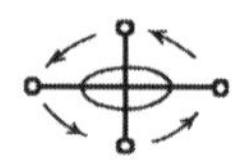

The cosmogram drawn above suggests an aerial view of the skiff, the old man in its center, and the great turns of the fish around and around the skiff.

The simplest form of this cosmogram, as Robert Farris Thompson notes, is the cross (+) that always constitutes its center. Such a mark is drawn on the ground for oath taking. This "Kongo cruciform [creates] a sacred 'point' on the ground of the dead and under all-seeing God" (Thompson 108). Thompson goes on to explain that "the Kongo *yowa* cross . . . signifies the vision of the circular motion of human souls about the circumference of its intersecting lines" (108). Thompson provides the following commentary on the cosmogram: "The horizontal line divides the mountain of the living world from its counterpart in the kingdom of the dead . . . God is imagined at the top, the dead at the bottom, and water in between. The four disks at the points of the cross stand for the four movements of the sun, and the circumference of the cross the certainty of reincarnation: *the especially righteous Kongo person will never be destroyed*" (109; my emphasis). It also should be noted that the summit of the cross symbolizes noon, maleness, north—the peak of a person's strength on earth, while the bottom represents midnight, femaleness, south—the highest point of a person's otherworldly strength (109).

Hemingway plots Santiago's journey on the Great Blue River along the cycle of the sun, day in and day out. He launches the skiff "in the dark" (*OMS* 26, 28, 29) of morning; then, "before it was really light he had his baits out" (30). Soon after, "The sun rose thinly from the sea" (32). Later in the morning we read that "the strange light that the sun made in the water, now that the sun was higher, meant good weather" (35). The attention paid by Hemingway and Santiago to the rising sun culminates on the first day with these words from the old man: "It was noon when I hooked him" (46).

The old man who has lost his love and all luck, the old man who has not caught a fish in eighty-four days, the old man who has lost his *aché,* his potency, accrues more power as the sun rises to its apex. His *aché* returns, his luck changes, and the hook is set in the great marlin at noon. Once the hook is set, the turn of life spins around the man and the skiff, testing the old man's renewed *aché* turn by turn, ultimately demonstrating that, as Thompson might have put it, he is "an especially righteous *Kongo* [who] will never be destroyed" (109).

It is "almost sunset" (*OMS* 80) when the old man hooks the dolphin, eats raw fish, then settles himself in the bow to rest. The moon had been up a long time when he is jerked awake. Midnight passes without explicit mention. The power of the feminine (night) has been powerfully at work. At first light the old man speculates that the fish will soon circle. Hemingway writes, "The sun was rising for the third time since he had put to sea when the fish began to circle"

(86). Much is made of the fish turning in a long cycle of circles. The words *circle* and *circling* are used twenty-one times in just nine pages, the words *turn, turns,* and *turned,* ten times. Clearly Hemingway has placed repetitive emphasis on the circle of life and death that is the struggle to land the fish.

Further, he has the old man stands at the crossroads, at the center (+) of the circle, as he begins the work of bringing in the line: "I'll rest now while he goes out on the circle and then stand up and work on him when he comes in . . . the old man rose to his feet and started the pivoting" (88–89). The old man is placed at the center/crossroads, where life and death pulse in and out of each other—and both have pulse: both, in Afro-Cuban terms, have *ache,* both are vital, and, as it nears noon, the "fish came alive with his death in him" (94). At the apex of power, epiphany: luck is restored, the fish is landed.

But not without a price. Santiago has gotten the luck he wanted; now he must "pay what they asked" (*OMS* 117). In the context of Afro-Cuban religion, the time has come for him to offer an *ebo,* a sacrifice. That *ebo* is contained in the epiphany that marks the return of luck and balance to Santiago's life. Hemingway uses a simile to present the epiphany. The fish "seemed to hang in the air above the old man in the skiff. Then he fell into the water with a crash that sent a spray over the old man and over the whole skiff" (94). This picture calls to mind a standard *ebo* ritual to cleanse a person afflicted by the dead (Santiago's wife) (Nodal and Ramos 182),[16] including the sacrifice of an animal and "passing it over the body of the afflicted" (182). In this process, the spirit is removed from the man and placed in the sacrificed animal. That done, luck and balance are restored. However, the ritual act is not complete until the animal's body is disposed of properly. And the ideal place to discard a contaminated body? A "garbage dumpster" (183). It seems, then, an extension of Afro-Cuban religious symbolism when Hemingway places the great white spine of the fish "in the water among beer cans and dead barracuda" (*OMS* 126).

The work of Ochún is complete. Santiago had great luck at a great price—and the price is paid. Balance is restored, and the old man can dream easily (and, perhaps, forever) about the lions.

Notes

1. In this essay I will confine my study to the two most prominent Afro-Cuban religions practiced in Cuba: Lukumi, the religion of Yoruba slaves, often referred to as Santería—I shall refer to it as Lukumi/Santería—and Palo Monte (the religion of slaves from the larger Kongo region of Africa. For a wonderfully illustrated study of the sorts of altars to which I refer, see Jasamur Flores-Pena and Roberta J. Evanchuk, *Santeria Gar-*

ments and Altars (Jackson, MS: Univ. Press of Mississippi, 1994). Practitioners of religion in Cuba are not homogonous. Their practice flows along a continuum outlined nicely by George Brandon in his *Santeria from Africa to the New World* (Bloomington, IN: Indiana Univ. Press, 1993), 172–75. This continuum moves from Spanish Official Catholic through Creole practice of Official Catholic and Folk Catholic, to Lukumi/Santería practice of Folk Catholic Yoruba, Yoruba Folk Catholic, and Yoruba, to Kongo practice of Folk Catholic Palo Monte, Palo Monte Folk Catholic, and Palo Monte, and on to still other forms of religious practice. A single practitioner may participate in religion at several points along the continiuum, depending on personal preference and immediate need.

2. Since at least 1997, attention has been paid to Afro-Cuban artifacts at the Finca Vigía. At the Hemingway Colloquia held in Havana, I gave a paper on Afro-Cuban influence in two short stories (adapted above), while Hemingway specialist Maria C. Valdes Fernandez spoke about Afro-Cuban artifacts at the Finca. Since then, as Hilary Hemingway notes in *Hemingway and Cuba* (New York: Ruggedland, 2003), 104–8, Valdes Fernandez has catalogued and studied those artifacts in considerable detail. As international scholars join Cubans in the study of Hemingway's life and work, much new information about both may come from careful study of "material culture."

3. In Lukumi/Santería and Palo Monte those who follow the *camino* ("way/path") of a particular *orishsa* ("deity/spirit") are given beads of a specific color during initiation; each *orisha* has a special color or colors. The beads referred to here as "voodoo beads" do not seem to match the *orisha* (the trickster figure known as Echu-Elegua) described in the scenes. This, I think, is because Hemingway had only a limited knowledge of Afro-Cuban religion in the 1930s. As his daily life was lived among people practicing these religions, both his interest and knowledge increased. He became interested enough in the matter that, according to Brasch and Sigman, he added a book treating the subject—Melville Herskovits's *Cultural Anthropology* (1955)—to his Finca Vigía library. An earlier book by Herskovits, *The Myth of the Negro Past* (1941), launched the serious study of African elements in slave and postslave cultures in the Americas. In their foreword to the Finca Vigía editon of their father's short stories, John, Patrick, and Gregory Hemingway confirm Ernest's interest in the survival of things African in the Americas when they write: "Papa told us some of the black slaves had escaped from the shipwreck of slave ships on the coast of South America, enough of them together with their language and culture intact so that they were able to live together in the wilderness down to the present just as they lived in Africa" (Hemingway, *Complete Short Stories* xi). It should be recalled that Hemingway "discovered" Cuba as the Afrocubanismo movement reached its apex. The movement, which celebrated Cuba's African traditions, flourished among Cuban artists of all sorts in the 1920s and 1930s, who integrated such traditions into their art, especially music.

4. As Fernández and Baravisini-Gebert note, "Congo traditions observe a different interaction with the spirits than Yoraba-based religions; focused less on a pantheon of deities, the Reglas Congas emphasize control of the dead and healing with the use of charms . . . formulas and spells" (79). At the philosophical center of this focus on the dead, according to Thompson, is "an ideal balancing of the vitality of the world of the living with the visionariness of the world of the dead" (106). Hemingway, like many Afro-Cuban religious practitioners, seems to borrow from both Yoruba and Kongo traditions as the need arises.

5. While Miguel Barnet (82) defines *aché* as "power in a state of pure-energy," Thompson gives the term more specificity, defining it as "spiritual command, the power-to-make-things-happen, God's own enabling light rendered accessible to men and women" (7). Literally, he says, it means, "So be it," "May it happen" (7). There are variant spellings of the word: "ache," "àshe," "axe."

6. Raul Villarreal, e-mail exchange with the author, 1 July 2008.

7. See Stoneback, passim.

8. Raul Villarreal, e-mail exchange with the author, 1 July 2008.

9. See Philip Melling (7–24), whose essay provides the first extensive analysis of Hemingway's Cuban works to focus on Afro-Cuban religion. Given the Marxist perspective of the essay, Afro-religions are necessarily deconstructed. In this essay, I have adopted the perspective of a historian of religion and have tried to present and validate these religions on their own terms. This leads to me to very different conclusions from those of Melling, conclusions I first published in "Lions on the Beach: Dreams, Place and Memory."

10. Such pictures are readily available on the Web. A quick "google" of "Virgin of Cobre" will take a reader to active sites featuring pictures of the Virgin of Cobre and pictures of the shrine in Santiago.

11. See Jasamur Flores-Pena and Roberta J. Evanchuk, *Santeria Garments and Altars.* Moreover, many websites discussing Ochún have pictures available. Olga Portuondo does "not believe that the adoption of the Virgin of Cobre's identifying yellow clothing in the 1930's is merely a coincidence. Rather, it reveals the growing influence of Santeria in the religious beliefs and practices of the people" (494).

12. Gerry Brenner, in his book-length reading of the novella, argues that Santiago is clinically obsessive, neurotic in his obsessions, perhaps even psychotic (35, 52). Brenner's psychological take on the old man is, I think, a classic example of a colonialist reading of the text. In contrast, a reading of *The Old Man and the Sea* through Afro-Cuban eyes would identify Santiago's behavior not as obsession but as possession. When possessed by Ochún, Santiago is able to exert her power against natural forces. It is possession that provides him with the *aché,* the power, needed to make good luck in the world—and good luck is what the plot seeks to bring into Santiago's life. There are many points in Brenner's essay, for example, his comments about Santiago's indifference toward his dead wife (37, 84) and his discussion of circles/cycles (43), where knowledge of Afro-Cuban concepts would have drastically changed his reading.

13. As Hemingway scholars become better acquainted with the Afro-Cuban traditon, it will be profitable, I think, to look at *la mar* through the complex relation of these water *orisha*s. To avoid confusion at this early stage of exploration, however, I will continue to focus on Ochún's role in the novel.

14. See note 11 above.

15. See the Levi Jordan Plantation web page, http://www.publicarchaeology.org/webarchaeology/html/kongocos.htm. Drawing adapted from Thompson, *Flash of the Spirit* 109.

16. The offering of ebó suggests that Santiago's wife has died and untimely death in one fashion or another. Ebó is necessary to tap into "ashé and its benefical, curative and harmonizing nature" (Nodal and Ramos 171).

Works Cited

Barnet, Miguel. "La Regla de Ocha: The Religious System of Santería." In *Sacred Possessions: Vodou, Santería, Obeah, and the Caribbean.* Edited by Margarite Fernández Olmos and Lizbeth Paravisini-Gebert. New Brunswick, NJ: Rutgers Univ. Press, 1997.

Beegle, Susan. "Santiago and the Eternal Feminine." In *Hemingway and Women: Female Critics and the Female Voice.*" Edited by Lawrence R. Broer and Gloria Holland. Tuscaloosa: Univ. of Alabama Press, 2002. 131–56.

Brandon, George. Santeria from Africa to the New World. Bloomington, IN: Indiana Univ. Press, 1993.

Brenner, Gerry. *The Old Man and the Sea: Story of a Common Man.* Twayne Masterwork Series. New York: Twayne Publishers, 1991.

Castellanos, Isabel. "A River of Many Turns: The Polysemy of Ochún in Afro-Cuban Traditon." *Osun Across the Waters: A Yoruba Goddess in Africa and the Americas.* Edited by Joseph M. Murphy and Mei-Mei Sanford. Bloomington, IN: Indiana Univ. Press, 2001. 34–45.

Fernández Olmos, Margarite, and Lizabeth Paravisini-Gebert. *Creole Religions of the Caribbean: An Introduction From Vodou and Santería to Obeah and Espiritismo.* New York: New York Univ. Press, 2003.

——, eds. *Sacred Possessions: Vodou, Santería, Obeah, and the Caribbean* (New Brunswick, NJ: Rutgers Univ. Press, 1997.

Flores-Pena, Jasamur, and Roberta J. Evanchuk. *Santeria Garments and Altars.* Jackson, MS: Univ. Press of Mississippi, 1994.

Gates, Henry Louis, Jr. "The Blackness of Blackness: A Critique of the Sign and the Signifying Monkey." In *Black Literature & Literary Theory.* Edited by Henry Louis Gates Jr. New York: Routledge, 1990. 285–322.

Grimes, Larry. "Lions on the Beach: Dreams, Place and Memory." In *Ernest Hemingway and the Geography of Memory.* Edited by Mark Cirino, and Mark P. Ott. Kent, OH: Kent State Univ. Press, 2012. 57–66.

Hemingway, Ernest. "Nobody Ever Dies." In *The Complete Short Stories of Ernest Hemingway.* Finca Vigía Edition. New York: Charles Scribner's Sons, 1987. 370–81.

——. *The Old Man and the Sea.* 1952. New York: Scribner, 2003.

——. "One Trip Across." In *Complete Short Stories.* 381–409.

Hemingway, Hilary. *Hemingway and Cuba.* New York: Ruggedland, 2003.

Hemingway, John, Patrick Hemingway, and Gregory Hemingway. Foreword to *The Complete Short Stories of Ernest Hemingway.* Finca Vigía Edition. New York: Charles Scribner's Sons, 1987. xi–xiii.

Melling, Philip. "Cultural Imperialism, Afro-Cuban Religion, and Santiago's Failure in Hemingway's *The Old Man and the Sea.*" *The Hemingway Review* 26.1 (Fall 2006): 7–24.

Murphy, Joseph M. *Santeria: African Spirits in America.* Boston: Beacon Press, 1993.

——. *Working the Spirit: Ceremonies of the African Diaspora.* Boston: Beacon, 1994.

——. "Yéyé Cachita: Ochún in a Cuban Mirror." *Osun Across the Waters: A Yoruba Goddess in Africa and the Americas.* Edited by Joseph M. Murphy and Mei-Mei Sanford. Bloomington, IN: Indiana Univ. Press, 2001. 87–101.

Nodal, Roberto, and Miguel "Willie" Ramos. "Let the Power Flow: Ebó as Healing Mechanism in Lukimí Orisha Worship." *Fragments of Bone: Neo-African Religions in a New World.* Edited by Patrick Bellegarde-Smith. Urbana, IL: Univ. of Illinois Press, 2005. 167–86.

Portuondo Zuníga, Olga. "The Virgin of Charity of Cobre, Cuba's Patron Saint." In *The Cuban Reader.* Edited by Aviva Chomsky, Barry Carr, and Pamela Maria Smorkaloff. Durham, NC: Duke Univ. Press, 2003. 490–97.

Stoneback, H. R. *Reading Hemingway's* The Sun Also Rises*: Glossary and Commentary.* Kent, OH: Kent State Univ. Press, 2007.

Sylvester, Bickford. "The Cuban Context of *The Old Man and the Sea.*" In *The Cambridge Companion to Hemingway.* Edited by Scott Donaldson. Cambridge, UK: Cambridge Univ. Press, 1996. 243–68.

Thompson, Robert Farris. *Flash of the Spirit: African & Afro-American Art and Philosophy.* New York: Vintage, 1984.

Villarreal, Raul. E-mail exchange with the author. 1 July 2008.

"You Know the Name Is No Accident"

Hemingway and the Matter of Santiago

H. R. STONEBACK

> "ISLE OF THE BLEST or FORTUNATE ISLANDS . . . placed in Greek mythology in the Western ocean, and peopled, not by the dead, but by mortals upon whom the gods had conferred immortality."
>
> *Encyclopaedia Britannica,* 1944 edition

For many years I shared the widespread assumption of many Hemingway readers and critics that *The Old Man and the Sea* was his most direct and straightforward work of fiction; that all that was there for the getting was more or less on the surface; that the "iceberg theory" did not apply to this work; that here—uniquely in Hemingway's fiction—we need not concern ourselves with theories of omission, with indirection and obliquity, with deep structure and buried allusions. Like so many others, I had been lulled into the ill-considered conclusion that there was little left to say, little new information to report, nothing left to clarify regarding *The Old Man and the Sea.* This is not to say that I ever agreed for one moment with those who have dismissed and debunked this work, or that I found the novel anything less than the moving, compelling, admirably realized masterwork that it is. I just thought that its many virtues were obvious to all those who would see them, a critical sin on my part, for which I hope to receive some absolution here.

For many decades, it seemed fairly clear that there were two irreconcilable critical camps: either *The Old Man and the Sea* was dreadful stuff, a thin soup, a sloppy pastiche, overstated sentimental uplift, or it was Hemingway's last polished work, a powerful narrative with a strong spiritual "message" for the millions of readers around the world who love this story and its style. Recently, however, in this age of the shining paths of ethnic, religious, cultural, critical, theoretical, and gender Puritanism and fundamentalism, it has become all too clear that there are more than two embattled camps. I have no desire to serve as negotiator, as Special Envoy to the MLA Security Council or to some Hemingway Disarmament Conference convened to draft a treaty that will accommodate radically disparate views of *The Old Man and the Sea.* I would prefer to say, simply and directly, that I am here to celebrate Hemingway's Cuba, Hemingway's Santiago, and to call attention to some allusions, some details regarding the *naming* and *placing* of Santiago that have not been noticed before.

Before I do that, however, allow me a reminiscence and permit me to engage briefly the current cultural modalities, the miasma that now enshrouds this work, the poisonous critical vapors that threaten to choke off understanding of this last great illumination and distillation of the Hemingway Code—or, as I prefer to say, the Hemingway Creed. What *is* and what *was,* really, this small novel that more than five million readers avidly devoured in *Life* magazine in that first memorable week of September 1952? That week when I—a kid hitchhiking through strange cities—saw people reading it on street corners, heard drivers who gave me a ride talk passionately about it; that week when I—not yet a teenager—first read *The Old Man and the Sea* at a truck stop in the Ozarks, at three A.M., after two waitresses and the truckdriver I had hitched a ride with were through reading it, long parts of it were read aloud to the cathedral-hushed truck stop—jukebox silent, all orders, all eggs and burgers and apple pie, on hold, coffee cups poised in midair, the timeless suspension of another dimension as Hemingway's words filled the truckstop, first in the lilting mountainy accent of that waitress, then in the clipped New Englandese of that truck driver. Then, after they were through reading, and after I had read it straight through, sitting at the truck stop counter, even forgetting to put extra sugar in my coffee for nourishment for the road, I handed the magazine back to the waitress. She said: "Honey, that old man is some kind of saint, ain't he? He's *my* kind of saint." I said nothing, for I knew nothing about saints and I was still deep inside the story. I smiled at her, however, for she was very nice and very pretty even with her streaky bleached hair, and I can still see that waitress's face and eyes as she read *The Old Man and the Sea,* and hear her proclamation of Santiago's sainthood. I wanted a copy of that magazine, but it cost 20¢ and I couldn't afford it, with 85¢ to my name to last me who-knew-how-long. Anyway, I had the story, I owned the story and its style; and for the next week or so, hitchhiking around the country, I talked about it with dozens of strangers who had also read it. There was even that farmer in the mountains of Pennsylvania, where I stopped off a day to help with hay baling, who read parts of

The Old Man and the Sea to his wife and children at the dinner table, after grace, before eating—but that's another story. When I finally went back to school, my English teacher read a little of it to the class and talked about it for a long time. It sounded like a different book; it was not the book I had read and had been discussing with truck drivers and waitresses and farmers. So I said nothing in that class. This, then, is one version of what *The Old Man and the Sea* was in 1952. It would seem now to be a different story altogether, and if, as *Time* magazine suggested (Dec. 7, 1992), the novel may have to be retitled *The Senior Person and the Sea,* it is surely a different age.

In recent years, in various academic settings—conferences and classrooms—I have heard Hemingway and/or Santiago charged with, and spuriously convicted of, the following grievous sins and crimes: 1) of inadequate "multiculturalism"; 2) of regarding Santiago's Cuban culture with the "Imperial Gaze" or the "Colonialist Gaze"; 3) of patriarchalism, of sexist aggression of the most flagrant DWEM variety; 4) of conflicted homosexuality (or was it homotextuality?), unwilling or unable to come out of the closet; 5) of "onanistic fantasy; 6) of a form of "parental abuse"; 7) of "ecocidal triumphalism"; and on and on goes the Contemporary Writ.[1]

Seeking some light in all this darkness, I turned to an issue of *The Hemingway Review* (12:1 [Fall 1992]), where I discovered evidence of yet another act of Hemicide: Robert Hogge's review of Gerry Brenner's 1991 critical volume on *The Old Man and the Sea,* in which Hogge announced that Brenner's study was "the best book I've read on . . . *The Old Man and the Sea.*" (Perhaps we can't argue with this since, at that time, it was the only book on *The Old Man and the Sea.*) Mentioning his initial resistance to Brenner's arguments, Hogge nevertheless goes on to praise the treatment of what Brenner calls Santiago's "egoism," "paternalism," "sexism," ecocidalism or "environmental nearsightedness"; his "feminization," "psychological confusions," "capitalistic consciousness," vindictiveness, fratricide, and macho pride; his "self-glorification" and "self-pity"; his pernicious influence on Manolin; his "latent homosexuality"; his insidious "passive-aggressive behavior"; and so on, through the jejune litany of the psychological primer and the current ABCs of the academically correct. For Brenner, it doesn't matter that—shall we say, generously—maybe five of fifty million readers might agree with any of this. For Brenner, there's nothing wrong with Santiago (and Hemingway) that five years of therapy, a subscription to *PMLA,* and attendance at MLA conventions and certain Hemingway Conferences wouldn't fix. Clearly, in Brenner's study and in much academic discourse, both Hemingway and Santiago are victims of *textual* harassment. The only thing to do with this laundry list of *-isms* is to render them *-wasms.* It's not that we haven't encountered this shock-schlock critical fast-food before; it's just that all of these tired old questions, these stale models of discourse, address issues that have outlived their uselessness.

Happily, however, there is some good news to report from the critical frontlines: the same issue of *The Hemingway Review* that carried Hogge's review of Brenner, for example, included a solid and useful treatment of Santiago as a Homeric hero (Kathleen Morgan and Luis Losada, "Santiago in *The Old Man and the Sea:* A Homeric Hero"). Also, the Hemingway session of the 1992 MLA convention that was devoted to a fortieth anniversary celebration of *The Old Man and the Sea* included three papers that substantially enhanced our understanding of the work: Allen Josephs's "Why Is Santiago Spanish?"; Kathleen Morgan's "Eating and Appetite in Homer and *The Old Man and the Sea*"; and Bickford Sylvester's "Cuban Ethnicity and Social Commentary in *The Old Man and the Sea:* The Neglected Dimension (Part II)." Morgan's essay extended and deepened our knowledge of Homeric resonances in Hemingway; Sylvester's essay presented invaluable details and stressed the specifically Cuban contexts of the work; and Josephs's essay skillfully navigated the question of Cuban models for Santiago and stressed, through his Canary Island background, Santiago's Spanishness.

On the one hand, if, as both Josephs and Sylvester cogently argue, Santiago's Cuban-Spanish ethnicity is crucial, perhaps we had better take an even closer look at his identity as a native of the Canary Islands. In fact, isn't it possible that Hemingway posits for his blue-eyed Santiago a background that is not necessarily Spanish at all, but true autochthonous Canary—that is, Guanche, the blue-eyed inhabitants of the islands who were there when first the French and then the Spanish came on their missions of conquest? Does it then signify and is it to Hemingway's point that these mysterious blue-eyed Guanches, these "strange" old people (the sources often note their strangeness), regarded suicide as honorable, preserved absolute respect for the dignity of women, and especially venerated the sun, moon, sea, and stars? That they believed that one of the Great Spirits lived on the snowcapped peak of Mount Teide (the highest mountain on Spanish soil), a mountain that fits Hemingway's description of the "white peaks of the islands rising from the sea," a bit of symbolic landscape as emblematic in this work as Kilimanjaro is in the short story?[2]

If, as has been suggested, Santiago may be from Lanzarote (as was one of his "models," Gregorio Fuentes) then we should know more about this island. It does not have snow-capped peaks, for example, nor, I am told, views of white peaks on neighboring islands. Lanzarote does have extraordinary caves—miles of underground galleries—where the Guanches would take refuge from Spanish marauders. It also has a rich *French* history, dating from 1334, when the Canaries were "rediscovered" by French sailors, and from the early 1400s, when blue-eyed Normans from La Rochelle established the first European settlements in the Canaries, when (blue-eyed?) Jean de Béthencourt was crowned king of the Canaries in 1404 and was much loved, so the story goes, by the native Guanches. As a Francophile I would love to prove that Santiago is really French, or French-Guanche, and I am reminded that Santiago de Cuba was settled by, and its culture influenced by, thousands of French emigrants in the late 1700s. However, in my reading of the novel, ethnicity—not the details of culture but *ethnicity*—is largely beside the point.

On the other hand, if our blue-eyed Santiago was from one of the more out-of-the-way Canaries, say, Goméra, where the Guanche *deus loci* is said to be the strongest and strangest and where the Guanche spirit of place lingers to this day, then Santiago may have grown up in the village of Santiago on Goméra, with the celebrated view of the snow-capped peak of Mount Teide rising across the water on Tenerife (a Guanche word meaning "snow capped mountain"). So perhaps we have both Homeric and Goméric resonances in *The Old Man and the Sea*. Moreover, it should be noted that the Canaries, and especially Goméra, are closely associated with Christopher Columbus; indeed, as the old saying has it, without the Canaries Columbus might never have discovered America. And the place in the Canaries where Columbus lingered the longest on his four voyages was Goméra—particularly in San Sebastian de la Goméra, near the village called Santiago. All of these reverberations add up to a reading of Santiago's Canary background that is more inclusive and richly resonant than, for example, Allen Josephs's conclusion that Santiago is from the Canaries because Hemingway wants to stress his Spanishness and because the Canaries join the three places Hemingway loved best in the world; Spain, Africa, and Cuba. Of course, Hemingway often varied and revised his statements of best-loved places, naming France on some occasions, Wyoming on others, and many other places; the point is that Hemingway loved all numinous places and was finely attuned to the spirit of place. And if we comprehend the Canary background fully, we must add French and Guanche influences—together with traces of Libyan, Berber, and Semitic—to the spirit of place thus evoked. Indeed, the entire Mediterranean world is thereby associated with Hemingway's Cuban protagonist, together with the sense of odyssey, voyage, pilgrimage, and discovery suggested by the matter of Homer, the matter of Columbus, and the matter of Santiago. If our strange, old, blue-eyed Santiago is even part Guanche, as these associations suggest, he is not just "pan-Hispanic," as Josephs asserts, but pan-Mediterranean, pan-Atlantic, pan-Euro-Afro-American. In fact, his panethnicity may be precisely the point.

Far more important than any of this is the primary reason, I believe, that Santiago is portrayed as from the Canary Islands, the most important, the best and earliest-known Canary identity, one to which Hemingway's creative imagination responded most profoundly. It is a Canary resonance that tells us precisely who Santiago is—and it has nothing to do with ethnicity. Remarkably, the force of this well-known Canary allusion has never been noted in Hemingway studies: the Canaries have long been celebrated in mythology and lore as the Fortunate Islands, the Isles of the Blest, the abode of the storied undead, the mortal heroes upon whom the gods confer immortality. Santiago's native place, then, is in the Islands of the Blessed, and Hemingway has conferred his immortality. This is the thrust of the Canary background that millions of readers understand, that my students, from China to France, New York to Kentucky, have immediately grasped in their blissful unconcern with ethnicity. This is the place-identity that a conductor of the Siberian Express understood, a man who, many years ago in the Soviet Union, mysteriously summoned me to the privacy of his compartment, where we sipped vodka and listened to his cassette recording of *The Old Man and the Sea* as he sighed about the Islands of Blessedness. Santiago's birthplace, and his ultimate "place" in literature, is the place of storied, immortal heroes. If this places Santiago properly and precisely, let us now try to name him eloquently and exactly.

> "You know about Santiago and you know the name is no accident."
> —Hemingway to Father Robert Brown, July 14, 1954

> "I prayed for you sincerely and straight in Chartres, Burgos, Segovia . . . Sorry not to have made the home office of Santiago de Compostela."
> —Hemingway to Bernard Berenson, August 11, 1953

Since the late 1970s, in the course of several essays and papers concerned with the pilgrimage theme in *The Sun Also Rises,* I have remarked in passing that one key to *The Old Man and the Sea* is provided if we understand that Santiago represents the culmination of Hemingway's lifelong preoccupation with the Pilgrimage of Santiago de Compostela. I have noted, for example, that although Jake Barnes is clearly a Compostelan pilgrim, he does not complete the pilgrimage, whereas Hemingway's Santiago does complete "the pilgrimage in a figurative or incarnational sense" (Stoneback 5). My concern here is to articulate whatever I may have meant when I wrote that sentence many years ago and to provide some evidence for such a reading of *The Old Man and the Sea.*

In 1954 Hemingway wrote to Father Robert Brown: "You know about Santiago and you know the name is no accident." This was at the beginning of an important correspondence of several years' duration, which had been initiated by Father Brown's general inquiries regarding Hemingway's Catholicism and specific inquiries about *The Old Man and the Sea.* We will focus here on that one telling sentence, where Hemingway is saying, in effect: "*You* know—that is, *you,* Father Brown, a priest with a sense of history and a knowledge of pilgrimage—*you* know, even if all the others do not know, about Santiago/Saint James/Saint-Jacques and the pilgrimage of Compostela. And *you* know—even if other readers are blind to the fact—that it is 'no accident,' that I have named my old Cuban fisherman after Saint James, and, more particularly, after the avatars of Saint James associated with Compostela."

So Father Brown knew about Santiago, and Hemingway knew—and, as informed readers, we need to know. To date, however, nothing of any substance has appeared in print concerning the ways in which the sense and sensibility of Santiago de Compostela informed *The Old Man and the Sea.* First, therefore, let's note briefly the facts of Hemingway's knowledge of Compostela. Even though Jake Barnes never finished the pilgrimage, Hemingway did, several times. Santiago was, for Hemingway, not just "the loveliest town in Spain" (Baker 186), but a shaping force in the patterns of both his life and his work. On June 24, 1929, for example, he wrote to Maxwell Perkins, noting that he is about to go to church for noon Mass, and, after the fiesta in Pamplona, he will "settle down in Santiago in August" (*SL* 299). (I remind the reader that, historically, the Pamplona Fiesta is one stage, one phase, in the carefully orchestrated pilgrimage to Compostela, which moves from religious festival to shrines to more fiestas, all across France and Spain; I also stress that there are no bullfights in Santiago, that loveliest Spanish town where Hemingway spent so much time.) Decades later, Hemingway's correspondence with Bernard Berenson, in the period of *The Old Man and the Sea* is replete with references to pilgrimage, to Compostela. On August 11, 1953, he tells Berenson that he prayed for him, "sincerely and straight in Chartres, Burgos, Segovia" but he is "sorry not to have made the home office" of Santiago de Compostela (*SL* 824; emphasis added). Two years later, on October 24, 1955, Hemingway is still writing to Berenson about Santiago, asking him if he likes the Portico de la Gloria, telling him he has been to Mass at the Cathedral, and noting that he stayed in Santiago "three summers trying to learn when I was working on my education" (*SL* 848). It is clear that Hemingway's knowledge of the matter of Santiago was extensive, his participation in the spirit of the pilgrimage profound. More important, for the reader of his fiction, is the use he makes of this in his work. I have argued in considerable detail that the deep structure of *The Sun Also Rises* is determined by the matter of Santiago and that we cannot connect truly with that novel at the deepest level (even at the surface level) if we do not bring to it some understanding of the Compostela Pilgrimage (Stoneback, *Reading Hemingway* passim). To what uses, then, does Hemingway put his knowledge of Santiago in *The Old Man and the Sea?*

The most obvious associations, some of which have often been noted, are those biblical resonances that link the old man, Santiago, to James the fisherman and the calling of St. James to apostleship. In the "fishers of men" passage from the Book of Matthew, for example, Jesus, at the sea of Galilee, sees "James the son of Zebedee, and John his brother, in a ship . . . mending their nets; and he called them" (4:21). Far more rarely noted, if ever, and far more pertinent to *The Old Man and the Sea,* is the passage from Luke concerning "the great catch of fishes" (5:1–11). There, you may recall, Simon Peter complains to Jesus that they have had bad luck, having fished all night long and caught nothing. Jesus tells Peter and James and John, "Put out into the deep" (or "launch out into the deep"). After going far out, they let down their nets and found a great catch, which left the fishermen "amazed" (or "astonished"). This tale of the great catch ends with Jesus telling the fishermen: "Do not be afraid; henceforth thou shalt catch men."[3] The situational and verbal parallels with *The Old Man and the Sea* are obvious: the bad luck of catching nothing; the injunction to "put out into the deep"; Santiago's drive, his compulsion, to go "far out" (28), perhaps "out too far" (120); and the similar amazement in response to the two great catches. Perhaps, too, there is an implicit apostleship in Santiago's situation, a "call" to be a "fisher of men" (e.g., to or of Manolin; to or of readers?). I will not argue that point here, for these biblical resonances are not, strictly speaking, the matter of Santiago with which Hemingway is most deeply concerned; his matrix of signification is primarily generated by Saint James of Compostela—by matter, that is to say, which is extrabiblical, which is specifically Catholic; and which concerns medieval legend, lore, and tradition.

Tradition holds that after St. James-Santiago was beheaded in Jerusalem, thus becoming the first martyred apostle, his body was transported by arduous sea voyage in a small open boat to the northwestern coast of Spain, near the site of what would become the city of Santiago de Compostela. At landfall, his body (and, in some versions, his boat, which is often a "stone boat") was held fast by a rock or stone which opened up to receive his body. The pagan queen of the region ordered twelve wild bulls to be harnessed to the stone to drag the relic into the sea. The bulls, however, were tamed by the sign of the cross and, in short, the pagan queen converted to Christianity and a shrine was created. We note here the landfall of Hemingway's Santiago, after his arduous sea journey in a small open boat, during which he worried much about becoming "unclear in the head" after a "strange" perception at the moment of the marlin's death (*OMS* 77). He pulls the boat up in the deserted harbor. And then—at the completion of this circular voyage/pilgrimage that has yielded a numinous vision—"he stepped out and made her fast to a rock" (120).

By the twelfth century, after the rediscovery of the tomb of St. James in 813, Santiago had assumed his full, complex identity, through the two principal configurations of St. James/St. Jacques/Santiago, the Pilgrim Saint for all of Europe, and Santiago Matamoros ("Moor-slayer"), champion of the Spanish armies in the reconquest of Spain for Christendom. In his manifestation as Santiago Matamoros, Patron of Spain, and one of the "Seven Champions of Christendom," he appears rather directly in *The Old Man and the Sea* as, in Hemingway's words, "Santiago El Campeón." For a long time after his epic struggle with and final conquest of the "great negro from Cienfuegos," everyone calls him "The Champion." The fact that Santiago becomes "The Champion" (in Hemingway's insistent upper-case) by virtue of his conquest of the "negro from Cienfuegos" constitutes a straightforward allusion to the identity of St. James as the Moor-slayer. However, Hemingway's Santiago grants his opponent his dignity and proclaims him "a fine man and a great athlete" (69–70). As I discern the patterns, then, Hemingway deliberately de-emphasizes Santiago Matamoros and emphasizes the avatar of Santiago that is the opposite of the knightly warrior-champion: the avatar evoking the feeling and vision, the humility and gentleness, the poverty, resolution and endurance of St. James the pilgrim.

Consider Hemingway's repeated references to the stars. On the first night at sea, the old man knows his location and direction "from watching the stars"; he repeatedly checks his course by looking "at the stars" (47). On the second night at sea, he watches the "first stars" appear and he knows that "soon they would all be out and he would have all his distant friends." He knows he must kill the great fish, but he is glad, he says aloud, "we do not have to try to kill the stars." He assures himself that he is "clear enough" in the head: "I am as clear as the stars that are my brothers" (74–77). These and other references to the stars function as a primary allusion to Santiago de Compostela, which has manifold associations with the stars. The popular derivation of Compostela is from *campus stellae,* the "field of the star," and the pilgrimage road to Compostela was known as the *via lactea,* the Milky Way, which pointed pilgrims toward the shrine of Saint James.[4]

In Hemingway's terms, then, Santiago the pilgrim-fisherman knows where he is and who he is ("brother" of the stars) because of the field of stars, the Compostela or *campus stellae.* But Hemingway also knows, as all students of Compostela do, that the more likely derivation of Compostela is from the Latin *compostum,* suggesting not only the "little graveyard" of Saint James, but death and the grave in general, and—perhaps for Hemingway's ear—the compost heap of dying, dead, and decaying matter that is the always-imminent destination of all nature, great fish and humble fisherman alike. The true pilgrim knows this well: that truth is why the pilgrimage is made.

At the heart of the "great strangeness" which is in the center of *The Old Man and the Sea* is what Bickford Sylvester calls "the heightened awareness of participation in nature's mysteries" (259); and the quintessential mystery of nature, I would add, has to do with the triumph of the human spirit. Hemingway and Santiago said it better: "A man can be destroyed but not defeated" (*OMS* 103). Pilgrims, above all others, know this truth of the spirit: pilgrims who suffer and endure much in their lonely journey through and struggle with nature; pilgrims who participate profoundly in "nature's mysteries"; pilgrims who seek expiation and redemption; pilgrims who sing the poetry of brotherhood, who practice humility and charity and compassion. The "great strangeness"—Hemingway's and Santiago's—is finally approachable only as mystery, through the discipline of mysticism, that mysticism which is a form of internalized pilgrimage, as pilgrimage is externalized mysticism.

There are many other details that resonate with the lore of Santiago. Think of Santiago's cramped hand, for example, and remember that Saint James, aside from being the patron of pilgrims, soldiers, horsemen, knights, peasants, and laborers, is also the patron saint of those, like Santiago with his cramped left hand, who suffer from rheumatism and arthritis (perhaps because of the aches and cramps associated with the long and physically demanding pilgrimage to Compostela). Since there is not space here to consider other pertinent allusions, it must suffice to declare that the primary strategy of allusion in *The Old Man and the Sea* reflects Hemingway's deep awareness and skillful narrative deployment of the pilgrim-saint of Compostela. We recall, too, that Hemingway's Santiago promises "to make a pilgrimage to the Virgin of Cobre" if he catches the great fish (65). We note that Nuestra Señora del Pilar, the virgin patroness of Spain who appeared to St. James on the banks of the Ebro, is associated with Santiago de Compostela. And fittingly, the Virgin of Cobre, Cuba's sacral image found floating in coastal waters in the early 1600s, is associated, first, with Santiago de Cuba where she was housed in the Cathedral of Santiago until 1677, and second, with Hemingway's Santiago, who has made the interior pilgrimage to the Virgin of Charity and promises the physical pilgrimage. Moreover, all of these avatars of Santiago and the Virgin are associated with the sea, with water. Yet the most intricate aspect of Hemingway's overall narrative strategy is, I suggest, that at the same time that he constructs a pattern of allusions to the universal matter of the Pilgrimage to Santiago, and to the local Cuban matter of Pilgrimage to the Virgin of Cobre, he presents the transcription of Santiago's actual pilgrimage at sea.

The pilgrimage motif was rounded off and underlined, extratextually, when Hemingway gave his Nobel Prize medal to the Virgin of Cobre. At a fiesta in his honor in San Francisco de Paula, with four hundred persons present (including forty-five fishermen of Cojímar), Hemingway presented his medal "to the Shrine of Our Lady of Charity of Cobre, patron of Cuba . . . It will be formally presented to the shrine in Santiago de Cuba September 8" (*The Catholic News,* August 25, 1956). To be more exact, the Sanctuary of Our Lady of Cobre is some twelve kilometers west of Santiago; and, to record precisely what Hemingway said and did that day, he gave his medal to the Virgin, not to her Shrine, not to the State: "Quiero dar esta Medalla," Hemingway said in his speech, "al Nuestra Señora la Virgin de Cobre" (August 1956). In that speech, more revealing than his Nobel Prize address, he also spoke of pilgrimage.

> "[Hemingway's] lifelong subject [was] saintliness."
> —Reynolds Price

> "This seems to be getting very solemn for the hour which is 0930 but then I have heard Mass at that hour in Santiago de Compostella [*sic*] . . . I stayed there three summers trying to learn when I was working on my education."
> —Hemingway to Bernard Berenson, October 24, 1955

In conclusion, I want to say a word about Santiago and saintliness. Some years ago, the novelist Reynolds Price made the observation that Hemingway's "lifelong subject" was "*saintliness.*" (141). Price believed, though, that this concern with saintliness was "generally as secret from [Hemingway] (a lapsing but never quite lost Christian) as from his readers" (141). Therefore, when I wrote to Price to thank him for his fine essay, I told him that I agreed that "saintliness" was indeed Hemingway's "lifelong subject," but, I insisted, Hemingway knew that very well; it was not a secret from him but from almost all his readers. I do not know whether I was thinking then of *The Old Man and the Sea,* which I am now inclined to call Hemingway's culminating and definitive study of saintliness. And I do not mean by that anything remotely resembling what Brenner seems to mean in the subsection of his study which he gives the title "Santiago as Saint" (32). Setting up categories of what he is pleased to regard as simplistic responses to *The Old Man and the Sea,* Brenner suggests that what he calls "new readers" will, at first, before the necessary skepticism is brought to bear, admire Santiago, "whose every act exhibits the altruistic behavior expected of a saint," who "exudes"—yes, he says *exudes*—"a strong religious sensibility," and who may seem to deserve, in the eyes of Brenner's imaginary, naïve "new reader," "the saint's halo" (32–33). One of the problems with Brenner's exudations regarding "Santiago as Saint" is that he shows no recognition of Santiago's complex associations with his namesake,

Santiago de Compostela, or even with the biblical Saint James.[5] Another problem is that he shows little comprehension of sainthood or saintliness, a status and quality that need to be addressed, apparently, in discussions of this novel.

My core notion is this: *The Old Man and the Sea* is a complex study of saintliness, not only in the way that it connects with the history and legend of a particular saint but in its deconstruction (for want of a better word) of Santiago de Compostela, not for purposes of debunking and dismissal but in order to reconstruct a version of the original, historical saint—anchored in time, immersed in nature, rooted in the bright particularity and dailiness of lived saintliness. That is to say, the old fisherman Santiago is Hemingway's version of Saint James the Fisherman grown old as a fisherman, not as an apostle; and he is also Hemingway's version of Santiago of Compostela, stripped of legend and lore, largely dissociated from his warrior avatar, presented in his fundamental human identity as pilgrim. Hemingway reconstructs the paradigm of sainthood, not to deny but to confirm, to reclaim the basic condition and state of beatification and canonization, the order of sanctity for which—as Hemingway's Church insists—all are eligible.

Finally, I nod to that dread category of discussion, over which critical wars have been fought and much ink has been exuded, and I utter the distasteful phrase which I have thus far rigorously avoided: Santiago as Christ-figure. The Christic associations are so obvious and so many that we need not mention them here. The reasons that so many critics have found the so-called Christ-figure pattern problematic or disturbing (see, for example, Brenner 37–38) are rooted, in particular, in an insufficient comprehension of Santiago and that name which was "no accident" and, in general, in a simplistic, ill-informed approach to literary texts, and to Christianity. Let me put this another way: 1) Santiago is *not* a Christ-figure; he is a Santiago figure; 2) allusions and resonances in literary texts are echoic overtones and undertones, not ironclad legal definitions or psychological case-histories or passport identities; Santiago may share some experiences and attributes with Christ, but he is not a Christ-figure—suggestion is not identity; and 3) in strict theological terms, which in their amplitude subsume and transcend mere sociological and psychological approaches to the matter, Christ participates in humanity just as Santiago participates in Christology or—in the words of Hemingway's Church—in the "Mystical Body of Christ," of which all are members incorporate through communion. Santiago may not be "religious," as he protests, but he is *devout.* And he knows about communion. Hemingway was pretty "religious" and very devout, much of the time. And without coming to rather exact terms with his religious and specifically Catholic thought and feeling, readers may sense, but are not likely to apprehend deeply, Santiago's state of blessedness.

. . .

Thus we leave Santiago, having properly *placed* him and *named* him: he is an immortal hero from the Isles of the Blessed, and an intentional reconfiguration of his namesake Saint James of Compostela. Simultaneously, he is a celebration of and a celebrant in the communion of all being, all nature, and an emblem of the dignity of working people, poor people, and of all who suffer and endure with courage, pride, humility, and compassion. That leaves just that extra quality of Santiago, his indefinable "strangeness." In his "strangeness" is his deepest saintliness. By whatever power granted me to beatify—and my power to do so, and yours, and every truckstop waitress's and truckdriver's, and every reader's is as infallible as the pope's—I submit Santiago as a candidate for veneration, for beatification, as the ultimate embodiment of Hemingway's values and vision. Canonization is another matter, requiring lengthy and rigorous examination and a few miracles, both in the Church and in literary circles. Maybe the miracles happen through the intercession of Hemingway's creative genius; maybe they happen every time a reader weeps for Santiago;[6] but in any case the verdict of history is about to come clear, through the all-but-universal approbation of millions and millions of readers worldwide, new readers and old readers and re-readers. And so I salute *Sant*-Iago, man, hero, mystic, pilgrim, saint, and undefeated fisherman of Cojímar.

Notes

1. These "charges" are drawn from my notes from twelve national and six regional conferences, and from classrooms and public lectures at four universities, between 1988 and 1995. Some of the papers, lectures, and discussions at these events were citing or simply parroting Gerry Brenner's study (discussed in the text); others were not. Obviously, since we began to hear such charges against Hemingway in the 1960s, and since such marginal and intensely politicized views grew ever more extreme throughout the 1970s and 1980s, we cannot blame such views on Brenner's 1991 critical study. However, his work does epitomize this vein of commentary.

2. For the most part, the information presented here regarding the Canaries and the Guanches is drawn from standard guidebooks—Baedeker's, Michelin's, and so forth—and from encyclopedias. This is deliberate, and very much to the point of Hemingway's likely knowledge of the Canaries, for these were precisely the sources he usually consulted.

3. Except for parenthetical citations of the King James Version, I quote here from the 1952 edition of the Douay-confraternity text of the Bible, because of its contemporaneity with *The Old Man and the Sea;* because Hemingway, as a Catholic, was likely to have consulted this version; and because the verbal resonances are more exact.

4. I have tried to refrain from citing any but the most widely known aspects of the matter of Santiago, details that are treated in most studies of the Pilgrimage and the

Saint of Compostela. Hemingway, I feel certain (but am as yet unable to demonstrate), seems to have known very well the source material on Santiago. In any case, the material cited here could be picked up in a day or two in Santiago, and Hemingway spent three summers there, "working," as he put it, "on my education"; the information also could have been obtained, for the most part, from standard guidebooks. For the student, useful points of entry to the matter of Santiago include Edwin Mullins, *The Pilgrimage to Santiago;* Marilyn Stokstad, *Santiago de Compostela: In the Age of the Great Pilgrimages;* and Brian and Marcus Tate, *The Pilgrim Route to Santiago.* Regarding the *campus stellae* derivation, it seems that Hemingway may have heard and pronounced Compostela in this fashion, since he often spells it "Campostella."

5. Oddly, the only saint that Brenner associates with Santiago is Saint Francis of Assisi, perhaps because he's the only popularized, media-hyped, politically correct saint he can think of, or, worse yet, because he assumes that Saint Francis may be the only saint his audience has heard of. I would hasten to point out that, over the years, a good number of my students, especially those with a Catholic background, have demonstrated that they know a good deal about Santiago and about his pilgrimage. As for the common perception, especially in American academic circles, that the pilgrimage is a thing of the past, an item of study for the medievalist, it is worth noting that an extraordinary renascence of the Compostela pilgrimage began during the twentieth century and has gathered momentum since about 1980. So it would seem that Hemingway was in the vanguard of this revitalization, this resurgence of the matter of Santiago. One might wish he had lived to see its most remarkable manifestation, World Youth Day, in August 1989, when Pope John Paul II addressed the pilgrims gathered at Compostela—more than half a million of them—an event variously characterized by the media as "the largest pilgrimage in history," "the largest gathering of young people in the history of Europe," "the largest public gathering in the history of Spain," and "the Catholic Woodstock." From my various peregrinations and sojourns along the pilgrimage route over the last five decades, I can attest to both its increasing popularity among true pilgrims and its growing trendiness as an occasion for travel articles, touristic outings, or fund-raising events by self-proclaimed atheists raising money for this or that cause. Indeed, the pilgrimage route to Compostela seems to be in danger of crossing into the terrain of the radical chic, flourishing with charlatans and con artists, vagabonds and poets—that is to say, it has returned to its medieval vitality as the world's highway of pilgrims, false and true.

6. There are widespread reports of tears for Santiago, of weeping over *The Old Man and the Sea;* indeed, it seems that in the 1950s such tears, softly falling, were general all over America. They were certainly general at the Finca, as numerous reports of prepublication readings by Hemingway's friends and guests attest. In conversations with Mary Hemingway and Bill Walton over the years, I heard numerous accounts of the persons who wept for Santiago in Hemingway's presence. Hemingway referred to this weeping in a number of letters; in one to Adriana Ivancich, for example, dated 3 Sept. 1952, just two days after publication in *Life,* he wrote that all kinds of people are calling him up about "*Old Man,*" and "everybody cries . . . I am very modest and good because I cried so many times myself (inside) when I wrote it." In earlier letters, he also told Adriana (as he did many others) that the book "has a strange effect on anyone who reads it and that it changes them some way and they are never the same" (12 Apr. 1952), and commented, "I have read the book more

than 200 times and it did something to me every time" (9 July 1952). I cannot testify to any personal tears for Santiago (except, as Hemingway said, inside). But I have seen students weep freely after reading aloud portions of the novel, and I do remember the shining wet eyes of that waitress and truck driver in the truck stop in the Ozarks where I stopped long ago, after they read *The Old Man and the Sea,* mostly aloud. Perhaps I should add that tears have always seemed somewhat suspect to me as a criterion for reckoning the power and greatness of literature; however, Hemingway and his friends report the tears, so I report them. Moreover, I am quite sure—oh yes, absolutely certain—that the tears here reported were miraculous tears, devout tears, tragic and joyful tears, cathartic and redemptive tears, tears far beyond the category of soap-opera tears, mere romantic or sentimental tears.

Works Cited

Baker, Carlos. Ernest Hemingway: A Life Story. New York: Scribner's, 1969.

Brenner, Gerry. *The Old Man and the Sea: Story of a Common Man.* New York: Twayne, 1991.

Hemingway, Ernest. Correspondence with Adriana Ivancich. Collection of the Humanities Research Center. University of Texas at Austin.

——. Correspondence with Robert Brown. Collection of the Humanities Research Center. University of Texas at Austin.

——. *Ernest Hemingway: Selected Letters, 1917–1961.* Edited by Carlos Baker. New York: Charles Scribner's Sons, 1981.

——. *The Old Man and the Sea.* New York: Scribner's, 1952.

——. Speech at honorary dinner, Aug. 1956. Item 683a. Hemingway Collection. John Fitzgerald Kennedy Library, Boston, MA.

Hogge, Robert M. "Review of *The Old Man and the Sea: Story of a Common Man,*" By Gerry Brenner. *Hemingway Review* 12.1 (Fall 1992): 88–90.

Josephs, Allen. "Why is Santiago Spanish?" MLA Convention. 27–30 Dec. 1992, New York, NY.

Morgan, Kathleen. "Eating and Appetite in Homer and *The Old Man and the Sea.*" MLA Convention. 27–30 Dec. 1992, New York, NY.

——, and Luis Losada. "Santiago in *The Old Man and the Sea:* A Homeric Hero." *Hemingway Review* 12.1 (1992): 35–51.

Mullins, Edwin. *The Pilgrimage to Santiago.* 1974. New York: Interlink Books, 2001.

Price, Reynolds. "For Ernest Hemingway." In *Ernest Hemingway.* Edited by Harold Bloom. New York: Chelsea House, 1985. 137–60.

Stokstad, Marilyn. *Santiago de Compostela: In the Age of the Great Pilgrimages.* Norman, OK: Univ. of Oklahoma Press, 1978.

Stoneback, H. R. "From the rue Saint-Jacques to the Pass of Roland to the 'Unfinished Church on the Edge of the Cliff.'" *Hemingway Review* 6.1 (1986): 2–29.

——. *Reading Hemingway's* The Sun Also Rises. Kent, OH: Kent State Univ. Press, 2007.

Sylvester, Bickford, "The Cuban Context of the *The Old Man and the Sea.*" *The Cambridge Companion to Ernest Hemingway.* Edited by Scott Donaldson. Cambridge, UK: Cambridge Univ. Press, 1996. 143–268.

"Papa" and Fidel

Cold War, Cuba, and Two Interpretive Communities

YOICHIRO MIYAMOTO

"I'm not a Yankee, you know."

—Ernest Hemingway at the Havana Airport, 1959.

Ernest Hemingway's 1952 novella, *The Old Man and the Sea,* portraying an old fisherman's mythic struggle with a gigantic fish, is an apolitical fiction as far as its thematic content is concerned. The milieu in which this novella was published, however, was highly political. *The Old Man and the Sea* appeared in the days of McCarthyism, when many writers were forced to abandon their political beliefs. Furthermore, the whole novella was published in *Life* magazine, whose major interest was in cold war politics rather than in literature of itself. Across the Gulf Stream, Fidel Castro's revolt against colonialism had just begun, and Hemingway's relations with Cuban revolutionaries continued all the way to the donation of his home in Cuba, Finca Vigía, to the revolutionary government. Publication of *The Old Man and the Sea* thus heralded the decades when cold war politics and global anticolonialism were articulated together.

Consideration of Cuba's cold war geopolitical landscape is sorely absent from U.S. scholarship on *The Old Man and the Sea.* As frequently as the novella is interpreted as a fable of one mode or another, even the old man's nationality can easily be forgotten. Except when it is occasionally discussed as a background of the novella, Cuba slips from critical attention in the United States.[1] Although Hemingway's presence in Cuba never escaped the attention of Hemingway biographers, his self-exile there—in contrast to his exile in Paris—has been curiously distanced from the interpretation of his literary works. The absence of Cuba from the map of Hemingway studies is all the more striking given that

Fidel Castro hailed *The Old Man and the Sea* as celebrating, if allusively, Cuba's struggle against U.S. imperialism. In an interview with Norberto Fuentes on February 6, 1984, Castro remarked that the message of *The Old Man and the Sea*—"A man can be destroyed but not defeated" (*OMS* 114)—has been "a slogan of meetings and marches, and has been the battle cry of the last twenty years of Cuban history" (quoted in Fuentes 531; my translation). This interview, included in the original of Fuentes's *Hemingway en Cuba*, has been mysteriously deleted from the heavily edited English translation available in the United States. For Castro, there was no distance between the novella and Hemingway's celebration of revolutionary struggle in *For Whom the Bell Tolls*. Castro's reading was, furthermore, echoed and perpetuated by such eminent Cuban scholars as Lisandro Otero and Mary Cruz. It is unfortunate that Fuentes's book has often been dismissed in the United States as a biography marred by minor inaccuracies; it actually opened the door to Hemingway scholarship in Cuba whose critical and ideological terrain stands in striking contrast.[2]

My goal here is not to argue for Cuban readings of Hemingway; to categorize literary responses by nationality is ultimately a lost cause. Yet my attention is irresistibly riveted by the ways in which U.S. readings and Cuban readings of *The Old Man and the Sea* so radically diverged during the cold war. The seemingly incommensurable gap between the two interpretative communities, the United States and Cuba, does not necessarily come from political biases that are extrinsic to the text. Rather, I would argue, it points to Hemingway's positioning within the text, oscillating and mediating between the United States and Cuba, between the colonial and the postcolonial. Hemingway himself reenacted this paradoxical stance outside the text in 1959, when, on his return to Havana Airport after the success of Castro's revolution, he kissed the Cuban flag and declared to the surrounding reporters: "I'm not a Yankee, you know."[3] I do not wish to suggest that Hemingway's life and text are simply (if vexingly) ambivalent toward Cuba. My point, rather, is that *The Old Man and the Sea* enables (and disables) both the U.S. and Cuban readings, thus allowing us to see the ways in which the colonial and the postcolonial are, in fact, not so much polarized as mutually reinforcing.

The Old Man and the Cold War

Appearing in 1952, at the height of the McCarthy era, Hemingway's *The Old Man and the Sea* was hailed in the United States as heralding Hemingway's "comeback." In the words of James Michener, in an editorial note in the August 25 issue of *Life* magazine, announcing *Life*'s forthcoming publication of

The Old Man and the Sea in the next number, "Old Man Hemingway . . . won back the championship" (186). *Life* magazine, where the novella first appeared, was committed to a campaign against "twisted" trends in American novels.[4] As James Steel Smith points out, *Life* editorial writers then "frequently addressed themselves to the question of alleged Communist leanings among American writers" and criticized the realism of "Mailer, Jones and the majority of modern war novelists" as depicting "solely the dirty surfaces of war" (28, 34). Their campaign against negative literary trends, observes Smith, extends all the way back to "Farrell, Sinclair Lewis, Dreiser, Norris, [and] Zola." (34). Papa Hemingway's mythic portrayal of the indomitable fisherman was precisely what *Life*, with its cold war editorial policy, was seeking. For the editors of *Life* magazine, *The Old Man and the Sea* was not only Hemingway's "comeback" from his unsuccessful *Across the River and into the Trees* (1950), which "hardly deserved the relish with which his critics and detractors put the boots to him when he was down" ("A Great American Storyteller" 20); the novella marked a "comeback" of American fiction from leftist political engagement.

Perhaps not coincidentally, Philip Young's *Ernest Hemingway* and Carlos Baker's *Hemingway: The Writer as Artist* were published in that same year. Young's seminal book placed Hemingway in the direct line from the writing of Mark Twain as part of the American mythic response to adversity. It thus institutionalized the apolitical reading of Hemingway, with the resulting effect of further distancing Hemingway's literary stature from prewar leftism. Aside from the notable exception of Keneth Kinnamon, who contends that Hemingway "had deep sympathy with the left, especially the revolutionary left" (159), U.S. critics since Philip Young have traditionally tended to focus on Hemingway's involvement with the national myth while dismissing his political engagement as naïve, if not totally irrelevant to his works.

Meanwhile across the Gulf Stream, through a different (though no less nationalistic) strategy, Cuban critics appropriated the novella for "revolutionary" Cuba. As Castro and Cuban critics proposed to read it, *The Old Man and the Sea* was less about recuperation than about a logical sequence from the leftism of the 1930s. Castro, as noted earlier, saw the message of *The Old Man and the Sea*—"A man can be destroyed but not defeated"—as a rallying cry of Cuban revolutionaries. Mary Cruz, echoing Castro's reading, is also adamant in arguing that Hemingway belongs to the Cuban people. "With unerring instinct, the people of Cuba always appreciated the worth of this American writer who, under cover of a careless attitude, observed with deep interest and affection the things of Cuba. Much to the displeasure of those who didn't know how or refused to interpret his writings correctly, and thus judge the man by them, there is the bust of Hemingway donated by the fishermen of Cojímar, and there is the museum in San Francisco de Paula, with a constant stream of visitors" ("Negation of Negation" 133).

Furthermore, Lisandro Otero claims in his monograph that Hemingway sincerely supported the Cuban Revolution: "Before the victory of the Cuban Revolution, and afterwards, Hemingway left various statements and testimonies of his support of Cuba and its social liberation process. With that he was doing nothing more than being consistent with his own past" (22; my translation). Otero clearly sees Hemingway's support of Castro's Revolution as being in line with his leftism during the 1930s. This is precisely the aspect of Hemingway's career that is downplayed in the United States, where *The Old Man and the Sea* is celebrated as a recuperation from Hemingway's past.

Cuban appropriation of Hemingway is not necessarily a bombastic gesture of chauvinism. Norberto Fuentes's *Hemingway in Cuba* gives evidence of Hemingway's close relationship with exiled Spanish communists in Cuba, including Doctor José Herrera Luis Sotolongo, Hemingway's personal physician and closest friend in Cuba.[5] Fuentes also cites the testimony of Roman Nicolau, a Cuban communist and veteran of the Spanish Civil War, that Hemingway, of all foreigners, "contributed most money to the Communist Party in Cuba" (188). Even a U.S. critic, Cary Nelson, suggests in his essay "Hemingway, the American Left, and the Soviet Union" that Hemingway stayed in contact with communists he met in Spain till 1953, a year after the publication of *The Old Man and the Sea* (42). In contradiction to James R. Mellow, who claimed that Hemingway's ties with Spanish communists ended in bitter disillusion by 1940, when *For Whom the Bell Tolls* was published, Nelson points out that Hemingway contributed to *Pravda* his statements in support of the Soviet causes in 1941, 1942, and 1943. Hemingway's last letter to Edwin Rolph, veteran of the Abraham Lincoln Brigade and a member of the Communist Party, is dated June 13, 1953.[6] Although Hemingway's relationship with the Communist Party may have been complex and variably nuanced, there is good reason to suspect that "evaluations [in the United States] of Hemingway's politics have been dominated by the Cold War ideologies" (Nelson, "Hemingway" 42).

Of course, Cuba's appropriation of Hemingway can be preserved only by downplaying the imperialist elements present in Hemingway's life and work; Hemingway's love of big game fishing and Daiquiris at El Floridita, for example, is flavored with imagery of U.S. imperialist pursuit of pleasures. But Mary Cruz dismisses this imagery as a sign of "his careless attitudes" ("Negation of Negation" 133). Also, in reading the closure of "The Snows of Kilimanjaro," Otero argues that the author-hero's arrival at Ngaje Ngai ("The House of God") does not symbolize Hemingway's escape from reality but rather signals his repudiation of U.S. capitalism. For Otero, Ngaje Ngai is an allegory of Hemingway's achievement in the socially aware novels he wrote in Cuba. Although it is not uncommon to equate Harry, the protagonist of the story, with Hemingway the artist, the Cuban critic's interpretation pushes it a step further: the leopard is Hemingway. Otero says that the leopard "had not wandered off," since Hemingway divorced Pauline Pfeifer and finished two books, *To Have and Have Not* and *For Whom the Bell Tolls* (34). The final chapter of Otero's book, "In Ngaje Ngai," concludes by saying "The leopard stepped into *Ngaje Ngai.*" In Otero's view, the author-hero's fictional arrival at Ngaje Ngai materializes into fact through the publication of *The Old Man and the Sea,* with which Hemingway "culminated all of his work into a great fable" (36). Otero's scenario, in which Hemingway's life in Cuba is an undistracted approach of the leopard to Ngaje Ngai, can be sustained only by ignoring Hemingway's epicurean lifestyle in Cuba.

In their respective ways, the two interpretative communities, the United States and Cuba, suppressed the traces of the relationship between the colonizer and the colonized across the Gulf Stream. Yet the gap in their readings of the novella, as I have suggested, does not speak to their political fissure. Instead it indicates Hemingway's positioning within the text, oscillating and mediating between the colonizer and the colonized, between their different social realities, and thus enabling (and disenabling) both the U.S. and Cuban readings. In the pages that follow, I take up key scenes in *The Old Man and the Sea* and demonstrate how Hemingway's text functions as a semiotic site where exchanges occur between the colonizer and the colonized. Through the dialogics of exchanges, *The Old Man and the Sea,* as I show, effects the reconfiguration of the (power) relationship between them but does not necessarily work to create equity. Rather, Hemingway's text displaces and mutates a violent hierarchy between them into a more empathic (hence ostensibly unproblematic) relationship of brotherhood.

Displacement of (Colonial) Violence

Unlike Herman Melville's Ahab and Moby Dick, Santiago and the marlin—and their relationship in particular—in Hemingway's novella are not created in terms of blatant antagonism. Hemingway does not, for instance, take the fisherman as subject and define the fish as the Other in need of subordination—a logic that justifies a unilateral violence on the part of the old man toward the game. Instead *The Old Man and the Sea* creates the moment of Santiago's intense, emotional exchanges with the marlin—exchanges that even evoke a bonding. The old man's violence to the fish is represented (if only linguistically) as an erotic bond between the fisherman and the game, the aggressor and the aggressed, fastened to each other by the harpoon line.

> "Fish," he said softly, aloud. "I'll stay with you until I am dead." (52)
> "Fish," he said, "I love you and respect you very much. But I will kill you dead before this day ends." (54)

Hemingway's text thus works to deflect the tensions and enmity (if any) between the aggressor and the aggressed.

Hemingway then unites the aggressor and the aggressed in pain—the "fish's agony" (93) and the old man's agonized body—as if the marlin is Santiago's mirror image. Toward the end of the battle, Santiago "took all his pain and what was left of his strength and his long gone pride and he put it against the fish's agony and the fish came over onto his side and swam gently on his side" (93). Even as the fisherman defeats the fish, then, Santiago is not a conqueror and master. He has killed his "brother" and "now [he] must do the *slave* work" (95; my emphasis). Hemingway's text goes on to suppress the violence of conquest on the part of Santiago. The moment Santiago kills the marlin, his "brother," Hemingway places him on the side of the aggressed, and Santiago emerges as the victim of the avarice of the sharks. In his classic essay "*The Old Man and the Sea*" (1955), U.S. critic Leo Gurko reiterates this rhetoric of displacement when he observes that "A sense of brotherhood and love, in a world in which everyone is killing or being killed, binds together the creatures of Nature, establishes between them a unity and an emotion which transcends the destructive pattern in which they are caught" (11–12). For Gurko, the destructive nature of the world is ultimately subsumed into "the profound harmony of the . . . universe" (12).

Gurko goes so far as to claim that "[e]ven the sharks have their place" in this universe, asserting that the Mako shark "shares the grandeur of the marlin" (12). Yet Hemingway's hauntingly real descriptions of the Mako shark disrupt such romanticized readings. The "destructive pattern" is inscribed in the physical presence of the shark in insistently material terms. "Inside the closed double lip of [the shark's] jaws all of his eight rows of teeth were slanted inwards. They were not the ordinary pyramid-shaped teeth of most sharks. They were shaped like a man's fingers when they are crisped like claws. They were nearly as long as the fingers of the old man and they had razor-sharp cutting edges on both sides. This was a fish built to feed on all the fishes in the sea, that were so fast and strong and well armed that they had no other enemy" (100–101).

Interestingly, Robert P. Weeks questions the zoological accuracy of this passage. Weeks points out that "only two rows of the shark's teeth are functional" and that "only the main teeth in the mid part of the shark's jaws are as long, slender, and sharp as Hemingway describes" (192). What Hemingway's realism in the passage above evokes, then, is not the zoological presence of the shark. Rather, it re-presents the violence inherent in the story, including Santiago's own. The shark's grotesque teeth are thus obliquely associated with "the old man's fingers," which killed the marlin. The aggressor's violence of conquest is no longer camouflaged by the bonding; it manifests itself and haunts the old man. The shark's ferociousness, furthermore, is virtually identified with the "well armed" imperial might that threatens to colonize the whole world.[7] Aggression in Hemingway's text is never subsumed into the mythic; it is somehow reinscribed into the realm of the real.

Displacement of violence is made complete and, at the same time, is revealed for what it is, when a U.S. tourist mistakes—or creatively misreads—the carcass of the marlin for that of a shark. "I didn't know sharks had such handsome, beautifully formed tails," she exclaims (127). The victim of predatory violence is finally conflated with the monstrous predator. In her eyes, there is no longer the distinction between the subject and the object of violence. When the tourist contemplates the rem(a)inder of violent conquest—a naked backbone—as an aesthetic object, the ending of Hemingway's text offsets violence and, at the same time, works to make what was ultimately a militant aggression appear aesthetic and apolitical. The U.S. tourist in Hemingway's text, then, is not so much an ignorant outsider to the combats unfolding in the narrative as a participant in the rhetorical network of the text that displaces and mutates the violence of conquest. Although her confusion itself derives from her linguistic problem, one should not miss the whole irony of the scene. The U.S. tourist's (mis)understanding of the Cuban waiter ultimately, and ironically, reveals the rhetorical strategy of displacement that penetrates the whole narrative, a strategy that works to mutate a colonial encounter with the Other into a more empathic (hence ostensibly unproblematic) relationship, deflecting and suppressing the "coercion, radical inequity, and intractable conflict" involved in the encounter (Pratt 6).

It is, I suggest, precisely this rhetorical strategy of displacement in Hemingway's novella that enables—and disables—both U.S. and Cuban readings. The readings of the two interpretive communities both reenact displacement, but in different directions. In the traditional U.S. reading of the text, for instance, Santiago's nationality is of secondary importance. *The Old Man and the Sea* is less a tale about a Cuban fisherman than it is a mythic parable about the tragic condition of the mankind. As Clinton S. Burhans Jr. summarizes, "Philip Young, Leo Gurko, and Carlos Baker have stressed the qualities of *The Old Man and the Sea* as allegory and parable" (446). American readers identify themselves with the Cuban Santiago while distancing themselves from the "unauthentic" female tourist from their own country. In empathizing with the Cuban fisherman, they participate in the same inverted logic that made Santiago feel the intense and potent bond with the marlin in spite of—or precisely because of—their antagonism. In a Cuban reading, the same logic works the other way around; for Cuban critic Mary Cruz, for example, the U.S. tourists are "Cuban": "The sky, the sea, the fish, and the birds that are part of the environment in the narration are Cuban. And 'Cuban'—precisely in the environmental sense—is the pair of American tourists who, at the end of the novella, show their ignorance and insensitivity" (Cruz 180–81; my translation).

The U.S. and Cuban readings, one mythic and the other nationalistic, both subsume the power relations across the Gulf Stream, deploying the same logic that informs Hemingway's text. The gap between the two interpretive communities, I repeat, does not come from the political fissure extrinsic to the text. Instead both communities are faithfully unfolding the intrinsic textual strategies.

I see the encounter between the Cuban fisherman and the U.S. tourist at the closure as a deconstructive moment in *The Old Man and the Sea* that supports—and at the same time undermines—the readings of both communities. At the ending of Hemingway's text, Santiago emerges both as a mythic hero in the U.S. imagination and as a national hero in the Cuban imagination. At the far end of the continuum of U.S. readings, Hollywood made the novel into a cold war film, starring Spencer Tracy as the Cuban Santiago—a film in which Ernest Hemingway made a cameo appearance as one of the onlookers of the hand-wrestling contest and Mary Hemingway appeared as one of the U.S. tourists in the closing sequence. At the far end of the Cuban continuum across the Gulf Stream, with Santiago's phrase "man is not made for defeat" as a rallying cry, Fidel Castro translated Hemingway's novella into revolutionary propaganda. While sustaining these readings, *The Old Man and the Sea* also stymies them. It undermines Castro's reading by pointing to the irony that Hemingway's sojourn in Cuba was inseparable from U.S. tourism, and that what reads as an anti-U.S. propaganda was written not by one of the Cuban fishermen but by a U.S. tourist who hires them. It also undercuts the U.S. readings by mocking the cold war–era readership that is compelled to displace the Cuban fisherman with a non-Cuban identity, even with Spencer Tracy.

Of course, this is not to suggest that *The Old Man and the Sea,* a text that (dis)enables both U.S. and Cuban readings, is simply ambivalent; instead, this exploration seeks to highlight the ways in which Hemingway's text functions as a transcultural space, in which different social realities are negotiated. It indicates what Mary Louise Pratt terms the "contact zone"—the space of "colonial frontier" (6)—where different cultures meet and negotiate their different social realities.

Kinds of Realism

The contest and negotiation between the two interpretive communities across the Gulf Stream raise the question of realism in Hemingway's text. In the United States—with the important exception of Bickford Sylvester's "The Cuban Context of *The Old Man and the Sea*," which calls for a reading that pays attention to the "topical and historical specificity" of Hemingway's writing (263)—*The Old Man and the Sea* is rarely discussed in terms of "realism." The symbolic, mythic mode of discourse that seemingly dominates the novella is emphasized in the U.S. readings, while the potentially realistic moments are significantly skirted. The interpretations of *The Old Man and the Sea* by Cuban critics, on the other hand, largely center around those realistic moments in Hemingway's text. Both Lisandro Otero and Mary Cruz see realism as central to Hemingway's writing. But once again, the interpretative gap, I suggest, does not speak to a gap between the two interpretative communities, for they do read Hemingway in dialogue, if in a covert and oblique way.

To take just one brief example here, Cuban critic Mary Cruz discusses Hemingway's realism by appropriating terminology from a U.S. critic. While admitting that *The Old Man and the Sea* is a mythic fable reminiscent of William Faulkner's "The Bear," Cruz nonetheless argues that Hemingway's text is geared toward upholding an "'extended vision' of reality," borrowing the term *extended vision* from Bickford Sylvester's earlier essay, "Hemingway's Extended Vision: *The Old Man and the Sea*" (1966). For Cruz, what is most commendable in Hemingway's text is its capacity for "learning reality and suggesting it in the smallest, most definitive details, which are primarily perceived through sight and sound" (Cruz 180–81; my translation). By "details" Cruz means Hemingway's ethnographical representation of Cuban folkways and dialects that are not consumable by U.S. tourism. Hemingway's "'extended vision' of reality," Cruz argues, problematizes and finally subsumes the imperial gaze itself. A U.S. scholar's words were thus used to support the Cuban reading. What is no less ironic, however, is that the U.S. scholar from whom Cruz borrowed, Bickford Sylvester (at least in his 1966 article), was not talking about realism in Hemingway's text; quite the contrary: he was arguing that the *mythic* "vision" in *The Old Man and the Sea* is "extended" from his earlier themes.

Indeed Cuban critics' emphasis on realism in Hemingway's text presents a striking contrast to mainstream U.S. readings that highlight the mythic, rather than the realistic, elements in the novella. But the mythic and the realistic readings, as I have suggested, are potentially not so much opposed as mutually constitutive and even reinforcing in the two interpretative communities. And this raises a certain possibility for rereading *The Old Man and the Sea*:

that Hemingway's text enables what may seem like two incompatible representational codes—the mythic and the realistic—within the same text. Departing from the traditional mode of realism, *The Old Man and the Sea,* I argue, leans heavily toward what is termed magic realism, a style that articulates the real and the magical at the same time. As Amaryll Chanady explicates, magic realism is a discursive site on which the binary between the Western subject and its "Other" dissolves and converges (140); it is a literary contact zone between the colonial and the postcolonial.

In seeking to account for Hemingway's realism, Cuban critic Lisandro Otero actually uses the term *magic realism.* Without specifying the source, Otero refers to John Brown's contention that Hemingway's text subscribes to magic realism, and claims that "Hemingway searches the world for symbolism that will help him to express his idea of the world" (39; my translation). Otero does not indicate any contextual link between Hemingway and Latin American magic realists. But Otero's reading of Hemingway seems to have particular affinity with the stylistic designation that has two separate origins across the Atlantic, an essay by a German art critic Franz Roh, "Magic Realism: Post-Expressionism" (1925), and the introduction by Cuban novelist Alejo Carpentier to his *El reino de este mundo* (The Kingdom of This World [1949]), with its oxymoronic implications of both the fantastic and the real, of the European as well as the non-European. Along with Mary Cruz, Lisandro Otero thus points up the realism and Cuban-ness of Hemingway's text but without dismissing the mythic and the symbolic mode in it.

Incidentally, Hemingway himself was concerned with ethnographical realism, if not magic realism, in *The Old Man and the Sea.* Generally indifferent to the filming of his novels, Hemingway made several suggestions to the studio with regard to *The Old Man and the Sea.* He was adamant that all Cuban fishermen in the film should be performed by native Cubans. He went so far as to fly to Peru, trying unsuccessfully to film the actual harpooning of a giant marlin in waters known for fish even larger than those in Cuba. Ernest Hemingway, able to tolerate Gregory Peck as the writer-hero in *The Snows of Kilimanjaro* and even happy with Gary Cooper as the hero of *For Whom the Bell Told* and *Farewell to Arms,* uncharacteristically resisted the language of Hollywood films by insisting on bringing non-Hollywood realism into the film production. Eventually Hemingway was "defeated"; Santiago was performed by Spencer Tracy and the sharks were portrayed by foam-rubber dummies. Yet clearly Hemingway did not want the ethnographical realism of the novella to be subsumed by the mythic.

In *Works and Lives: The Anthropologist as Author,* Clifford Geertz dwells on the crux of an ethnographical text, "the oddity of constructing texts ostensibly scientific out of experiences broadly biographical" (10). While maintaining scientific objectivity to the extent of evacuating the existence of the author, an ethnographical text has to inscribe in itself the presence of the author who claims, "I was not only there, I was one of them, I speak with their voice" (Geertz 22). Ernest Hemingway, especially in the 1950s, personifies this kind of ethnographic dilemma. The "being there" tradition of ethnographical writings has always dictated Hemingway's authorship. Hemingway was "there" on the Italian battlefield, in Spanish bullfight rings, in Kenyan highlands, and in the Spanish Civil War. Hemingway's major texts are inseparable from the dynamic literary figure that has "been there." During the 1950s, Hemingway pushed this dilemma to the limit. In the posthumously published *True at First Light* (1999), written during the 1950s shortly after the publication of *The Old Man and the Sea,* the author-protagonist, who is "burned dark enough to pass as a half-caste," feels that it is "stupid to be white in Africa" and fashions himself a quasi-ethnic pontifex of "Gitchi Manitou the Mighty" (199, 78). During the safari in 1953–54, Hemingway went so far as to adopt the hairstyle of Masai girls.

Returning to the Havana Airport in November 1959, after Fidel Castro's revolution, Hemingway reportedly kissed the Cuban flag and declared to the reporters, "I'm not a Yankee, you know." A writer who has "been there" at the forefront of U.S. expansionism thus declares that he is *not* an agent of that expansionism. Whether to read *The Old Man and the Sea* as a novella of mythic transcendence with an exotic setting (as U.S. critics have done) or as a postcolonial text with specific topical and historical settings (as Cuban critics have done), then, is beside the point. *The Old Man and the Sea* is an oscillating text written by a Yankee who not only has "been there" but also is "one of them," hence who is "not a Yankee."

Through my readings of the two interpretative communities, I have offered an argument that *The Old Man and the Sea* is a semiotic site or "contact zone" where exchanges may occur from both sides: the United States and Cuba, the imperial power and the fish-shaped island-nation once under U.S. control. *The Old Man and the Sea* enables (and disables) both the U.S. and Cuban readings, and the Gulf Stream or the sea that divides the two interpretive communities is not a gap but potentially a contact zone where interaction may occur, albeit in asymmetrical relations of power. Hemingway's sympathy for Castro's revolution may not have been as unequivocal as the Cuban revolutionary government wanted to believe; Hemingway's commitment to Castro was, after all, as questionable and as variable as his relationship with the Communist Party. Nonetheless, his statement that he was "not a Yankee" is a charged one. Whatever his political platform was, we know it can have come only from an author who has located himself in the contact zone. *The Old Man and the Sea,* hailed at once by the reactionary editorial board of *Life* magazine and by the revolutionary Cuban dictator, has brought to the fore the gulf between the two interpretative communities. And Hemingway inexorably urges us to read the gulf as an important space of encounter that may effect social changes.

Notes

I am grateful to Alicia Moyer for her help in researching and translating Cuban texts.

1. For discussions of the Cuban background of *The Old Man and the Sea,* see Bickford Sylvester, "The Cuban Context of *The Old Man and the Sea,*" and Patricia Dunlavy Valenti, *Understanding* The Old Man and the Sea *: A Student Casebook to Issues, Sources, and Historical Documents.*

2. Michael Reynolds, in his review of *Hemingway in Cuba,* advised the readers to "discount these minor flaws and read the book for what it is: a treasure trove of new data and the most important biographical study we have of Hemingway's final years" (344–45). For alleged inaccuracies in Fuentes's book, see also Walter Houk, "Lessons from Hemingway's Cuban Biographer, with a Note on the Introduction to *Hemingway in Cuba* by Gabriel García Márquez."

3. Typically, this episode is not mentioned in major U.S. biographies of Hemingway, except for Michael Reynolds's three volumes, while it has a place in a three-page chronology of Hemingway's life in the pamphlet of Museo Ernest Hemingway in Cuba. Gabriel García Márquez also refers to this incident in his introduction to Fuentes's book.

4. An unattributed editorial entitled "A Great American Storyteller" delineates the importance of Hemingway's comeback as follows: "[*The Old Man and the Sea*] is a tragedy, but it tells of the nobility of man. . . . If he has influenced any of the twisted young men now writing fiction, he hasn't influenced them enough in this respect." See "A Great American Storyteller," *Life* 1 Sept. 1952: 20.

5. U.S. critic Stephen Cooper questions the credibility of Fuentes's account. He contends that Fuentes is motivated by eagerness "to have the renowned Ernest Hemingway as a partisan to his cause" and that Fuentes's argument is based largely on "often inconsistent and contradictory stories" (127). As a prime example of the book's unreliability, Cooper cites Fuentes's recounting of Herrera Sotolongo's story that Hemingway was accused of being a communist during the McCarthy period. Cooper refutes the veracity of this anecdote on the grounds that Mary Hemingway and Carlos Baker mention no such stories, and that it is unconceivable that such charges against Hemingway could go unreported in the United States, as both Hemingway's life and McCarthy's hearings were closely covered by the U.S. media (128). Cooper's argument, however, seems to ignore the FBI file on Hemingway, already declassified by the time of his book's publication. According to Jeffrey Meyers, the FBI kept a 124-page file on Ernest Hemingway from 8 Oct. 1942 to 25 Jan. 1974, documenting the bureau's fluctuating suspicion that Hemingway maintained ties with communists (215). Given the cold war cultural imperative to promote Hemingway as one of the literary representatives of American values, it is questionable that the U.S. biographers of Hemingway, including Carlos Baker, were totally free of the kind of bias of which Cooper accuses Fuentes.

6. This letter, written by Hemingway to Rolfe on 13 June 1953, is reproduced in *Remembering Spain: Hemingway's Civil War Eulogy and the Veterans of the Abraham Lincoln*

Brigade, edited by Cary Nelson (Urbana, IL: Univ. of Illinois Pres, 1994), 33–35. In this letter, Hemingway gives Rolph permission to read his 1939 Spanish Civil War eulogy, "On the Americans Dead in Spain," at a meeting commemorating the seventeenth anniversary of the outbreak of Spanish Civil War.

7. Hemingway's use of figures in the quoted passage accommodates, if it does not justify, Fidel Castro's idiosyncratic reading of the famous motto that appears two pages later: "A man can be destroyed but not defeated." For Castro, as I have pointed out, this motto is none other than the rallying cry of the Cuban revolt against U.S. imperialism.

Works Cited

Burhans, Clinton S., Jr. "*The Old Man and the Sea:* Hemingway's Tragic Vision of Man." *American Literature* 31.4 (1960): 446–55.

Chanady, Amaryll. "The Territorialization of the Imaginary in Latin America: Self-Affirmation and Resistance to Metropolitan Paradigm." In *Magical Realism: Theory, History, Community.* Edited by Lois Parkinson Zamora and Wendy B. Faris. Durham, NC: Duke Univ. Press, 1995. 125–144.

Cooper, Stephen. *The Politics of Ernest Hemingway.* Ann Arbor, MI: UMI Research, 1987.

Cruz, Mary. *Cuba y Hemingway en el gran río azul.* Havana: Ediciones Union, 1981.

——. "Hemingway and Negation of Negation." In *Hemingway in Cuba,* by Norberto Fuentes. Edited by Larry Alson; translated by Consuelo E. Corwin. Secaucus, NJ: Lyle Stuart, 1984.

Fuentes, Norberto. *Hemingway en Cuba.* Havana: Editorial Letras Cubanas, 1984.

Geertz, Clifford. *Works and Lives: The Anthropologist as Author.* Palo Alto, CA: Stanford Univ. Press, 1995.

"A Great American Storyteller." Editorial. *Life* 1 Sept. 1952: 20.

Gurko, Leo. "*The Old Man and the Sea.*" *College English* 17.1 (1955): 11–15.

Hemingway, Ernest."From Ernest Hemingway to the Editors of *Life.*" Letter. *Life* 25 Aug. 1952: 186.

——. Letter to Edwin Rolfe, 13 Jun. 1953. In *Remembering Spain: Hemingway's Civil War Eulogy and the Veterans of the Abraham Lincoln Brigade.* Edited by Cary Nelson. Urbana, IL: Univ. of Illinois Press, 1994. 33–35.

——. *The Old Man and the Sea.* 1952; reprint, New York: Charles Scribner's Sons, 1980.

——. *True at First Light: A Fictional Memoir.* New York: Scribner, 1999.

Houk, Walter. "Lessons from Hemingway's Cuban Biographer, with a Note on the Introduction to *Hemingway in Cuba* by Gabriel García Márquez." *North Dakota Quarterly* 68.2–3 (2001): 132–55.

Kinnamon, Keneth. "Hemingway and Politics." In *The Cambridge Companion to Ernest Hemingway.* Edited by Scott Donaldson. Cambridge, UK: Cambridge Univ. Press, 1996. 149–69.

Meyers, Jeffrey. *The Spirit of Biography.* Ann Arbor, MI: UMI Research Press, 1989.

Nelson, Cary. "Hemingway, the American Left, and the Soviet Union: Some Forgotten Episodes." *The Hemingway Review* 14.1 (1994): 36–45.

Otero, Lisandro. *Hemingway.* Havana: Cauldrons de la Cassia de Las Americas, 1963.
Pratt, Mary Louise. *Imperial Eyes: Travel Writing and Transculturation.* London: Routledge, 1992.
Reynolds, Michael. "Review of *Hemingway in Cuba* by Norberto Fuentes." *American Literature* 57 (1985): 344–45.
Smith, James Steel. "*Life* Looks at Literature." *The American Scholar* 27.1 (Winter 1957–58): 23–42.
Sylvester, Bickford. "The Cuban Context of *The Old Man and the Sea.*" In *The Cambridge Companion to Ernest Hemingway.* Edited by Scott Donaldson. Cambridge, UK: Cambridge Univ. Press, 1996. 243–68.
Valenti, Patricia Dunlavy. *Understanding* The Old Man and the Sea: *A Student Casebook to Issues, Sources, and Historical Documents.* Westport, CT: Greenwood Press, 2002.
Weeks, Robert P. "Fakery in *The Old Man and the Sea.*" *College English* 24.3 (1962): 188–92.

Into the Terrain of the Bull

Hemingway's "The Undefeated"

ANN PUTNAM

In his *Reader's Guide to the Short Stories of Ernest Hemingway,* Paul Smith suggests that the story "The Undefeated" reveals a "pattern" of action that would come to "[serve] Hemingway well in later fiction" (108). Though Smith does not specifically mention *The Old Man and the Sea,* his comment is significant because it implies that there is indeed an overreaching pattern evident in Hemingway's fiction from the very beginning. I would like to suggest that there is a strange and provocative connection between the form and vision of "The Undefeated" and *The Old Man and the Sea,* two works written thirty years apart but that tell essentially the same tale. That the tragic vision came so early and with such fully rendered awareness reveals the astonishing strength and unity of Hemingway's creative vision present from almost the very beginning. Seen in the context of Hemingway's developing short fiction of the twenties and early thirties, "The Undefeated" appears to be an anomaly in every way. It is a strange story in several respects. We find it in the third collection of stories, *Men Without Women* (1927), but it was written in the fall of 1924, a year before the publication of *In Our Time,* and first saw publication in a German periodical in the summer of 1925, then in *This Quarter* a few months later. The dates are important because they reveal that Hemingway was working on the story a year before the publication of *In Our Time.*

What is so striking about this story is that with its linear unfolding it prefigures *The Old Man and the Sea* during a time when Hemingway was experimenting with quite a different form: lyric, sketch-like stories revealing a different sort of heroism—a heroism found in the posture of holding steady, waiting for the end with quietude and dignity. These stories suggest a nihilism that assumes the inevitability of catastrophe and the impossibility of any significant action with which to oppose it: in story after story blows fall unexpectedly and without reason upon characters whose only reaction is a dazed and bewildering silence.

In these lyric stories, characters learn to hold steady against the chaos and pain of existence by exhibiting a gesture of defiance, however small, in refusing to lose control: Nick building his camp and fishing the stream with precision and love; the major returning to the machines he knows will never heal him; Ole Andreson lying, fully dressed, waiting for the end; the old man in the café watching the shadows of the leaves against the light. These are characters who learn to hold themselves with dignity and grace through the creation of their own clean, well-lighted places. Thus the Hemingway protagonist confronts the overpowering presence of the thing called *nada* in his walk home late into the night, or in the black form of a raging buffalo, or in the tangled mysteries of the swamp, or in two men with an odd bulk under their overcoats—in whatever it is that keeps him awake all night listening to the radio, or staying late at the cafe, or seeking oblivion from the point of a needle. With its mode of indirection, the lyric form provided Hemingway with the perfect vehicle for these stories of tenuous holds and motionless posturings, a perfect form for a nihilistic vision that precludes the possibility of meaningful action.

Yet "The Undefeated" reveals a fully formed vision of the tragic nature of human existence that emerges once protagonists move out of their long-suffering, careful stances and on toward ends they themselves have made. They meet disaster head on, knowing they have helped bring it about, even while they have prevailed over it. Here Hemingway fashions a classical pattern of struggle against fate, defeat on one level but triumph on another.[1] What results is not only a conventional, linear structure but a fulfillment of the tragic potential latent in the lyric stories. Here the protagonist takes an active stance against what is always the inevitability of defeat. Catastrophe comes as much from Manuel Garcia's decision to act as from the way things are. His decision to persist, against all reason, in saying "'I am a bullfighter'" brings him both triumph and defeat. It anticipates Hemingway's move from the lyric to the linear story years later, and prefigures the shift from nihilism to tragedy that is the key thematic and formal movement in the progression of Hemingway's short fiction.

"The Undefeated" introduces a protagonist who risks everything in a confrontation with the very forces that would destroy him, illuminating a tragic vision in which the futility of human endeavor becomes, finally, a belief in one's ability to wrest meaning from chaos through created action. For this kind of action, a linear form that observes an Aristotelian notion of narrative was required. Rather than revealing truth in an instant of time, as the lyric story does,

"The Undefeated" tells its truth in a sequence of moments that unfolds in syllogistic fashion. Here the protagonist, taking some kind of action against coming defeat, becomes as responsible for his fate as circumstances are.

In Hemingway's short stories there are three postures protagonists may assume: they may retreat through denial, madness, or opiate; they may learn to hold steady with control and style; or, much more rarely, they may risk the "tragic adventure" (*IOT* 155), going out past all other people in defiance of human limitation. In "The Undefeated," the act of defiance is no symbolic gesture with only private meaning but a gesture played out in such a way that it precipitates the very misfortune the clean, well-lighted place was constructed to avoid. Private ritual now becomes public spectacle, as the imaginative construct of the clean, well-lighted place becomes an actual game with its own set of rules. The rush of the black bull becomes both a metaphoric figure for the disorder and danger of existence and a real danger for the game player who confronts it. Thus through the metaphor of the game Hemingway fashions a mode for the objectification of forces which in everyday life are too scattered to be plainly beheld.

The arena of the bullfight provided Hemingway with the perfect setting for the development of his tragic sense. From this design, centuries old, as formulaic and intricate as a classical ballet, comes this artifice, in time, yet timeless in its repetition, and as such a striking paradigm for the tragedy of the human condition. The bullfight, in its purity and created form, becomes a place where honor, dignity, and courage could be made visible in the poetry of the sequence. The ritual of the bullfight becomes an objective correlative for the tragic experience which contains both inevitable death and the active struggle against it. In the matador's control and manipulation of the bull, in this brilliantly executed series of calculated risks, a stay is found against the chaos of the real world, where wounds come unexpectedly and for no reason. Thus the bullfight is both real and artificial. It may serve as a metaphor for the writer, a mode of catharsis for the spectator, but for the bullfighter, for Manuel Garcia, it is something infinitely real. To stay in the lighted circle of the arena is the whole point of Manuel's story. Outside it his life is meaningless. "I am a bull-fighter," he says, and the whole story could be read as proof of that statement. Outside the bullring Manuel knows that "it was all a nothing and a man is nothing too" (*SS* 383).

Thus the bullring becomes like the café: a clean, well-lighted place where the darkness beyond the lighted circle can be confronted according to rules and, for the moment, beaten. Here darkness comes in the form of a big, black bull who may kill but for whom death is certain. The rules of the bullfight insist that the bull must die. In what manner he is killed becomes the only variable, and here is where the tension of playing the game lies. The principal action of "The Undefeated" occurs at night, as Manuel secures only a position in a night bullfight, or *novillada.* The yawning circle of light in the center of the bullring emphasizes the artificial quality of this created form. This well-lighted circle is rimmed by darkness, holding an audience Manuel can neither see nor control. And it becomes a visual statement of the relationship between the created form of the clean, well-lighted place and the forces of darkness just beyond. It is the bull that represents the dark terror in this drama choreographed to subdue it.

Yet "The Undefeated" is a complex story in its presentation of the tragic pattern, for the heroism of the story is threatened by both the presence of an alternative stance and by the comic potential hovering at the edges. For Hemingway gives us not one protagonist but a *pair* of protagonists, and through the contrast between them we can see the extraordinary innovation, both thematically and formally, that this story represents. In undercutting the very courage that is at the heart of the story, Hemingway is working as close to the bull as a fine matador. He presents two protagonists—one who stands firm and the other who braves a risky advance into the terrain of the bull.[2] In the sharp-edged contrast between Manuel and Zurito the picador, Hemingway creates a graceless moment that in the end shows the stuff of true grace under pressure.[3] This distinction clearly illustrates the reach of Hemingway's vision, present from the beginning, and marks the path toward the tragic adventure that would reach its deepest affirmation in *The Old Man and the Sea.*

Like Hemingway's ancient mariner, Manuel is presented as well past his prime, working under extreme conditions, degraded, made awkward and graceless through age. Again and again Manuel attempts to drive the sword between the shoulder blades of the bull, an uncanny echo of Santiago's repeated attempts, almost thirty years later, to raise the fish out of the ocean.[4] Both Manuel and Santiago have stepped outside the clean, well-lighted place that marks the landscape of mastery and control, and in essence, have entered the "terrain of the bull."[5]

However, one of the chief differences between the two works is tonal. As with his use of the character Zurito, Hemingway undercuts the potential heroism of the story through the intrusion of comic moments at key points within it. It is a daring strategy. Throughout the story, the formal cadences of stylistic repetition are contrasted with the comic in the awkwardness of the very action that style describes. In this, Hemingway plays the tonal aspects of the story as closely as he does the thematic ones, because the potential for comedy is present from the beginning. This particular kind of bullfight, the *novillada,* has certain comic aspects traditionally associated with it. There are the "Charlie Chaplins" who precede the bullfight, performing a burlesque of the *corrida* itself: "Around the edge of the ring were running and bowing two men dressed like *tramps* followed by a third in the uniform of a hotel bell-boy who stooped and picked up the *hats and canes thrown down onto the sand* and tossed them back up into the darkness" (245; my emphasis). Hemingway's choice of the *novillada* for the setting is a daring one: from the beginning this carnival atmosphere almost transforms Manuel into a clown for whom we may feel great sympathy but no tragic sense. From the beginning Manuel is identified with the buffoon. "You in the Charlie Chaplins?" asks one of the waiters (240).

Hemingway also permits comic elements to intrude at other points in the narrative. Ineffectual picadors account for more circus-like mood. Here the repetition in the stylistic sequence barely controls the comic potential: "Finally the bull charged, the horse leaders ran for the barrera, the picador hit too far back, and the bull got under the horse, lifted him, threw him onto his back. . . . The picador, now on his feet, swearing and flopping his arms. . . . *And the bull, the great black bull, with a horse on his back, hooves dangling, the bridle caught in the horns. Black bull with a horse on his back, staggering short-legged, then arching his neck and lifting, thrusting, charging, to slide the horse off, horse sliding down*" (252; my emphasis).

In the last act of the bullfight, Hemingway again permits the intrusion of a comic note. After Manuel has unsuccessfully attempted to kill the bull, it turns, then charges one of the dead horses covered with canvas, hooking the canvas to one of his horns: "[The bull] charged Fuentes' cape, with the canvas hanging from his splintered horn, and the crowd laughed. Out in the ring, he tossed his head to rid himself of the canvas" (261).

Positioned between Manuel's first and second attempts to kill the bull, this sequence illustrates the tight tonal control and balance Hemingway was working for. All these elements—the "Charlie Chaplins," the picadors, the bull with the canvas on his horn—prefigure the comic potential in the drama of the final moments of the narrative, when Hemingway allows Manuel to become a Charlie Chaplin too. Manuel runs toward the bull and then falls back, his sword turning end over end into the crowd, provoking the laughter that becomes part of the humiliation he must endure and part of his final heroism. But the use of stylistic repetition creates an intensity in the prose that also elevates Manuel's graceless moments into genuine pathos, acquiring a grace even in their gracelessness: "He hit the ground and the bull was on him. Manuel, lying on the ground, kicking at the bull's muzzle with his slippered feet. Kicking, kicking, the bull after him, missing him in his excitement, bumping him with his head, driving the horns into the sand. Kicking like a man keeping a ball in the air, Manuel kept the bull from getting a clean thrust at him" (261). In both the stylistic and structural repetition, Hemingway creates a pattern of foreshadowing that prepares for the tragic unfolding of events. The narrative reveals a tightly knit progression toward a conclusion as inevitable as the unalterable sequence of the *corrida* itself, for although the story is called "The Undefeated," it is permeated with defeat.

The story is divided into three separate scenes. The bullfight is divided into three acts: the *tercio de varas,* the planting of the pics; the *tercio de banderillas,* the planting of the banderillos; and the *tercio del muerte,* the death of the bull with muleta and sword.[6] The *corrida* pattern illustrates the ways in which theme and structure mirror one another, for Manuel's defeat is as carefully choreographed as is the bullfight sequence itself. The first act of the bullfight involves the preparation of the bull by the picadors in an effort to slow him down for the final killing in the third act. In the first scene in Retana's office, the conditions for Manuel's comeback are determined. They prepare for his defeat in the arena as surely as a skilled picador prepares the bull for the kill. Retana finally agrees to put Manuel, just out of the hospital, into a *novillada.*[7] But Manuel is reluctant to be a substitute in this bullfight where the picadors are inferior and the bulls more dangerous. "'That was the way they all got killed,'" he says (237). As Hemingway explains in *Death in the Afternoon,* the bulls in a *novillada* are often "larger and more dangerous" than those used in a regular bullfight, being those bulls that are "refused by the stars of their profession. It is in the *novilladas* that the majority of the bullfighters who die in the ring are killed each year" (427). When Manuel pleads with Retana to put him in a regular bullfight, arguing, "'They'd come to see me get it,'" Retana tells him, "'They don't know who you are anymore. . . . Why don't you get a job and go to work?'" But Manuel insists, "'I don't want to work. . . . I am a bull-fighter.'" Throughout the interview, hovering above them like some grotesque omen, is a black bull's head. "Manuel looked up at the stuffed bull. He had seen it often enough before. He felt a certain family interest in it. It had killed his brother, the promising one, about nine years ago" (236–37).

The second scene of the narrative and the second act of the bullfight present a repetition, with variation, of the first. The second act, consisting of the planting of the *banderillos,* is designed to complete the work of slowing the bull begun in the first act with the pics. In the second scene of the narrative, Manuel goes to a café where he hopes to meet his friend Zurito, the picador. The waiter, noticing his *coleta* and his age, mocks him, pretending to mistake him for one of the clowns. But the coffee-boy senses the disrespect and looks away. When Zurito arrives, he echoes what Retana had said: "'Why don't you cut off your *coleta?* What do you keep doing it for?'" But Manuel answers, "'I've got to stick with it, Manos'" (243).

The third act of the bullfight and the third scene of the narrative confirm the pattern of defeat begun in the first two scenes. For Manuel, the third scene provides both the final humiliation and the final triumph, his defeat becoming the very basis of his victory in all its inglorious disorder. In most of Hemingway's lyric stories, fate delivers the blow. Circumstances decree that the young wife will die, that love will perish, that the pain will not abate. In this story, too, fate decrees that Manuel is too old, too ill, and the bulls far too dangerous. But here, circumstances only partly determine what happens: Manuel contributes equally to his defeat in his desire to push beyond human limitation.

The bullfight sequence consists of a varying series of three repeated actions: a retreat from the bull, a holding still against his rush, and an advance into the bull's terrain. The three kinds of movements can be seen as metaphorical extensions of the attitudes characters assume toward life, where wounds are inevitable and only the circumstances are variable. In this story Manuel Garcia makes all three kinds of moves. In the *tercio del muerte,* Manuel completes a series of veronicas judged "acceptable" by the critic (249). However, the critic calls the second series "vulgar," rating "no applause," for Manuel "side-steps" (253) at the last moment to avoid contact with the bull. In *Death in the Afternoon,* Hemingway explains how the veronica is "tricked by the man making a side-step as the bull charges . . . [then] by the man putting his feet together once the horn has passed . . . and leaning or stepping toward the bull once the horn has passed to make it look as though he had passed the horn close" (460).

But there are other directions in which Manuel moves. He gathers his will and stands firm against the rush of the bull:

> Manuel turned as the bull came and raised the muleta so that it passed over the bull's horns and swept down his broad back from head to tail. The bull had gone clean up in the air with the charge. *Manuel had not moved.*
>
> The bull recharged as the pase natural finished and Manuel raised the muleta for a pase de pecho. *Firmly planted,* the bull came by his chest under the raised muleta. Manuel leaned his head back to avoid the clattering banderillo shafts. The hot, black body touched his chest as it passed. (258; my emphasis)

After the work with the cape has been completed, the third act of the bullfight, the *tercio del muerte,* the death of the bull, commences. Here "the bull is faced by only one man, who must, alone, dominate him by a piece of cloth placed over a stick, and kill him from the front, going in over the bull's right horn to kill him with a sword thrust between the arch of his shoulder blades" (*DIA* 98). A bullfighter may, if he knows some tricks, cheat the requirements and kill the bull easily and more safely by avoiding the dangers at the tip of the right horn. Yet Manuel's honor prevents him from taking the easier way. As Hemingway explains of another Manuel in *Death in the Afternoon,* "Now at any time he could have, without danger or pain, slipped the sword into the neck of the bull, let it go into the lung or cut the jugular and killed him with no trouble. But his honor demanded that he kill him high up between the shoulders, going in . . . over the horn, following the sword with his body" (77–83).

Manuel tries five times to kill the bull. On the sixth he is successful.[8] In his first attempt, Manuel's sword hits bone and buckles high into the air. The bull charges the dead horse, hooks the canvas on his horn and the crowd laughs. For a moment it is as though we are seeing the Charlie Chaplins again. The second attempt ends the same way. This time the bull bumps Manuel and pushes his face into the sand. The progression becomes both more comical and more dangerous.

But Manuel's ordeal is a public one, and the forces he must overcome include not only the danger of the bull but the crowd high up in the darkness. Manuel's isolation, the hostility of the audience, the humiliation of his awkward movements, all merge into the final pattern of defeat that is part of the sequence begun in Retana's office. It is something out of which Manuel must fashion his triumph. Critical to Manuel's role as performer, as game-player, is the presence of an audience. Various characters in the story observe Manuel's performance and comment on it. Zurito's appreciation of Manuel's courage is balanced against the judgment of the bullfight critic who is, like the audience, only "second string," who is "slightly bored" with the whole thing, and who drinks warm champagne from a bottle, which he eventually tosses into the arena. He is poignantly juxtaposed with Manuel, who is also a "substitute," who drinks water from a "heavy porous jug," who is giving the performance of his life, and who is hit on the foot by the bottle thrown by the critic.

In "chapter 14" of *In Our Time,* Hemingway describes the moment in which Villalta the bullfighter becomes one with the bull and the audience through the triumphant enactment of the timeless ritual of the *corrida.*

> When he started to kill it was all in the same rush. The bull looking at him straight in front, hating. He drew out the sword from the folds of the muleta and sighted with the same movement and called to the bull, Toro! Toro! and the bull charged and Villalta charged and just for a moment they became one. Villalta became one with the bull and then it was over. Villalta standing straight and the red hilt of the sword sticking out dully between the bull's shoulders. Villalta, his hand up at the crowd and the bull roaring blood, looking straight at Villalta and his legs caving. (*IOT* 105)

It is the ideal moment: bull, matador, and audience come together in a communal celebration of victory over the forces of death. For Manuel in "The Undefeated," it is too late to know this kind of unqualified triumph. Yet it is the moment against which Manuel's actual achievement is measured. On Manuel's third attempt, the bull refuses to charge. "The bull's eyes watched it [the muleta] and turned with the swing, but would not charge. He was waiting for Manuel" (262). As Hemingway explains, the *novillada* is dangerous precisely because the bulls are "defective" in some manner—behavior, vision, size, horn, proportions. It is precisely here that Manuel steps outside the sequence, leaves the well-lighted place that marks his own terrain, and enters the terrain of the bull. "Manuel was worried. There was nothing to do but go in" (262). Because the bull will not budge, Manuel must leave the place of control and enter the far more dangerous terrain of the bull. To kill the bull on this night, Manuel must risk the tragic adventure. As Jake Barnes explains in *The Sun Also Rises,* "as long as the bull-fighter stays in his own terrain he is comparatively safe. Each time he enters into the terrain of the bull he is in great danger" (213). So Manuel gathers himself and rushes at the bull. But again the sword does not go in. "There was the bull. He was close to the barrera now. Damn him. Maybe he was all bone. Maybe there was not any place for the sword to go in. The hell there wasn't. He'd show them" (263).

For the fourth time Manuel drives in upon the bull, and now the sword buckles, flying end over end into the crowd. It is then that the cushions begin to come down out of the darkness. It is over one of these cushions that Manuel trips as he makes his fifth run at the bull, feeling the horn go into his side as he grabs for the horn, then riding backward, "holding tight onto the place" where the horn had gone in. "He got up coughing and feeling broken and gone" (264). But there is the bull, impassive and unmoving as ever. "'Don't be a fool,' someone says" (264). Yet for the bullfighter there is nothing to do but advance and confront the bull. The next action confirms the simplicity and truth of Manuel's assertion: "I am a bull-fighter": "Manuel drew the sword out of the muleta, sighted with the same movement and flung himself onto the bull. He felt the sword go in all the way. Right up to the guard. Four fingers and his thumb into the bull. The blood was hot on his knuckles *and he was on top of the bull*" (264; my emphasis).

Thinking he ought to salute the president, Manuel finds instead that he is not standing at all but sitting in the sand looking at the dead bull. He starts to get up, begins to cough, and sits down again. Someone comes and pushes him up. Although we see the sequence of events from Manuel's eyes, Hemingway also permits us to see Manuel as we would sitting high up and looking down at a little man in the center of a great bullring. It is a perspective that undercuts the clarity we expect to find in the presentation of a hero.

In the end scene we see Manuel lying on the operating table, looking up at the picador Zurito, massive and looming, standing above him. The contrast between Manuel and Zurito is nowhere more evident than at this moment.

Through this contrast, Hemingway isolates the single quality that distinguishes one posture from the other. Certainly both are heroes of a kind. From the first, Hemingway distinguishes Zurito from the other picadors through his great size and his careful professionalism. The other waiting picadors talk, but "Zurito said nothing. He had the only steady horse of the lot. . . . He had already, since he had mounted, sitting in the half-dark, in the big quilted saddle, waiting for the passeo, pic-ed through the whole corrida in his mind. The other picadors went on talking on both sides of him. He did not hear them" (246).

"'Why do you do it? Why do you keep on?'" Zurito had asked Manuel (243). He does not seem to understand Manuel's answer any better at the end than he did originally. In having the good sense to quit, to go no place where control may be lost, Zurito shows the courage to stand firm in the presence of the bull. Graceful and imposing, Zurito's strong and unfaltering presence brings to mind other heroes who fashion a cool style from holding steady—Ole Andreson, Nick in "Big Two-Hearted River," the old waiter, Cayetano the gambler, and perhaps even another old warrior who also has no illusions, living in a holding pattern of graceful control, Count Mippipopoulos of *The Sun Also Rises.* All have learned to accommodate with style, risking nothing that might unbalance them. "'One should not place himself in a position to lose,'" the major of "In Another Country" explains, a lesson he has learned after he has lost everything. "'Find things [one] cannot lose'" (271). Just holding steady takes a powerful act of will, and one had best not risk anything that might loose the fragile hold. Risking loss is what Nick of "Big Two-Hearted River" cannot do. He cannot enter the swamp and bear the inevitable loss that comes from leaving the clean, well-lighted place. Thus Nick's journey stops just short, for he knows that "in the fast deep water, in the half light, the fishing would be tragic" (231).

However Manuel's posture is different. Zurito had pleaded with him to give it up. "'It isn't right . . . You ought to get out and stay out.'" But Manuel insists, "'I got to stick with it, Manos, I've tried keeping away from it. . . . I got to do it'" (243). What is it that compels him to keep on, knowing the probable cost? The young waiter of "A Clean, Well-Lighted Place" had been "all confidence." The young bullfighter called Fuentes is all confidence too. "[He] came running along the barrera toward Manuel, taking the applause of the crowd. His vest was ripped where he had not quite cleared the point of the horn. He was happy about it, showing it to the spectators. He made the tour of the ring. Zurito saw him go by, smiling, pointing at his vest" (256). Never having known the pain of a horn wound in the side, Fuentes can afford to be "all confidence." He has yet to know the cost of his obsession. But Manuel knows all too well what it costs to say, "'I am a bull-fighter.'" When the wound comes, Manuel recognizes the old familiar sequence—the rush across the ring to the infirmary, the electric lights above the operating table, the scalding pain inside his chest. "They had put something over his face. It was all familiar. He inhaled deeply. He felt very tired. He was very, very tired" (265–66).

It is not "confidence" that drives Manuel, against all reason, to confront the bull, which on this night is all too big and dangerous. In his heroic inflexibility, Manuel refuses to quit the arena that defines him. If he is following a "code," it is one that surely leads to destruction. Yet what is outside the arena? Manuel would be nothing outside the arena of the bullfight. He is almost that even with his *coleta* and this black bull, who is all horns and bone. What impels Manuel to continue is his determination not to become "displaced," his refusal to be "torn away from [his] chosen image of what and who [he is] in this world" (Miller 149). It is this, Arthur Miller claims, that evokes the "tragic feeling": when we are "in the presence of a character ready to lay down his life, if need be, to secure one thing—his sense of personal dignity" (148). In a world in ontological disorder, self-definition becomes the only possible way to meaning. But neither is it pride that keeps Manuel rushing at the bull the fourth time, the fifth time, the final time. Pride has long since been burned away by the pain and humiliation, and by the loss of dignity the awkward moments have stripped away.

In the contrast between the bullfighter and the picador in "The Undefeated," Hemingway defines the distinction between the nihilism implicit in holding steady against inevitable blows and the tragic stance that emerges from a protagonist's unwillingness to let holding steady be enough. Yet Hemingway seemingly abandoned this venture into the tragic arena in his short fiction for more than ten years, until the mid-1930s, when he once again explored its possibilities in the African stories. When he had created the outline of the tragic encounter so early on, why did Hemingway avoid it during all those intervening years? Why did the lyric form come to dominate virtually all of his stories?

There are several reasons. When Hemingway began his experiments in form, the lyric mode was the emerging structure as he saw it, looking as he did to Pound, Anderson, and Joyce. Hemingway, who had begun as a poet, was instinctively drawn to the subtlety and power that could come from this mode of indirection, which submerged the narrative within constellations of images that seemed to halt the time-governed urgings of the narrative. And so he had apparently wanted to master what he considered the newer, more experimental form of the lyric story, with its tonal subtleties and luminous effects. We can see this clearly in a letter Hemingway wrote to Ernest Walsh on January 2, 1926, in which he expresses uncertainty about his bullfight story, which Walsh had accepted for the second issue of *This Quarter*. Hemingway writes that he had re-read the story twice and still found it unsatisfactory:

> I thought it was a great story when I wrote it. Don't think I am vacillating or doubtful about my stuff and do not, for instance, think it is a hell of a lot better story than my well known contemporaries can write. But the hell of it is that I am not in competition with my contemporaries but with the clock—which keeps on ticking and if we figure out some way to stop our own particular clock all the other clocks keep on ticking. For instance, of the two I would much rather have written the story by Morley Callaghan. Though, to him, the Bull fight story will be much the better story. Oh Christ I want to write so well and it makes me sore to think that at one time I thought I was writing so well and was evidently in a slump. Callaghan's story is as good as *Dubliners*. (*SL* 187)

In another letter to Walsh dated a month later, on February 1, 1926, Hemingway writes that he had rediscovered that "'The Undefeated' *is* a grand story and I'm very proud I wrote it" (*SL* 192). This "vacillation," as he called it, came in part from his desire to write in the lyric mode, sensing, as he must have, the great difference between lyric and linear structures. Callaghan's story, printed just after "The Undefeated" in *This Quarter*, is a fine story in the lyric tradition, called "A Girl with Ambition." Another reason Hemingway apparently preferred the lyric form came from his sense that the philosophical stance of disillusionment and graceful resignation was in some important way less risky than that of active opposition. But what does a writer risk who accepts the implications of a vision demanding that action be taken against inevitability and that that very action be given directly? If we look for a moment longer at the two protagonists of "The Undefeated," we can see how, in a metaphoric sense, they emblemize the structures of the two story forms competing for dominance in the Hemingway aesthetic. Zurito, who is positioned just at the edge of the scene as its watchful observer, is contrasted with the more dangerous posture Manuel assumes in the center of the action, where he risks the very control Zurito manages to retain.

Hemingway was well aware of the dangers of attempting to endow a protagonist with tragic characteristics. To present unqualified heroic action would risk not only a terrible sentimentality, but a falsification of his vision, which insists that victory is as limited as defeat is inevitable. But by presenting his protagonist in comic, humiliating postures in contrast to the dignity of Zurito the picador, Hemingway undercuts the very premises he wishes to affirm. And in doing so he achieves the tragic dimension. Yet had Hemingway undercut his presentation of Manuel too much, the matador would have appeared not tragic, but only pathetic.

Hemingway the writer takes as many risks in drawing Manuel as does Manuel himself when he leaves the safety of his own terrain for the terrain of the bull.

Manuel will either triumph or go down to defeat in the bull ring before an audience, where, under the brilliant arc-lights, his every gesture is exposed. Thus it is with the writer when he risks a tragic structure that brings the story out into the open through a direct rendering of the sequence of motion and fact. The strategies Hemingway employed in "The Undefeated" outline clearly the great risks he took thirty years later in his linear unfolding of the old fisherman's tale, with all the attendant dangers of sentimentality and falsification. The little man on the operating table struggling to keep his *coleta* is transformed thirty years later into the old fisherman who lies with arms outstretched, dreaming of the lions.

And so Hemingway wrote stories of catastrophe, stories revealing the world as he saw it: brutal and unyielding, yet beautiful as well. But he hid the catastrophe at the bottom of his great iceberg, in the shadows of his portraits, preferring the still, mysterious surfaces of the lyric to the restless, urgent demands of a linear narrative. He created protagonists who wait for the catastrophe to come, or who hold steady in the bewildering silence after, fixed to the terrain of the clean, well-lighted place, graceful posturings rendered in elliptical fragments and brilliant images. Later, when his protagonists take up action, they move out of their watchful, waiting stances toward catastrophes of their own making, even while they have triumphed over them.

And to what end? To reveal emotions that are perhaps more safely positioned in the shadows of suggestiveness. To unmask truths too terrible to tell, yet telling them anyway. When Hemingway accepted the implications of telling the stories of protagonists who act rather than react, and the risks of using the structures in which these actions are embedded, then both form and vision came together in a perfect union that produced not only "The Undefeated" but also "The Short Happy Life of Francis Macomber" and "The Snows of Kilimanjaro"—a union that reached its apotheosis in *The Old Man and the Sea.*

For Hemingway, the ultimate test of courage is how one performs when control is lost, when luck has gone bad, when everything is lost except the one thing not lost—the irreducible sense of *I am* that Manuel imposes upon the darkness. In every way, we can see how closely this early story is related to *The Old Man and the Sea.* Both Santiago and Manuel have gone out beyond all people, beyond the clean, well-lighted places, out into the swamp where they have both, in a sense, hooked fish impossible to land. Both Manuel and Santiago suffer the indignity of both private and public failure, in agonizing moments of loss of control. Santiago knows the pattern of inevitability he begins when he hooks the fish in waters outside the boundaries of control. It is where the big fish stays, but it is also where the sharks wait. Likewise, Manuel knows what will happen when he enters the terrain of the bull. For a bullfighter there is nothing else to be done but to go in. “And what beat you?” the old man thinks. “‘Nothing,’ he said aloud. ‘I went out too far’” (133).

In Hemingway’s world of unexpected blows and certain defeat, it is only by risking everything that one can gain a measure of triumph. Either way, the story ends in death. But it is only by saying, then let it be *here,* that one can take some meaning from it. Let it come blowing this bridge, which will count for nothing. Let it come even now, on this African plain, when it would be, finally, most propitious to live. Or let it come with this strange black bull who has only bone where the soft place should be. Thirty years before the story of an old man and a great fish, Hemingway told the story of an aging bullfighter who wrests triumph out of defeat, and fashions a momentary stay against the dark. Both bullfighter and fisherman are truly of the “undefeated,” and both are at the very center of a complex but sustaining vision, part and parcel of the same creative whole.

Notes

1. In *The Tragic Art of Ernest Hemingway,* Wirt Williams includes a fine description of Manuel as a “tragic” character who reaches “redemption,” even “transcendence” (90–91).

2. Since Philip Young defined the “code hero,” as distinguished from the “Hemingway Hero,” in his groundbreaking study, *Ernest Hemingway,* and later in *Ernest Hemingway: A Reconsideration,* most critics at some point note Hemingway’s use of a *pair* of characters in the short stories, though with differing views. Earl Rovit calls them the “tutor” and the “tyro”(53–57); Joseph DeFalco, the “father-son” (198); Leo Gurko, “the open figure” and the “hidden figure”(175–203); and Jackson Benson, the “protagonist of courage” and simply “the protagonist”(129–49), to name several. This debate has had its day and though most critics have moved on or rather built upon these distinctions, it remains a useful model to start from. However they are labeled, they call attention to recognizable pairs of characters whose relationships determine the form and effect of the stories they inhabit. The essential dynamic between the pair is often something more complicated than this binary way of thinking would suggest.

3. Not all readers, of course, see Manuel’s actions as “heroic” or Manuel as “hero.” In fact, it is tempting to see Zurito as the hero of the story, and the rightful bearer of the title of the story. Representative of this familiar position is Scott Donaldson’s fine article, “Implications of Narrative Perspective in Hemingway’s ‘The Undefeated.’” He explores the thesis that Manuel’s supposed victory is so consistently undercut by other perspectives in the story (Retana’s man, the bullfight critic, the audience, and, most importantly, Zurito the picador) that Manuel emerges as no hero at all, neither heroic nor undefeated, but instead not only an embarrassment but a danger to both Zurito and the other bullfighters, as well as defrauding the public of its right to a genuine performance. Donaldson argues that it is Zurito, in his undiminished stature, dignity, and courage, who is the truly undefeated character. Yet this argument perhaps does not recognize Hemingway’s

purpose in contrasting the two, for Hemingway provides this other, equally admirable protagonist in order to firmly define the stance Manuel assumes.

4. Melvin Backman's essay "Hemingway's The Matador and the Crucified," written in 1955, remains to my mind the quintessential essay and the first to look in depth at the comparison between Santiago and the matador figure, principally Pedro Romero. Philip Young makes this comparison in 1966, in *Ernest Hemingway: A Reconsideration* (124–25), as do others subsequently.

5. See also *DIA* 455–56 for an explanation of the importance of terrain or position and the accompanying dangers.

6. For a description of the function of each of the three acts, see Hemingway's account of bullfighting, *Death in the Afternoon,* pages 434–36, 386, 454, and 423, in that order. Hemingway explains how "the first act is the trial, the second act is the sentencing, and the third the execution." See *DIA* 98.

7. Hemingway describes the conditions of the *novillada* or nocturnal, and also its audience: "The admission to a novillada is usually about half that of an ordinary corrida." This fact suggests that the audiences are "second rate," as well as the critics assigned to review them. See *DIA* 426–29.

8. Here Hemingway describes the ordeal of Manuel Garcia Maera in his six attempts to kill the bull, the account upon which the story of the fictional Manuel is modeled. See *DIA* 77–83. For a description of the bulls which are used in the *novilladas,* see the same pages.

Works Cited

Backman, Melvin. "Hemingway's The Matador and the Crucified." *Modern Fiction Studies* 1 (Aug. 1955), 2–11.

Benson, Jackson J. *Hemingway: The Writer's Art of Self-Defense.* Minneapolis, MN: Univ. of Minnesota Press, 1969.

DeFalco, Joseph. *The Hero in Hemingway's Short Stories.* Pittsburgh, PA: Univ. of Pittsburgh Press, 1963.

Donaldson, Scott. "Implications of Narrative Perspective in Hemingway's 'The Undefeated.'" *Journal of Narrative Technique* 5 (1972): 1–14.

Gurko, Leo. *Ernest Hemingway and the Pursuit of Heroism.* New York: Thomas Y. Crowell Company, 1968.

Hemingway, Ernest. *Death in the Afternoon.* Lyceum Edition. New York: Charles Scribner's Sons, 1960.

——. *Ernest Hemingway: Selected Letters, 1917–1961.* Edited by Carlos Baker. New York: Charles Scribner's Sons, 1981.

——. *In Our Time.* New York: Charles Scribner's Sons, 2003.

——. *The Old Man and the Sea.* New York: Charles Scribner's Sons, 1952.

——. *The Short Stories of Ernest Hemingway.* Scribner Library Edition. New York: Charles Scribner's Sons, 1966.

——. *The Sun Also Rises.* Scribner Library Edition. New York: Charles Scribner's Sons, 1954.

Miller, Arthur. "Tragedy and the Common Man." *New York Times,* 27 Feb. 1949. Reprinted in *Tragedy: Vision and Form,* edited by Robert W. Corrigan. San Francisco, CA: Chandler Publishing Co., 1965. 148–51.
Rovit, Earl H. *Ernest Hemingway.* New York: Twayne Publishers, 1963.
Smith, Paul. *Reader's Guide to the Short Stories of Ernest Hemingway.* Waterville, ME: G. K. Hall, 1989.
Williams, Wirt. The Tragic Art of Ernest Hemingway. Baton Rouge, LA: Louisiana State Univ. Press, 1981.
Young, Philip. *Ernest Hemingway.* New York: Holt Rinehart and Winston, 1952.
———. *Ernest Hemingway: A Reconsideration.* University Park, PA: Pennsylvania State Univ. Press, 1966.

Islands in the Stream

Death by Drowning

Trauma Theory and Islands in the Stream

KIM MORELAND

Islands in the Stream has attracted relatively little attention from readers and critics, in part because of its posthumous publication and vexed composition history.[1] But such explanations do not hold up for *A Moveable Feast,* embraced by readers and critics alike, and *The Garden of Eden,* which has garnered great critical attention and even encouraged a reinterpretation of the Hemingway canon. *Islands'* relative lack of popularity thus requires additional explanation. The unsympathetic nature of the novel's protagonist, Thomas Hudson, may help in this regard. He is a hard man to like, and we cannot escape him in this novel, which focuses almost exclusively on his actions and thoughts. We not only observe him from the outside but also are almost claustrophobically located within his thoughts. He is the novel's Jamesian center of consciousness, and we are granted extraordinary access to his interiority. His unsympathetic nature therefore colors our reading experience. Moreover, as the novel progresses, he grows not more but less sympathetic, and so we experience not relief but an increase in the tension of dislike. We grow increasingly uncomfortable as we follow—indeed, intimately accompany—Hudson on his journey through the novel, which ends not with a catharsis but with a dying fall. Reading *Islands* is a depressing and enervating experience not redeemed by sympathy, which helps to explain why neither readers nor critics have embraced the novel.

However, if we read *Islands in the Stream* through the lens of trauma theory, our experience of Thomas Hudson will change. *Islands* is a narrative of profound loss marked by uncanny repetition. Though Hudson is unable to integrate his traumatic past into his present and thereby afford himself a future, trauma theory will enable us to understand and sympathize with him rather than rejecting him in distaste.

In *Unclaimed Experience: Trauma, Narrative, and History,* Cathy Caruth asserts that "trauma describes an overwhelming experience of sudden or catastrophic events in which the response to the event occurs in the often delayed, uncontrolled repetitive appearance of . . . intrusive phenomena" (11). Noting that Freud "describes a pattern of suffering that is inexplicably persistent in the lives of certain individuals," she adds that he "wonders at the peculiar and sometimes uncanny way in which catastrophic events seem to repeat themselves for those who have passed through them" (1). In her discussion of Freud, she further notes that "these repetitions are particularly striking because they seem not to be initiated by the individual's own acts but rather appear as the possession of some people by a sort of fate, a series of painful events to which they are subjected, and which seem to be entirely outside their wish or control," such that "the experience of a trauma repeats itself, exactly and unremittingly, through the unknowing acts of the survivor and against his very will" (2).

Hudson's traumatic experiences are prominent in the novel, as are the uncanny repetitions he experiences. He has two failed marriages, and he obsesses about the failure of his first marriage and about his first wife, whom he wishes he had never left and who makes an unlikely appearance in the second section of the novel. He subsequently marries a third time during the course of the novel—in fact, in the white space between the first and second sections of the novel ("Bimini" and "Cuba," respectively), which encompasses the passage of about seven years—but this marriage too is unhappy, and he and his third wife are estranged. She is only an absent presence in the novel, nameless, never actually appearing except in his thoughts and, very occasionally, his conversation. His two younger sons—David and Andrew—are killed in an automobile accident in France with their mother, as Hudson learns via telegram at the end of the first section—and these deaths gain resonance from the focus of the first section on Hudson's holiday with the boys at his home in Bimini. His oldest son, young Tom, who shared the holiday with his half-brothers, is killed in action during World War II, his plane shot down over the English Channel by a flak ship, again during the white space between the first and second sections; we learn this only in the second section—and indeed, not until halfway through this section does Hudson mention young Tom's death. Hudson himself is mortally wounded in the third section ("At Sea"), while he is on voluntary submarine-hunting duty in the Caribbean with a crew of irregulars, troubled outsiders all.

While such a constellation of traumatic incidents would typically evoke compassion in the reader, Hudson's reactions limit this response. He silently acquiesces to the unlikely suggestion that young Andrew was driving the automobile and caused the fatal accident, effectively blaming Andrew for his own death and that of his brother and mother. This disturbing response gains resonance from Hudson's troubled and complicated relationship with Andrew, whom he identifies as "a bad boy," "a boy born to be quite wicked," and "a devil" (*IS* 53), and whom he seems at a basic level to dislike.

Hudson's obsessive reliving of his first marriage—a marriage that he chose to end—and his profound regret at the loss of his first wife is undercut by his behavior with her when she appears in Cuba during the second section. Though they share loving moments and make love, their encounter soon degenerates into arguments and rancor, undermining the fantasy that all would have been well if he had not originally left her. When she asks about young Tom, their son, he first lies to her, saying, "He's fine" (*IS* 318), but when she presses, "Tell me. Is he dead?" he responds curtly, "Sure" (*IS* 319).

Hudson is also pressed into sharing the news of Tom's death with a few others, but he is unable to express his emotions or accept consolation, and he rigidly limits conversation about Tom, escaping into bouts of drinking and into his sub-hunting adventures. When his acquaintance Ignacio Natera Revello brings up young Tom in casual conversation in the bar, Natera (and we readers) learn for the first time about Tom's death. Natera says, "I've known you and your boy Tom for years. By the way how is he?" to which Hudson replies merely, "He's dead." When Natera appropriately responds, "I'm so sorry. I didn't know," Hudson responds oddly: "That's all right. . . . I'll buy you a drink" (*IS* 262). Hudson's response is guardedly detached: "He could feel it all coming up; everything he had not thought about; all the grief he had put away and walled out and never even thought of on the [sub-hunting] trip nor all this morning" (*IS* 263). He has remained silent about Tom's death for several weeks, having "walled out" his grief until this moment, when he first shares the news with a man whom he does not even particularly like; he then dismisses all attempts at conversation and consolation, first by Natera, then by his comrade Willie, and finally by his friend Lil. Hudson later regards his own fatal wounding more as a relief than a tragedy—a judgment with which the reader is likely to agree.

Hudson's responses to the various traumas of his life are a catalogue of the responses to trauma elucidated by Judith Herman in *Trauma and Recovery.* She taxonomizes these responses into three categories.The first category is hyperarousal: "The traumatized person startles easily, reacts irritably to small provocations, and sleeps poorly" (35). The second category is intrusion:

> Long after the danger is past, traumatized people relive the event as though it were continually recurring in the present. They cannot resume the normal course of their lives, for the trauma repeatedly interrupts. It is as if time stops at the moment of trauma. The traumatic moment becomes encoded in an abnormal form of memory, which breaks spontaneously into consciousness,

> both as flashbacks during waking states and as traumatic nightmares during sleep. . . . Trauma arrests the course of normal development by its repetitive intrusion into the survivor's life. . . . [Traumatic memories have a] frozen and wordless quality. (37)

The third category is constriction, or numbing:

> The helpless person escapes from [the] situation . . . by altering [his] state of consciousness. . . . Perceptions may be numbed or distorted, with partial anesthesia or the loss of particular sensations. . . . These perceptual changes combine with a feeling of indifference, emotional detachment, and profound passivity in which the person relinquishes all initiative and struggle. . . . Traumatized people who cannot spontaneously dissociate may attempt to produce similar numbing effects by using alcohol or narcotics. . . . Although dissociative alterations in consciousness, or even intoxication, may be adaptive at the moment of total helplessness, they become maladaptive once the danger is past. Because these altered states keep the traumatic experience walled off from ordinary consciousness, they prevent the integration necessary for healing . . . [and they] interfere with anticipation and planning for the future. (42–45)

While hyperarousal and intrusion initially predominate in the traumatized person, "numbing or constrictive symptoms later come to predominate . . . [resulting in a sense of] alienation and inner deadness" (48–49).

Thomas Hudson manifests all these responses: hyperarousal, intrusion, and constriction. He exhibits hyperarousal through his quick temper and difficulty in sleeping. He relives his traumatic experiences in the form of flashbacks, nightmares, and uncontrolled and uncanny repetitions—classic examples of intrusion. Yet while these symptoms are apparent, perhaps the most obvious response he displays is constriction, or numbing. Like so many Hemingway protagonists, he wills himself not to think, detaches himself emotionally, and drinks alcohol—all maladaptive means of coping. Ultimately, he fixates on his sub-hunting adventures as though he is in a timeless space, with no thought for the future. If not actively seeking death, he seems at least to be accepting it with passive resignation.

Hudson's disastrous marriages and especially the deaths of his three sons seem to be sufficiently traumatic to elicit these symptoms. But his inability to integrate the traumas into his life—to "encode [them] like the ordinary memories of adults in a verbal, linear narrative that is assimilated into an ongoing life story" (Herman 37)—suggests that he experiences these clearly horrific traumas with particular intensity. Herman notes that individuals who have experienced traumas early in their lives are particularly susceptible to the destructive nature of later traumas; later traumas reengage the initial trauma, just as the responses to that initial trauma are recapitulated in later traumas—unless, that is, one has integrated the early trauma, narrativizing it and thereby integrating it as a chapter in one's life story rather than the whole of the story relived again and again in a version of the Freudian repetition compulsion. Herman also notes that "survivors [of trauma] challenge us to reconnect fragments, to reconstruct history, to make meaning of . . . present symptoms in the light of past events" (3). As readers of *Islands in the Stream,* we are challenged to do exactly that. But Herman also notes that "it is difficult for an observer to remain clear-headed and calm, to see more than a few fragments of the picture at one time, to retain all the pieces, and to fit them together, [and] it is even more difficult to find a language that conveys fully and persuasively what one has seen" (2). In effect, the witness—here, the reader—is also susceptible to the symptoms of trauma. Constriction or numbing may be one response of readers of *Islands,* resulting in their disengagement from the novel.

However, the experience of trauma contains within it a particular dialectic, causing the traumatized person to "simultaneously call attention to the existence of an unspeakable secret and deflect attention from it [which is] most apparent in the way traumatized people alternate between feeling numb and reliving the event" (Herman 1). As readers of *Islands,* our task is to recognize the dialectic of trauma and to attend to "the ways it simultaneously defies and demands our witness" (Caruth 5)—to hear the voice that proclaims the trauma and to recognize in the voice that denies it those clues to the experience of trauma.

Thomas Hudson's inability to integrate his own traumas and the increasing intensity of his constriction or numbing as the novel proceeds both point to an earlier trauma that is largely repressed in the narrative. Hudson's acknowledgment about "grief hoard[ing]"—that he was "brought up on the goddamned stuff" (*IS* 271)—points to a youthful trauma to which he responded with constriction: "Telling never did me any good. Telling is worse for me than not telling" (274). Hudson's assertion that he was "brought up on the goddamned stuff" suggests that his family environment was not supportive of his telling of his trauma, that his family was not willing to truly hear it. Indeed, in a novel that focuses much of its attention on memories, it is notable that Hudson recalls his childhood only a handful of times—and in all but one of those memories he is alone. In only one memory does a family member, his father, appear, and this in the context of a bird-hunting adventure. But there is no emotional content in his memory of his father, and the rest of his family—his mother? his siblings?—remain only as an absent presence, a gap in the narrative.

Hudson alludes to this original trauma in the "Cuba" section of *Islands,* in a drunken conversation with Honest Lil, the proverbial whore with a heart of gold. Hudson suddenly describes her drink with peculiar specificity, "That is the color of the water in the Firehole River before it joins the Gibbon to become the Madison. If you put a little more whisky in it you could make it the color of a stream that comes out of a cedar swamp to flow into the Bear River" (277). When she asks him about this place in Montana, he recounts in a detached way his traumatic youthful experience there: "One time I had been fishing and I wanted to cross the river and I crawled across on the logs. One rolled with me and I went into the water. When I came up it was all logs above me and I could not get through between them. It was dark under them and all I could feel with my hands was their bark. I could not spread two of them apart to get up to the air" (278). When she asks him what happened, he makes the startling comment, "I drowned" (278). When Lil objects, he explains how he managed to push against the logs to create a space for himself: "I lay there like that a long time between them. That water was brown from the logs in it. The water that's like your drink was in a little stream that flowed into that river" (278)—the place of confluence "called Wah-Me-Me" (*IS* 277), a telling name that evokes the sound of a child crying. The relationship that he draws between the color of Lil's drink and the deadly water into which he fell points to his own means of numbing his experience of this traumatic event: through drinking alcohol; coupled with his refusing to speak at length or with emotion about the incident.

More significant, however, is his utterance, "I drowned"—not "I almost drowned," or "I could have drowned." In a very real sense, Hudson's life stopped at that traumatic moment, and he relives his near encounter with death over and over again, exactly because he has repressed it rather than narrativizing it and thereby incorporating it into his life. His surname, Hudson, points to the centrality of water—his place of drowning—in his life story. There is no mention of his having painted the watery scene of his trauma, even though his reputation is based on his seascapes. This absence evidences one aspect of the defining dialectic of trauma—that is, deflecting attention from it. Conversely, Hudson's presence throughout the novel always in proximity to water evidences the other and opposite aspect of this dialectic—that is, "call[ing] attention to [the] unspeakable [trauma]" (Herman 1); he lives surrounded by water first on the island of Bimini and then that of Cuba, and he finally leaves land altogether for life at sea on his sub-hunting boat.[2]

It is telling that Thomas Hudson recounts the story of his near-drowning—a story that he otherwise "hoards"—at the very time when he is grappling with the recent news of his son Tom's death. Hudson knows the terrifying circumstances, though he shares them with no one, even lying about the circumstances to Tom's mother. He knows that Tom was not killed by the flak that hit the plane—as he encourages his wife to believe—but that after the flak hit, Tom parachuted out of the plane, his parachute caught fire, and he plummeted to the water below. While the youthful Thomas Hudson had survived his own fall into the water, his son and namesake, young Tom—in this regard his twin—did not. Thomas Hudson's own trauma of near death by drowning is thus exacerbated by survivor guilt.

Provocatively, there is still another story of drowning recounted in the novel. During an extended visit, Hudson's good friend of many years, Roger Davis, for the first time shares his story of the drowning of his younger brother when both were boys. It is a harrowing account. Unaware that Davis had even had a brother, Hudson asks where he is and hears a one-word response to his question, "Dead" (*IS* 75)—a response that in its brevity is echoed by Hudson's later assertions in response to the questions of Natera, Lil, and his first wife, respectively: "He's dead" (*IS* 262), "I drowned" (*IS* 278), and "Sure [he is dead]" (*IS* 319).

In a series of brief questions and answers, we learn from Davis that "a canoe turned over with us" (*IS* 75) when Davis was twelve and his brother a year younger. Hudson's response to this startling information is to urge, "Don't talk about it if you don't want to" (*IS* 75), but Davis goes on: "For a long time I thought everybody in the world knew about it. It's strange when you are a boy. The water was too cold and he let go" (*IS* 75).

In contrast to Davis's brother, who let go and drowned, Hudson had hung onto the logs and survived. However, his having been trapped under the water's surface caused him to experience the trauma of a drowning only narrowly escaped. The story of Davis's brother's drowning is yet another uncanny repetition of Hudson's trauma.

To Hudson's distress, Davis inexorably continues telling his story, his own traumatic response revealed not only by the story's content but also by its hypnotic repetition: "What it added up to was that I came back and he didn't. . . . It was early to learn about that stuff. And then I loved him very much and I'd always been afraid something would happen to him. The water was cold for me too. But I couldn't say that. I don't think my father ever forgave me although he tried to understand it. I've wished it was me every day since. I tried to go down after him. But I couldn't find him. . . . It was too deep and it was really cold" (*IS* 75–76).

Hearing this story proves too much for Hudson, who anxiously asks for reassurance: "Roge, you did get over it, though"; but Davis does not reassure him: "You never get over it and sooner or later I have to tell it. I'm ashamed of that" (*IS* 76). Davis's occasional but overwhelming compulsion to speak of his brother's death and of his own survivor guilt is a manifestation of the voice that speaks the trauma. His childhood inability to share the whole story with his disapproving father is repeated in his shame as an adult at needing sometimes to tell the story, which is coupled with his repression of the identities of those with whom he has shared it. These manifestations of the voice that disguises the trauma powerfully reflect his hidden anger at his brother's inability to hang on, to survive, as manifested in his silently accusatory statement: "The water was cold for me too."

Davis's difficulties as a writer are linked to his inability to narrativize this trauma. His writer's block and his production of trivial fictions are a means for him to numb himself to his own story. Though Hudson urges him to use his personal material as the foundation for a serious novel, Davis shrugs off the suggestion, indicating that he would inevitably introduce a pretty girl and create a happy ending—a falsification that would serve to deny the traumatic incident expressed in the core of the novel.

The two never talk again about this seminal event in Davis's life; neither does Hudson share at this appropriate time his own experience of near-drowning. In yet another example of constriction, we learn nothing about Davis's brother except his name, David, and his age. The lack of information and David's closeness to Roger Davis's own age at the time of the incident cause the boys to merge in the reader's mind, effectively twinning them. This twinning is underscored by Davis's own assertion that he "wished it was me every day since." For all that Davis does not talk about the incident, his survivor guilt and his inability to directly address the traumatic event except occasionally and dispassionately cause it to intrude "every day since" it happened. In effect, each day he dies again as his brother died, and each day he survives again as he did in fact survive. Caruth's question is singularly relevant here: "Is the trauma the encounter with death, or the ongoing experience of having survived it?" (7). She argues that the trauma story enacts "a kind of double telling, the oscillation between a *crisis of death* and the correlative *crisis of life;* between the story of the unbearable nature of an event and the story of the unbearable nature of its survival" (7).

The name of Roger Davis's brother, David, of course aligns him with Hudson's middle son, David, who also becomes twinned with the dead boy. Roger Davis is especially close to David Hudson, understanding him better than his own father does. Notably, Davis is particularly protective of David, the relationship between Roger Davis and David Hudson essentially replicating that between Roger Davis and his brother David Davis.

However, Roger Davis is unable to protect David Hudson when David and his brothers are spear-fishing in the ocean and a shark, attracted by the smell of the fish David has speared, speeds toward him to attack him. Because Davis has lingered by the small boat near Andrew, he is too far away to swim to David in time to save him. Similarly Hudson, on the boat itself, tries to shoot the shark but repeatedly fails, despite his excellent marksman skills. It is Eddy, Hudson's right-hand man, who successfully shoots and kills the shark, thereby saving David from death.

David's reaction to this near-death experience is relatively calm, in contrast to the "shaken" response of Davis and Hudson. While there are "goose pimples still over his legs and back and shoulders" when he safely boards the boat, he is largely "excited" by the experience (*IS* 87). He is most absorbed by the possibility of landing the dead shark, which proves impossible. When asked later if he was "very scared," he responds with a simple "yes," but he "cri[es] like a little boy" only when young Tom proudly talks about telling the boys at school about David's adventure, because David fears that they will doubt its authenticity. In response to David's tears, Eddy reproves him by asking "What's the matter with you, Davy?" (*IS* 88), to which David replies, "Nothing" (*IS* 89), thereby denying the trauma that he has just experienced. He asks to go goggle-fishing in the low tide, to return, in effect, to the site of his trauma virtually immediately, as if nothing has happened. While Thomas Hudson and Roger Davis are uneasy at the thought, they allow him to do so.

This traumatic incident has happened so suddenly that David cannot fully experience its impact in the moment but only later, for "the story of trauma . . . is the narrative of a belated experience" (Caruth 7). According to Caruth, "Trauma is experienced too soon, too unexpectedly, to be fully known and is therefore not available to consciousness until it imposes itself again, repeatedly, in the nightmares and repetitive actions of the survivor" (4). Thus, David's response is far more intense after a subsequent and far less dangerous but still parallel event, when his long and torturous fishing battle ends with defeat in the form of the loss of the swordfish just at the moment of seeming victory. While David is not at risk of drowning during this painful adventure, the possibility of drowning emerges in disguised form when Eddy "lunge[s] down into the water with the gaff and then [falls] overboard" (*IS* 139). That David's reaction to the loss of the fish is much more disturbed than his reaction after his near-death by shark attack suggests that he is experiencing a kind of delayed or projected reaction. Not only is he physically injured but he is both exhausted and emotionally distraught. He sobs, his "shoulders shaking" (139), at the loss of the swordfish. Lying face down on the bed while his injuries are treated, he speaks "in a toneless voice" (140). Rather than eating a big meal, as he did after the shark attack, he is not hungry and must be coaxed to eat an invalid's meal. He is initially reluctant to talk about the incident, but when given permission by his father he speaks of his "crazy" sense of not being able to distinguish between the swordfish and himself (142)—a disguised version of his fear at almost being consumed by the shark. As Caruth notes, "Trauma is not locatable in the simple violent or original event in an individual's past, but rather in the way that its very unassimilated nature—the way it was precisely *not known* in the first instance—returns to haunt the survivor later on" (4).

That neither Davis nor Hudson is able to save David in the shark incident, nor to enable his triumph in the fishing incident, suggests their complicity in his potential death—yet another such potential death, recapitulating aspects of both Hudson's and Roger Davis's own near-death experiences, as well as David Davis's actual death by drowning. That David Hudson ultimately does die shortly after this incident adds heft to the significance of this event. Moreover, that Hudson seems to acquiesce to the suggestion that Andrew was driving the automobile and thus bore responsibility for the deaths is significant insofar as Andrew "was a copy of Thomas Hudson" and "had a dark side to him that nobody except Thomas Hudson could ever understand." Thomas Hudson and Andrew "were very close to each other although Thomas Hudson had never been as much with this boy as with the others" (*IS* 53). Here, Thomas Hudson and Andrew are twinned, and so the responsibility for the deaths imaginatively borne by Andrew is thus borne by Thomas Hudson as well.

The four incidents of drownings or near-drownings in the novel—Hudson's own near-drowning under the logs in the river, Davis's near-drowning, his younger brother's actual drowning, and David Hudson's near death in the waters of the Atlantic ocean (later followed by his death across the ocean)—all coalesce into a single drowning event. This coalescence is emphasized by the twinning relationships in the novel. Not only are Roger Davis and his younger brother David twinned, as are David Hudson and David Davis, and Thomas Hudson and Andrew Hudson, but so too are Roger Davis and Thomas Hudson, who "don't look too different" and who, according to their friend, the bar owner Bobby, "look like quarter brothers" (*IS* 155). They shared essentially the same past during their early manhood in France; as Hudson notes, they "used to live in the same town and ma[d]e some of the same mistakes" (155). The walk-on character Audrey loves both of them. They both function in a parental manner toward Hudson's sons. Moreover, both are artists, Hudson a painter and Davis a writer.[3] At least initially in the novel, Hudson is the successful artist to his alter-ego's failed artist, but by the opening of the second section, Hudson has ceased his artistic work, in this regard replacing Davis, who disappears completely from the novel.

Thomas Hudson's youthful near-drowning recalls both Roger Davis's youthful near-drowning and David Hudson's youthful near-death by shark attack. David Davis's actual death by drowning suggests the possibility of death that Roger Davis escaped and that fills him with survivor guilt and unspeakable anger at his dead brother; it also suggests the possibility of death that David Hudson escapes in the waters off Bimini yet meets shortly thereafter in the automobile accident across the water in France—a death that inevitably fills Thomas Hudson with survivor guilt. Roger Davis's inability to save his brother David is recapitulated in his inability to save David Hudson from the shark attack; Thomas Hudson is similarly unable to save his son, David surviving only because of the first mate Eddy's successful shooting of the shark. Both Roger Davis and Thomas Hudson feel guilt at David Hudson's near death, holding themselves responsible for allowing the boys to swim in dangerous waters and for not watching David closely enough. Hudson's "some sort of special guilt" (*IS* 90) at not being able to save his son, despite his usually masterful marksmanship, must inevitably inform his reaction at hearing of his sons' deaths later, in an automobile accident occurring shortly after they leave Bimini. Hudson's last sight of his sons is their departure by hydroplane, lifting off the waters of Bimini, and his last imaginative vision of young Tom Hudson is his plummeting into the waters off France, the country in which David and Andrew were killed.[4]

The various permutations of death by drowning are each traumatic events in their own right, but they also create a complicated nexus, each death or near-death informing the others—indeed, absorbing the others into a single traumatic incident that haunts Thomas Hudson, recalling his own primary traumatic experience. Within the text, these various events operate as a sort of repetition compulsion.

Roger Davis's curiously sudden disappearance from the novel in the latter part of the first section is psychologically meaningful in this regard. Critics agree that Roger Davis is Thomas Hudson's alter-ego. He is the artist who has dissipated his creative energies by allowing himself to be distracted by alcohol and women. He is a man who has not grown up, lacking adult discipline. Thomas Hudson, by contrast, is the successful artist of the novel, one who has constructed a rigidly disciplined life that locates painting at its center. While Davis and Hudson shared wild times as young men, Hudson has seemingly grown up, as evidenced by his learning the importance of discipline to his art. Roger Davis is, in effect, the failed artist whom Hudson fears in himself.[5] But in the white space between the first and second sections, Thomas Hudson in effect becomes Roger Davis, engaging in extended bouts of drinking and most significantly abandoning the discipline of his art. Davis is no longer necessary to the text because he has been absorbed into Thomas Hudson.

While Hudson's drinking and abandonment of his art are presented as traumatic responses to his sons' deaths, his work itself has long been a response to his own primary trauma:

> He thought that on the ship [to Europe to claim his sons' bodies] he could come to terms with sorrow, not knowing, yet, that there are no terms to be

> made with sorrow. It can be cured by death and it can be blunted or anesthetized by various things. . . . One of the things that blunts it temporarily through blunting everything else is drinking and another thing that can keep the mind away from it is work. Thomas Hudson knew about both these remedies. But he also knew the drinking would destroy the capacity for producing satisfying work and he had built his life on work for so long that he kept that as the one thing that he must not lose. But since he knew he could not work now for some time he planned to drink. (197)

Notably, even before his sons' deaths, work is presented as an adaptation to trauma—that primary trauma of which he speaks only later, and briefly, to Lil at the bar, where he is breaking his own drinking record for double frozen daiquiris. Having abandoned his painting by this point, he numbs his trauma alternately with alcohol and his new work, sub-hunting—a type of work focused on destruction rather than creation. When not sub-hunting he drinks, and when sub-hunting he keeps rigidly away from alcohol, recapitulating in exaggerated form his previous alternation between drinking and painting.[6]

The white space between the first and second sections of the book marks a gap, a disruption, a wound, a trauma. The deaths of Thomas Hudson's two younger sons occur immediately before it, and the death of his oldest son occurs within it, as does Hudson's third failed marriage—itself a gap in the text. In the "Bimini" section, Hudson sleeps in a bed in a well-managed house; in the "Cuba" section, he suffers from insomnia while lying on the floor in an ill-managed house; in the "At Sea" section, he sleeps only fitfully and occasionally on the deck of his boat and on beaches. He is increasingly deracinated—not at home but truly at sea in his life. Much of the "At Sea" section has a nightmarishly repetitive quality, as he and his crew seek the German submariners in key after seemingly identical key, down channel after seemingly identical channel, seldom even catching sight of the Germans but always warily on guard. He is lost in the nightmare his life has become. Because he does not drink alcohol while on duty, he loses one of his two preferred anesthetics for his pain. Because he has given up painting, he loses the other—the discipline of a work that not only distracted him from his pain but that also gave vent to his constructive and creative impulses. He has replaced the work of painting with the work of sub-hunting, the "duty" (*IS* 418) with which he attempts now to palliate his pain, but which is destructive in nature while also insignificant in light of the larger war effort. As he says, the result is, "I just don't give a damn" any longer (*IS* 360). As his crew realizes, he has "ceased to be careful of [him]self" (*IS* 358). He identifies to a great extent with the Germans he seeks to kill, who have a "fellow death-house feeling about them" (*IS* 376). In Herman's terms, he has reached the irreversible terminal point for a trauma victim, "losing the will to live," operating only as "the living dead" (85).

Thomas Hudson's living death is inevitably followed by his actual death, which he passively accepts.[7] Rather than allow himself to be cared for after he has been wounded by three gunshots, he continues to stand upright to steer the boat during the battle and then directs the crew to dismantle a trap before leaving the scene of the battle in search of medical care. As he bleeds to death from internal wounds, "he ha[s] time to realize that he [is] probably going to die" (*IS* 460). He expresses only mild regret, and this only at the paintings he has not painted over the past seven years and now will never paint. But this regret is accompanied by a palpable sense of relief: "He felt far away now and there were no problems at all" (*IS* 466).

The apocalyptic imagery that fills the novel thus points appropriately to Hudson's living and actual deaths. Allusions to "the Second Coming" (11), "the End of the World" (19), and the return of "the ice age" (447) are accompanied by references to destructive hurricanes, dangerous waterspouts, "the sinking of the *Titanic*" (18), "Custer's Last Stand" (459), and "the extinction of the passenger pigeon" (447). And this apocalyptic imagery reflects "the end of a man's own world" (194)—an ending that we witness recurring throughout the novel, as each new trauma recalls Hudson's original trauma, each engaging the others in a complicated dialectic.

But Hudson can only occasionally speak the voice that proclaims his trauma, more often speaking the voice that denies it. We readers, however, are in a privileged position in this third-person omniscient novel. We have the opportunity to "listen to a voice that [we] cannot fully know but to which [we] nonetheless bear witness . . . [because] this listening to the address of another, an address that remains enigmatic yet demands a listening and a response" (Caruth 9) is a privilege, while also a sometimes difficult burden to bear.

Caruth argues that the trauma story is an "attempt to tell us of a reality or truth that is not otherwise available" (4). In this regard, *Islands in the Stream* is not only the story of Thomas Hudson's traumas, but also the story of Ernest Hemingway's.[8] In "the complex ways that knowing and not knowing are entangled in the language of trauma and in the stories associated with it" (Caruth 4), *Islands in the Stream* simultaneously addresses and denies Hemingway's own experience of loss of control—loss of control over his writing ability, his physical health, and his psychological stability, as well as loss of control over his relationships, notably with his mother, his first wife, Hadley Richardson, his third wife, Martha Gellhorn, and his youngest son, Gregory. At this late point in his life, Hemingway must have felt that he was drowning in words, but words that he could no longer control as he had done in his earlier years. The insistent intrusion of his own traumas into his story speaks the voice that proclaims and the voice that denies trauma, and we readers have the privilege and the responsibility of bearing witness to these voices in *Islands in the Stream.*

Notes

1. In *Hemingway: The Postwar Years and the Posthumous Novels,* Rose Marie Burwell provides a detailed explanation of the composition and publication history of *Islands.* She notes that two of Hemingway's posthumously published texts, *Islands* and *A Moveable Feast,* along with *Across the River and into the Trees* and *The Old Man and the Sea,* began as part of "an ur-text" that he started writing in early October 1945 and that "he sometimes referred to as 'The Land, Sea, and Air Book'" (1). He "finished what is now the final section of the book he thought of as 'The Islands and the Stream' on 18 May 1951" (57). Burwell addresses what Hemingway called "the African book," which was posthumously published as *True at First Light* (1999) in a heavily edited and abbreviated form by Patrick Hemingway, and then as *Under Kilimanjaro* (2005) in a scholarly edition by Robert W. Lewis and Robert E. Fleming. She argues that "the African book" and *The Garden of Eden* "were not part of the ur-text; but they grew out of the same thematic concerns with the creative imagination that had driven the ur-text" (1). She further argues that "the result is four schizophrenic fictional structures that he could neither complete, nor expose, nor destroy; but that he did intend for publication after his death" (6). She notes that Carlos Baker was "the dominant force in the project" of editing the novel, but that Charles Scribner, Jr. and Mary Hemingway also participated in the editing project (94).

2. For a discussion of the significance of islands in Hemingway's life and art, see my "Hemingway's I-Lands in the Streams."

3. Burwell argues that "the observation made by several critics—that in the novel Roger Davis and Thomas Hudson are one character—is a recognition that Hemingway was dealing with the unitary origin of creativity and was using the *remate* technique to explore problems common to a writer and a painter" (61).

4. Burwell argues that "the near obliteration of David and Andy from Hudson's memory after 'Bimini,' the silence of the text on his relationship with young Tom during the seven years that have passed, and the disappearance of Roger from the narrative cause a textual gap that leaves Hudson's creative decline unexplained, and his alternating self-hatred and grandiosity unconvincing" (64). She explains this "textual gap" as "evidence of Hudson's and, by extension, Ernest Hemingway's inability to either develop and sustain intimate human relationships or function creatively without them" (70).

5. Robert Fleming compares the two as follows: "Hudson and Roger are doubles who illustrate two versions of the modern artist: Hudson is the pure artist for whom everything else is relegated to a secondary rank; Roger is the flawed artist who is more human

and more vulnerable than the perfect artist. Hudson enjoys having his sons with him, but there is a reserve in his attitude toward them—and toward all of humanity. . . . At times it seems that Hudson has taken refuge in art because his relationships with people have disappointed him; he seems actively to crave isolation. . . . He isolates himself from women. . . . He holds the commercial world at bay. . . . In contrast to Hudson, Roger illustrates most of the pitfalls to which an artist can fall victim. He continues to make disastrous alliances with women. . . . He continues to lead an adventurous life. He has aimed his writing at commercial markets for so long that he has lost all artistic integrity. . . . If, as Carlos Baker has maintained, Thomas Hudson represents a narcissistic and idealized picture of Hemingway's own life at middle age, Roger suggests the dark self that Hemingway might have feared he had become. . . . If Hudson bears away the palm as true artist, however, Roger's fallibility lends him a saving humanity. The boys enjoy a closeness with Roger that they cannot hope to achieve with their father" (133–34).

6. G. R. Wilson Jr. presents a Christian argument that "Thomas Hudson is suffering not just . . . deep-seated anxiety and existential emptiness . . . but is rather living in spiritual despair, the greatest of all Christian sins because it denies faith, indeed, the very possibility of faith" (28). Wilson is not interested in the source of this despair, but in contrasting it with the spiritual state of Santiago in *The Old Man and the Sea*, once a part of *Islands in the Stream*: "Santiago triumphs through faith, Thomas Hudson fails through despair" (28). In short, Wilson posits Hudson's state without exploring its source—indeed, deems its source unimportant—while I focus on Hudson's primary trauma as the source of his state, exacerbated by the later traumas that recall the initial trauma.

7. Burwell rightly notes, "As Hudson acknowledges that the duty he chose over his painting is murder, he becomes a man waiting for an opportunity to give his life away" (58). She further notes that "when Hudson leaves his home at the end of 'Cuba,' he is like a resolved suicide awaiting the action of an assassin with whom he has made a contract to surprise him" (86).

8. Donald Junkins argues that "Hudson the painter is Hemingway, and Roger the writer is Hemingway, and Davy and young Tom and Andrew are Hemingway. . . . The Hudson-Roger-Davy-young Tom-Andrew-Eddy-Joseph character is the real Hemingway biography" (109).

Works Cited

Burwell, Rose Marie. *Hemingway: The Postwar Years and the Posthumous Novels*. Cambridge, UK: Cambridge Univ. Press, 1996.

Caruth, Cathy. *Unclaimed Experience: Trauma, Narrative, and History*. Baltimore, MD: Johns Hopkins Univ. Press, 1996.

Fleming, Robert E. "Hemingway's Late Fiction: Breaking New Ground." In *The Cambridge Companion to Hemingway*. Edited by Scott Donaldson. Cambridge, UK: Cambridge Univ. Press, 1996. 128–48.

Hemingway, Ernest. *Islands in the Stream*. New York: Charles Scribner's Sons, 1970.

Herman, Judith. *Trauma and Recovery*. New York: Basic Books, 1997.

Junkins, Donald. "Rereading *Islands in the Stream.*" *North Dakota Quarterly* 68.2–3 (2001): 109–22.

Moreland, Kim. "Hemingway's I-Lands in the Streams." *North Dakota Quarterly* 68.2–3 (2001): 123–31.

Wilson, G. R., Jr. "Saints and Sinners in the Caribbean: The Case for *Islands in the Stream.*" *Studies in American Fiction* 18.1 (1990): 27–40.

Sea of Plenty

The Artist's Role in Islands in the Stream

LAWRENCE R. BROER

"A book must be the axe for the frozen sea inside us."
—Franz Kafka

"What a book . . . would be the real story of Hemingway, not those he writes but the confessions of the real Ernest Hemingway."
—Gertrude Stein

In his review of James Mellow's biography, *Hemingway: A Life Without Consequences,* Donald Lyons reminds us how much of Hemingway's writing is *about* writing: "Nick, the fisherman hero of 'Big Two-Hearted River' . . . is not just a man escaping some unspecified awful past and healing some unspoken wound, but is a writer. The hero of *The Sun Also Rises* is a writer, if a journalist (as was Hemingway, of course); more covertly, all the analysis of bullfighting is a metaphorical analysis of writing. And how much of later (and poorer) Hemingway is about writers and writing! *Green Hills of Africa* discourses at great length on the subject; *For Whom the Bell Tolls* has a writer for hero, and so forth" (73).[1]

Lyons's summary of Hemingway's artist-protagonists serves my purpose here in two respects, first by wrongly excluding Thomas Hudson of *Islands in the Stream* (1970), my focus in this paper, and then by referring to Hemingway's "later" works as "poorer." Lyons thus reflects the tendency in Hemingway studies to praise the author's early work at the expense of the later. (It is, indeed, curious that in the case of F. Scott Fitzgerald, for example, we cite his weaker work to accentuate his strengths, while in Hemingway's, we pounce on his perceived failures to downgrade his work as a whole.)

Lyons's dismissal of Hemingway's later work seems to me misinformed, both because it limits our understanding of the merit of individual works, such as *For Whom the Bell Tolls* and *The Old Man and the Sea,* and because it obscures the meaning of Hemingway's career as a whole. We cannot quarrel with Lyons's admiration of Hemingway's application of "verbal spareness" and "emotional indirection" in such stories as "Big Two-Hearted River," which he terms "elusively beautiful," and "Soldier's Home," which he calls "one of the finest stories in Hemingway's first—and likely his best—book, the 1925 collection *In Our Time*" (73). However, Lyons cannot resist the familiar codicil that "this was Hemingway's modernism, but it was a modernism of the sketch; he had no architectonic knack and the traditional structures of his later novels rather imprison than enable his talent" (73).

We are aware that there are shark attacks not only in, but also on the later novels. A summary of these critical assaults would include the view, even of *The Old Man and the Sea,* that these works are less compelling for two reasons. They are less imagistic, devoid of the continuous high intensity and ambiguity of the early work. In addition, they present heroes—Jordan, Cantwell, Hudson, Santiago—who are simpler and more self-possessed—hence, less interesting—than the more uncertain and angst-filled figures of Nick Adams, Frederic Henry, and Jake Barnes! As Kelli Larson observes, *The Old Man and the Sea* remains "a distant fourth" in the order of Hemingway texts written about. *Islands in the Stream* is, well, a distant, distant" (22). The fact is that Faulkner was on target when he said that "Time may show [*The Old Man and the Sea*] to be the best single piece of any of us . . . This time, he discovered God, a Creator. . . . this time, he wrote . . . about something somewhere that made them all: the old man who *had* to catch the fish and then lose it, the fish that *had* to be caught and then lost, the sharks which *had* to rob the old man of his fish; made them all and loved them all and pitied them all" (qtd. in Baker 503–4; my emphasis). What Hemingway had discovered, of course, were the wonderful creative possibilities of God-in-the-Sea, the energy of creation, paradoxical creator, preserver, destroyer. That is the boundless sphere, the true sea the Hemingway hero has always yearned to believe in, which dissolves or reconciles all opposites. As Baker explained it, all Hemingway knew was that *The Old Man and the Sea* "was the best he had ever done in his life. It could well stand as an epilogue to all his writing and to all he had learned, or tried to learn, while writing and trying to live" (499).[2]

If we substitute "painting" for "writing," Hemingway's summation of his best efforts as a man and a writer at the time of his writing of *The Old Man and the Sea* sounds remarkably like Thomas Hudson's mature comments in *Islands in the Stream.* Hudson paints what Hemingway writes—and in the manner Hemingway writes. As Wirt Williams says, "No other persona is so close to Hemingway the writer as Thomas Hudson the painter, down to wives, sons, experiences, and grief" (199).[3] What Hemingway has learned, Hudson has learned as well. Imagine, then, what we are invited to miss of insight into the most prominent features of Hemingway's art, at the point of its arguable summit, if we ignore, or look reductively at, these final versions of Hemingway's artist-hero, Thomas Hudson and Santiago. Together, they represent the climax and crystallization of Hemingway's evolving creative vision. Thomas Hudson-Hemingway tells us not only *how* Hemingway does it, but *why* he does it, and what he hopes it will finally mean. Both know, for instance, that the artist's integrity resides not in strict fidelity to actual experience, but to the truthfulness of the idea or the emotion produced. "You have to make it inside of yourself," Hudson explains (*IS* 16). "Make something happen," Tommy exhorts his father about his Paris memories (59). When Roger Davis, Hudson's corrupted secret-sharer, complains of writer's block, Hudson suggests that he "make it up after the canoe" (77). He advises Roger to combine experience with imagination, to invent his characters from fragmented experience, just as Hemingway does in this novel with Roger, his boys, and his divorced first wife, the last a composite of Marlene Dietrich and Hemingway's real wives Hadley and Mary. The resulting work of imagination is neither fictional nor autobiographical, as those terms are traditionally understood; rather, explains Millicent Bell, it is Hemingway's virtual creation of his own literary genre. She describes the author's (hence, Hudson's) use of personal experience as a deliberate and complex artistic reworking of life experience that makes it seem that he was yielding to memory to make it more authentic (114).[4] To paraphrase Faulkner's description of the process of writing *The Sound and the Fury,* understanding Thomas Hudson teaches us not just how to read *Islands in the Stream* and *The Old Man and the Sea,* but also how to assimilate what we have "already read" of earlier Hemingway. Just as Faulkner—having "as much as ten years before . . . consumed whole and without assimilating at all" Flaubert, Conrad, and Turgenev—was able to rediscover them "in a series of repercussions like summer thunder" after completing *Sound and Fury,* so Hudson helps us to rediscover Hemingway's earlier work with the same sense of revelation (qtd. in Lyons 73).

In a handful of rare, admirably careful readings of *Islands in the Stream,* Joseph DeFalco, James Justus, G. R. Wilson, Francis Skipp, Wirt Williams, Rose Marie Burwell, and Robert Fleming disagree about the final fate and character of Thomas Hudson. They concur, however, that *Islands* and *The Old Man and the Sea* were clearly parts of a single conception in Hemingway's mind, a shared vision of a universe in harmony with itself, whose major symbols are the life-giving and spiritually regenerative sea, the Gulf Stream, the islands of the Caribbean, and the creatures of the ocean world. DeFalco describes what he calls a vision and a system of aesthetics of a very different order that evolved once

Hemingway "adopted" the Gulf Stream as a major metaphor and abandoned his long-favored use of the bullfight. This was a major shift to the affirmative mode, with "new and fresh ways" of rendering reality in his work (40). The "need to find meaningful metaphors and images to express themes of human solidarity and brotherhood, DeFalco argues, "led Hemingway away from the sophisticated rituals of the bullring to the pastoral primitiveness of the Gulf Stream."[5] This is a universe shared as well, DeFalco explains, by Colonel Cantwell and Robert Jordan, a universe where man's "willed actions have meaning in a way they do not for a compromised Jake Barnes or a despairing Frederic Henry." I submit that it is the increasingly introspective capacity of Cantwell and Jordan that prepares for the greater understanding of self and world that climaxes in the joined artistic identity and transcendent vision of Thomas Hudson and Santiago. For the earlier hero, DeFalco explains, "the estrangement between man and forces he cannot understand remains," while the greater life experience and the capacity for intense self-analysis in Cantwell, Jordan, Hudson, and Santiago provide a resolution of the dilemma inherent in the essential duality of the universe (42). Robert Jordan's epiphany in *For Whom the Bell Tolls* appears to define the moral progress of these later heroes: Envisioning Madrid "just over the hills there . . . rising white and beautiful," he declares, "That part is just as true as Pilar's old women drinking blood down at the slaughterhouse. There's no one thing that's true. It's all true" (*FWBT* 467). The unifying image of the sea (Whitman's "eternal float of solution" [137]) allows these later heroes the possibility of reconciling the painful duality, the identity of opposites, in external nature as well as within themselves. Hudson, for instance, knows that there are bad things as well as good above and below the sea (*IS* 80), that the same wind and sea that produce cooling breezes and wonderful fishing also create tidal waves that "submerge every living thing" (5) or "God's own hell of a waterspout" (17). One can observe here the complex mythological implications of the novel's extensive fire and water imagery. These fused motifs symbolize the contending forces of good and evil in the universe that I call the forces of "cosmic plenty." On just one page, for example, Hemingway produces thirteen references to fire that join with the sea imagery to portray Thomas Hudson's reconciliation of opposites in himself and his world. "He could feel the pounding of the surf," Hudson says, "the way he remembered feeling the fury of heavy guns" (*IS* 5).

Joseph Campbell sees this acceptance of opposites as necessary to the questing hero's transcendence of ego and transformation into "eternal" or "universal" man. To experience the "lofty light," Campbell explains, requires facing not only the perils of descent, but the assimilation of his opposite or unsuspected self. The hero must find that he and his opposite are not of differing species but one flesh. For Hudson this means, first, the knowledge that such opposites as

German and American, East and West, the one and the many, light and dark, conscious and unconscious, and masculine Yang and feminine Yin are "evolved by the one-same power of nature or spirit." Second, the hero must see a related kind of "otherness," a balancing act that Hudson masters as no hero before but that Santiago, the true "universal man," brings to perfection. That demiurge within himself comes from the same power of nature or spirit that unites Hudson to that eternal sea for which he and Santiago feel such great love.

It is not my intention here to discuss Hudson's achievement in detail—this balancing or assimilation of opposites that prepares us for Santiago and that climaxes the Hemingway hero's long quest for integration of self and world. But it is Hudson's and Santiago's resolution of what DeFalco and Campbell intend as "the basic dualism of the human predicament" (qtd. in Cirlot 106) that separates Hudson and Santiago from earlier protagonists and allows them to make peace with cosmic order. In contrast to the more hostile universe of their predecessors, the sea that Hudson and Santiago know and accept is a sea that represents the totality of what can be known and experienced; it is, therefore, both their cross and their joy. Though the sea deceives at times "Hudson looked ahead at the smooth sea and the innocent-looking deadliness of the reef" (*IS* 391)—Hudson realizes that it is this same ubiquitous energy of creation—a marriage of heaven and hell, birth and dissolution—that bonds them to the sea and its creatures, and whose paradox they carry within themselves. Although he refers to it once as the "puta sea" (*IS* 230), Hudson reflects: "You know you love the sea and would not be anywhere else. . . . She is not cruel or callous nor any of that Quatsch" (239–40). This spirit of acceptance carries no sentimental illusions about man's fate. Hudson knows that the same force that supports and fills him during his time of life is that sea into which he must ultimately dissolve. Acknowledging life's necessary cycles, which ebb and flow throughout the story, he also acknowledges his feelings: the "happiness of the summer began to drain out of him as when the tide changes on the flats and the ebb begins in the channel that opens out to sea. He watched the sea and the line of beach and he noticed that the tide had changed and the shore birds were working busily well down the slope of new wet sand. The breakers were diminishing as they receded" (191).

While, as Wirt Williams explains, *Islands in the Stream* may not be among Hemingway's greatest three or four novels, detailed explications by the novel's major critics show that the novel's three sections are meticulously and subtly crafted, interwoven with rich ironies and possessing a complexity of construction that ease of reading is apt to conceal. Williams refers to the novel's "tonal" qualities and notices an "intricate contrapuntal development" that he compares with Beethoven's Ninth Symphony (216). Therefore, Skipp, Wilson, and Justus are wrong, I think, in finding Hudson both a failed painter and a failed human being: the "dreadfully depressed" end product (Skipp 27), of (in Justus's words) a "battered lifetime of constant threats, tests, and disappointments" (108). The novel, Justus asserts, is "studded with the diction of defeat: unhappiness, suffering, loss, sorrows, and cries of grief, hopelessness, blankness, wickedness" (111). Wilson likewise argues that whereas Santiago triumphs through faith, Hudson fails through despair, a figure too isolated from his world to hope for recovery (28–29). Justus faults Hudson's "stoic imperturbability" as protection against "psychic hurt" (113), while Skipp writes that Hudson fails to improve on Jake Barnes's sense of "how to live in it" by "narrowing his life, reducing his exposure, cutting his risks, holding tight" (137). In fact, Skipp concludes, Hudson retreats "further and further within the confines of nostalgia, into an even narrower life, until at last in a channel along the Cuban coast, where the mangroves press close on either hand, he finds his death" (137).[6]

Such assessments, I suggest, are off the mark. Rather than fearing to make himself vulnerable, rather than resorting to detachment or withdrawal (the emotional adjustment of the Hemingway hero and of Hudson, too, at an *earlier* phase of development), I contend that Thomas Hudson, with the exception of Hemingway himself in *Under Kilimanjaro,* is Hemingway's most inclusive and integrated artist-protagonist. He is gentle, open to himself and the world, and expressive in a way that challenges the discourse of silence of Nick Adams, Jake Barnes, and Frederic Henry. Rather than a surrender to defeat, Hudson's frequent sojourns in nostalgia are both a heroic reconciliation to the inevitability of loss—the negative side of "plenty"—and a way of sustaining memories that nourish his mind and art. He wishes that many things about his life were different, better: that he could "be able to draw like Leonardo or paint as well as Pieter Brughel"; that he could have "absolute veto power against all wickedness," especially his own; that he could "be always healthy" and "not decay in mind or body"; that he "could have the children" and have back alive all those "who you loved" and who had "gone out from your life" (97). Anticipating the most resonant of Hemingway's themes that climax in *The Garden of Eden*—the knowledge of "the garden a man must lose," as Hemingway put it in a letter to Buck Lanham, dated June 12, 1948 (qtd. in Baker 460)—Hudson knows he cannot regain his losses. Even Tom's death, he decides is "something that happens to everybody" (*IS* 449).

Yet Hudson also knows that all experience, whether of sorrow or happiness, can contribute to the "great intensity" (96), the dualistic "plenty" that feeds his art. "Everything that a painter did or that a writer wrote," Hudson declares, "was a part of his training and preparation for what he was to do" (103). Moreover, while nostalgia can kill you—"Nostalgia hecha hombre" (237)—he knows that it is a powerful tool of the creative imagination. It allows him to travel in his mind to where he wants to be: "Now when he was lonesome for Paris he would remember Paris instead of going there. He did the same thing with all of Europe and much of Asia and Africa" (7).

Hudson acknowledges his past sins: the disastrous errors of judgment, the selfishness that many women had told him about but which now "he had finally discovered for himself" (9). In a reversal of the iceberg principle, what might be called an aesthetics of "superconsciousness" or an "awakening of soul" (Campbell 8), Hudson summons his past to face and to denounce the sins of his darker self, his underwater self, an act that produces a fully mature hero, more open to the unconscious, more able to talk about repressed experience than any Hemingway hero before him.[7] There is indeed a persistent sadness about Thomas Hudson, but Wirt Williams is right in seeing this as "tragic emotion" that builds in intensity through the novel's three sections (200).[8] Hudson's detractors fail to see that Hudson is his own most severe critic, that his remembrances of things past are not just of happy surface events, like Tom's wonderful experiences in Paris as a baby: "Que muchacho más lindo y más guapo!" (280). They are about what went on "down below." "He could feel it all coming up," he says, "all the grief he had put away and walled out" (263). When Willie feels the confessions loosening Thomas up, he remarks, "Now you got the old pecker up," and "see what I meant by sharing it?" (272).

One might discuss here the myriad ways Thomas Hudson and Santiago complete what Carl Bredahl and Susan Lynn Drake call "the larger integrating vision that drives Hemingway's work" (22), especially their view of the "creative advance" of the later heroes, in which each protagonist assimilates the creative energies of the former, then passes that energy on, as Hudson does to Santiago. "*The Old Man and the Sea,*" they explain, "offers both an appropriate and necessary conclusion to the narrative efforts of Ernest Hemingway's creative genius. He could take his story no further" (131). There is more to be said about Thomas Hudson's acquisition of pity; his celebration of art and renunciation of war; and, most notably, his acceptance of the female in himself and finally even of the necessity of his own death.

Recent studies by Ann Putnam, "On Defiling Eden: The Search for Eve in the Garden of Sorrows," and by Susan Beegel, "Santiago and the Eternal Feminine: Gendering La Mar," show us that Hemingway's efforts to resolve the feminine/masculine duality in himself was always at the heart of his work. The quest for wholeness was the object of the hero's anytime quest for Eden across paradisal landscapes in such works as "Big Two-Hearted River," *Green Hills of Africa, The Old Man and the Sea,* and *The Garden of Eden.* But, they argue, it is Hemingway or his protagonist's habit of associating the feminine with the dark or destructive aspects of nature that stand in the way of successful integration of these divided feminine/masculine selves. The feminine, Putnam says, is always the "other" that threatens the essential male self: the lure and danger of the swamp, for instance, in "Big Two Hearted River" and "The Last Good Country," a female landscape to be avoided, taken, or destroyed (124). But it is precisely the fact that first Hudson and then Santiago no longer associates the feminine with evil that completes their humanity and ironically restores the old feeling of Edenic harmony and wholeness. The Garden must perish, but Eve is no longer the culprit.

This development in Hemingway's protagonists entails discussion of Hemingway's ingenious use of the Dantesque and Conradian "heart of darkness" theme, that manifests in *Islands* through Hudson's exploration of his dark side that, he says, he has "to look at" (*IS* 247). This is the night hunter that nature has built into him along with the artist (239), which Donald Junkins sees as a necessary source of Hemingway's creativity (143). It is the self-conscious allegory of self-examination and discovery that culminates in *Under Kilimanjaro,* a version of the descent-journey that finds the author repentant over the slaying of beautiful animals and sensitive to his more humane potential as artist, husband, father, friend, and caretaker of animals, rather than as the hunter-killer who has so often commanded his allegiance. As *Under Kilimanjaro* closes, the author's "child's heart," as he calls it (*UK* 23), comes to the fore. A lion is assumed, but not definitely known, to be raiding the Masai. But "that was conjecture," Hemingway reflects, "and no evidence to kill him on" (440). In the final scene, Hemingway and his wife hold one another gently, and with those contrary forces in balance—man, woman; night, day; animal, human; light, dark—the lion feels far away (441).[9]

I will conclude by describing what I see in *Islands* as the deeper sea-source of Hudson's salvation as a man and making as an artist—the doctrine of plentitude, which in turn produces the humanity of Santiago in *The Old Man and the Sea.* "Plenty," Hudson announces. "The land of plenty. The sea of plenty. The air of plenty" (*IS* 237). Hudson's and Santiago's "plenty" is *both* the "puta sea" (*IS* 230) and "the promising sea" (*IS* 372). And it is the tension born of this eternal paradox that Hemingway conveys to us in the book's many juxtapositions—nada and fullness, pain and pleasure, loss and replacement: these constitute the mutual canvas of Hemingway's writing and Hudson's painting.[10] Hudson, for instance, paints two pictures of the terrible sadness of loss and desire when David's wonderful fish gets away. But both highlight the boy's courage and fortitude. David has been called Santiago in embryo. Hudson also paints massive destruction by waterspouts and hurricanes, and even an apocalyptic death scene he calls "The End of the World." Yet Hudson's art redeems nature's destructive fire by transforming it into the spiritual fire of Yeats's Byzantium. "That was the great thing about pictures," Hudson explains. "You could love them with no hopelessness at all—because they had done what you always tried to do" (238). Throughout the novel we experience with Hudson what Campbell calls the "inexhaustible and multifariously wonderful divine existence that is the life in all of us" (12)—a product of the sea's palpably rich gifts. We respond happily or sadly to the creative fire of sex, food, drink, love, and art, and to the opposing destructive fire, the loss and grief of flux and dissolution, the killing fire of war. Yet if, as Hudson says, "Plenty is wrong with me" (237), plenty is also right. Someone tells him, "Hudson, you've had it. And you've rehad it. And you've had it doubled" (*IS* 256). When Lil at the Floridita asks him what he's sad about, he says, "El mundo entero" (282). But when he finds himself growing morbid with thoughts of the death of Tom, his son, he rebukes himself for not remembering the good: "You had plenty," he says (448). Hudson has indeed learned plenty about both life's fecundity and its emptiness. For every destructive fire, there is a creative one, for every receding tide, a replenishing fullness. Numerous references to "burning charcoal" ingeniously compress the contrary associations of cooking food with charred human beings, the "plenty" of "frags" with which they burn Germans (455). Of this "hell," whether from German guns or the sea's sudden and violent squalls, they know they will certainly "have plenty" (382). Burning driftwood makes Hudson "both sad and happy": "He thought that it was probably wrong to burn it when he was so fond of it" (5). The war suddenly brings Thomas Hudson back together with his first wife, as suddenly as their domestic war had torn them apart (305, 311). Hudson's losses are potentially overwhelming, especially the deaths of all three of his sons and the loss of his first wife. Both haunt him ever afterward. But life has also brought Hudson the "solid, prominent Bimini house that has withstood three hurricanes, a Finca in Cuba, a ranch in Idaho—and a boat with a flying bridge that ranges all over the Gulf Stream, first for fish, finally for German submarines (Justus 115). At a point when life looks bleakest for Hudson's crew, Hudson wants to know if they have "plenty" to eat. When Antonio explains that there is Spanish sauce and black beans and rice and apricots, Hudson asks, "Have you plenty of soup?" "Plenty," Antonio assures him. "How is the rice?" "Plenty . . ." (44) "Is there coffee below?" "Plenty" (349). There's also "plenty" of scotch and gin and coconut water with lime in it, and even "plenty" of cognac and morphine for their wounded German prisoner. To encourage Hudson's morale, Antonio makes him a "peanut butter and onion sandwich, with plenty of onion" (390), called "the Mount Everest Special for Commanders only" (391). In the midst of their life-threatening chase of the Germans, when Willie advises them that they have to "get the *hell* along," Hudson nevertheless thinks, "I bet we could catch plenty of good fish all along here" (390). Central to Hudson's ironic and life-affirming approach to plentitude is not just his knowledge that for every "bad" there is an offsetting "good," but that the good sometimes requires the bad as a regenerating force, and that the existence of the bad may sharpen sensitivity to the good in a way that intensifies one's appetite for experience, and certainly one's ability to make art. Hudson knows that the brown-red roots beneath the green mangrove key contain the best of oysters. Cuba, a "country of so many greens," quickly becomes brown from the drought (243), the "green tops" of palms become "slanted" by the harsh wind and made "hard and cold." But this makes the fire of his drink all the better, "a hell of a good drink": "fresh green lime juice mixed with . . . tasteless coconut water . . . [and] real Gordon's gin that made it alive to his tongue and rewarding to swallow, and all of it tautened by the bitters that gave it color" (244). When Hudson's first wife asks him, "How many times have we made love *because* there was a norther?" he answers: "Plenty" (276). She wants "a big, big bed, to forget all about the army" (312). It is the sea itself here that is the Goddess of Plenty, that not only guides Hudson to his knowledge and embrace of the "other," but that rewards him for living and doing disciplined work by providing sensuous experience and then artistic creation: what Hudson calls the "palliative measures" (282) he takes that feed not only his art but his emotional needs as well.

Cuba, a microcosm of the paradoxical world that Hudson has learned not just to accept but to love, seems to heighten his capacity for sensuous pleasure. He is troubled by the "illogical and neurotic Cuban traffic" (244–45), but the sensuous names for things buoy him up: San Isidro street, Cojímar, Floridita. He is moved by the brightness of a Cuban winter morning (241), by "the smell of roasting coffee that was a stronger sensation than a drink in the morning" (252), and by the "smell of tobacco" as his car approaches the Floridita. A meal at the Floridita is plenty wonderful: "A plate of bits of pork, fried brown and crisped, and a plate of red snapper fried in batter so that it wore a yellow crust over the pink-red skin and the white sweet fish inside" (281–82).

Knowledge of life's brevity makes Hudson extraordinarily careful with time and relationships. He knows how to extract the maximum value and pleasure from life-heightening experiences by paying them complete and focused attention, while shaping them with artistic finesse. "Out of all the things you could not have," Hudson says, "there were some that you could have and one of those was to know when you were happy and to enjoy all of it while it was there and it was good" (97). Hence Hudson gives himself completely to his boys while they are with him, because "he would have his habits again long after he would no longer have the boys" (52). Even little pleasures, James Justus explains, are carefully planned. Hudson puts away the mainland newspaper—"to save it for breakfast" (49). He reads *The New Yorker* as a magazine "you can read on the fourth day after something happens" (200). Directed to Obispo, a street he particularly loves, he reflects that "he did not like to ride down it because it was over so quickly." He "saved the street for later when he could walk it" (252–53).

Halliday is right that Hudson's heightened appreciation of the beauty of the physical world has always been a part of the Hemingway hero's "passionate fondness for being alive" (36). But no prior Hemingway protagonist has so developed his ability to elevate life's simplest elemental experiences literally and figuratively to an art form. And this is my final point. When Hudson's first wife years later reminds him that it was because of his dark side that they parted, he responds: "You'd have asked Toulouse-Lautrec to keep away from brothels, and Gauguin not to get the syphilis, and Baudelaire to get home early" (*IS* 317–18). He underscores the main theme of his—and Hemingway's—life and work: that learning to live *and* practicing your art are often damnably difficult accomplishments. Hudson's ex-wife tells him, "The one thing you were always faithful to was good wine" (323). But Hudson has managed much more than this. Though he quips that learning not to quarrel with women anymore was as difficult to learn as learning "how to settle down and paint in a steady and well-ordered way," he believes that he has learned more every year about living with both compassion for people *and* discipline for his work, and that he "had learned them permanently" (8). Noting that Hudson is now more caring and selfless than she can ever remember, Hudson's first wife declares, "You *are* changed" (325). This is a line, I think, as weighted with meaning for our understanding of Hemingway's more open and expressive later heroes, Thomas Hudson, Santiago, David Bourne, and the narrating Hemingway of *Under Kilimanjaro,* as is that "heavy sea" that draws Hudson to it in the final episode of his life, and *from* which Santiago makes a triumphant return.

Notes

1. Rose Marie Burwell notes that even Santiago in *The Old Man and the Sea* is an "avatar of the author" (59). See also Robert Gajdusek's discussion of the ingenious ways by which Hemingway writes himself as artist into *For Whom the Bell Tolls.* Appropriate to what I say here about Hemingway the writer is Thomas Hudson the painter in *Islands in the Stream.* Gajdusek notes that Hemingway "*paints* himself, the artist, in the very center of his art" (23; my emphasis).

2. As we now know, the fullest understanding of "all he [Hemingway] had learned" requires reading *Islands in the Steam* and *The Old Man and the Sea* in conjunction with *The Garden of Eden* and *Under Kilimanjaro.* For further discussion of the bedeviling paradox of Mother Sea that Hudson's more courageous art brings to life, see chapter 8 of *Vonnegut and Hemingway: Writers at War.* As early as 1966, Bickford Sylvester cogently argued that the later Hemingway had neither abandoned nor parodied his early work but had extended and perfected it.

3. Rose Marie Burwell, Robert Fleming, and Robin Gajdusek offer provocative ways of understanding what Fleming calls "the face in the mirror," the autobiographical projection of the author as character or as artist creator. See particularly Fleming's excellent extended discussion of Hemingway's treatment of Thomas Hudson and Roger Davis as a single artist, one whose split reflects the conflict between artist and man in Hemingway himself.

4. Each of the critics discussed here shows Hemingway's remembrances of things past to be a deliberate and complex reworking of life experience. I especially like what Robin Gajdusek says about Hemingway as "the double thinker," immersing himself in, yet transcending, his artist heroes. The heroes are "simultaneously" versions of himself *and* (my emphasis) *other* than himself. Burwell and Fleming treat the posthumous novels *Islands* and *A Movable Feast* as a single tapestry in which Hemingway explores the cost of the creative process to the artist and to those whose lives (children, parents, loves, wives, comrades, even pets) are united with his own.

5. Bickford Sylvester finds the worlds of the bull ring and the Gulf Stream more connected than disconnected, joined by the "compassionate violence" implicit in the slaying both of the bull and of Santiago's marlin. Sylvester suggests that such opposites, love and violence, do not lead away from the "meaningful continuity of the universe, but are only another part of its endless flux" (89).

6. Robert Fleming and Rose Marie Burwell agree that *Islands in the Stream* is important for its extensive commentary on the problems of the artist-writer, and they acknowledge that in both *Islands* and *The Garden of Eden* Hemingway addresses questions close to his own heart with a frankness not paralleled in any of the works published in his lifetime, with the possible exception of "The Snows of Kilimanjaro." They cite Hudson's occasional willingness to look at the darker implications of killing and the abuse of children and former wives. Burwell recognizes a new degree of conscience, introspection, and self-criticism in Hudson. More than any prior hero, she says, Hudson accepts responsibility for the destruction of the two personal relationships "that had been most sustaining to him as a man and writer and thus gains in integrity and self-knowledge" (2). However, Burwell also interprets Hudson's story as a movement from self-discipline to dissipation and the pursuit of violence, while Fleming concludes that as Hudson surrenders his absorption in his art and reveals his more vulnerable self, he regains his humanity (122–23). Nevertheless, Fleming and Burwell would agree that Hemingway could not complete *Islands* or *The Garden of Eden* precisely because these works demanded a more probing exploration of the writer's psyche than he was prepared to give (114).

7. Burwell notes paradoxically that whereas Hemingway was a writer whose ethos and style seemed "forged as a protection against introspection" (5), his later heroes—Jordan, Cantwell, Santiago—turn increasingly inward, so that writing for Hemingway becomes a form of self-examination in the novels published posthumously. In venturing from the old narrative form, Burwell believes, Hemingway had "descended into the iceberg" (5), a technique he called "remate" (61) that facilitated the twinning, cloning, and splitting of painters and writers in *Islands* and *The Garden of Eden* (54). Fleming notes that it is especially in the second and third books of *Islands* that Hudson reveals his more vulnerable self, becoming more sensitive to the feelings of others (122–23).

8. Burwell explains that in the self-reflexivity of his portrait of the artist, Hemingway's view from inside the hero was "fear-like."

9. For further discussion of Hemingway's incorporation of Dante's allegorical descent in *Islands in the Stream*, see *Hemingway and Vonnegut: Writers at War*, pp. 132–33.

10. Sylvester and I essentially concur as to the nature of Hemingway's later creative vision—that Hemingway discovers in what I call the doctrine of plenitude and Sylvester calls a "philosophical naturalism" a principle of harmonizing oppositions that gives "transcendental meaning to life's harsh inevitabilities" (Sylvester 81). Sylvester explains that Hemingway was preoccupied during the last of his productive periods with exploring the paradoxical fusion of affection and violence more centrally in his fiction than he ever had before—"the idea of an immanent order based upon the tension between opposed forces" (91). But whereas I see a humanism at work here, an embracing of one force by the other, Sylvester specifies that both figures participate in a spiritual victory, although material defeat is inevitable for one or the other or both.

Works Cited

Baker, Carlos. *Ernest Hemingway: A Life Story.* New York: Scribner's, 1969.

Beegel, Susan. "Santiago and the Eternal Feminine: Gendering La Mar." *Hemingway and Women: Female Critics and the Female Voice.* Edited by Lawrence Broer and Gloria Holland. Tuscaloosa, AL: Univ. of Alabama Press, 2002.

Bell, Millicent. *Ernest Hemingway: The Writer in Context.* Edited by James Nagel. Madison, WI: Univ. of Wisconsin Press, 1984. 107–28.

Bredahl, A. Carl, Jr., and Susan Lynn Drake. *Hemingway's* Green Hills of Africa *as Evolutionary Narrative.* Lewiston, NY: Edwin Mellen Press, 1990.

Broer, Lawrence. *Vonnegut and Hemingway: Writers at War.* Columbia, SC: Univ. of South Carolina Press, 2011.

Burwell, Rose Marie. *Hemingway: The Postwar Years and the Posthumous Novels.* Cambridge, UK: Cambridge Univ. Press, 1996.

Campbell, Joseph. *The Hero with a Thousand Faces.* Princeton, NJ: Princeton Univ. Press, 1973.

Cheatham, George. "Androgyny and *In Our Time,* Chapter VII." *Hemingway Review* 14.1 (Fall 1994): 67–71.

Cirlot, J. E. A Dictionary of Symbols. Translated by Jack Sage. New York: Philosophical Library, 1971.

D'Agostino, Nemi. "The Later Hemingway." In *Hemingway: A Collection of Critical Essays.* Edited by Robert P. Weeeks. Englewood Cliffs, NJ: Prentice Hall, 1962. 152–60.

DeFalco, Joseph M. "Hemingway's Islands and Streams: Minor Tactics for Heavy Pressure." In *Hemingway in Our Time.* Edited by Richard Astro and Jackson J. Benson. Corvallis, OR: Oregon State Univ. Press, 1974. 34–51.

Fleming, Robert E. *The Face in the Mirror.* Tuscaloosa, AL: Univ. of Alabama Press, 1994.

Gajdusek, Robert. "Artists in Their Art: Hemingway and Valaquez—The Shared Worlds of *For Whom the Bell Tolls* and "Los Meninas." In *Hemingway Repossessed.* Edited by Kenneth Rosen. Westport, CT: Greeenwood, 1994.

Halliday, E. M. "Hemingway's Ambiguity: Symbolism and Irony." In *Ernest Hemingway: A Collection of Criticism.* Edited by Arthur Waldhorn. New York: McGraw-Hill, 1973. 35–55.

Hemingway, Ernest. *Islands in the Stream.* New York: Charles Scribner's Sons, 1970.

——. *The Old Man and the Sea.* New York: Charles Scribner's Sons, 1952.

——. *Under Kilimanjaro.* Edited by Robert W. Lewis and Robert E. Fleming. Kent, OH: Kent State Univ. Press, 2005.

Junkins, Donald. "Shadowboxing in the Hemingway Biographies." In *Hemingway: Essays of Reassessment.* Edited by Frank Scafella. New York: Oxford Univ. Press, 1991. 142–53.

Justus, James H. "The Later Fiction: Hemingway and the Aesthetics of Failure." In *Ernest Hemingway: New Critical Essays.* Edited by A. Robert Lee. Totowa, NJ: Barnes and Noble, 1983. 103–22.

Larson, Kelli A. "Stepping into the Labyrinth: Fifteen Years of Hemingway Scholarship." *Hemingway Review* 11.2 (Spring 1992): 19–24.

Lyons, Donald. Review of *Hemingway: A Life without Consequences,* by James R. Mellow. *American Spectator,* Oct. 1994: 72–73.

Putnam, Ann. "On Defiling Eden: The Search for Eve in the Garden of Sorrows." *Hemingway and Women: Female Critics and the Female Voice.* Edited by Lawrence Broer and Gloria Holland. Tuscaloosa, AL: Univ. of Alabama Press, 2002.

Skipp, Francis E. "Memempsychosis in the Stream, or What Happens in 'Bimini'?" *Fitzgerald/Hemingway Annual,* 1974. Edited by Matthew J. Binecoli. Washington, DC: Microcard, 1974. 137–43.

Stein, Gertrude. *The Autobiography of Alice B. Toklas.* New York: Random House, 1955.

Stephens, Robert O. *Hemingway's Nonfiction: The Public Voice.* Chapel Hill, NC: Univ. of North Carolina Press, 1968.

Sylvester, Bickford. "Hemingway's Extended Vision: *The Old Man and the Sea.*" In *Twentieth Century Interpretations of* The Old Man and the Sea. Edited by Katherine Jobes. Englewood Cliffs, NJ: Prentice Hall, 1968.

Waldneir, Joseph. "Confiteor Hominess: Ernest Hemingway's Religion of Man." In *Hemingway: A Collection of Critical Essays.* Edited by Robert Weeks. Englewood Cliffs, NJ: Prentice Hall, 1962.

Whitman, Walter. "Crossing Brooklyn Ferry." In *Leaves of Grass.* 1855; New York: Bantam Dell, 1983. 133–38.

Williams, Wirt. *The Tragic Art of Ernest Hemingway.* Baton Rouge, LA: Louisiana State Univ. Press, 1981.

Wilson, G. R., Jr. "Saints and Sinners in the Caribbean: The Case for *Islands in the Stream.*" *Studies in American Fiction* 18:1 (Spring 1990): 27–41.

Hemingway's Impressionistic *Islands*

JAMES NAGEL

By the time Grace Hall arrived in New York in 1895, the air was electric with the phenomenon of impressionism. She was there to study voice as a prelude to a life as a wife and mother, but she was also deeply interested in painting, as her frequent visits to the Art Students League testify. She had seen the French impressionists at the Columbian Exposition in Chicago in 1893, the World's Fair that demonstrated the resurgence of the city after the devastating fire of 1871, and she had a serious interest in painting, an art that would occupy the last two decades of her life. There was no avoiding impressionism in America: it had swept the country in the 1890s, and frequent exhibitions were held in various parts of the country while articles on painting and literature appeared in the periodicals nearly every month, especially in the leading magazine, the *Atlantic Monthly.* It would not have been lost on her that a local Midwestern writer, Hamlin Garland, had been chosen to explain impressionism to the American public in Chicago, nor that the paintings had attracted so much attention at the exposition that they were loaded on an exhibition train and taken on a national tour, complete with Garland's explanatory essay. A year later, he published his views on impressionism in his artistic credo, *Crumbling Idols,* which remained an influential statement for several decades.

America had been much more receptive to impressionism than had France, where its first exhibition in Paris had been greeted with confusion and derision. The painters loved it, but the audiences could not figure it out: not the technique, not the subjects, and not the point of it all. So it was natural that as the movement grew, a flood of speeches and essays issued forth to discuss the nature of this sensational new trend in art. What quickly became clear was a core principle of the movement: that what the artist was recording was not nature as it is *understood* to be but nature as it is *perceived* to be by the senses in a moment of experience, what the Italians called the *vistazo.* A concern for the artistic representation of immediate impressions required an intense interest in the fluctuation of light and color, in movement, depth, and the special effects inherent in fog, haze, snowfall, distance, and reflections on the water. The sight was to be rendered with objectivity, without the imposition of the artist's personal feelings about the scene, without preconceptions, historical backgound, classical allusions, or symbolic references. The philosophical implications of the movement are perhaps most significant in the concern for the transcience of reality, for the ineluctable flux in human perceptions of even the most stable of objects, so that Monet could paint numerous pictures of haystacks from the same perspective at different times, and the light, the color, the emphasis, the essence of reality would have changed each time.

All of these ideas were received enthusiastically in America from the first important show in New York in 1886, which exhibited more than three hundred paintings by Degas, Monet, Manet, Pissarro, and Renoir. In 1892, when Stephen Crane was living in the Art Students League, Cecelia Waern published "Some Notes on French Impressionism" in the *Atlantic Monthly,* emphasizing that "the great secret of all impressionism lies in aiming to reproduce, as nearly as possible, the same kind of physical impression on the spectator's eye that was produced on the eye of the artist by the object seen in nature" (537). Waern was talking about the aesthetic principles of painting, but an identical artistic creed had rapidly formed in literature, influencing the work of Stephen Crane, Kate Chopin, Ambrose Bierce, and a host of other writers of the period.

Perhaps the most influential theoretical formulation of the idea was offered by Joseph Conrad in 1897 in the preface he wrote for *The Nigger of the Narcissus,* in which he argued that fiction must appeal to the senses: "My task which I am trying to achieve is, by the power of the written word, to make you hear, to make you feel—it is, before all, to make you *see.* That—and no more, and it is everything" (xlix). Once Ernest Hemingway arrived in Paris and began writing fiction as a professional, he endorsed a virtually identical artistic creed. As he explained to his father, C. E. Hemingway, in a letter dated March 20, 1925, "you see I'm trying in all my stories to get the feeling of the actual life across—not to just depict life—or criticize it—but to actually make it alive. So that when you have read something by me you actually experience the thing" (*SL* 153). Nearly eight years later, in February 1933, he once again explained his objectives in writing fiction in a letter to Everett R. Perry: "I am trying, always, to convey to the reader a full and complete feeling of the thing I am dealing with; to make the person reading feel it has happened to them" (380). Hemingway was endorsing the central tenets of the rapidly growing tradition of literary impressionism.

The literary tradition of impressionism grew rapidly, manifesting in subtle and dynamic ways that changed the fiction and poetry of the next three decades. William Dean *Howells* published a series of prose sketches in 1890 under the title *Pastels in Prose,* and Stephen Crane wrote his "London Impressions" later in the decade. By the early years of the new century, Hamlin Garland was working on his "Chicago Studies," brief impressionistic prose sketches capturing the sensation of a moment: "The cold rain sailed in over the wild lake on the remorseless wind. The sky to the northeast had an illimitable and desolate look. It was a deep blue-black at the water's edge but grew more luminous as it rose, until at the zenith the yellow-gray of the city's reflected light met it and edged it with weird radiance" (qtd. in Stronks 49). Here was a new literature, one that attempted to render the sensory nature of human life, to present the sensations of a character so graphically that the reader would experience the scene directly, participating in the action on the same epistemological plane as the character.

These ideas evolved in the second decade of the century into two movements that directly influenced the work of Ernest Hemingway: imagism and polyphonic prose. Imagism, the poetic manifestation of impressionist ideas, presented verse that contained direct, concrete images in compressed language with no emotional intrusion by a narrator. The emotional impact of an image was in the reader, not expressed overtly in the verse itself. John Gould Fletcher's poem "VII" from his 1915 collection, *Irradiations: Sand and Spray,* is a good example:

Flickering of incessant rain
On flashing pavements:
Sudden scurry of umbrellas:
Bending, recurved blossoms of the storm.

The winds came clanging and clattering
From long white highroads whipping in ribbons
  up summits:
They strew upon the city gusty wafts of
  apple-blossoms,
And the rustling of innumerable transluscent
  leaves.

Uneven tinkling, the lazy rain
Dripping from the eaves. (qtd. in Hughes 126)

The speaker does not talk about himself; he presents the details of life that inspired emotion, a sensory evocation of scene that elicits vicarious participation in the experience and creates a similar emotion in the reader. There is no doubt that Hemingway was aware of the principles of imagistic verse even in high school, since he wrote and published several poems based on these ideas, such as "The Punt":

> Twenty-two mud-daubed figures battling together on a muddy field.
>   A sharp barking of numbers.
> The front line of figures pile up together.
> The back line crouch and throw themselves
>   at the men coming through.
> The sodden thump of a pigskin being kicked,
>   and the ball rises higher and higher in the air
> While the grimy, muddy figures race down the field. (*88 Poems* 11)

The visual depiction of scene, the kinetic images of the game, the sound of the ball being kicked, the objective stance of the narrator, and the restriction to a sensory description of the moment are all the essence of imagism.

The prose expression of impressionistic technique was allied to imagist poetry, although it had started much earlier. Amy Lowell gave the form the name "Polyphonic Prose," somewhat inaccurately describing the concept, since what was at issue was not multivoiced prose but fiction that captured the impressionistic sensations of a moment of human experience, precisely as the painters had attempted to do in their medium. All of the imagists were sensitive to this kind of fiction, and many volumes of very brief fictional prose poems, often restricted to a single paragraph, were published, such as Amy Lowell's *Can Grande's Castle,* John Gould Fletcher's *Breakers and Granite,* or in the fragmentary images of John Dos Passos:

> Rosey yellow and drab purple, the buildings of New York slide together into a pyramid above brown smudges of smoke standing out in the water, linked to the land by the dark curves of the bridges.
>
> In the fresh harbour wind comes now and then a salt-wafting breath off the sea. (Dos Passos 12)[1]

Hemingway exhibits no influence from these works in his fiction until he comes under the sway of Ezra Pound in Paris; prior to that, his stories often had the feel of Ring Lardner or Jack London. In 1922, however, he began working seriously on his writing, and one experiment, consisting of six one-sentence vignettes that he titled 'Paris 1922,' was quintessential polyphonic prose; for example: "I have stood on the crowded back platform of a seven oclock Batignolles bus as it lurched along the wet lamp lit street while men who were going home to supper never looked up from their newspapers as we passed Notre Dame grey and dripping in the rain" (*88 Poems* xxiii). The feel of the swaying of the bus, the look and smell of the wet street in Paris, the color of the cathedral in the rain, all are the stuff of impressionistic fiction, as is the fact that this passage constitutes an entire story.

Hemingway wrote a series of such sketches in the formative period of the development of his aesthetic, and they led naturally to the slightly longer works in the mode that constituted the first *in our time*, which was not an anomalous collection, as many reviewers assumed, but simply a continuation of the volumes of polyphonic prose produced throughout the teens. That Hemingway then progressed to the longer stories in the expansion of *In Our Time* did not constitute a rejection of impressionistic aesthetics but rather an expansion of his capabilities to the creation of more complex works; the central principles of impressionism, imagism, and polyphonic prose were part of his central artistic creed throughout his life, from the vignettes of *in our time* to the highly visual descriptions in *The Sun Also Rises* to the evocation of war and the thematic epiphany of *A Farewell to Arms* to the wonderfully sensory story Pilar tells in *For Whom the Bells Tolls* about the taking of the fascist village. What is remarkable is that Hemingway continues to employ these techniques throughout his life, informing passages in even the most unlikely of posthumous works, including the loose and baggy monster that was ultimately published as *Islands in the Stream.*

In *Islands in the Stream* Hemingway uses the concepts of impressionism and the techniques of polyphonic prose in ways that provide a sensory evocation of scene, establish a frame for dialogue or action, and create a cinematic immediacy, as in the opening part, "Bimini." This section begins from a distance, with Thomas Hudson's house set in context as viewed from afar, perhaps from above, as in the establishing shot of a motion picture. The description is highly visual, with an emphasis on color:

> The house was built on the highest part of the narrow tongue of land between the harbor and the open sea. . . . It was shaded by tall coconut palms that were bent by the trade wind and on the ocean side you could walk out of the door and down the bluff across the white sand and into the Gulf Stream. The water of the Stream was usually a dark blue when you looked out at it when there was no wind. But when you walked out into it there was just the green light of the water over that floury white sand and you could see the shadow of any big fish a long time before he could ever come in close to the beach. (*IS* 3)

The emphasis in the opening is on the outside of the house, its position and setting on the peninsula, the color of the sand and water, and the concept of the shadow on the sea bottom, which will figure later in the chapter, when the hammerhead shark comes over the reef, headed for David.

The opening paragraph could have been published as a work of polyphonic prose, complete in itself as an impressionistic description of a scene. But the important action of the opening occurs not in the sea but in the house, and a more detailed description of the interior follows as the viewpoint, the "camera," moves inward, onto the land itself: "The house was the highest thing on the island except for the long planting of tall casuarinas trees that were the first thing you saw as you raised the land out of the sea. Soon after you saw the dark blur of casuarinas trees above the line of the sea, you would see the white bulk of the house. Then, as you came closer, you raised the whole length of the island with the coconut palms, the clapboarded houses, the white line of the beach" (4). The narrative perspective moves in, using kinetic imagery in a manner unique to literature and film but impossible in painting. The progression is then into the house, where Hudson is on the floor in front of the fireplace. "On a cold night he would sit in the big chair in front of the fire, reading by the lamp that stood on the heavy plank and look up while he was reading to hear the northwester blowing outside and the crashing of the surf and watch the great, bleached pieces of driftwood burning. . . . On the floor he could feel the pounding of the surf the way he remembered feeling the firing of heavy guns when he had lain on the earth close by some battery a long time ago when he had been a boy" (5). This passage establishes the sensory immediacy of the thumping surf, of coldness, of sound, of the kinetic visual play of burning firewood, of the feel of the crashing waves hitting the shore, a sensation that evokes the memory of World War I, supplying, gracefully, some background for Hudson that will be pertinent in the third part, "At Sea." All of this is standard impressionistic technique, evoking sensations to draw the reader into the scene, forcing a participation in the sound of the ocean, feeling its heavy surf, seeing the white sand and green water and the house set against the line of trees receding behind it. As Stephen Mathewson has indicated, "Hemingway's descriptions of what Hudson sees and paints in the 'Bimini' section of the novel illustrate his impassive, scrupulously objective recording and ordering of 'empirical phenomena'" (141). A vivid participation in the scene evolves, gradually, into a more subtle involvement in the personality of the protagonist as he deals with his loneliness and the remnants of his family life, as his three sons come from the mainland for a summer visit.

"Bimini" is filled with sensory evocations: the feel of Hudson's bathing, "rinsing under the prickling drive of the sharp, jetted shower" (12), for example. Section 4 of "Bimini" opens with the sensory suggestion of movement and sight and sound on the island: "It was dark now and there was a breeze blowing so that there were no mosquitoes nor sand flies and the boats had all come in, hoisting their outriggers as they came up the channel, and now were lying tied up in the slips of the three docks that projected out from the beach into the harbor. The tide was running out fast and the lights of the boats shone on the water that showed green in the light and moved so fast it sucked at the piling of the docks and swirled at the stern of the big cruiser they were on" (22). This passage is pure polyphonic prose, identical to the abbreviated fiction Hemingway was writing in his early years in Paris, when he came under the influence of Ezra Pound and the imagists. There is darkness, movement as the boats come in, the sharp picture of the lights on the water, the synaesthetic sucking of the current against the piles and the stern of the boat. The viewpoint once again moves from a distance progressively inward to the immediate situation of Hudson. What follows is an even more visual masterpiece describing the surface of the water, its depth, and the movement of fish in the light: "Alongside in the water where the light was reflected off the planking of the cruiser toward the unpainted piling of the dock where old motorcar and truck tires were tied as fenders, making dark rings against the darkness under the rock, garfish, attracted by the light, held themselves against the current. Thin and long, shining as green as the water, only their tails moving, they were not feeding, nor playing; only holding themselves there in the fascination of the light" (22–23). This visual feast of light and dark and movement is the fulfillment of Monet's desire to paint not only the surface of water but its depth, a wish that remained unsatisfied in his lifetime.

Section 5 of "Bimini" opens with a similar visual symphony of color and movement: "When Thomas Hudson woke there was a light east breeze blowing and out across the flats the sand was bone white under the blue sky and the small high clouds that were traveling with the wind made dark moving patches on the green water. The wheel of the wind charger was turning in the breeze and it was a fine fresh-feeling morning" (49). This is the kind of writing that Hemingway learned from the imagists, broadening his aesthetic from the journalistic stance of the *Kansas City Star* and its stylebook, outdistancing Ring Lardner and his sardonic wit, and moving into territory unmatched by either Sherwood Anderson or Gertrude Stein, who had deeply influenced some of his early work. The evocation of color and distance and movement is precisely the artistic aim of polyphonic prose.

Part 2, the "Cuba" segment of the novel, focuses thematically on variations of the theme of love: Thomas Hudson's love of his cats, especially Boise, the purest affection in his life; his devotion to his sons, whom he will lose before the novel is over; his love of the women in his life, particularly his first wife; his somewhat more conditional but sincere affection for the prostitute Honest Lil, whom he admires as an truthful woman; his carnal love for the three Chinese whores, with whom he experiences a memorable adventure; and the consummation of his love for his first wife, with whom he shares unfathomable grief at the loss of their son. These thematic variations, jazz riffs on a central melody, are once again rendered with tactile acuity in brief passages of impressionistic prose.

Boise is described in great sensory detail, from the feel of his coat to the sound of his purr, his weight on the bed, the sensation of Hudson's pushing against the cat's stomach with his foot, the visual sense of the sun glistening on his black and white coat. Other experiences are given a similar sensational base. Hudson's hunger and the cold front that moves in one morning provide the sensory transition to similar feelings during his affair with a princess in Marseilles. The memory is alive with acute sensation: "It reminded him of the cold day there on the steep street in Marseilles that ran down to the port, sitting at the café table with their coat collars up eating the *moules* out of the thin black shells you lifted from the hot, peppery milk broth with hot melted butter floating in it, drinking the wine from Tavel that tasted the way Provence looked, and watching the wind blow the skirts of the fisherwomen, the cruise passengers and the ill-dressed whores of the port as they climbed the steep cobbled street with the mistral lashing at them" (230). It is a great passage, full of the feel of life, including taste and sight and sound and the movement of the wind and the people walking, and it matches exactly the polyphonic paragraphs Hemingway wrote in the early years of his apprenticeship.

Another *tour de force* of impressionistic style in this section is found in Hudson's long conversation with Honest Lil, when Hudson tells about waking up when he was a boy:

> In the morning I was always hungry when I woke and I could smell the dew in the grass and hear the wind in the high branches of the hemlock trees, if there was a wind, and if there was no wind I could hear the quietness of the forest and the calmness of the lake and I would listen for the first noises of morning. Sometimes the first noise would be a kingfisher flying over the water that was so calm it mirrored his reflection and he made a clattering cry as he flew. Sometimes it would be a squirrel chittering in one of the trees outside the house, his tail jerking each time he made a noise. But whenever I woke and heard the first morning noises and felt hungry and knew I would not have to go to school nor have to work, I was happier than I have ever been. (286)

It is a quintessential Hemingway passage, an evocative word picture with movement, acute visual points of focus, sound, and odor, that communicates Hudson's intense memories and requires Lil's participation in the life of the past.

This heightened evocation of the sensation of life is an important prelude to the concluding section, which ends in death.

Part 3 of *Islands,* "At Sea," consists of movement and sharp visual descriptions, appropriately so since Hudson is hunting for a German submarine that was recently spotted in the region. The opening paragraph is once again a perfect passage of polyphonic prose: "There was a long white beach with coconut palms behind it. The reef lay across the entrance to the harbor and the heavy east wind made the sea break on it so that the entrance was easy to see once you had opened it up. There was no one on the beach and the sand was so white that it hurt his eyes to look at it" (331). The intensity of the moment is directly related to the heightened sensitivity of Hudson's search for an enemy capable of killing him and his men, a device that dominates the section. There is an expansion of the sensory appeals as Hudson comes on shore to continue his pursuit of the Germans: "The water was clear and lovely over the white sand bottom and he could see every ridge and wrinkle in the sand. As they waded ashore when the dinghy grounded on a ridge of sand he felt small fish playing around his toes and looked down and saw they were tiny pompano" (334). It is a sharp visual picture, augmented by the feel of the grounding of the boat and the tickling of the fish on his toes, a passage that creates equivalent sensations in anyone who reads it. Many of the descriptive passages add the color an artist would be particularly aware of, although nearly always the palette consists of the primary colors of the impressionists: "They came in toward the line of green keys that showed like black hedges sticking up from the water and then acquired shape and greenness and finally sandy beaches" (372).

This cinematic technique of progressive movement into a scene is reminiscent of the device Stephen Crane used repeatedly in *The Red Badge of Courage.* Hemingway uses it often in "At Sea": "Thomas Hudson saw the high lookout post on the sandy key and the tall signalling mast. They were painted white and were the first things that showed. Then he saw the stumpy radio masts and the high cocked wreck of the ship that lay on the rocks and obscured the view of the radio shack" (350). As Hudson moves onto land, the descriptions become even more impressionistic, using synaesthesia, kinetic imagery, and a spectrum of sensory imagery: "There was a sandy half-moon of beach and the island was covered with dry grass on this side and was rocky and flat on its windward end. The water was clear and green over the sand and Thomas Hudson came in close to the center of the beach and anchored with his bow almost against the shore. The sun was up and the Cuban flag was flying over the radio shack and the outbuildings. The signaling mast was bare in the wind. There was no one in sight and the Cuban flag, new and brightly clean, was snapping in the wind" (351). The poetic "snapping" of the flag provides movement, sight, and sound in a single figure.

Hudson naps at one point, and his dream once again evokes the sharp memories of childhood, when he was full of life and close to the innocence of nature: "He was a boy again and riding up a steep canyon. The canyon opened out and there was a sandbar by the clear river that was so clear he could see the pebbles in the bed of the stream and then watch the cutthroat trout at the foot of the pool as they rose to flies that floated down the current" (384). At another point, Hudson's memories of Paris are directly related to the impressionistic painting of Manet: "The trees would be black in the dusk as he pedalled now toward the Place de la Concorde and the upstanding blooms would be white and waxen. He would get off the racing bicycle to push it along the gravel path and see the horse chestnut trees slowly, and feel them overhead as he pushed the bicycle and felt the gravel under the thin soles of his shoes" (448). The effect of the constant sensory evocation of scene is to emphasize how much Hudson loves life, how acutely he feels it, how immediate is the stuff of life to his every waking moment. The intensity of these memories also has the function of taking his mind off the proximity of danger, the death of his wife and three sons, the emptiness of his present life apart from his suicide mission against the crew of the German submarine. As Stephen Tanner has commented, "in the case of *Islands in the Stream,* the narrative is permeated with the flavor or fragrance of nostalgia. A simple page count shows a singular amount of space devoted to the past; but it is not the past treated as Faulkner treats it: extended narrative flashbacks providing information essential to the plot. The past in this novel is islands of nostalgic recollection that, without being directly related to the plot, nevertheless provide the real substance and tone of the story" (74).[2] In this sense, Hemingway, in *Islands in the Stream,* has once again created a novel that looks backward to previous experience rather than to the present or the future for the emotional context of the central character.

The ultimate effect of Hemingway's use of impressionistic techniques is not to suggest that his protagonist is essentially a painter in that mode but rather to bring alive, in an immediate, tactile way, the world Hudson lives in and his relation to it. It is this emphasis that establishes how much he loves his cats, his children, and his first wife, as well as the sound of the waves and the feel of the sand and the smell of the sea. Thomas Hudson is in love with life, and that is the meaning of his painting, and that is the meaning of his novel. The ultimate tragedy at the end is the impending death of a man who so relishes being alive, who has a rich involvement in the simple things around him, things forever lost in Hemingway's impressionistic *Islands.*

Notes

1. John Dos Passos changed the title of his book to *First Encounter* when it appeared in 1946 in this edition, which is more readily available than *One Man's Initiation*.

2. For Tanner's perceptive discussion of the novel, please see Stephen L. Tanner, "Hemingway's Islands," *Southwest Review*, 61 (1976): 74–84.

Works Cited

Conrad, Joseph. Preface. *The Nigger of the Narcissus*. Edited by Cedric Watts. New York: Penguin, 1988.

Dos Passos, John. *First Encounter*. New York: Philosophical Library, 1946. Originally published as *One Man's Initiation* (1917).

Fletcher, John Gould. "VII." In *Imagism and the Imagists: A Study in Modern Poetry*. By Glen Hughes. New York: Humanities Press, 1960. Originally published in Fletcher, *Irradiations: Sand and Spray* (Boston: Houghton Mifflin, 1915).

Hemingway, Ernest. *Ernest Hemingway: 88 Poems*. Edited by Nicholas Gerogiannis. New York: Harcourt Brace Jovanovich, 1979

——. *Ernest Hemingway: Selected Letters, 1917–1961*. Edited by Carlos Baker. New York: Charles Scribner's Sons, 1981.

——. *Islands in the Stream*. New York: Charles Scribner's Sons, 1970.

Hughes, Glenn. *Imagism and the Imagists: A Study in Modern Poetry*. New York: Humanities Press, 1960. 126.

Mathewson, Stephen. "Against the Stream: Thomas Hudson and Painting." *North Dakota Quarterly* 57 (Fall 1989): 141.

Stronks, James B. "A Realist Experiments with Impressionism: Hamlin Garland's 'Chicago Studies.'" *American Literature* 36.1 (1964): 38–52.

Tanner, Stephen L. "Hemingway's Islands." *Southwest Review* 61 (1976): 74–84.

Waern, Cecelia. "Some Notes on French Impressionism." *Atlantic Monthly* 69 (1892): 535–41.

The Context of Hemingway's Personal Art and the Caribbean Subject

JOSEPH M. DEFALCO

In *Islands in the Stream,* Ernest Hemingway appropriated materials from Homer's *Odyssey,* as James Joyce did before him in *Ulysses.* For Hemingway, however, these appropriations serve somewhat different ends than did the literary borrowings of his accomplished contemporaries, James Joyce, Ezra Pound, and T. S. Eliot. Like them, Hemingway generated a quasi-mythic and historical portrayal of the ontological reality of a modern man's life "in being" (Hemingway's phrase) in the period preceding and encompassing the world of World War Two. Hemingway accomplished this portrayal while adhering in his usual way to the strictures of Jamesian realism in his primary or surface narrative structure. In other words, he "back- grounded" his classical subtext, whereas his distinguished contemporaries "foregrounded" theirs, letting their subtexts become, in effect, their surface narratives—a technique most patently obvious, of course, in Joyce's *Ulysses.* Hemingway also kept his classical source from intruding on his surface narrative by limiting the similarities between *Islands in the Stream* and *The Odyssey* to what I will refer to as *resemblances,* rather than the more conspicuous *parallels.*

Hemingway delivered his views on the subject of literary borrowings in his 1935 nonfiction work, *The Green Hills of Africa,* when he asserts, in his own voice as a character, that "a new classic does not bear any resemblance to the classics that have preceded it. It can steal from anything that it is better than." Refining and qualifying this view, he adds that, "Some writers are born only to help another writer to write one sentence. But [a classic] cannot derive from *or resemble* a previous classic" (21; my emphasis). I take Hemingway's meaning here to be that "true" original works cannot be derivative or obviously imitative in *a literal* sense. But they can exhibit an original relationship to reality, the reality called for by Wallace Stevens in *The Necessary Angel* when he asserts that "reality is the central reference for poetry"—and prose, I would add—and that "there is a structure of reality, which is the resemblance of things" (85). Resemblance in this sense, he adds, need not be imitative, for that would produce inferior art. Hemingway's later works, particularly those set in the Caribbean, reveal a shift from his earlier views and illustrate his agreement with Stevens's definition of resemblances.

The use of literary and historical allusions was usual for Hemingway throughout his career, of course, but they became increasingly evident in later works, and his preference for the use of resemblances rather than parallels will be clear in the following analysis of *Islands in the Stream* and its Homeric antecedents.

Two resemblances will serve as introductory examples. , the first from the opening section of part 1, "Bimini," is characterized by settled, domestic scenes and evasively tranquil artistic pursuits, just as Homer's Calypso episode presents Odysseus during a passive moment in his journey. The second resemblance is from part 2, "Cuba," which focuses on Hudson's alcoholic escape into a Circean world of "pig-like things," the phrase Honest Lil, a prostitute at the Floridita, employs to describe sexual acts she considers perverse (275). What is noteworthy here is Hemingway's use of allusion to represent Hudson's personal moral decline in "Cuba." Rather than emphasizing the many one-for-one parallels, he accomplishes this by association, allowing his readers to observe these allusions for themselves. These sordid reminders of Circean transformations of men into beasts are also associated, appropriately, with details of war and of Hudson's persistent nostalgia for the sheltered home life he left behind on the symbolically smaller island of Bimini, as a momentarily "static" wanderer, like Homer's Odysseus.

Important differences between Joyce's and Hemingway's narratives become apparent in their structures, relative to the three-part divisions in Homer's *Odyssey:* Telemachia, Wandering, and Nostos. On the one hand, the divisions in Joyce's *Ulysses* form a parallel, with eighteen chapterlike subdivisions, each dealing with a specific Homeric subject, *viz.* Telemachus, Nestor, and Calypso. In *Islands,* on the other hand, Hemingway's division of the text into thirty-six chapters, both in the manuscript and in the published work, organizes the narrative action in terms of scene or episode. Although we cannot be sure what the final organization might have been had Hemingway finished the book himself, the three parts of the published work, as edited by diverse hands, closely resemble Homer's structure.

Joyce's and Hemingway's narrative structures indicate different mimetic concerns, and the characterization of their heroes points to still further differences.

From an Aristotelian perspective, Hemingway's hero is an artist–warrior whose station—being considerably above the average—is closer in this respect to Homer's Odysseus than to Joyce's protagonist. Yet the modernist heroes of both Hemingway's and Joyce's works share the plight of the Homeric original, adapted to the modern idiom.

While both Hudson (*Islands*) and Bloom (*Ulysses*) languish, as I have said, in a gentle captivity, resembling the captive state of Odysseus on Calypso's island, Hemingway's resemblance in his novel's first part, "Bimini," is more direct than Joyce's, for Joyce mainly suggests the resemblance through allusions, while Hemingway gives Hudson a geographical location and setting on a Caribbean Island that literally resembles Calypso's paradisiacal isle. Joyce's very different decision was to locate his hero in a modern city and to meticulously plot his parallel Homeric course through that city. This decision provided Joyce with a subject matter that best served his parodic and satiric purposes, as opposed to Hemingway's more somber view.

The Caribbean obviously resembles Homer's Mediterranean because it allows for the kind of verisimilitude that Homer himself was able to achieve, as, for example, in portraying the conflict between Odysseus and the offended sea god, Poseidon, through whose domain the hero had to pass in order to return finally to his home. Hemingway's modern Odysseus similarly attempts to thwart the forces of time, eventual experience, and all of existence that is represented by the sea. Furthermore, in Hemingway's portrayal, as in Homer's, such avoidance is moral death. And just as forces in *The Odyssey* dislodge Homer's hero whenever he would turn aside from his destined task in his wanderings, so Hemingway thrusts his hero back into the ontological flux whenever Hudson would demur.

In part 1 of *Islands,* "Bimini," Hudson broods over his divorced but still beloved wife, the mother of his oldest son, just as Homer's Odysseus broods over his possibly remarried wife, Penelope, the mother of his son Telemachus. Odysseus ponders over faraway Ithaca, the homeland of his young manhood, while in parts 1 and 2 of *Islands,* Hudson continues to long for his "Ithaca," the city of Paris, the site of his (and, indeed, Hemingway's) magical "Movable Feast" during early manhood. In "Bimini," the emotional constriction Hudson has undergone is demonstrated by his rationalization of his real reasons for remaining on his secure island rather than wandering and "doing" (or "be"ing)—for no longer challenging life or seeking experience in the stream of life. Hudson can only look backward and take false journeys, instead of real ones: "Now," we are told, "when he was lonesome for Paris he would remember Paris instead of going there. He did the same thing with all of Europe and much of Asia and Africa" (7).

Hudson's true odyssey begins in a way that reflects Hemingway's conflation of several early books in Homer's text. Specifically, they are Book I. "What went on in the house of Odysseus"; Book V. "Hermes is sent to Calypso's island"; and the several books constituting the Telemachiad (the story of Odysseus's son's life). Again, the revelation of the similarities between Hemingway's sources and his narrative is not a portrayal of parallels. It is the process of fabricating resemblances that also serves to distract readers from dwelling primarily on the otherwise all-too-obvious parallels between *Islands* and Hemingway's personal life. Accordingly, for example, Hudson has three sons, instead of the one son featured in *The Odyssey*, each bearing some resemblance to the Homeric model, Telemachus. Hemingway also effects transformations in his characterizations of Hudson's three sons, and his portrayals of each boy, in one way or another, raise the question of which is the true son of Hudson—that is, which most resembles him and offers the greatest continuity with the rest of the classical plot. (By effecting a composite Telemachus, Hemingway also avoids some artistic difficulties later in the work, when Tom, Hudson's first son, thought to be dead, emerges alive as the lost Telemachus of Hudson's Paris/Ithaca past.)

In part 2 of *Islands*, the now dislodged and wandering Hudson has arrived on a larger island, Cuba, which is portrayed, as we have seen, as a composite of Homer's island of the lotus-eaters and Circe's different kind of escape and degrading denial. Here, unlike Odysseus, who resisted the temptation to win forgetfulness through lotus-eating, Hudson chooses alcohol and further rationalization as his responses to the death of two of his sons. The rationalization is an egocentric irony that proves to be a continuing, weak defense against the forces of existence in a contingent world. "You should not have loved them so damn much in the first place," he says, referring to his two truly dead sons (199). Hudson's heavy drinking at the Floridita, along with the name of the establishment (Floridita means "little flower"), suggests more pointedly a wish for Homeric lotus-eating and forgetfulness, and provides a setting for Hudson's attempts to avoid a new intrusion of reality, the supposed death of his remaining third son.

The action in the rest of *Islands*, however, reveals a significant difference between Hemingway's classical model and his protagonist's portrayal, reflecting the former's modern mindset. For Odysseus, love and honor are concomitant virtues of duty, and as a Greek of his times he accepts a moral and spiritual responsibility to exert his whole being in the enterprise of returning his shipmates and himself to his homeland. For him, duty is not an anchor but an honor, part of an acculturated worldview; for Hudson, in contrast, duty is a burdensome self-concern that marks the depth of his forlorn emotional and spiritual modern condition, alienated from all eternal values.

In part 3 of *Islands*, "At Sea," Hemingway creates an amalgamation of the historical context (the enveloping action of war) with the Homeric resemblances of just such a time. After his period of depressed dissipation in Havana, Hudson leads his crew on a search down the northern coast of Cuba, east of Havana, for a murderous crew of German sailors from a submarine sunk among the islands. Here, Hemingway takes advantage of the convenient connotations of several real place-names to give his narrative a mythic frame, just as he exploits the historical reality of underwater German sailors as resemblances of the sons of Poseidon, who are in conflict with Homer's Odysseus. The initial direction of Hudson's search is east, the direction of "home" in Homeric geography, although not in Western history. Some of the Spanish names of the islands—such as Paredon, Lobos, Sabinal, Confites, Romano, Cruz—enhance the metaphorical and mythic content by their suggestion of dangers, barriers, temptations, and obstructions, and as ciphers of Western secular and religious history. These suggest Homeric resemblances to Scylla and Charybdis, the Lestrogonians, Sirens, and others. Seeking resemblances, not parallels, Hemingway makes no attempt to include all or even most of their names. But the "Rome" (Romano) and "Cross" (Cruz) allusions relate Hudson's journey to the Western religious past and its spiritual significance for the modern world, as Odysseus's journey had spiritual significance for Homer's world.

A major thematic purpose of these latter tropes, then, is to evoke the universality of the journey, and prompt the revelation that Hudson, as a modern man of the West, must follow the ancient patterns inherent in the Christian scenario, patterns dictating that one must lose one's life to gain eternal life, a view that has not provided for Hudson the certitude Odysseus found in his cultural tradition.

After leaving Circe's island, Odysseus had journeyed to Hades. In a close Homeric resemblance, the opening of the third part of *Islands,* "At Sea," signals Hudson's similar Nekuia (his journey to the underworld). In *The Odyssey,* Circe describes the approach to Hades in these terms to Odysseus: "When you have crossed over the ocean, you will see a low shore, and the groves of Persphoneia, tall poplars and fruit-wasting willows; there beach your ship beside deep-eddying oceanos, and go to the moldering house of Hades" (72). Hemingway's opening line of "At Sea" is a descriptive passage that echoes Homer's passage: "There was a long white beach with coconut palms behind it . . ." (331). Although Hudson does not beach his boat, as does Odysseus, he in fact anchors it inside the reef, and this area is a place of death, since the Germans have killed the villagers. It also resembles the place where Odysseus performed his ritual sacrifices. Here, the native shacks have been burned, bodies lie in the ashes, and the land crabs are feeding on them, just as the shades of fallen heroes in Hades came to feed on the blood of Odysseus's sacrificed animals.

Hudson, like Odysseus before him, brings questions to this place of death. Odysseus had found no answers in Hades until after he talked with Teiresias, the seer, who revealed the key to conversing with the dead. Thereafter, each shade in turn fed on the blood of Odysseus's sacrifices and then answered all his questions about his family and his journey home. So it is with Hudson, who, having changed direction from the original search to the east, now searches to the west, the direction of darkness and Hades itself in Homeric geography. As Hudson and his crew search the decimated village and probe its dead bodies for the bullets that killed them, they find answers to some of their questions about the Germans. Here, too, Hudson finds a "seer" when his crew captures a badly wounded German sailor, who had been left behind. On the brink of death, the German, who "looked like a saint," answers with the cryptic, oracular "Nothing is important. . . . It doesn't hurt anymore" (362–63). For Hudson, still grieving over the death of his sons, these prophetic responses point to a way of reconciling himself to their deaths. The German's words forewarn him of his own death and remind him that death is the cessation of pain. Gloomy and negative as that is, it provides Hudson with the only solution available to an alienated modern protagonist beset by the spiritual weariness that has dominated his life for so long. When Hudson is later mortally wounded in an ambush by the last of the remaining Germans, his quest comes to an end, and he experiences an ironic "Nostos" (homecoming) by coming home to death.

If we are mindful that Hudson's journey, like Odysseus's, is twofold, physical and moral, with a large psychological component added for Hudson's modern sensibility, the novel's end is not as bleak as a reading of a single aspect of the Homeric referent would suggest. The German sailors (Homeric sons of Poseidon) seem to have won a victory and ended Hudson's wandering quest, but Hemingway's coda modifies the bleakness when Willie, Hudson's friend and crewman, attempts to soothe the dying Hudson by articulating in a masculine way the nature of the bond achieved by Hudson with his crew after the long and difficult journey, a bond that Hemingway intends the reader to acknowledge as one of a different order of reality that transcends the immediate and temporal. "I love you, you son of a bitch, and don't die," Willie pleads to Hudson, whose response is, "I think I understand." Tentative as his response is, Hudson does accept Willie's positive assertion and acknowledges a brotherhood of man founded on mutual struggle and the need for survival. Hudson's final acknowledgment is a complete reversal of his earlier commitment to a "death-house" brotherhood. The "turn" for Hemingway is of a kind with that found in *The Old Man and the Sea,* the companion piece from Hemingway's manuscript, "Sea-Book." Both sea works required newer methods of rendering a newer spirit in the fiction. In *The Old Man and the Sea,* the religiomythic metaphorical vehicle worked with astonishing effectiveness, while in *Islands,* Hudson's radically opposite "agon" is carried effectively by the Homeric resemblances.

Insofar as the similarities between the lives of characters approximate

Hemingway's life-experiences, the metaphorical groundings of the "Sea-Book" manuscript work to clearly reveal Hemingway's awareness of the dangers of isomorphisms to his art, for both works effect a distancing of the personal from the fictional.

Works Cited

Hemingway, Ernest. *Green Hills of Africa.* 1935. Rpr. New York: Collier, 1987.
——. *Islands in the Stream.* New York: Charles Scribner's Sons, 1970.
Homer. *The Odyssey.* Translated by W. H. D. Rouse. New York: N.A.L., 1937.
Stevens, Wallace. *The Necessary Angel.* New York: Random House, 1951.

Selected Bibliographies

Trolling the Deep Waters

Hemingway's Cuban Fiction and the Critics

KELLI A. LARSON

While many scholars have eagerly welcomed a new literary era with the arrival of the twenty first century, critical interest in the twentieth century's best-known American author has yet to wane. Hemingway scholarship progresses at a feverish pace with more than two hundred articles, essays, and books published annually on the man and his work. With Hemingway studies long established as a cottage industry, finding open areas for critical exploration can prove frustrating—unless one knows where to search. For those interested in exploring some of Hemingway's lesser-critiqued works, the Cuban fiction provides abundant opportunities for close readings, biographical approaches, and theoretical applications. Perhaps it is the exclusion of these works (with the possible exception of *The Old Man and the Sea*) from the typical college syllabi that has contributed to their critical neglect when compared to the overwhelming bulk of scholarship devoted to such college classroom mainstays as *The Sun Also Rises* and *A Farewell to Arms.* After all, teaching scholars tend to write about what they teach and thus know well. Certainly *The Old Man and the Sea* enjoys popularity among college faculty, but many may be reluctant to include the novella because of its heavy use within secondary school curricula (Donahue D4+). Having encountered once too often that resisting undergraduate, clinging to the erroneous supposition that the depths of *The Old Man and the Sea* had been plumbed in high school, college teachers may be reluctant to assign the novella in their courses. Thus *The Old Man and the Sea,* while cornering the critical market among the Cuban texts, still lags a clear third overall behind *The Sun Also Rises* and *A Farewell to Arms* in published criticism.

The publication of *The Old Man and the Sea* in 1952 restored Hemingway's sagging reputation, a feat he'd hoped to achieve back in 1937 with the publication of *To Have and Have Not.* Although some current criticism of *To Have and Have Not* focuses on the novel's deficiencies in character and dialogue development, which may explain in part the limited scholarly interest in the text, other critics have seized the opportunity to reconstruct Hemingway's method of composition through a firsthand examination of the author's manuscript drafts and revisions, resulting in a keener appreciation of the novel's subtleties. Indeed, recent analysis of Hemingway's experimental style within *To Have and Have Not* suggests greater narrative complexity than previously thought and points the way for future scholars, especially those interested in the application of new critical approaches and theoretical lenses.

Manuscript studies, like those mentioned above on *To Have and Have Not,* very wisely have not been confined to Hemingway's completed works. The warnings heralded by many regarding the distortions, errors, and misrepresentations in Hemingway's posthumous publications have been heeded in the case of *Islands in the Stream,* though clearly more needs to be done. At the time of Hemingway's death, the novel still lacked a clear narrative structure, necessitating extensive editing by Mary Hemingway, Charles Scribner Jr., and Carlos Baker to meld the three sections of the manuscript into a coherent whole. Because the editors did not document their deletions and alterations of the text, scholars are compelled to dig into the original manuscripts, however unformed or unfinished, to recover the authentic Hemingway. Although it is tempting to stand on a soapbox and prattle on about authorial integrity and editorial responsibility, I am ever mindful that without the efforts of various editors over the years, these posthumous contributions to the Hemingway canon might never have reached the vast majority of Hemingway aficionados. Publication of the manuscripts brings them to the larger reading public and grants scholars a wealth of critical fodder in both published and manuscript form (with the latter readily accessible in collections at the John F. Kennedy Library in Boston and elsewhere) for years to come. Thus, this may be one of those rare instances of the end justifying the means.

In looking over criticism pertaining to the short stories, a quick perusal of the MLA bibliographical listing reveals that, at least in Hemingway studies, size does matter. Scholars of Hemingway have long favored the novels over the short stories, despite the richness and complexity several of those stories reveal. Certainly heavily anthologized works, such as "The Short Happy Life of Francis Macomber" and "A Clean, Well-Lighted Place," have received their fair share of scholarly attention over the years. But many of Hemingway's more than fifty short stories remain overlooked in the critical stakes. The two Cuban stories, "Nobody Ever Dies" and "After the Storm," prove no exception to this neglect.

Hemingway traveled to Cuba during a fishing trip in 1932 and visited periodically over the next few years before eventually settling, in 1940, in a hilltop house near a small village not far from Havana. For the most part, he lived and wrote in that house for the next twenty years, and all of us are the better for it.

This annotated bibliography on Hemingway's Cuban fiction begins where Larson's *Ernest Hemingway: A Reference Guide* (1990) left off and includes materials published into 2013. Entries are arranged alphabetically by author's last name within the year of their publication. Items that were unavailable for reading are marked by an asterisk (*), with the source of their listing given in place of the usual summary annotation. With the exception of dissertations, which are listed in *Dissertation Abstracts International,* I have attempted to include all serious contributions to scholarship focused on Hemingway's Cuban fiction published in English. However, I am a realist and thus apologize to those scholars I've overlooked or misconstrued.

1988

Murphy, John. "Unspoken Depths in *The Old Man and the Sea.*" *CEA Forum* 18.2–4: 18–20.

Discusses the reader's contribution to the process of creating and understanding meaning in *The Old Man and the Sea,* suggesting that the novella's hidden depths are made up of a "string of images that can be wound into a sphere of reference."

Van Woensel, Maurice. "Hemingway's *Old Man:* An Agnostic Agonistes." *Estudos anglo-americanos* 12–13: 51–57.

**Hemingway Review* 10. 2 (1991): 92.

1989

Buffet, Jimmy. "Hooked in the Heart." *Tales from Margaritaville: Fictional Facts and Factual Fictions.* New York: Harcourt Brace Jovanovich. 189–96.

Reminisces on his adventures with a documentary film crew retracing Hemingway's footsteps in Cuba, meeting with Gregorio Fuentes, and love for *The Old Man and the Sea.*

Fleming, Robert E. "The Libel of Dos Passos in *To Have and Have Not.*" *Journal of Modern Literature* 15.4: 597–601.

Manuscript study, arguing against the long-held assumption that Hemingway had John Dos Passos in mind when creating the character of Philip Gordon and asserting instead that Gordon represents a type of opportunistic and morally corrupt author that Hemingway despised.

Flora, Joseph M. *Ernest Hemingway: A Study of the Short Fiction.* Boston: Twayne. 98–100.

Values "Nobody Ever Dies" for its experimental narrative form and its thematic links to *For Whom the Bell Tolls,* but for little else.

Leahy, Robert. "Concept Mapping: Developing Guides to Literature." *College Teaching* 37.2: 62–69.

Heuristic device for teachers and students showing the relationships between the ideas of autonomy and authority within *The Old Man and the Sea* and Camus's *The Stranger.*

Mathewson, Stephen. "Against the Stream: Thomas Hudson and Painting." *North Dakota Quarterly* 57.4: 140–45.

Argues that the realist painter Thomas Hudson in *Islands in the Stream* must free himself of the "anxiety of influence" arising from contemporary artists in order to pursue his own aesthetic vision. Cites allusions in Hudson's work to nineteenth-century American realist painter Winslow Homer.

Smith, Paul. *A Reader's Guide to the Short Stories of Ernest Hemingway.* Boston: G. K. Hall. .

Reference guide devoting a chapter to the composition and publication history, sources and influences, and criticism of each of the fifty-five short stories published during Hemingway's lifetime. Stories are arranged chronologically by composition date.

Re "After the Storm," 240–45. Smith's summary of existing criticism reveals the dearth of serious attention, with the exception of two articles, that this story has received.

Re "Nobody Ever Dies," 382–84. Smith's summary of existing criticism notes only one serious study to date.

Timms, David. "Contrasts in Form: Hemingway's *The Old Man and the Sea* and Faulkner's 'The Bear.'" In *The Modern American Novella.* Edited by A. Robert Lee. New York: St. Martin's. 97–112.

Working from various critical definitions of the term *novella,* Timms contrasts the thematic, structural, and stylistic differences between the two works. Compares their thematic treatment of women, confinement of action, and character development, concluding that *The Old Man and the Sea* conforms to the traditional definition of the genre, making it a "model novella."

1990

Edgerton, Larry. "'Nobody Ever Dies!': Hemingway's *Fifth* Story of the Spanish Civil War." In *New Critical Approaches to the Short Stories of Ernest Heming-*

way. Edited by Jackson J. Benson. Durham, NC: Duke Univ. Press. 331–40. Reprint from *Arizona Quarterly* 39.2 (Summer 1983): 135–47.

Fleming, Robert E. "The Hills Remain: The Mountain West of Hemingway's *Islands* Manuscript." *North Dakota Quarterly* 58.3: 79–85.

Manuscript study, noting that Hemingway's original draft of *Islands in the Stream* portrayed the American West in a positive light, as a place for renewal and creative growth. Because Hemingway deleted this early section from the posthumously published novel, most readers know only Hemingway's negative depiction of the West found in stories such as "The Gambler, the Nun, and the Radio" and "A Man of the World."

———, and Warren Wheelock. "Hemingway's Last Word on Stein: A Joke in the Manuscript of *Islands.*" *Hemingway Review* 9.2: 174–75.

An examination of the manuscripts reveals both an obscure joke aimed at Gertrude Stein and Hemingway's capacity to hold a grudge.

Hays, Peter L. *Ernest Hemingway.* New York: Continuum.

Concise biography of Hemingway's life, encompassing his works.

Re *To Have and Have Not,* 75–80. Criticizes the author's inept dialogue, failure to create convincing and sympathetic characterization, and racism in *To Have and Have Not.*

Re *The Old Man and the Sea,* 102–9. Discusses the restoration of Hemingway's reputation with *The Old Man and the Sea,* briefly commenting on the biblical and Christian imagery and echoes of Greek tragedy found within the novella.

Re *Islands in the Stream,* 120–24. Outlines the unusual publication history of *Islands in the Stream,* lamenting the lack of anything new in the novel; whether subject matter, characterization, or philosophy, it has been encountered before in other Hemingway works.

Morgan, Kathleen. *Tales Plainly Told: The Eyewitness Narratives of Hemingway and Homer.* Columbia, SC: Camden House. 78–80.

Compares similarities between Hemingway's and Homer's narrative styles. Reprints a portion of Hemingway's letter to Bernard Berenson denying his use of symbolism in *The Old Man and the Sea* and soliciting a blurb for the novel. Berenson's assessment of the novel as Homeric in his endorsement echoes much in Hemingway's original letter.

Spilka, Mark. "Marie Morgan." *Hemingway's Quarrel with Androgyny.* Lincoln, NE: Univ. of Nebraska Press. 243–46.

Considers the character Marie Morgan as a proletarian tribute to Pauline Pfeiffer, Hemingway's second wife. While the wealthy couples around them fight, Harry and Marie exemplify a successful, albeit androgynous, middle-aged relationship.

Stoltzfus, Ben. "Hemingway's 'After the Storm': A Lacanian Reading." In *New Critical Approaches to the Short Stories of Ernest Hemingway.* Edited by Jackson J. Benson. Durham, NC: Duke Univ. Press. 48–57.

Lacanian approach to the details of the short story, revealing a series of metaphors of repression, impotence, death, and desire.

Wilson, G. R., Jr. "Saints and Sinners in the Caribbean: The Case for *Islands in the Stream.*" *Studies in American Fiction* 18.1: 27–40.

Reads *Islands* as a structural and thematic inversion of *The Old Man and the Sea.* Although both protagonists struggle in a hostile and alienated world, Santiago triumphs through his faith in the heroic human spirit while Hudson fails through spiritual despair. Provides a close examination of the complicated structure of *Islands,* arguing that despite the commonly held belief that it is structurally loose, the novel's careful crafting ensures a consistent and balanced narrative that enhances its thematic coherence.

1991

Brenner, Gerry. *The Old Man and the Sea: Story of a Common Man.* New York: Twayne.

Brenner summarizes the varied critical responses to the novella over the years, arguing against the simplified portrait of the dignified, benevolent, and noble hero. Rather, Brenner views Santiago as morally complex, noting a host of negative qualities that point to his flawed character, including his passive-aggressive and sexist behavior and his emotional abuse of Manolin, arising from latent homosexual desire. Connects elements of the text, such as the bringing in of the great fish and the relationship between Santiago and Manolin, with professional and personal anxieties Hemingway was experiencing at the time of composition. Most helpful is Brenner's overview of the important political and cultural currents of the time period.

Byrne, Janice F. "New Acquisitions Shed Light on *The Old Man and the Sea* Sources." *Hemingway Review* 10.2: 68–70.

An early notebook in Hemingway's own handwriting and the log of his fishing boat the *Pilar* suggest the author began recording material for *The Old Man and the Sea* as early as 1932.

Fleming, Robert E. "Roger Davis of *Islands:* What the Manuscript Adds." In *Hemingway: Essays of Reassessment.* Edited by Frank Scafella. New York: Oxford Univ. Press. 53–60.

Recaps the plot line of the early manuscript, which reveals Davis as the main character, struggling to heal the division between his artistic and personal lives. Fleming hypothesizes that the thematic shift away from the difficulties of the writer in the final version may have reflected Hemingway's wish to avoid having the work considered autobiographical; the vulnerable, troubled writer of the holograph manuscript may have paralleled too closely Hemingway's own anguished life.

Petite, Joseph. "Hemingway and Existential Education." *Journal of Evolutionary Psychology* 12.1–2: 152–64.

Argues that in much of Hemingway's fiction, the author pairs a naïve student with a worldly teacher, who then instructs the uninitiated, though often unsuccessfully, on the ways of living in a chaotic world, but that this pattern changed near the end of Hemingway's career. At that point, most notably with the Bimini section of *Islands in the Stream* and *The Old Man and the Sea,* Hemingway abandoned the model, along with the notion that teachers should instruct others, instead presenting a world in which the naïve must learn firsthand, directly from life.

Simmons, Marc, et al. *Santiago: Saint of Two Worlds.* Albuquerque, NM: Univ. of New Mexico.

Though Hemingway's Santiago is not studied here, the authors attempt to provide a comprehensive overview of the history largely dominated by myth—of St. James (known in Spain as Santiago). Includes memorable photographs of art depicting Santiago as well as the pilgrimage route to Santiago de Compostela.

Stoltzfus, Ben. "*The Old Man and the Sea:* A Lacanian Reading." In *Hemingway: Essays of Reassessment.* Edited by Frank Scafella. New York: Oxford Univ. Press. 190–99.

Lacanian approach attempting to define the iceberg beneath the surface of *The Old Man and the Sea.* Stoltzfus focuses on three areas: Hemingway's conscious text; the reader's construction of meaning; and Hemingway's unconscious. Contends that Santiago (and Hemingway) wishes to supplant the law of the father, which emphasizes "meekness, humility, and self-abnegation, with more elemental virtues stressing pride, honor, and killing."

1992

Culver, Michael. "Sparring in the Dark: Hemingway, Strater and *The Old Man and the Sea.*" *Hemingway Review* 11.2: 31–37.

Source study. Recounts Hemingway's Bimini fishing trip with artist friend Henry "Mike" Strater, whose hooking of a giant marlin served as a model for *The Old Man and the Sea.* Sums up Hemingway's troubled relationship with the painter, which essentially dissolved over the events of that trip.

Hurley, C. Harold, ed. *Hemingway's Debt to Baseball in* The Old Man and the Sea: *A Collection of Critical Readings.* New York: Mellen.

Collection of mostly previously published material. Contents:

"Introduction," by C. Harold Hurley, 1–6. Brief overview of Hemingway's fascination with baseball in *The Old Man and the Sea,* along with summaries of articles included in the volume.

"Hemingway's Praise of Dick Sisler in *The Old Man and the Sea,*" by Samuel E. Longmire, 9–11. Reprint from *American Literature* 42.1 (1970).

"Carelessness and the Cincinnati Reds in *The Old Man and the Sea,*" by Richard Allan Davison, 13–17. Reprint from *Notes on Contemporary Literature* 1.1 (1971).

"Hemingway's Pleiade Ballplayers," by George Monteiro, 19–23: Reprint from *Fitzgerald/Hemingway Annual* (1973).

"The Reds, the White Sox, and *The Old Man and the Sea,*" by George Monteiro, 25–27. Reprint from *Notes on Contemporary Literature* 4.3 (1974).

"Santiago, DiMaggio, and Hemingway: The Ageing Professionals of *The Old Man and the Sea,*" by George Monteiro, 29–38. Reprint from *Fitzgerald/Hemingway Annual* (1974).

"Baseball and Baseball Talk in *The Old Man and the Sea,*" by James Barbour and Robert Sattelmeyer, 39–47. Reprint from *Fitzgerald/Hemingway Annual* (1975).

"Hemingway: *The Writer as Artist,*" by Carlos Baker, 51–52. Excerpt from "The Ancient Mariner" in *Hemingway: The Writer as Artist,* edited by Carlos Baker (Princeton, NJ: Princeton Univ. Press, 1952).

"Hemingway's Tragic Fisherman, Review of *The Old Man and the Sea,*" by Robert Gorham Davis, 53. Excerpt from *New York Times Book Review* 7 September 1952, sec. 7: 10.

"The Sham Battle over Ernest Hemingway," by Ray B. West Jr., 54. Excerpt from *Western Review* 17 (Spring 1953).

"The Heroic Impulse in *The Old Man and the Sea,*" by Leo Gurko, 55. Excerpt from *English Journal* 44 (1955).

"*The Old Man and the Sea:* Hemingway's Tragic Vision," by Clinton S. Burhans Jr., 56–57. Excerpt from *American Literature* 31 (1960).

"The Marlin and the Shark: A Note on *The Old Man and the Sea,*" by Keiichi Harada, 58–59. Excerpt from *Journal of the College of Literature* (Aoyama Gakuin University, Tokyo) 4 (March 1960).

"A Ritual of Transfiguration: *The Old Man and the Sea,*" by Arvin R. Wells, 60–61. Excerpt from *University Review* 30 (Winter 1963).

"Hemingway's Extended Vision: *The Old Man and the Sea,*" by Bickford Sylvester, 62. Excerpt from *PMLA* 81 (1966).

"*Ernest Hemingway: A Reconsideration,*" by Philip Young, 63. Excerpt from "Death and Transfiguration," in *Ernest Hemingway: A Reconsideration* (University Park, PA: Pennsylvania State Univ. Press, 1966).

"New Worlds, Old Myths," by Claire Rosenfield, 64–67. Excerpt from *Twentieth Century Interpretations of* The Old Man and the Sea: *A Collection of Critical Essays,* edited by Katharine T. Jobes (Englewood Cliffs, NJ: Prentice, 1968).

"*Hemingway's Craft,*" by Sheldon Norman Grebstein, 68. Excerpt from "Hemingway's Humor," in *Hemingway's Craft* (Carbondale, IL: Southern Illinois Univ. Press, 1973).

"Biblical Allusions in *The Old Man and the Sea,*" by Joseph M. Flora, 69. Excerpt from *Studies in Short Fiction* 10 (1973).

"The Poem of Santiago and Manolin," by Linda W. Wagner, 70. Excerpt from *Modern Fiction Studies* 19 (1973–74).

"When Did Hemingway Write *The Old Man and the Sea?*" by Darrel Mansell, 71. Excerpt from *Fitzgerald/Hemingway Annual* (1974).

"The Facts Behind the Fiction: The 1950 American League Pennant Race and *The Old Man and the Sea,*" by C. Harold Hurley, 77–93. Detailed study of the factual events of the 1950 baseball season, relating the public American League pennant race to Santiago's heroic and private struggle with the marlin and sharks. "Against the games of baseball's "September Stretch," Santiago's ordeal at sea achieves temporal and thematic synchronism with the larger order of a sport whose contests seem to many a paradigm of the human condition."

"Just 'a Boy' or 'Already a Man'?: Manolin's Age in *The Old Man and the Sea,*" by C. Harold Hurley, 95–101. Argues against the long-held assumption by many critics that Manolin is a teenager, on the verge of adulthood. Suggests that an exchange between Santiago and Manolin regarding the "great Sisler's father" sets Manolin's age at about ten years. Expanded version of *Hemingway Review* 10 (Spring 1991).

"The World of Spirit or the World of Sport? Figuring the Numbers in *The Old Man and the Sea,*" by C. Harold Hurley, 103–17. Gives a broad overview of the varying critical responses, often related to religion, aimed at explaining Hemingway's fascination throughout the novella with the numbers eighty-four and eighty-five. Notes the chronological correspondence between the two numbers and events of the 1950 American League pennant race, suggesting that the numbers reflect Santiago's enthusiasm for baseball and high regard for Joe DiMaggio.

Mellard, James. "Homer, Hemingway, and the Oral Tradition." *Style* 26.1: 129–41. Review of Kathleen Morgan's *Tales Plainly Told: The Eyewitness Narratives of Hemingway and Homer* (1990), arguing that Morgan should have been comparing both Homer and Hemingway to the broad tradition of oral narrative to which both authors belong. Mellard goes on to discuss Hemingway's adherence to the oral tradition's dominant principles of economy and scope in *The Old Man and the Sea.*

Mellow, James R. *Hemingway: A Life Without Consequences.* Boston: Houghton Mifflin.

Re "After the Storm," 361–62. Recounts the actual event upon which "After the Storm" is based.

Re *To Have and Have Not,* 484–88. Biographical overview of the writing of *To Have and Have Not,* criticizing the novel's lack of unity, improbable characterization, and obvious social commentary. Remarks on early versions of the novel, noting Hemingway's numerous deletions and citing several sources among Hemingway's friends, acquaintances, and literary rivals (e.g., Dos Passos as source for Richard Gordon).

Re *The Old Man and the Sea,* 578–83. Biographical overview of the writing, publishing, and critical reception of *The Old Man and the Sea,* identifying Santiago with the author. Mellow briefly outlines the novel's use of Christian symbolism and Hemingway's denial of such use.

Messent, Peter. *Ernest Hemingway.* New York: St. Martin's.

Re *To Have and Have Not,* 63–68. Notes Hemingway's significant shift toward the theme of class in *To Have and Have Not,* criticizing the novel for its disjointed narrative voice and characterization and its lack of subtlety. Argues that while the novel's modern context may be heavily deterministic, Hemingway celebrates Harry Morgan's self-sufficiency and heroic individualism.

Re *Islands in the Stream,* 79–82. Messent suggests that despite the obvious flaws in *Islands in the Stream* (reliance on partial narrative, plot turns, and an unstable central protagonist), the novel resists easy interpretation and results in an interesting "hotch-potch."

Morgan, Kathleen, and Luis Losada. "Santiago in *The Old Man and the Sea:* A Homeric Hero." *Hemingway Review* 12.1: 35–51.

Source study, comparing Santiago with Homer's heroes from the *Iliad* and the *Odyssey.* Sees the old fisherman demonstrating three fundamental heroic characteristics. Santiago is born to fulfill his destiny as a fisherman and to be the best at it. In so doing, he reflects upon his experiences and makes conscious choices based on thoughtful analysis. Reads Santiago's struggle with the marlin as an epic battle between two champions. Not only does Santiago share physical characteristics with his Trojan predecessors, such as Achilles and others, he also demonstrates empathy with and respect for his enemy. In the end, he succeeds through his wits, strength, and tenacity.

Morrison, Toni. "Disturbing Nurses and the Kindness of Sharks." *Playing in the Dark: Whiteness and the Literary Imagination.* Cambridge, MA: Harvard Univ. Press, 61–91.

Criticizes Hemingway's treatment of African American characters in his texts, most specifically the silencing of Wesley from *To Have and Have Not.*

Sees Hemingway's discrimination against the "nameless, sexless, nationless Africanist presence" as a narrative strategy to establish and confirm the superiority of the novel's white characters, namely Harry and Marie.

Prasad, Murari. "The Sea as Symbol in *Moby Dick, Lord Jim* and *The Old Man and the Sea.*" *Indian Journal of American Studies* 22.2: 89–95.
Compares the common sea symbol found in the three novels, examining how each protagonist must face differing existential challenges set against the limitless and inscrutable backdrop of the sea. "The Seascape in Hemingway's story becomes the operative alternative reality on which man can impose order, exercise his will, and attain selfhood through his exertion and strenuous work."

Pressman, Richard S. "Individualists or Collectivists? Steinbeck's *In Dubious Battle* and Hemingway's *To Have and Have Not.*" *Steinbeck Quarterly* 25.3–4: 119–33.
Comparison of the left-wing political ideology espoused in each novel, summing up the long-running critical debate over whether or not the novels' central themes support collectivism or individualism. Contends that these proletarian works served as each author's reaction to the Great Depression, and that while they engage the Depression, they also evade it; internal conflict within each novel reflects the author's own ambivalent feelings on the subject.

Salick, Roydon. "Selvon's Santiago: An Intertextual Reading of *The Plains of Caroni.*" *Journal of West Indian Literature* 5.1–2: 97–105.
Influence study, examining similarities between *The Old Man and the Sea* (1952) and *The Plains of Caroni* (1969), including the creation of peasant heroes who preserve an obsolete way of life and their reliance on young initiates (Manolin and Popo). Reads Hemingway's novel as the more parabolic of the two.

Viertel, Peter. *Dangerous Friends: At Large with Hemingway and Huston in the Fifties.* New York: Doubleday, 183–84, 242–43, 248–50, 254–59, 264–65, 274–80. Peter Viertel, novelist and screenwriter for the film of *The Old Man and the Sea* recounts his time spent with Hemingway and the various production difficulties associated with the screen adaptation of Hemingway's novella.

1993

Miller, Paul W. "Hemingway's Posthumous Fiction, 1961–87: A Rorschach Test for Critics." *Midamerica: The Yearbook of the Society for the Study of Midwestern Literature* 20: 98–107.
Remarks on the overall decline of interest in the posthumous works. Divides critics into two camps, those biographical critics who promote the posthumous works because they illuminate Hemingway's life or embody his writing

style and aesthetic critics, who decry the continued publication of inferior texts that fail to meet the author's earlier generic and thematic standards. Briefly comments on the "divided" critical response to *Islands in the Stream.*

Morris, Daniel. "Hemingway and *Life:* Consuming Revolutions." *American Periodicals* 3: 62–74.
Chronicles Hemingway's close association with *Life* magazine from 1940 to his suicide in 1961. Notes that the publication of *The Old Man and the Sea* in *Life* fit well the magazine's traditional image. Comments on *Life*'s marketing strategies regarding Hemingway (his image and works) and on Hemingway's advertisement for Ballantine Ale, which made use of his recently published *Old Man and the Sea.*

Murphy, Charlene M. "Hemingway, Winslow Homer, and *Islands in the Stream:* Influence and Tribute." *Hemingway Review* 13.1: 76–85.
Source study, examining how American artist Winslow Homer's Caribbean paintings not only influenced Hemingway's descriptions of the landscape and the artistic creations of his character Thomas Hudson but also contributed to larger themes within the novel. "The struggle to endure, the paradox of the struggle between man and nature and the harmony between man and nature—all of it is shown in its complexity by both artists."

Prescott, Jeryl J. "Liberty for Just(us): Gender and Race in Hemingway's *To Have and Have Not.*" *College Language Association Journal* 37.2: 176–88.
Looks at Hemingway's treatment of gender and race. Contends that while a strong sympathy for the plight of women emerges, minorities (including African Americans and Cubans) are marginalized and stereotyped.

Salick, Roydon. "Selvon and the Limits of Heroism: A Reading of *The Plains of Caroni.*" In *Shades of Empire in Colonial and Post-Colonial Literatures.* Edited by C. C. Barfoot and Theo D'haen. Atlanta, GA: Rodopi. 221–34.
In comparing Balgobin with Santiago, Salick argues that while *The Plains of Caroni* is not as parabolic as *The Old Man and the Sea,* both protagonists fall into the category of traditional epic hero. In their courageous struggles to preserve their obsolete ways of life, Santiago and Balgobin are men to be honored and emulated.

1994

Comley, Nancy R., and Robert Scholes. *Hemingway's Genders: Rereading the Hemingway Text.* New Haven, CT: Yale Univ. Press. 40–43.
Defines the "rich bitch" as primarily concerned with sex, money, and power. Contrasts the sexual appetites of the poor Marie Morgan with the rich Dorothy Hollis and Helene Bradley.

Fleming, Robert E. *The Face in the Mirror: Hemingway's Writers.* Tuscaloosa, AL: Univ. of Alabama Press.

Re "*To Have and Have Not:* Portrait of the Artist as a Bad Man," 66–76. Reprints portions of "Portrait of the Artist as a Bad Man," from *North Dakota Quarterly* 57.1 (Winter 1987), with additional manuscript evidence to support his original thesis that *To Have and Have Not* demonstrates Hemingway's ambivalence over the role of the writer and his responsibility to his fellow human beings.

Re "Posthumous Works: *Islands in the Stream,*" 102–28. Manuscript study. Fleming suggests that Hemingway's usual distance from his fictional artists diminished in *Islands in the Stream* to the extent that he was unable to finish the novel. Sees painter Thomas Hudson and author Roger Davis as doubles articulating the plight of the artist, who must balance his family life with his professional responsibilities. Fleming details the extensive revisions in the manuscripts regarding this theme and points to numerous biographical connections between the characters and Hemingway himself. Hemingway's revisions may have reflected his growing concern regarding the "confessional" turn the novel was taking. "Torn between his commitments to his art and his children, the artist chooses the former, but only at the cost of being tormented by guilt."

Gajdusek, Robert. "Sacrifice and Redemption: The Meaning of the Boy/Son and Man/Father Dialect in the Work of Ernest Hemingway." *North Dakota Quarterly* 62.2: 166–80.

Traces the pattern of the necessary sacrifice of the boy-son figure as a means of redemption for the lost man-father figure throughout much of the Hemingway canon. Looks at the significance of giving characters two first names in several texts, including *To Have and Have Not* (e.g., Harry Morgan and Richard Gordon), as a way of eliminating the father.

Losada, Luis A. "George Sisler, Manolin's Age, and Hemingway's Use of Baseball." *Hemingway Review* 14.1: 79–83.

Close reading of the "great Sisler's father" passage in *The Old Man and the Sea* in light of Hemingway's habit of conflating historical facts to fit his artistic purposes. Argues that the passage alone should not be relied upon to determine Manolin's exact age.

Miller, Paul W. "Hemingway's Posthumous Fiction: From Brimming Vault to Bare Cupboard." *Midamerica: The Yearbook of the Society for the Study of Midwestern Literature* 21: 98–111.

Contends that despite Mrs. Hemingway's stated principles of publication regarding the posthumous works, violations and abuses of those principles have reduced Hemingway's stature as an author. Gives a summary to date of Hemingway's posthumously published fiction, noting editorial procedures and significant alterations between manuscript and published text. Sums up the critical reception of *Islands in the Stream* along with the debate over whether or not it should have been published at all.

Oberhelman, Harley D. "Hemingway and Garciá Márquez: Two Shipwreck Narratives." *International Fiction Review* 21.1–2: 1–6.
Influence study, examining similarities between *The Old Man and the Sea* (1952) and Márquez's *Relato de un náufrago* [The Story of a Shipwrecked Sailor] (1982), noting that they share the theme of "winner take nothing." Focuses on the intense public reaction and political turmoil created by the 1955 publication in serial form of Márquez's text.

Philbrick, Nathaniel. "A Window on the Prey: The Hunter Sees a Human Face in Hemingway's 'After the Storm' and Melville's 'The Grand Armada.'" *Hemingway Review* 14.1: 25–35.
Comparison of Hemingway's short story with Melville's earlier piece from *Moby-Dick,* asserting that both authors undermine the traditional hunter-prey relationship by "humanizing" the prey. Although no direct evidence exists that Hemingway read Melville, Philbrick argues that thematic and structural parallels, such as the use of the storm and the chase, suggest Hemingway may have sought out the works of the great sea writer before attempting "After the Storm," his first mature sea fiction.

Plath, James. "'After the Denim' and 'After the Storm': Raymond Carver Comes to Terms with the Hemingway Influence." *Hemingway Review* 13.2: 37–51.
Influence study, charting Carver's eventual acceptance of Hemingway's effect on his writing, especially his indebtedness to Hemingway's minimalist style. Noting thematic and structural parallels between the two stories, Plath suggests both are about timing, luck, and the will to survive in the face of defeat.

Smith, Jayne R. "*The Old Man and the Sea.*" The Old Man and the Sea/Ethan Frome: *Curriculum Unit.* Rocky River, OH: The Center for Learning. 1–37.
Instructional materials aimed at the high school level. Smith provides lesson plans, study questions, essay topics, and reading quizzes on a variety of subjects, including the themes of isolation and nature and Christian symbolism.

1995

Croft, Steven. "Karl Jasper's Ideas on Tragedy and Hemingway's *The Old Man and the Sea.*" *Notes on Contemporary Literature* 25.3: 7–8.
Notes similarities between Santiago and Karl Jasper's definition of the tragic hero in *Tragedy Is Not Enough,* also published in 1952. Croft emphasizes the notions of mythic struggle and the role of guilt/free choice in both texts.

Donaldson, Scott. "Protecting the Troops from Hemingway: An Episode in Censorship." *Hemingway Review* 15.1: 87–93.

Examination of military memoranda reveals an unsuccessful attempt by military personnel to destroy Armed Services Editions of *To Have and Have Not* and *Selected Short Stories,* because of their detrimental effect on "the culture and simple virtue of American civilization."

Mandel, Miriam B. *Reading Hemingway: The Facts in the Fictions.* Metuchen, NJ: Scarecrow Press.

Reference guide, annotating the real people, fictional characters, animals, and cultural constructs found in each of Hemingway's nine novels. Entries are arranged alphabetically and include information on such diverse topics as music, sports, politics, art, marine exploration, and history. Thorough index.

Re *To Have and Have Not,* 164–97.

Re *The Old Man and the Sea,* 346–63.

Re *Islands in the Stream,* 364–441.

Strauch, Edward H. "*The Old Man and the Sea* as Testament." *Aligarh Journal of English Studies* 17.1–2: 66–81.

Archetypal approach, first examining the novella's contrasts and distortions and then tracing comparisons between characters, situations, space, and time. Relates Santiago's struggle to the larger physical and spiritual struggle for survival of all humanity. Sees the underlying message of the story to be one of hope, love, and faith.

1996

Boker, Pamela A. *The Grief Taboo in American Literature: Loss and Prolonged Adolescence in Twain, Melville, and Hemingway.* New York: New York Univ. Press.

"*Islands in the Stream:* Hitting the Wall of the Heroic Code," 270–80. Psychoanalytic approach. Discusses Hudson's strategies for dealing with his emotional pain and fear of loss, including ritualized drinking and work. Far from relieving him of his grief, Hudson's strict adherence to these defense tactics accelerates his emotional decline.

"*The Old Man and the Sea:* Transcending the Fear of Loss," 281–86. Contrasts Santiago with Hudson. Unlike Hudson, who represses his emotions out of fear of loss, Santiago loves deeply and unconditionally because he "is resigned to the very idea of loss and grief."

Bruccoli, Matthew J., with the assistance of Robert W. Trogdon. *The Only Thing That Counts: The Ernest Hemingway–Maxwell Perkins Correspondence, 1925–1947.* New York: Scribner. 187–88, 191, 195, 199, 202, 245, 248–51, 253.

Reprints selected correspondence between Hemingway and his editor, with numerous references to the writing, publication, and sales of *To Have and*

Have Not and the writing and positioning of "After the Storm" within the short story collection *Winner Take Nothing* (1933).

Burwell, Rose Marie. *Hemingway: The Postwar Years and the Posthumous Novels.* New York: Cambridge Univ. Press.

Critical biography, arguing that Hemingway's four posthumous works, *A Moveable Feast, Islands in the Stream, The Garden of Eden,* and the African journal, form a tetralogy of his vision of the artist "as writer and painter, and as son, husband and father" but that their publication history obscured their connection. Examines Hemingway's focus on the life of the artist from childhood through middle age and his use of memory, paired painter/writer character relationships, and thematic concern with the artist's growth and decline over time. Argues that Hemingway's distance from his fictional artists diminished in these later works, demonstrating the author's own anxieties and fears. Asserts that despite his difficulties in completing the four works, Hemingway did intend them to be published after his death. Burwell devotes a chapter to each of the four posthumous works, with the greatest attention given to *Islands in the Stream.* Extensive endnotes.

"*Islands in the Stream:* A World of Men Without Women," 51–94. Relying on Hemingway's manuscripts and correspondence with editors, Burwell reconstructs the writing history of *Islands in the Stream,* including the evolution of *The Old Man and the Sea.* Details the numerous revisions of the various manuscripts that eventually comprised *Islands.* Also chronicles Hemingway's troubled relationship with Martha Gellhorn and developing relationship with Mary Welsh. Suggests that Hudson's lack of true parental concern reflects Hemingway's failure at intimacy in his personal life; unlike many of Hemingway's other protagonists, Hudson is unable to heal his inadequacies through his art and fails to reconcile his creativity with domestic life.

Donaldson, Scott, ed. *The Cambridge Companion to Hemingway.* New York: Cambridge Univ. Press.

"Hemingway's Late Fiction: Breaking New Ground," by Robert E. Fleming, 128–48. Far from seeing Hemingway resting on his literary laurels, Fleming praises the experimental nature of Hemingway's later works, including *Islands in the Stream.* Provides a composition history of the posthumous novel along with an analysis of the artistic doubles and father-son relationship found within it. Frequently notes connections to *The Old Man and the Sea.*

"The Cuban Context of *The Old Man and the Sea,*" by Bickford Sylvester, 243–68. Argues for a close reading of narrative detail in order to reconstruct the novella's cultural context and thus understand the plot and its multilayered meanings. Advises scholars to look to a Cuban explanation of puzzling details before leaping to "symbolic" interpretations. Provides important information on topics such as turtle hunting, the Virgin of Cobre, baseball, and New Testament Gospels. Comments on the parallels between the two champions, Santiago and Joe DiMaggio, and on their larger thematic relationship to society as a whole. Sets the record straight, citing historical and topical detail, regarding the protracted debate over Manolin's age. Asserts that allusions to American baseball player Dick Sisler and various fishing equipment, as well as a Cuban consciousness about the patriarchal family structure, establish Manolin's age at twenty-two, far older than most scholars and readers have assumed.

Meyers, Jeffrey. "Bogart and Hemingway." *Virginia Quarterly Review* 72: 446–49.
Draws biographical comparisons between Hemingway and Humphrey Bogart, who starred in the film version of *To Have and Have Not.*

Moreland, Kim. *The Medievalist Impulse in American Literature: Twain, Adams, Fitzgerald, and Hemingway.* Charlottesville, VA: Univ. Press of Virginia. 181–83.
Although identifying Santiago with Christ, Moreland reads the fishing trip as a mythic quest or joust. Makes thematic connections with *Green Hills of Africa* regarding the transitory nature of such mythic places.

Plath, James. "Santiago at the Plate: Baseball in *The Old Man and the Sea.*" *Hemingway Review* 16.1: 65–82.
Provides an overview of the diverse criticism concerning baseball references in *The Old Man and the Sea.* Adds to the critical debate by asserting that "baseball serves not only as a metaphorical or allegorical underpinning, but as a structural element as well." The numerous references create a pattern "which suggests player at-bats during a crucial game." Connects Santiago's struggle at sea with hitting balls. Though Santiago succeeds in the first two instances with the marlin and mako, in his third time at bat he goes "down swinging against the shovel-nosed sharks." Explicates the cultural and historical context of many of the baseball allusions.

Putnam, Ann. "Across the River and into the Stream: Journey of the Divided Heart." *North Dakota Quarterly* 63.3: 90–98.
Broad overview of the pastoral landscape found in many Hemingway works, including *The Old Man and the Sea.* Discusses Santiago's tragic adventure, to kill that which he loves and respects.

Tessitore, John. *The Hunt and the Feast: A Life of Ernest Hemingway.* New York: Franklin Watts. 133–35, 175–78.
Briefly notes Hemingway's hurtful parody of friend John Dos Passos and others in *To Have and Have Not.* Mentions the author's nervousness over the impending publication of *The Old Man and the Sea* in *Life,* and its subsequent success with readers and critics alike.

Tyler, Lisa. "'Women Have a Bad Time Really': Gender and Interpretation in *To*

Have and Have Not." *Marjorie Kinnan Rawlings Journal of Florida Literature* 7: 57–66.

Takes issue with previous criticism, contending that male critics, like the men in the novel, have failed to understand its female characters. Focuses primarily on Richard's misinterpretations regarding his wife and others. Argues that *To Have and Have Not* "suggests, obliquely, that women are more skilled at interpretation than men, and he [Hemingway] implies that women might make better writers."

1997

de Koster, Katie, ed. *Readings on Ernest Hemingway.* San Diego, CA: Greenhaven Press.

Collection of previously published material. Contents:

"Rejecting 'A Separate Peace,'" by Edgar Johnson, 85–89. Excerpt of "Farewell the Separate Peace: The Rejections of Ernest Hemingway," *Sewanee Review* 48.3 (Summer 1940). Focused on *To Have and Have Not.*

"Women and Minorities in *To Have and Have Not*" by Jeryl J. Prescott, 155–61. Reprint of "Liberty for Just(us): Gender and Race in Hemingway's *To Have and Have Not,*" *CLA Journal* (December 1993).

Galeano, Juan Carlos. "By the River." *ANQ: A Quarterly Journal of Short Articles, Notes, and Reviews* 10.2: 38.

Brief reflection on his appreciation of *The Old Man and the Sea.*

Hurley, C. Harold. "Letter." *Hemingway Review* 16.2: 120–22.

Responds to James Plath's "Santiago at the Plate: Baseball in *The Old Man and the Sea,*" *Hemingway Review* 16.1 (Fall 1996). Hurley takes issue with Plath's factual misstatements and misinterpretations of the baseball references in *The Old Man and the Sea.*

Knott, Toni D. "Playing in the Light: Examining Categorization in *To Have and Have Not* as a Reflection of Identity or Racism." *North Dakota Quarterly* 64.3: 82–88.

Contests Toni Morrison's thesis (in *Playing in the Dark: Whiteness and the Literary Imagination* [Cambridge, MA: Harvard Univ. Press, 1992]) that Hemingway's treatment of African American characters in *To Have and Have Not* enhances the status of whites in the novel. Rather, Knott asserts that such a reading misses the implications of Hemingway's irony, designed to enlighten his readers on the difficulties of making judgments based on appearance. Portions of this article were reprinted and expanded upon in Knott's *One Man Alone: Hemingway and* To Have and Have Not (Lanham, MD: Univ. Press of America, 1999).

Listoe, Daniel. "Writing Toward Death: The Stylistic Necessities of the Last Journeys of Ernest Hemingway." *North Dakota Quarterly* 64.3: 89–95.

Notes Hemingway's thematic preoccupation with imminent death in his later works. Examines Robert Jordan, Richard Cantwell, and Santiago as artists who prepare for their inevitable deaths by finishing their projects—in Santiago's case, for example, bringing in the fish.

Monteiro, George. "Grace, Good Works, and the Hemingway Ethic." In *The Calvinist Roots of the Modern Era.* Edited by Aliki Barnstone, Michael Tomasek Manson, and Carol J. Singley. Hanover, NH: Univ. Press of New England. 73–90.

Examines the evolution of the theme of grace and good works in several of Hemingway texts, beginning with "Today is Friday" (1926) and concluding with *The Old Man and the Sea* (1952). Compares Hemingway's vision of Jesus with that found in Bruce Barton's best seller, *The Man Nobody Knows,* and Max Weber's *The Protestant Ethic and the Spirit of Capitalism.* Both Barton and Hemingway envision Jesus as a "he-man" and an "outdoor man." Sees Santiago and DiMaggio as having achieved grace through their courage, suffering, and professionalism.

Nyman, Jopi. "A Tragedy of Idealism in *To Have and Have Not.*" In *Men Alone: Masculinity, Individualism, and Hard-Boiled Fiction.* Atlanta, GA: Rodopi. 272–91.

Treats the loss of idealism, suggesting that the novel's stance on the topic is paradoxical: without idealism, a character's value is questionable, but to believe in any ideology is impossible within the modern world. Though Nyman discusses the loss of idealism pervading society as a whole, he focuses on Morgan's fatal flaw—his inability to adapt his individualism and idealism in a changing world. Interestingly, he asserts that the novel fails to provide an alternate vision or ideology, resulting in an overpowering mood of bleakness. Briefly discusses the connection between language and morality within the novel.

Reynolds, Michael. *Hemingway: The 1930s.* New York: W. W. Norton.

Re "After the Storm," 86–87. Comments briefly on the source for and lack of sentiment in "After the Storm."

Re *To Have and Have Not,* 236–42, 269–71, 274–75. Biographical overview of the writing and publication history of *To Have and Have Not,* noting sources among Hemingway's friends and Key West locales. Notes the author's numerous revisions and deletions in preparing the final manuscript.

Rogal, Samuel J. *For Whom the Dinner Bell Tolls: The Role and Function of Food and Drink in the Prose of Ernest Hemingway.* Bethesda, MD: International Scholars Publications. 156–61.

Distinguishes Santiago from Hemingway's other protagonists for his spare and practical eating and drinking habits.

Sabetelli, Arnold E. "The Re-forming of Word and Meaning in *Islands in the Stream.*" *North Dakota Quarterly* 64.3: 177–83.
Uses *Islands in the Stream* and an essay by Maurice Merleau-Ponty, "Indirect Language and the Voices of Silence," to explore the similarities between the painter's act of expression and the writer's. Both texts aid in our understanding of how language is formed and used.

1998

Bandyopadyay, Soma. "The Ancient Mariner, the Tainted Mariner and Hiawatha: Studies in Pride." *Journal of the Department of English: Hemingway Centennial Tribute* (Rabindra Bharati University, Calcutta, India) 5 (1998–99): 158–66.
Comparison study of *The Old Man and the Sea* with Melville's *Moby Dick* and Longfellow's *Son of Hiawatha,* identifying each protagonist's struggle as a test of manhood resulting in his transcendence over pride.

Barua, D. K. "*The Old Man and the Sea:* A Humanist Parable." *Journal of the Department of English: Hemingway Centennial Tribute* (Rabindra Bharati University, Calcutta, India) 5 (1998–99): 142–48.
Contrasts Hemingway's humanistic approach in *The Old Man and the Sea* to Melville's theologically framed *Moby Dick.*

Chakrabarti, Santosh. "*The Old Man and the Sea:* A Story of Conviction." *Journal of the Department of English: Hemingway Centennial Tribute* (Rabindra Bharati University, Calcutta, India) 5 (1998–99): 194–98.
Briefly looks at Santiago's convictions of strength as a fisherman and social acceptance resulting from killing the marlin.

Choudhury, Sheila Lahiri. "Re-inventing the Whale: Hemingway's *The Old Man and the Sea.*" *Journal of the Department of English: Hemingway Centennial Tribute* (Rabindra Bharati University, Calcutta, India) 5 (1998–99): 174–83.
Compares Hemingway's reinvention of the paradoxical hunter/prey motif to Melville's *Moby Dick,* identifying key characteristics of the quest found in both works.

Knott, Toni D. "One Man Alone: Dimensions of Individuality and Categorization in *To Have and Have Not.*" *Hemingway Review* 17.2: 78–87.
Argues that Hemingway's categorization of people within the novel (often derogatory and disparaging) reveals the limitations of stereotyping, a common societal practice then and now. Identifies three potential heroes within the text (Harry Morgan, Professor MacWalsey, and Helen Gordon) because

they accept responsibility for their actions and value human relationships. Portions of this article were reprinted and expanded upon in Knott's *One Man Alone: Hemingway and* To Have and Have Not (Lanham, MD: Univ. Press of America, 1999).

Mandal, Somdatta, "The Itinerant American Traveller [*sic*]: Settings and Locales in Ernest Hemingway's Fiction." *Journal of the Department of English: Hemingway Centennial Tribute* (Rabindra Bharati University, Calcutta, India) 5 (1998–99): 83–97.
Focuses on the relationships between geography, experience, and identity in Hemingway's texts and personal life. Argues that setting plays a strong role in reflecting Hemingway's commitment to both total sensual engagement and the creation of a "picture of the whole world." Discusses Michigan, Paris, Spain, and Cuba, with brief references to the major novels and short stories set in those locales.

Prasad, Murari. "The Sea as Symbol in *The Old Man and the Sea*." *Journal of the Department of English: Hemingway Centennial Tribute* (Rabindra Bharati University, Calcutta, India) 5 (1998–99): 184–93.
Asserts that the sea symbolizes Hemingway's worldview, representing man's struggle against and integration with the natural environment.

Rudra, Arup. "The Ways of Images and Languages in Hemingway's *The Old Man and the Sea*." *Journal of the Department of English: Hemingway Centennial Tribute* (Rabindra Bharati University, Calcutta, India) 5 (1998–99): 149–57.
Explicates the imagery of *The Old Man and the Sea* by comparing Hemingway's visual descriptions with impressionist paintings.

Sengupta, Pallab. "The Isomorphs of Santiago-Myth." *Journal of the Department of English: Hemingway Centennial Tribute* (Rabindra Bharati University, Calcutta, India) 5 (1998–99): 167–73.
Examines the influence of *The Old Man and the Sea* upon Gabriel Marquez's *The Story of the Shipwrecked Sailor* (1970) and George Pierre's *Autumn's Bounty* (1972). Notes overarching thematic similarities, such as the protagonists' struggle with nature.

Waggoner, Eric. "Inside the Current: A Taoist Reading of *The Old Man and the Sea*." *Hemingway Review* 17.2: 88–104.
Explores the relationship of *The Old Man and the Sea* to Taoist thought (particularly the Taoism of Lao-Tzu and the *I Ching*), noting similarities in their treatment of the natural world and Santiago's desire to follow a path of correctness while on his spiritual journey. Traces three main Taoist principles throughout the novella: 1) balance between oppositional forces; 2) connection between one's inner self and outer world; and 3) cyclic movement of

earthly and spiritual life. Argues that reading the novella "in terms of victory and defeat is to reduce *The Old Man and the Sea* to a simple story of action rather than a rumination on the awareness of essence and precision from which that action arises."

Watson, William Braasch. "The Other Paris Years of Ernest Hemingway: 1937 and 1938." In *French Connections: Hemingway and Fitzgerald Abroad.* Edited by J. Gerald Kennedy and Jackson R. Bryer. New York: St. Martin's Press. 141–58. Comments briefly on the limitations of "Nobody Ever Dies," suggesting it "should not have been published." Notes Hemingway's focus on the themes of death and rejection in the short story, arguing that the conditions surrounding Hemingway at the time contributed to the story's oppressive air of defeat.

1999

Adair, William. "Hemingway's Sense of an Ending: Repetitious and Pathetic." *ANQ: A Quarterly Journal of Short Articles, Notes, and Reviews* 12.2: 32–34. Laments the romantic pathos and lack of variety in Hemingway's endings. In *The Old Man and the Sea, To Have and Have Not,* and *Islands in the Stream,* the protagonist lies near death while someone close to him cries.

Bloom, Harold, ed. *The Old Man and the Sea.* Philadelphia: Chelsea House. Collection of previously published material. Contents:

"Introduction," by Harold Bloom, 1–3. Characterizes *The Old Man and the Sea* as both "repetitive and self-indulgent." With so little respect shown for either the author or novella, one wonders why Bloom bothered to edit the volume.

"Review of *The Old Man and the Sea,*" by William Faulkner, 5. Reprint from *Ernest Hemingway: Six Decades of Criticism,* edited by Linda W. Wagner (East Lansing, MI: Michigan State Univ. Press, 1987).

"The Boy and the Lions," by Carlos Baker, 7–12. Excerpt from *Hemingway: The Writer as Artist* (Princeton, NJ: Princeton Univ. Press, 1952).

"The Heroic Impulse in *The Old Man and the Sea,*" by Leo Gurko, 13–20. Reprint from *Twentieth Century Interpretations of* The Old Man and the Sea, edited by Katharine T. Jobes (Englewood Cliffs, NJ: Prentice-Hall, 1968).

"*The Old Man and the Sea* and the American Dream," by Delmore Schwartz, 21–26. Excerpt from "The Fiction of Ernest Hemingway," in *Perspectives USA* 13 (Autumn 1955).

"Confiteor Hominem: Ernest Hemingway's Religion of Man," by Joseph Waldmeir, 27–33. Reprint from *PMASAL* 42 (1956).

"The Later Hemingway," by Nemi D'Agostino, 35–43. Reprint from *Sewanee Review* 68 (Summer 1960).

"*The Old Man and the Sea:* Hemingway's Tragic Vision of Man," by Clinton S. Burhans Jr., 45–52. Reprint from *American Literature* 31 (January 1960).

"Fakery in *The Old Man and the Sea*," by Robert P. Weeks, 53–59. Reprint from *College English* 24 (1962).

"Hemingway's Extended Vision: *The Old Man and the Sea*," by Bickford Sylvester, 61–72. Reprint from *PMLA* 81 (1966).

"*The Old Man and the Sea*: Vision/Revision," by Philip Young, 73–80. Excerpt from *Ernest Hemingway: A Reconsideration* (University Park, PA: Pennsylvania State Univ. Press, 1966).

"New World, Old Myths," by Claire Rosenfield, 81–94. Excerpt from *Twentieth Century Interpretations of* The Old Man and the Sea, edited by Katharine T. Jobes (Englewood Cliffs, NJ: Prentice-Hall, 1968).

"Hemingway's Craft in *The Old Man and the Sea*," by Sheldon Norman Grebstein, 95–103. Reprint from *The Fifties: Fiction, Poetry, Drama*, edited by Warren French (Deland, FL: Everett/Edwards, 1970).

"The Poem of Santiago and Manolin," by Linda W. Wagner, 105–17. Reprint from *Ernest Hemingway: Six Decades of Criticism* (East Lansing, MI: Michigan State Univ. Press, 1987).

"Incarnation and Redemption in *The Old Man and the Sea*," by G. R. Wilson Jr., 119–23. Reprint from *Studies in Short Fiction* 14.4 (Fall 1977).

"The Later Fiction: Hemingway and the Aesthetics of Failure," by James H. Justus, 125–39. Reprint from *Ernest Hemingway: New Critical Essays*, edited by Robert A. Lee (Totowa, NJ: Barnes and Noble, 1983).

"A Not-So-Strange Old Man: *The Old Man and the Sea*," by Gerry Brenner, 141–51. Reprint from *Concealments in Hemingway's Works* (Columbus, OH: Ohio State Univ. Press, 1983).

"Contrasts in Form: Hemingway's *The Old Man and the Sea* and Faulkner's 'The Bear,'" by David Timms, 153–64. Reprint from *The Modern American Novella*, edited by A. Robert Lee (New York: St. Martin's, 1989).

"The Cuban Context of *The Old Man and the Sea*," by Bickford Sylvester, 165–84. Reprint from *The Cambridge Companion to Hemingway*, edited by Scott Donaldson (New York: Cambridge Univ. Press, 1996).

Brenner, Gerry. "Manolin on Hemingway's Santiago: A Fictive Interview." *Thalia: Studies in Literary Humor* 19.1–2: 3–13.

Tongue-in-cheek interview with an older and "wiser" Manolin, reflecting on his experiences as a boy with Santiago.

Dillon-Malone, Aubrey. *Hemingway: The Grace and the Pressure*. New York: Robson/Parkwest.

Re *To Have and Have Not*, 155–9. Criticizes *To Have and Have Not* as banal, stylistically messy, and flat. Lacking strong authorial direction, readers are unable to empathize with characters or even become involved in the action. Suggests the Bogart/Bacall film as a successful alternative to the novel.

"The Old Man and the Prize," 238–52. Gives a brief biographical background on the writing of *The Old Man and the Sea,* including Hemingway's infatuation with Adriana Ivancich at the time, his desire to reestablish his sagging reputation, and his winning of the Pulitzer and Nobel prizes. Discusses Hemingway's dissatisfaction with the casting of Spencer Tracy as Santiago in the screen version and his rocky relationship with screenwriter Peter Viertel.

Eby, Carl P. "*Islands in the Stream,* Perversion, and Creativity." In *Hemingway's Fetishism: Psychoanalysis and the Mirror of Manhood.* New York: State Univ. of New York Press. 263–75.

Psychoanalytic approach to three deleted chapters of *Islands in the Stream.* Suggests Hemingway's fascination with sweaters, mirrors, hair, and gender transformation in the original manuscript made up a "perverse scenario" that played itself out over and over in Hemingway's canon.

Gajdusek, Robin. "Hemingway's Late Life Relationship with Birds." In *Hemingway and the Natural World.* Edited by Robert E. Fleming. Moscow, ID: Univ. of Idaho Press. 175–87.

Surveys Hemingway's fascination with birds throughout his lengthy career, citing passages from various essays, short stories, and novels, including *Death in the Afternoon, The Old Man and the Sea,* and *For Whom the Bell Tolls.* Primarily focuses on "At Sea," the third book of *Islands in the Stream,* connecting birds thematically to the human life/death cycle, strategies of war, and Hudson's artistic identity. As a structuring device, the birds serve as "harbingers and prophesiers," signaling "both safety and danger."

Jones, Oliver. "*The Old Man and the Sea.*" *Variety,* 13 September 1999, sec. 4: 42. Print.

Positive review of the latest screen adaptation of the novella, an animated feature film, shot on giant-screen Imax, which remains faithful to the text.

Kinnamon, Keneth. "The Politics of 'The Snows of Kilimanjaro.'" In *Value and Vision in American Literature.* Edited by Joseph Candido and Ray Lewis White. Athens, OH: Ohio Univ. Press. 15–31.

Notes briefly that Hemingway's ambivalence toward the wealthy as expressed in *To Have and Have Not* are reminiscent of that found in the earlier "Snows of Kilimanjaro."

Knott, Toni D., ed. *One Man Alone: Hemingway and* To Have and Have Not. Lanham, MD: Univ. Press of America. 250.

"The Critical Reception—through Time," by Toni D. Knott, 11–46. Broadly surveys the critical response to the novel from its publication to the present, grouping this criticism according to its primary focus (e.g., characterization, title, proletariat and sexual themes, treatment of minorities and women, Morgan as hero, or narrative structure). Concludes by summing up those praising the novel's extensive literary experimentation. This article was derived in part from "Playing in the Light: Examining Categorization in *To Have and Have Not* as a Reflection of Identity or Racism," in *North Dakota Quarterly* (Summer 1997), and from "One Man Alone: Dimensions of Individuality and Categorization in *To Have and Have Not,*" in *Hemingway Review* (Spring 1998).

"'Their Money's Worth': The Composition, Editing, and Publication," by Robert W. Trogdon, 47–64. Delivers what the title promises: an account of the composition history, editorial relationship between Hemingway and Maxwell Perkins, publication, and marketing strategies for the novel.

"The Setting," by Toni D. Knott, 65–80. Explores the validity of several geographical and historical elements Hemingway uses in the novel. Examines the tension between the native Key West/Cuba population and the outsiders, especially tourists, drawn in through the efforts of the Federal Emergency Relief Administration (FERA) and other New Deal agencies to alleviate the area's depressed economy. Discusses Hemingway's treatment of prohibition, bootlegging, and Cuban politics within their historical and cultural contexts.

"Winner Takes Winner Takes Winner: Social Darwinism," by Randall A. Meeks, 81–90. After summing up the "evolving" philosophy of social Darwinism, Meeks argues that the grain broker's reading about a trip to the Galapagos Islands refers to Charles Darwin's *On the Origin of Species by Means of Natural Selection* (1859). *To Have and Have Not* can then be read as a predatory/prey scenario in which many of its characters, including Harry Morgan, attempt to survive the Great Depression, with its savage competition for limited resources.

"Sacrifice and Redemption: The Meaning of the Boy/Son and Man/Father Dialectic in the Work of Ernest Hemingway," by Robert E. Gajdusek, 95–111. Reprinted from *North Dakota Quarterly* (Spring 1994–95).

"Dimensions of Love," by Toni D. Knott, 113–30. Discusses Hemingway's frequent reliance on derogatory terms in the novel (e.g., *yellow rat, nigger, bum*) to mirror societal conditioning and prejudice. Argues against Toni Morrison's well-known thesis that Hemingway maligned African American characters to elevate Morgan (see her "Disturbing Nurses and the Kindness of Sharks," in *Playing in the Dark: Whiteness and the Literary Imagination* [Cambridge, MA: Harvard Univ. Press], 61–91). Focuses on the flawed characters of Morgan and Gordon, arguing that Hemingway creates complex central characters whose many errors in judgment take them far from the moral center. This article was expanded from "Playing in the Light: Examining Categorization in *To Have and Have Not* as a Reflection of Identity or Racism," in *North Dakota Quarterly* (Summer 1997) and from "One Man Alone: Dimensions of Individuality and Categorization in *To Have and Have Not,*" in *Hemingway Review* (Spring 1998).

"'Juxtaposition' and 'Contrast': Unifying Hemingway's *To Have and Have Not,*" by Tracy Banis 131–54. Traces the influence of the metaphysical poetry of John Donne on Hemingway's notion of love in *To Have and Have Not.* Sees the novel's greatest unifying principle of subject and theme to be the metaphysical union of Harry and Marie. Banis contrasts the beauty and depth of the Morgans' monogamous marriage with the empty and unfulfilling relationships of the other couples to prove Morgan's powerful statement on the human condition: "A man alone ain't got no bloody fucking chance." Discusses Hemingway's use of the iceberg principle, which depends on the reader's active participation, thus resulting in a kind of "perpetual now" (fifth dimension) each time the novel is read anew.

"A Farewell to Arm: Amputation, Castration, and Masculinity," by Carl P. Eby, 155–72. Psychoanalytic reading, interpreting Morgan's testicular boasting as overcompensation for his castration anxiety. Explores Hemingway's fetishistic attraction to hair throughout the novel, looking to the author's unusual childhood as the probable source of the fetish. Explains Marie's excitement over Harry's stump as a split in the author's ego.

"Key West Shine," by Toni D. Knott, 173–84. Reminiscence of Knott's road trip to Key West, perusal of the galleys for *To Have and Have Not* at the Key West Library, and meeting with Kermit "Shine" Forbes (Hemingway's sparring partner during the 1930s).

"'Some Nigger. . . . Some Mr. Johnson': Getting the Reels and the Lines Together," by Robert E. Gajdusek, 187–200. Close analysis of Hemingway's language at the word level, examining the use of *and* in the novel's title as well as the novel's opening sentence and initial scene. Suggests that "Hemingway's prose in this work is highly contrived and endlessly intricate in its every detail." Argues that the function of the novel's title, to connect one side with the other, is integral to the novel's theme of redemptive crossover.

"Bad Luck or No Luck at All: Religion, Magic, and Chance," by Larry E. Grimes, 201–12. Analyzes the roles of chance and luck in *To Have and Have Not,* pointing to Hemingway's extensive world travels as the source for his magico-religious knowledge. In the Darwinian world of chance that Harry Morgan inhabits, luck and voodoo provide alternatives to the ineffective presence of Western Christianity. Theorizes that the cursed Gordon represents a warning to all irresponsible writers.

"Time Will Tell: Toward an Understanding of Hemingway's Religious Aesthetic," by Toni D. Knott, 213–26. General overview of Hemingway's religious aesthetic, summarizing existing criticism on the subject along the way. Contends that in *To Have and Have Not* transcendence of earthly sorrow can be achieved when one connects in a meaningful way with other individuals and with nature (i.e., with all of God's creation). Harry's death in winter will be followed by the rebirth of spring. Compares the suffering Morgan to Christ.

"Afterword: The Manuscript," by Toni D. Knott, 227–33. Calls for greater scholarly attention to the galleys and manuscripts of *To Have and Have Not,* noting that recent attention to the manuscripts has engendered as much critical debate as the published version of the novel.

Lawrence, H. Lea. "A Turbulent Time." In *A Hemingway Odyssey: Special Places in His Life.* Nashville: Cumberland House. 169–74.
Biographical travelogue, mentioning in passing the writing, publication, reception, and filming of *The Old Man and the Sea.*

Moddelmog, Debra A. "The Disabled Able Body and White Heteromasculinity." In *Reading Desire: In Pursuit of Ernest Hemingway.* Ithaca, NY: Cornell Univ. Press. 119–30.
Inventories the health problems of several Hemingway heroes, including Santiago and Harry Morgan. By connecting wounds to a character's worth or virility, Moddelmog argues that for white, heterosexual males, disability enhances ability.

Murphy, Charlene M. "Hemingway's Gentle Hunters: Contradiction or Duality?" In *Hemingway and the Natural World.* Edited by Robert E. Fleming. Moscow, ID: Univ. of Idaho Press. 165–74.
Compares excerpts of a number of Hemingway's works, including *Islands in the Stream,* with paintings by Winslow Homer to reveal Hemingway's sensitivity to nature.

Oliver, Charles M. *Ernest Hemingway A to Z.* New York: Facts on File.
Comprehensive guide to the facts of Hemingway's life and works, providing biographical information along with information on the "who, what, where and when" of the author's short stories, novels, poems, newspaper articles, and nonfiction books. Includes plot summaries for each work of fiction and synopses of the nonfiction. Entries are arranged alphabetically. Helpful appendices include a map from the "At Sea" section of *Islands in the Stream* and a chronology that places Hemingway's life and work within the larger cultural context by listing important literary and historical events.

Ray, Mohit K. "*The Old Man and the Sea:* An Archetypal Perspective." *West Bengal: A West Bengal Government English Fortnightly* 41.23: 71–74.
Explores the archetypal theme of the hunter/prey, contending that Santiago possesses an ancient "collective memory of the race."

Reynolds, Michael. *Hemingway: The Final Years.* New York: W. W. Norton.

"The Artist's Rewards: March 1952 to June 1953," 249–63. Biographical overview. Provides a publication history of *The Old Man and the Sea,* including the author's numerous clashes with critics, scholars, and William Faulkner during this time period. Briefly surveys the generally positive reception of the novella and remarks on Hemingway's unprecedented interest in its filming.

Re *The Old Man and the Sea,* 293–96. Briefly comments on the disruption of Hemingway's professional and private life during the filming of *The Old Man and the Sea,* in part because of Hemingway's instance on being an integral part of the project.

———. "A View from the Dig at Century's End." In *Value and Vision in American Literature.* Edited by Joseph Candido and Ray Lewis White. Athens, OH: Ohio Univ. Press. 1–14.

Overview of where we've been and where we might profitably head in Hemingway studies by the author's premier biographer. Takes exception to the oft-voiced criticism that *To Have and Have Not* holds little of value for present-day scholars and urges a close examination of this critical period in Hemingway's development.

Sanyal, Jharna. "'No Man Should Be Alone in His Old Age': A Gerontological Reading of *The Old Man and the Sea.*" *West Bengal: A West Bengal Government English Fortnightly* 41.23: 75–80.

Analyzes Santiago's physical and psychological struggles associated with aging. Concludes with a biocritical reading of the novel, suggesting the old man's problems might be read as Hemingway's "alternate life-script."

Sarkar, Subhas. "A Modernist Quest for Martyrdom: Hemingway's *The Old Man and the Sea* and T. S. Eliot's *Murder in the Cathedral.*" *West Bengal: A West Bengal Government English Fortnightly* 41.23: 67–70.

Comparison study of Santiago to Eliot's Becket, detailing their search to find meaning in life and Christocentric imagery.

Sipiora, Phillip. "Hemingway's Aging Heroes and the Concept of *Phronesis.*" In *Aging and Identity: A Humanities Perspective.* Edited by Sara Munson Deats and Lagretta Tallent Lenker. Westport, CT: Praeger. 61–76.

Rhetorical reading of Hemingway's aging heroes, who possess the quality of *phronesis,* commonly translated as practical sense or "judicial thinking." Sees Santiago's *phronesis* as evident in his creation of life-sustaining metaphors and interior monologues that aid him during his struggle.

Szumski, Bonnie, ed. *Readings on* The Old Man and the Sea. San Diego, CA: Greenhaven Press.

Collection of previously published material. Contents:

"*The Old Man and the Sea* as Fable," by Delbert E. Wylder, 32–41. Excerpt from *Hemingway's Heroes* (Albuquerque, NM: Univ. of New Mexico Press, 1969).

"*The Old Man and the Sea* Is an Allegory of the Artist," by Wirt Williams, 42–51. Reprint from *The Tragic Art of Ernest Hemingway* (Baton Rouge, LA: Louisiana State Univ. Press, 1981).

"Aging in *The Old Man and the Sea*," by Stanley Cooperman, 52–58. Excerpt from "Hemingway and Old Age," *College English* (December 1965).

"*The Old Man and the Sea* Is A Love Story," by Linda W. Wagner, 59–68. Excerpt from "The Poem of Santiago and Manolin," *Modern Fiction Studies* 19.4 (Winter 1973).

"Hemingway's Battle with God," by Ben Stoltzfus, 69–77. Excerpt from *Gide and Hemingway: Rebels Against God* (Port Washington, NY: Kennikat Press, 1978).

"Excerpt from *A Reader's Guide to Ernest Hemingway*," by Arthur Waldhorn, 79–87. Excerpt from *A Reader's Guide to Ernest Hemingway* (New York: Farrar, Straus and Giroux, 1972).

"Symbolism in *The Old Man and the Sea*," by Keiichi Harada, 88–95. Reprint of "The Marlin and the Shark: A Note on *The Old Man and the Sea*," in *Hemingway and His Critics*, edited by Carlos Baker (New York: Hill and Wang, 1961).

"Hemingway's Religious Symbolism," by Joseph Waldmeir, 96–103. Reprint of "Confiteor Hominem: Ernest Hemingway's Religion of Man," *Papers of the Michigan Academy of Science, Arts, and Letters* 42 (1956).

"Biblical Allusions in *The Old Man and the Sea*," by Joseph M. Flora, 104–8. Reprint from *Studies in Short Fiction* 10 (1973).

"A Lack of Realism Mars *The Old Man and the Sea*," by Robert P. Weeks, 109–16. Reprint of "Fakery in *The Old Man and the Sea*," *College English* 24 (December 1962).

"The Old Man Maintains a Fighting Code," by Wolfgang Wittkowski, 118–27. Excerpt from "Crucified in the Ring: Hemingway's *The Old Man and the Sea*," *Hemingway Review* 3.1 (1983).

"The Old Man Is a Spiritual Figure," by William J. Handy, 128–38. Excerpt from "A New Dimension for a Hero: Santiago of *The Old Man and the Sea*," in *Six Contemporary Novels: Six Introductory Essays in Modern Fiction*, edited by William O. S. Sutherland Jr. (Austin, TX: Univ. of Texas, 1962).

"The Old Man's Classic Quest," by Robert O. Stephens, 139–46. Excerpt from "Hemingway's Old Man and the Iceberg," *Modern Fiction Studies* 7 (Winter 1961–62).

"The Old Man's Heroic Struggle," by Leo Gurko, 147–56. Reprint of "The Heroic Impulse in *The Old Man and the Sea*," *English Journal* 44 (October 1955).

"The Old Man Is Not a Heroic Figure," by Chaman Nahal, 157–64. Excerpt from *The Narrative Pattern in Ernest Hemingway's Fiction* (Rutherford, NJ: Fairleigh Dickinson Univ. Press, 1971).

Trogdon, Robert W., ed. *Ernest Hemingway: A Documentary Volume.* Vol. 210 of *Dictionary of Literary Biography.* Detroit, MI: Gale Group. Paperback edition: *Ernest Hemingway: A Literary Reference.* New York: Carroll and Graf Publishers, 2002.

Biographical and bibliographical guide to Hemingway's life and writings. In addition to detailed chronologies, the volume also provides scholarly criticism on individual works. Reprints letters, dust jackets, interviews, reviews, and advertisements.

"1936–1940," 184–233. Covers the move to Finca Vigía and *To Have and Have Not.*

"1941–1952," 234–86. Covers relationships with Martha Gellhorn, Mary Welsh Monks, and Adriana Ivancich, and *The Old Man and the Sea.*

"1953–July 1961," 287–327. Covers Pulitzer Prize for and movie production of *The Old Man and the Sea.*

"3 July 1961–1999," 328–56. Covers the posthumous publication of *Islands in the Stream.*

Wyatt, David. "Hemingway at Fifty." *Southern Review* 35.3: 595–607.

Brief mention of Thomas Hudson's growing reliance on alcohol in *Islands in the Stream.*

2000

Clark, Brock. "What Literature Can and Cannot Do: Lionel Trilling, Richard Rorty, and the Left." *Massachusetts Review* 41.4: 523–39.

Contends that Trilling and Rorty still have much to offer contemporary criticism on the relationship between politics and literature. Recaps Trilling's well-known criticism of Hemingway's more political works, including *To Have and Have Not,* in which he lays partial blame for the novel's weakness at the door of "leftist" critics.

Fuentes, Norberto. *Ernest Hemingway Rediscovered.* Hauppauge, NY: Barron's.

French translation of *Ernest Hemingway Retrouvé,* published in French in 1987. Biography covering the last two decades of Hemingway's life. Outstanding photographs. Numerous references sprinkled throughout to *The Old Man and the Sea,* and, to a lesser extent, to *To Have and Have Not* and *Islands in the Stream.*

Izquierdo, Isabel Garciá, and Josep Marco Borillo. "The Degree of Grammatical Complexity in Literary Texts as a Translation Problem." In *Investigating Translation: Selected Papers from the 4th International Congress on Translation.* Edited by Allison Beeby, Doris Ensinger, and Marisa Presas. Philadelphia: J. Benjamins. 65–74.

Compares Spanish and Catalan translations of passages from *The Old Man and the Sea* to show that in each version the translator has preserved "the same degree of grammatical complexity found in the original text." Notes that Hemingway's stylistic simplicity reflects his central character's simplicity, a correlation not lost upon his translators.

Kwon, Seokwoo. "Harry Morgan's Dismemberment and Hemingway's Critique of Violence: *To Have and Have Not*." *English Language and Literature* 46.4: 1041–60.

Reads Morgan as an emasculated antihero of the bourgeoisie. Relying on the gender theory of social construction, Kwon contends that Hemingway is critiquing the cult of masculinity and violence in *To Have and Have Not*. Thus Morgan's use of excessive violence eventually leads to the degeneration of his manhood rather than its regeneration.

Llosa, Mario Vargas. "Hemingway." *Salmagundi* 128–29 (2000–2001): 42–47.

Broad overview of the origins, composition, and critical reception of *The Old Man and the Sea*. Comments on the novel's reliance on Darwinism, chivalry, and realistic detail, suggesting that through Hemingway's masterful attention an individual anecdote transforms into archetype.

Meyers, Jeffrey. "Bogart and Hemingway." In *Hemingway: Life into Art*. New York: Cooper Square Press. 83–86.

Reprint from *Virginia Quarterly Review* 72 (Summer 1996): 446–49.

Nänny, Max. "Formal Allusions to Visual Ideas and Visual Art in Hemingway's Work." *European Journal of English Studies* 4.1: 66–82.

Looks at Hemingway's narrative technique of repetition as a chiastic ordering that alludes to visual arts and ideas. Closely reads passages relating to painting in the "At Sea" section of *Islands in the Stream* and elsewhere. Comments briefly on the parallels between Hemingway's writing and Cezanne's painting.

Rao, E. Nageswara, ed. *Ernest Hemingway: Centennial Essays*. Delhi: Pencraft International.

"Hemingway: The Quintessential American?" by Alladi Uma, 26–30: Laments the "maleness" of *The Old Man and the Sea*, noting Hemingway's reliance on male characters and attitudes.

"Foregrounding the Sea: A Reading of Hemingway's *The Old Man and the Sea* and Thakazhi's *Chemmeen*," by S. Josh, 71–77. Comparison of the central sea symbol used in both texts, focusing on the dichotomy of the feminine sea as both nurturing and hostile to those who must struggle against it.

"Why Should We Read Kesava Reddy's Hemingway in English?" by M. Sridhar, 78–83. Influence study, noting the thematic and stylistic impact of *The Old Man and the Sea* on Reddy's *Athadu Adavini Jayinchadu*, which has recently been translated into English. Finds that despite Reddy's acknowledgement of heavy borrowing on his part, a thorough comparison of the two is warranted for a deeper understanding of both cultures.

"The Hemingway Cattery: The Feline in Hemingway's Life and Letters," by E. Nageswara Rao, 99–106. Recounts the importance of cats in Hemingway's personal life before briefly discussing the inclusion of Thomas Hudson's close association with cats in *Islands in the Stream* and Santiago's inspirational lion dreams in *The Old Man and the Sea,* among others.

"From Page to Screen: Hemingway, *To Have and Have Not* and Hollywood," by Somdatta Mandal, 136–47. Compares the three Hollywood and one Iranian film versions of the novel, wondering why Hollywood has devoted so much attention to one of Hemingway's inferior works.

Szalay, Michael. "The Politics of Textual Integrity: Ayn Rand, Gertrude Stein, and Ernest Hemingway." In *New Deal Modernism: American Literature and the Invention of the Welfare State.* Durham, NC: Duke Univ. Press. 75–119.
Drawing an analogy between human and artistic forms, Szalay compares several of Hemingway's texts with bodies to show the relation between parts and wholes. Discusses Hemingway's obsession with textual accuracy, the wound theory, the negative treatment of the New Deal in *To Have and Have Not* and that novel's complex narrative voice.

Young, Philip. "To Have Not: Tough Luck." In *American Fiction, American Myth: Essays by Philip Young.* Edited by David Morrell and Sandra Whipple Spanier. University Park, PA: Pennsylvania State Univ. Press. 87–96.
Reprint of original 1968 article, "Focus on *To Have and Have Not:* To Have Not: Tough Luck." In *Tough Guy Writers of the Thirties.* Edited by David Madden. Carbondale, IL: Southern Illinois Univ. Press. 42–50.

2001

Eddins, Dwight. "Of Rocks and Marlin: The Existentialist Agon in Camus's *The Myth of Sisyphus* and Hemingway's *The Old Man and the Sea.*" *Hemingway Review* 21.1: 68–77.
Explores the relationship of Camus's existential philosophy to *The Old Man and the Sea,* comparing Santiago to Sisyphus. Each is alone and isolated in his "repetitive struggle that must end in defeat, but who refuses the escape of some ultimate religious consolation." Gives an existentialist reading of the novella's Christian allegory, climaxing in Santiago's "crucifixion."

Florczyk, Steven. "Hemingway's 'Tragic Adventure': Angling for Peace in the Natural Landscape of the Fisherman." *North Dakota Quarterly* 68.2–3: 156–65.
Treats fishing in *The Old Man and the Sea, Islands in the Stream,* and "Big Two-

Hearted River," arguing that man's interdependent relationship with the natural world, as portrayed through these three fisherman, serves as a grounding force against the encroaching dangers of the modern world. Only by establishing a connection with nature and nurturing the natural order can Hemingway's protagonists find strength and fulfillment as they struggle against great loss.

Gajdusek, Robert E. "The Hemingway of Cuba and Bimini and His Later Relationship to Nature." *North Dakota Quarterly* 68.2–3: 91–103.

Comments on the openness of the Finca Vigía's structure, which enables a continual relationship between man and nature. Argues that the later *Islands in the Stream* differs from Hemingway's earlier works because, although the novel contains natural imagery and action, the real subject matter is interpersonal relationships, of how people relate to and affect one another. Hemingway's increased attention to natural detail in his later works further proves the author's shift in focus to the "other"—his shift toward reflection and understanding, and movement away from urgency and obsession.

Horowitz, Richard M. "On Hemingway's *The Old Man and the Sea.*" *Another Chicago Magazine* 39: 131–46.

Undergraduate essay on *The Old Man and the Sea* embedded within a fictive narrative about the student who wrote the essay.

Hotchner, A. E. *Ernest Hemingway's "After the Storm": The Story, Plus the Screenplay and a Commentary.* New York: Carroll and Graf Publishers.

Recounts his challenges over the years in adapting Hemingway's work to the screen (sixteen works to date). Comments that though Hemingway's minimalist style was effective on paper, revealing more of Hemingway's iceberg to meet the needs of the dramatic form engenders numerous pitfalls. Reprints both the original six-page short story and Hotchner's 119-page screenplay.

Houk, Walter. "Lessons from Hemingway's Cuban Biographer." *North Dakota Quarterly* 68.2–3: 132–55.

Takes issue with Norberto Fuentes's *Hemingway in Cuba* (1984), correcting a number of biographical fallacies, including the most likely source for Harry Morgan's boat in *To Have and Have Not,* Thomas Hudson's Q-boat route in *Islands in the Stream,* and the model for Santiago in *The Old Man and the Sea.* However, Houk's main complaint is the biographer's tendency to read Hemingway's Cuban fiction as real life fact.

Junkins, Donald. "Rereading *Islands in the Stream.*" *North Dakota Quarterly* 68.2–3: 109–22.

Sees the subject of the novel to be the creative process itself, with Roger the writer and Hudson the painter representing Hemingway. Analyzes the central themes of sorrow and loss that permeate *Islands* and concludes with a personal reflection on his own time spent in Bimini retracing Hemingway's footsteps.

Mann, Harveen. "South Asian Partition Literature and the Gendered Rape and Silence of the National Body." *South Asian Review* 22: 3–22.

*MLA Bibliography 1989–2002/12, online. www.mla.org/bibliography. Treats "After the Storm."

Moreland, Kim. "Hemingway's I-Lands in the Streams." *North Dakota Quarterly* 68.2–3: 123–31.

Examines the function of islands in several Hemingway texts, including *The Old Man and the Sea, Islands in the Stream,* and *To Have and Have Not,* representing them as a means for reinventing one's identity. Despite the appeal of creating a new life, Hemingway's protagonists learn that such freedom ultimately comes at the price of isolation and loneliness.

Pratt, John Clark. "My Pilgrimage; Fishing for Religion with Hemingway." *Hemingway Review* 21.1: 78–92.

Memoir from 1952 to the present detailing the author's intellectual journey from student to professor, held together by his unwavering interest in Hemingway's use of religious allusions in his writings. Frequent references to *The Old Man and the Sea* scattered throughout.

Stoltzfus, Ben. "Political Commitment in Hemingway and Sartre." *North Dakota Quarterly* 68.2–3: 182–88.

Compares Hemingway's political writings, including *To Have and Have Not,* with Sartre's oeuvre, suggesting the depth of Hemingway's social consciousness. Both authors opposed fascism in Spain, capitalistic excess, and American's economic policies in Cuba.

Stoneback, H. R. "*Poireaux* and *Pétanque:* Or, Games and Crops, Sport and Harvest, Place and Memory, and Hunger and Art in Hemingway's Works." *North Dakota Quarterly* 68.2–3: 14–27.

Taking his initial cue from the scene in chapter 5 of *Islands in the Stream* that joins together games and crops with place (Paris), memory, and hunger, Stoneback notes similar patterns in other Hemingway works, including *The Sun Also Rises* and several short stories. Stoneback examines the significance of Pétanque, the national game of France, and Hudson's knowledge of French leeks, arguing that this oft-undervalued portion of the novel "is a scrupulously orchestrated litany, with movements and motifs that anchor the novel, that resonate with and signify the central concerns of *Islands in the Stream.*"

Tyler, Lisa. *Companion to Ernest Hemingway.* Westport, CT: Greenwood Press.

"*The Old Man and the Sea,*" 129–35: Generalist approach geared to high school and college students. Examines the novel's plot and character development and its major themes, such as luck, baseball, and religion. Includes a brief reading from an ecofeminist perspective treating the relationship between nature and women in the novel.

"*Islands in the Stream*," 141–46: Generalist approach geared to high school and college students. Examines the novel's plot and character development and such major themes as loss, violence, and suicide.

2002

Biesen, Sheri Chinen. "Bogart, Bacall, Howard Hawks and Wartime *Film Noir* at Warner Bros.: *To Have and Have Not* and *The Big Sleep*." *Popular Culture Review* 13.1: 35–51.

Recounts Hollywood's shift toward heightened sex and violence to meet the changing needs of wartime and postwar audiences. Details Hawks's considerable creative influence in bringing *To Have and Have Not* to the big screen, including detailed information on early Warner Bros. synopses of the novel, contract negotiations, and production and promotion strategies.

Broer, Lawrence R., and Gloria Holland, eds. *Hemingway and Women: Female Critics and the Female Voice*. Tuscaloosa, AL: Univ. of Alabama. 353.

"To Have and Hold Not: Marie Morgan, Helen Gordon, and Dorothy Hollis," by Kim Moreland, 81–92. Contends that Hemingway's narrative experimentations in *To Have and Have Not* resulted in the creation of fully rounded and realistic female characters who survive the absence of their husbands in different ways. Suggests the sympathetic portraits of these three women may have been the author's way of expiating his guilt over leaving Pauline Pfeiffer for Martha Gellhorn.

"Santiago and the Eternal Feminine: Gendering *La Mar* in *The Old Man and the Sea*," by Susan F. Beegel, 131–56. Ecological approach elevating the sea setting to protagonist status (e.g., "sea as wife"). Rather than engaging in a violent contest with the sea, Santiago's loving treatment epitomizes the correct relationship between man and nature, a relationship that Manolin will continue to honor long after Santiago's passing.

"West of Everything: The High Cost of Making Men in *Islands in the Stream*," by Rose Marie Burwell, 157–72. Analyzes the novel within the genre of the Western. Argues that in editing, Baker ignored and deleted key thematic material on gender and creativity central to the reader's understanding of the younger Hudson.

Capshaw, Ron. "Hemingway: A Static Figure Amidst the Red Decade Shifts." *Partisan Review* 69.3: 441–45.

Argues that *To Have and Have Not* and *The Fifth Column* do not reveal

Hemingway's sudden political activism, but rather display the author's growing confidence regarding a subject area in which he had long been interested.

Gajdusek, Robert E. *Hemingway in His Own Country.* Notre Dame, IN: Univ. of Notre Dame Press.

"Sacrifice and Redemption: The Meaning of the Boy/Son and Man/Father Dialectic in the Work of Ernest Hemingway," 221–36. Reprint from *North Dakota Quarterly* 62 (1994–95) and from *One Man Alone: Hemingway and* To Have and Have Not, edited by Toni D. Knott (Lanham, MD: Univ. Press of America, 1999).

"Hemingway's Late-Life Relationship with Birds," 368–82. Reprint from *Hemingway and the Natural World,* edited by Robert E. Fleming (Moscow, ID: Univ. of Idaho Press, 1999).

Hurley, C. Harold. "The World of Spirit or the World of Sport? Figuring the Numbers in Hemingway's *The Old Man and the Sea.*" In *The Faith of Fifty Million: Baseball, Religion, and American Culture.* Edited by Christopher H. Evans and William R. Herzog II. Louisville, KY: Westminster John Knox Press. 83–95.

Expanded version of an original chapter with a similar title appearing in *Hemingway's Debt to Baseball in* The Old Man and the Sea: *A Collection of Critical Readings,* edited by Harold C. Hurley (New York: Mellen, 1992). Includes additional analysis of Santiago's parallel to and fictional competition with Joe DiMaggio, both aging heroes who, despite their resolve and strength of will, must ultimately face defeat.

Jenkins, John, ed. *Travelers' Tales of Old Cuba: From Treasure Island to Mafia Den.* Melbourne, NY: Ocean Press.

"Aboard the *Pilar* with Hemingway, Havana, 1934," by Arnold Samuelson, 138–44. Reprint from *With Hemingway: A Year in Key West and Cuba* (1984).

Mandal, Somdatta, ed. *The Ernest Hemingway Companion.* New Delhi, India: Prestige Books.

"Intertextualities: *The Old Man and the Sea* and *Islands in the Stream,*" by Sobha Chattopadhyay, 150–61. Reads *The Old Man and the Sea* in light of its origins in *Islands in the Stream,* citing evidence of numerous thematic connections, such as the struggle for existence, preoccupation with death, and the hunter/prey relationship.

"*The Old Man and the Sea* and *Riders to the Sea:* An Inter-textual Encounter," by Dipendu Chakrabarti, 181–87. Comparison study. Contends that reading the differing male and female perspectives in conjunction leads to an awareness of the necessity of dignity in a futile battle with forces that neither gender fully comprehends.

"*The Old Man and the Sea* in the Light of *Rasa* Theory: An Indian Reading of Hemingway," by Priyadarshi Patnaik, 188–205. Reads the novel through an ancient Indian aesthetic focusing on emotion or rapture. Identifies *bhavas* (psycho-physiological states), as well as *sancharibhavas* (various fleeting states), at work throughout the novel, focusing on courage and wonder, which culminate in peace. Contends that when Santiago admits defeat he transcends his ego and emotions.

"Santiago: A Sinless 'El Campeon'" by Pralhad A. Kuklarni, 206–9. Overview of events in *The Old Man and the Sea,* contending that Santiago is a Christ-figure.

McIver, Stuart B. *Hemingway's Key West.* Rev. 2nd ed. Sarasota, FL: Pineapple Press.

"Cuba," 129–51. Brief biography of Hemingway's time spent in Cuba, covering the usual topics: fishing; relationships with Jane Mason, Martha Gellhorn and Mary Welsh Monks; writing *For Whom the Bell Tolls, Across the River and into the Trees, Islands in the Stream* and *The Old Man and the Sea;* and chasing German submarines.

"Hemingway Trail in Cuba," 152–54. Outlines Hemingway haunts frequented by tourists.

Phillips, Jenny. "The Finca Vigía Archives: A Joint Cuban-American Project to Preserve Hemingway's Papers." *Hemingway Review* 22.1: 9–18.
Maxwell Perkins's granddaughter chronicles collaborative efforts to preserve thousands of personal photographs, letters, and manuscript fragments (including a rejected epilogue for *For Whom the Bell Tolls*) stored in the basement of the Finca Vigía.

Proctor, Minna. "Reader's File: The Fascist Archives." *The Literary Review* 45.3: 479–98.
Translates and reprints Italian reader's reports of several modernist novels from the archives of the Mondari publishing house, written during Italy's Fascist period. Report on *To Have and Have Not* seems more concerned with recommending a novel that won't offend the censors than with the value of the novel itself.

2003

Dowell, Peter W., and Lee A. Pederson. "Baseball and Ernest Hemingway." In *The Cooperstown Symposium on Baseball and American Culture 2002.* Edited by William M. Simmons. Jefferson, NC: McFarland.
**Hemingway Review* 24.1 (2004): 123.

Fantina, Richard. "Hemingway's Masochism, Sodomy, and the Dominant Woman." *Hemingway Review* 23.1: 84–105.

Psychoanalytical approach, focusing on male heterosexual masochism (sexual submission of the male body to the female body). Argues that during the dream sequence of *Islands in the Stream,* Hudson's ex-wife sodomizes him with his pistol. Points to other instances of sodomy in the author's canon, including *The Garden of Eden,* despite Hemingway's opposition to homosexuality. "Hemingway's work often dethrones the male phallus and . . . celebrates sodomy performed on the man by the woman."

Hemingway, Hilary, and Carlene Brennen, eds. *Hemingway in Cuba.* New York: Rugged Land.

Biography of the coffee table variety, showcasing original and never published photographs and holographs. Abundant quotations from *Islands in the Stream, The Old Man and the Sea,* and other writings support the biographical content. Covers the usual material of the period: writing; fishing; relationships with Jane Mason, Martha Gellhorn, and others; and the hunt for German submarines. Includes an overview of current research and restoration efforts at the Finca Vigía. Also prints Castro's comments on Hemingway's legacy.

Houk, Walter. "In 1948 Havana, Revolutionaries as Literary Inspiration." *North Dakota Quarterly* 70.4: 196–213.

Recounts little-known events surrounding Hemingway's Havana encounters with writer Thomas Heggen and filmmakers Peter Viertel and John Huston. The three had come to Cuba seeking story material regarding two revolutionary episodes, the 1947 attempted invasion of the Dominican Republic and the failed 1932 Cuban bombing plot. Suggests Hemingway's inclusion of specific historical incidents in *To Have and Have No*t reveals the author's keen awareness of Cuban politics of the period.

Love, Glen A. "Hemingway among the Animals." In *Practical Ecocriticism: Literature, Biology, and the Environment.* Charlottesville, VA: Univ. of Virginia Press. 117–34.

Characterizes Hemingway's primitivism in *The Old Man and the Sea* and elsewhere as an aggressive battle against both the natural environment he reveres and his own mortality. Sees Hemingway's need as a literary modern to "make" his world, to proclaim his uniqueness, at the expense of the earth he loved so much. Reads Santiago as a tragically flawed character whose pride and individualism conflict with the nobility of the natural world.

Nakjavani, Erik. "The Prose of Life: Lived Experience in the Fiction of Hemingway, Sartre, and Beauvoir." *North Dakota Quarterly* 70.4: 140–65.

Recounts his 1995 visit to the Finca Vigía and explores the philosophical bond between Hemingway, Sartre, and Beauvoir. Compares Hemingway's concept of "lived experience," as found in both his fiction and nonfiction, to the fiction of Sartre and Beauvoir. Argues that while all three writers stylistically engage in silence as omission, Hemingway achieves the greatest success in his short stories and *The Old Man and the Sea.*

Sanford, John. "Hemingway: Painting and Writing, Omissions and Connections." *North Dakota Quarterly* 70.4: 232–53.

Focuses on the artistic talents of Grace Hall Hemingway, briefly connecting her and painter Winslow Homer to *Islands in the Stream.* Raises the idea that Hemingway's mother may have had a greater influence on the novel than previously suspected.

Stoneback, H. R. "Pilgrimage Variations: Hemingway's Sacred Landscapes." *Religion and Literature* 35.2–3: 49–65.

Begins by outlining Hemingway's commitment to Catholicism to support his contention that nearly all Hemingway's canon demonstrates his Catholic vision, explicitly expressed through the recurring image of the pilgrimage. Theorizes that Hemingway's lifelong fascination with this motif culminated in the completion of the Pilgrimage of Santiago de Compostela in *The Old Man and the Sea.* The true pilgrim "salutes all sacred landscapes, but holds fast to his own God."

Strychacz, Thomas. "Reading the Bones: Santiago's Audiences in *The Old Man and the Sea.*" In *Hemingway's Theaters of Masculinity.* Baton Rouge, LA: Louisiana State Univ. Press. 235–58.

Drawing on performance studies, Strychacz argues that the author's awareness of an audience influenced his creation of masculine roles. Contends that audience response to Hemingway's representation of manhood reveals richness in the author's narrative strategies long overlooked by critics more interested in preserving idealized codes of masculinity. Concludes by examining the reader's spectatorial role in *The Old Man and the Sea.*

Valenti, Particia Dunlavy. *Understanding* The Old Man and the Sea: *A Student Casebook to Issues, Sources, and Historical Documents.* Westport, CT: Greenwood Press.

Generalist approach geared to high school students. Examines the novel's plot, setting, character development, style, and major themes. Includes reprinted articles, interviews, and charts reconstructing the cultural and political currents of the time period. Covers topics such as Cuba's geography, economics, ethnic influences, and sports. Concludes with topics for writing assignments and classroom discussion.

2004

Adams, Jon Robert. "'The Great General Was a Has-Been': Homoerotic Re-Definitions of Masculinity in 1950s Conformist Culture." *Harrington Gay Men's Fiction Quarterly* 6.3: 117–35.

Argues that the "aging" and "useless" Santiago of *The Old Man and the Sea* represents a transformation of the American heroic ideal following World War II. Compares *The Old Man and the Sea* to James Jones's *The Thin Red Line* and Gore Vidal's *The City and the Pillar,* claiming that all three authors reveal a fundamental shift during the cold war era regarding America's views on masculinity.

Ako, Edward O. "Ernest Hemingway, Derek Walcott, and Old Men of the Sea." *College Language Association Journal* 48.2: 200–12.
Compares *The Old Man and the Sea* to Walcott's *The Sea at Dauphin* (1954), discussing their respective sociohistorical environments and noting similarities in characterization and theme. Santiago and Afa, acknowledging their isolation in an indifferent universe, must find strength within themselves.

Jungman, Robert. "Hemingway's *To Have and Have Not.*" *Explicator* 62.4: 224–27.
Examines Harry's dying words in light of Ecclesiastes, identifying a number of religious allusions throughout the final portions of the novel. Thus, Harry's final words should be read "as an affirmation of the value of the 'warmth' of his relationships with Marie and his daughters."

Mandal, Somdatta. *Reflections, Refractions and Rejections: Three American Writers and the Celluloid World.* Naperville, IL: Wisdom House. 28, 60, 85–86, 95, 130–31, 212–13, 230, 248, 253, 255, 260, 267, 270–71, 273, 281, 321, 332–33.
Focuses largely on Hemingway's cinematic technique, commenting on the author's use of structural, thematic, and dynamic juxtaposition. Brief references to *To Have and Have Not, Islands in the Stream,* and *The Old Man and the Sea* scattered throughout. Characterizes Harry Morgan and Thomas Hudson, among others, as typical Western heroes: stoic, violent, and independent.

2005

Abdulla, Adnan K. "Hemingway in Arabic: A Study of Literary Transformation." In *Identity and Difference: Translation Shaping Culture.* Edited by Maria Sidiropoulou. Bern, Switzerland: Peter Lang. 151–65.
Discusses the difficulties of successfully translating Hemingway's terse style into Arabic, a language with a completely different culture and poetics. Focuses on biases found in various Arabic translations of *The Old Man and the Sea* that turn Hemingway into a "verbose, repetitive, and religious writer."

Anon. "Preservation Ordered—The Beguiling Hemingway Museum in Havana Faces Both Archival and Building Challenges." *Museums Journal* 105.5: 34–37.
Chronicles efforts made at the Finca Vigía to preserve Hemingway's papers, books, and home.

Barnes, Cynthia. "Documenting Hemingway." *Humanities* 26.4: 22.

After a brief overview of the contents of the Hemingway collection at the JFK Library, Barnes comments on preservation efforts regarding the more recent material from the basement of Finca Vigía.

Beegel, Susan F. "A Guide to the Marine Life in Ernest Hemingway's *The Old Man and the Sea.*" *Resources for American Literary Study* 30: 236–315.

Extensive reference to the marine life, both plants and animals, found within the novel. Opens with overviews of Hemingway's interest in marine science and experience as a deep-sea fisherman. Entries are arranged alphabetically, drawing upon Hemingway's personal library and other sources contemporary with *The Old Man and the Sea's* composition "to recapture the flavor of Hemingway's understanding." In addition to presenting natural histories for all of the species mentioned in the novel, including the lions on the beach, Beegel also details relevant contemporary events, issues, and attitudes surrounding particular species, e.g. sharks and the 1945 sinking of the USS *Indianapolis.* Beegel's clarification and identification of species reveals Hemingway's extensive knowledge of Gulf Stream marine life and lays the foundation for future interpretative studies in this area.

Fantina, Richard. *Ernest Hemingway: Machismo and Masochism.* New York: Palgrave Macmillan.

Psychoanalytical approach, focusing on male heterosexual masochism in Hemingway's works. Finds the author's emphasis on "masculine" virtues compatible with the tradition of literary masochism (sexual submission of the male body to the female body).

"1930s: Guilt in Life and Art: 'The Snows of Kilimanjaro' and *To Have and Have Not,*" 96–100. Biographical approach, connecting both texts to Hemingway's guilt over his treatment of second wife Pauline Pfeiffer. Fantina concludes, "The two works can be read as humiliating public confessions."

Re *Islands in the Stream,* 103–8. Reads the dream sequence in *Islands in the Stream* involving Hudson and his ex-wife as an incident of sodomy. Revised excerpt from *Hemingway Review* 23.1 (2003).

Justice, Hilary K. "Music at the Finca Vigía: A Preliminary Catalog of Hemingway's Audio Collection." *Hemingway Review* 25.1: 96–108.

Covers just what the title says, including the sound system and eclectic collection of phonograph records. Assesses the architecture of the Finca (open floor plan with high ceilings) as nearly acoustically perfect. Describes Hemingway's taste in classical music as "predictably bourgeois."

Oates, Joyce Carol. "Ernest Hemingway." *Uncensored: Views (Re)views.* New York: Ecco, 259–71.

Includes reviews of *The Old Man and the Sea* and *To Have and Have Not.*

Rovit, Earl, and Arthur Waldhorn, eds. *Hemingway and Faulkner in Their Time.* New York: Continuum.

Re *To Have and Have Not,* 66. Reprints portion of letter from Edmund Wilson to Malcolm Cowley, referring to *To Have and Have Not* as "Hemingway's Popeye-the-Sailor novel."

Re *The Old Man and the Sea,* 108, 129, 164–65. Reprints portions of letters from Elizabeth Bishop, William Faulkner, and John Steinbeck praising *The Old Man and the Sea.*

Seals, Marc. "Reclaimed Experience: Trauma Theory and Ernest Hemingway's Lost Paris Manuscripts." *Hemingway Review* 24.2: 62–72.

Psychoanalytic trauma theory approach, contending that Hemingway's continued inclusion of the loss of his Paris manuscripts in his major posthumous works (e.g. *A Moveable Feast, Islands in the Stream, The Garden of Eden,* and *True at First Light*) helped him to deal with the traumatic episode. Briefly discusses the deleted "Miami" section of *Islands in the Stream,* later published as "The Strange Country." Considers the rewriting of the episode therapeutic for Hemingway, thus explaining the shift from bitterness and despair in the earlier works—*The Garden of Eden* and "The Strange Country"—to forgiveness in the later work, *A Moveable Feast,* which was published posthumously.

Strathern, Paul. *Hemingway in 90 Minutes.* Chicago: Ivan R. Dee.

Geared to a general audience. Concise biography and limited commentary on Hemingway's larger works, including *The Old Man and the Sea.* Concludes with a chronology of Hemingway's life and recommendations for further critical reading (the most current published in 1991).

2006

Cain, William E. "Death Sentences: Rereading *The Old Man and the Sea.*" *Sewanee Review* 114.1: 112–25.

Invites the reader to reassess Hemingway's "most misunderstood" novel. Praises the author's control over language and style. "In *The Old Man and the Sea* Hemingway recounts Santiago's story to express the majesty and the pointlessness of human effort." Cain argues that despite the novella's biblical symbolism, salvation awaits neither Santiago nor Hemingway. Only through the act of writing could Hemingway achieve a feeling of immortality, and that was only temporary.

Eby, Carl P. "Wake Up Alone and Like it! Dorothy Hollis, Marjorie Hillis, and *To Have and Have Not.*" *Hemingway Review* 26.1: 96–105.

Reads Dorothy's last name as a bitter allusion to Pauline Pfeiffer's friend Marjorie Hillis, author of *Live Alone and Like It.* Interprets the reference as both a symbol of Hemingway's deteriorating relationship with Pauline and a note on the novel's theme regarding the tragic plight of the isolated individual.

Giguette, Ray. "Building Objects Out of Plato: Applying Philosophy, Symbolism, and Analogy to Software Design." *Communications of the ACM* 49.10: 66–71.

Software developers outline a computer game based on *The Old Man and the Sea,* in which built-in variations of goals, heroes, and settings maximize the reusability of the game.

Houk, Walter. "A Sailor Looks at Hemingway's Islands." *North Dakota Quarterly* 73.1–2: 7–74.

Drawing upon nautical charts, war records, the *Pilar* log, and personal experience, Houk examines the physical setting of Part III, "At Sea," of *Islands in the Stream* to demonstrate Hemingway's extensive knowledge of boating and local terrain. Finds numerous correlations between real life places and experiences and the fictionalized adventures of Thomas Hudson and the Q-boat in "At Sea." Houk navigates Hemingway's course to prove that the author "gets it right physically and metaphorically as he leads his adversaries at last to discover that there is truly no way out." Concludes by noting parallels between Andrew Geer's 1948 *The Sea Chase* and the later *Islands in the Stream.*

Kelley, James. "Maternal Records and Male Modernist Identities: The Family Albums of Ernest Hemingway and Christopher Isherwood." In *The Scrapbook in American Life.* Edited by Susan Tucker, Katherine Ott, and Patricia P. Buckler. Philadelphia, PA: Temple Univ. Press. 235–50.

Examines the influence of mothers' photograph albums and other maternal materials on the writings of Hemingway and Isherwood. As representations of traditional family identity, these records can reveal much about family dynamics. Drawing on Grace Hall-Hemingway's photograph albums covering Hemingway's childhood and early adulthood, Kelley connects the mother's shifting focus on gender identity (from gender flexibility to fixity as Hemingway matured) to the author's own interest in androgyny and twinning in his later works. Notes the collapsing identities in several novels, including those of Hudson and his wife of *Islands in the Stream.* Though resistant at first, the male in each work eventually concedes to the female's insistence on merged gender and sexual identities.

Melling, Philip. "Cultural Imperialism, Afro-Cuban Religion, and Santiago's Failure in Hemingway's *The Old Man and the Sea.*" *Hemingway Review* 26.1: 6–24. Reprinted in *Critical Insights: Ernest Hemingway.* Edited by Eugene Goodheart. Pasadena, CA: Salem Press, 2010.

Argues that in *The Old Man and the Sea* "the quest for human perfectibility in baseball is not transferable to the spiritual landscape of the Caribbean." Santiago resists the influence of Afro-Cuban religions in favor of imperial faiths and American popular culture deities like Joe DiMaggio. Reads Santiago's failure to preserve the cultural integrity of Cuban life as a product of the American government's use of mass culture to fight communism.

Moran, Stephen T. "Autopathography and Depression: Describing the 'Despair Beyond Despair.'" *Journal of Medical Humanities* 27.2: 79–91.

Examines how Hemingway, Fitzgerald, and Styron wrote about their depression as a way of understanding it. Contending that Hemingway filled his fiction with characters suffering from psychiatric conditions and alcoholism much like his own, Moran argues that Hemingway's metaphor of illness as a "generation's outlook" allowed him to deny the personal relevance of his psychiatric disorders. Comments briefly on the theme of suicide in *To Have and Have Not.*

Perry, Suzanne. "Cuban Embargo Hinders Efforts to Restore Hemingway Estate." *Chronicle of Philanthropy* 18.15: 11.

Outlines past and present preservationist efforts to restore and protect Finca Vigía.

Sanders, Jaimé L. "The Journalistic and Philosophic Observation of Men in Hemingway's 1930s Literature." *Florida Studies Proceedings of the 2005 Annual Meeting of the Florida College English Association.* Edited by Steve Glassman and Karen Tolchin. Newcastle upon Tyne, England: Cambridge Scholars. 157–63.

Brief discussion of *To Have and Have Not* and other works of the 1930s, connecting them to Hemingway's growing despair over the corruption and destruction of his favorite places and people. Reads the loss of self reflected in the works of this period as a result of Hemingway's fear of modernism and change.

Scott, Steven. "Santiago, Scheherazade, and Somebody: Storytelling from Hemingway to Barth." *Mattoid* 55: 74–88.

Reads *The Old Man and the Sea* as a modernist experiment bridging the gap between modernism and postmodernism. Suggests Scheherazade's fifth tale of Sinbad from *The Thousand Nights and One Night* as source for the novel, noting numerous similarities including the title. Closes with a discussion of Barth's use of the travels of Sinbad in his novel *The Last Voyage of Somebody the Sailor* but argues that while the general reader need not be aware of the source when reading *The Old Man and the Sea,* a knowledge of the voyages of Sinbad is essential when reading Barth's version because he retells and interprets the original tale.

Sova, Dawn B. *Banned Books: Literature Suppressed on Social Grounds.* New York: Facts on File, 116–20, 227–32. Reprinted from 1998.
Provides a brief censorship history of *To Have and Have Not,* outlining objections and bannings based on offensive language and sexual explicitness/situations in the novel.

Whiting, Jim. *Ernest Hemingway.* Hockessin, DE: Mitchell Lane.
Biography geared to young adult readers, with brief interchapters on other American Nobel Prize winners, the Spanish-American War, bullfighting, and the Cuban Revolution.

2007

Dempsey, George T. "Justice for Ernest Hemingway." *Antioch Review* 65.2: 239–55.
Assesses "the true state" of Hemingway's output in his final two decades, lamenting the publication of nearly all of the author's later texts, including *The Old Man and the Sea.* Calls for the scholarly reediting of all of Hemingway's posthumous works, similar to that of *Under Kilimanjaro,* "so that those of us who care can see the terrible reality of this master struggling to regain his mastery of his craft."

Hediger, Ryan. "Hunting, Fishing, and the Cramp of Ethics in Ernest Hemingway's *The Old Man and the Sea, Green Hills of Africa,* and *Under Kilimanjaro.*" *Hemingway Review* 27.2: 35–59.
Hediger relies on ethical theory to redefine the traditional notion of ethics so as to focus on "openness to experience and to aesthetics." Examines Hemingway's evolving attitudes toward hunting and fishing, as evidenced in the two safari books and *The Old Man and the Sea.* Argues "that in Hemingway's later texts, dead animals—the number of trophies, the size of their horns, or the weight of their flesh—becomes less necessary as a measure or memento of his hunting and fishing experience, and ethical experience itself takes greater emphasis."

Oliver, Charles M. *Critical Companion to Ernest Hemingway: A Literary Reference to His Life and Work.* New York: Facts on File.
Extensive revision of Oliver's 1991 *Hemingway A to Z,* an encyclopedic companion to the author's life and works, including *To Have and Have Not, The Old Man and the Sea,* and *Islands in the Stream.* Includes synopses, publication histories, and critical commentaries on the works, along with alphabetically arranged entries defining important characters, people, places, and subjects. Biographical sections provide overviews of the author's life and assess his legacy. Alphabetically listed biographical entries focus not only on family and friends but also on other people, places, and things helpful for understanding the author and his work. Extensive appendices include an updated bibliography of works by and about the author.

Ott, Mark P. "Ernest Hemingway's Caribbean Gulf Stream Frontier: An Evolving Ecological Perspective." In *This Watery World: Humans and the Sea*. Edited by Vartan P. Messier and Nandita Batra. Mayagüez, Puerto Rico: College English Association–Caribbean Chapter. 71–91.

Ecological approach tracing Hemingway's complex and evolving perspective on the Gulf Stream. Initially, as evidenced in early magazine articles and *To Have and Have Not,* Hemingway saw the stream as a frontier to be conquered. As his interest in and knowledge of the Gulf Stream grew over years, his vision transformed, culminating in the view, depicted in *The Old Man and the Sea,* of the stream as a harmonious Eden with rejuvenating powers.

Pridemore, Adam. "Decolonizing the Native Conch in Ernest Hemingway's *To Have and Have Not:* Harry Morgan as a Cautionary Tale against Tourism." *Florida Studies Proceedings of the 2006 Annual Meeting of the Florida College English Association.* Edited by Steve Glassman and Karen Tolchin. Newcastle upon Tyne, UK: Cambridge Scholars. 91–97.

Drawing on postcolonial theory, Pridemore argues that *To Have and Have Not* "predicts, confirms, and bemoans the commercialization and exploitation that have become second nature to the conflicted neocolonial colossus that is the United States of America." Sees tourists as the ultimate colonizers, corrupting and destroying the native culture of Key West to meet the prescribed cultural representation of their dominant imagination. While Harry may lament the burning down of shacks to make room for tourist apartments, his recognition in the end is not enough to stop the rampant commercialism that surrounds him.

Thomas, Gordon. "An Immovable Feast? Another Look at Henry King's The Sun Also Rises." Bright Lights Film Journal 55 (February). http://www.brightlightsfilm.com/.

Pans several Hollywood film adaptations of Hemingway's works, including The Old Man and the Sea.

Wagner-Martin, Linda. *Ernest Hemingway: A Literary Life.* Basingstoke, UK: Palgrave Macmillan.

Literary biography tracing Hemingway's development as a professional writer. Describes and interprets the author's unfolding life history from Oak Park to Ketchum, focusing on those influential relationships with family and especially wives and "significant others" that helped shape his life and writing. Contends that Hemingway's need to write was rivaled by his need for romantic love. Briefly writes on Adriana Ivancich's influence on the composition of *The Old Man and the Sea.* Covers the writing, revision, publication and critical reception of *To Have and Have Not,* focusing in particular on

Hemingway's troubled relationship with Pauline Pfeiffer. Includes information on Hemingway's publishing career, critical reputation, and the changing social context of the twentieth century.

2008

Ashe, Fred. "'A Very Attractive Devil': Gregory Hemingway in *Islands in the Stream. Hemingway Review* 28.1: 89–106.
Biographical reading paralleling Thomas Hudson's troubled relationship with his youngest son Andrew with Hemingway's own conflicted relationship with youngest son Gregory. Written during a period when Hemingway was exploring gender issues in both his life and writings and coming to terms with Gregory's transvestism, the father-son relationship of *Islands in the Stream* depicts Hemingway's "anger toward and identification with Gregory."

Bender, Bert. "Harry Burns and Professor MacWalsey in Ernest Hemingway's *To Have and Have Not.*" *Hemingway Review* 28.1: 35–50.
Identifies and explores Professor Harry Burns as the real-life model for Hemingway's fictional protagonist. Relies on Burns's correspondence with Hemingway and with Carlos Baker to reconstruct Hemingway's relationship with Burns from their initial 1936 meeting in Key West through Burns's final 1951 visit with the author in Cuba.

Bloom, Harold, ed. *Ernest Hemingway's* The Old Man and the Sea. New York: Bloom's Literary Criticism.
Collection of twelve previously published essays on the novel. Contents:
"Introduction," by Harold Bloom, 1–3. Negatively characterizes the novel as a "period piece" and self-parody of the author.
"Dynamics of Narration: Later Novels," by P. G. Rama Rao, 5–30. Reprint from *Ernest Hemingway: A Study in Narrative Technique* (New Delhi, India: Chand, 1980).
"*The Old Man and the Sea:* The Culmination," by Wirt Williams, 31–52. Reprint from *The Tragic Art of Ernest Hemingway* (Baton Rouge, LA: Louisiana State Univ. Press, 1981).
"The Later Fiction: Hemingway and the Aesthetics of Failure," by James H. Justus, 53–67. Reprint from *Ernest Hemingway: New Critical Essays*, edited by Robert A. Lee (Totowa, NJ: Vision Press, 1983).
"The Angler," by Gregory S. Sojka, 69–79. Reprint from *Ernest Hemingway: The Angler as Artist* (New York: Peter Lang, 1985).
"Contrasts in Form: Hemingway's *The Old Man and the Sea* and Faulkner's 'The Bear,'" by David Timms, 80–94. Reprint from *The Modern American Novella* (Totowa, NJ: Vision Press, 1989).

"Up to the End," by Peter L. Hays, 95–107. Reprint from *Ernest Hemingway* (New York: Continuum, 1990).

"Psychology," by Gerry Brenner, 109–23. Reprint from The Old Man and the Sea: *Story of a Common Man* (New York: Twayne Publishers, 1991).

"Inside the Current: A Taoist Reading of *The Old Man and the Sea,*" by Eric Waggoner, 125–41. Reprint from *Hemingway Review* 17.2 (Spring 1998).

"Of Rocks and Marlin: The Existentialist Agon in Camus's *The Myth of Sisyphus* and Hemingway's *The Old Man and the Sea,*" by Dwight Eddins, 143–51. Reprint from *Hemingway Review* 21.1 (Fall 2001).

"Santiago and the Eternal Feminine: Gendering *La Mar* in *The Old Man and the Sea,*" by Susan F. Beegel, 153–78. Reprint from *Hemingway and Women: Female Critics and the Female Voice,* edited by Lawrence R. Broer and Gloria Holland (Tuscaloosa, AL: Univ. of Alabama Press, 2002).

"The Self Offstage: 'Big Two-Hearted River' and *The Old Man and the Sea,*" by Thomas Strychacz, 179–212. Reprint from *Hemingway's Theaters of Masculinity* (Baton Rouge, LA: Louisiana State Univ. Press, 2003).

"Ernest Hemingway, Derek Walcott, and Old Men of the Sea," by Edward O. Ako, 213–23. Reprint from *CLA Journal* 48.2 (Dec. 2004).

Boon, Kevin Alexander. *Ernest Hemingway:* The Sun Also Rises *and Other Works.* New York: Marshall Cavendish.

Biography geared to young adult readers, with a chapter devoted to *The Old Man and the Sea.* Includes chronology and filmography.

Kroupi, Agori. "The Religious Implications of Fishing and Bullfighting in Hemingway's Work." *Hemingway Review* 28.1: 107–21.

Addresses the problem of redemption, appearing metaphorically in fishing and bullfighting passages taken from several Hemingway's novels and short stories. Very brief nod to *The Old Man and the Sea.*

Mangum, Bryant. "Ernest Hemingway." In *Notable American Novelists.* Edited by Carl E. Rollyson. Pasadena, CA: Salem Press. 578–89.

Overview of Hemingway's life and major works. Discusses *The Old Man and the Sea* stylistically, thematically, and in light of the Hemingway code.

Ott, Mark P. *A Sea of Change: Ernest Hemingway and the Gulf Stream, A Contextual Biography.* Kent, OH: Kent State Univ. Press.

Literary biography, drawing on Hemingway's fishing logs, correspondence (published and unpublished), and newspaper articles to reconstruct the author's complex relationship with the Gulf Stream and its influence on his writing. Ott traces Hemingway's stylistic and philosophic transformation from Cézanne-inspired abstraction in the 1920s to the realism of the 1950s, contending that a close reading of the fishing logs reveals both Hemingway's growing understanding of the natural world and his evolution as a writer. Focuses on *To Have and Have Not* and *The Old Man and the Sea.* Includes a chronology of Hemingway's time spent in the Gulf Stream and a list of books from Hemingway's library that may have influenced the composition of both novels.

Rossow, Francis C. "*The Old Man and the Sea* by Ernest Hemingway." In *Gospel Patterns in Literature: Familiar Truths and Unexpected Places.* Minneapolis, MN: Lutheran Univ. Press. 71–78.
Argues that Hemingway's goal in inserting gospel imagery into the novel was to elevate and ennoble Santiago's heroic struggles with nature rather than promote any serious Christian message. Rossow enumerates several parallels between Santiago and Christ "designed to win our admiration for Santiago."

Strychacz, Thomas. "The Construction of Hemingway: Masculine Style and Style-less Masculinity." In *Dangerous Masculinities: Conrad, Hemingway, and Lawrence.* Gainesville, FL: Univ. of Press of Florida. 73–103.
Reception-based approach focusing on the first half of the twentieth century. Strychacz analyzes the theatrical nature of Hemingway's work, an area largely overlooked by scholars. Treats the overriding professional anxieties present in male scholars in relation to constructions of manhood and masculine style in Hemingway's fiction. "Those men demonstrated powerful yearnings for stable, self-evident, and universal masculine attributes, and for comprehensible, solid-seeming texts of masculine awakening. And they strove to maintain the hegemony of their conventional ways of thinking about manhood-fashioning even as the very nature of their professional work seemed to insist on a very different and much more problematic relationship." Gives passing commentary on the ultra-masculine Morgan of *To Have and Have Not.*

Xie, Yaochen. "Hemingway's Language Style and Writing Techniques in *The Old Man and the Sea.*" *English Language Teaching* 1.2: 156–58.
Commentary on Hemingway's deliberate manipulation of language and facts in *The Old Man and the Sea,* resulting in both a seemingly natural prose style and a believable fictional narrative.

2009

Becnel, Kim E. *Bloom's How to Write About Ernest Hemingway.* New York: Bloom's Literary Criticism.
Designed to help high school students write essays on Hemingway's works. Provides an overview of Hemingway's important themes (e.g., love and war) and stylistic techniques. Offers individual chapters on specific major works, examining theme, character, and literary elements, followed by sample essay

topics and open-ended questions designed to inspire students to develop their own topics for investigation. Covers *The Old Man and the Sea.*

Beegel, Susan F. "Thor Heyerdahl's *Kon-Tiki* and Hemingway's Return to Primitivism in *The Old Man and the Sea.*" In *Hemingway: Eight Decades of Criticism.* Edited by Linda Wagner-Martin. East Lansing, MI: Michigan State Univ. Press. 513–51.

Parallel reading of both texts, suggesting that Hemingway's return to primitivism in *The Old Man and the Sea* (1957) may have been influenced by the immense popularity of Heyerdahl's 1948 narrative. Examines similarities in subject matter, arguing that the "back to nature" philosophy of both texts appealed to a modern generation overwhelmed by advancements in technology. Simplistic escape from civilization via the sea provides the heroes with a comforting sense of self-reliance and solitude. And yet their detailed environmental observations reveal not only their intimacy with the natural world but also their deep understanding of how that natural world might serve to measure man's progress away from nature's violence.

Curnutt, Kirk and Gail D. Sinclair, eds. *Key West Hemingway: A Reassessment*. Gainesville, FL: Univ. Press of Florida.

"Only in Key West: Hemingway's Fortunate Isle," by Lawrence R. Broer, 44–58. Describes the positive effects of island living on Hemingway's life and writing, particularly its remoteness and stability, which helped him to resolve conflicting roles in his life, such as "artist as husband and father, artist as friend, artist as public figure, and artist as man of action." Details his close friendships with sporting and drinking companions during this era and the importance of his balancing work and play (writing and fishing). Passing references to works of the period, including *To Have and Have Not.*

"Beleaguered Modernists: Hemingway, Stevens, and the Left," by Milton A. Cohen, 77–90. Characterizing both Hemingway and Wallace Stevens as "apolitical by temperament," Cohen compares how each dealt with the pull of the left during the economic crisis of the 1930s. Although rejecting Marxism, each gradually integrated political and economic issues into their writings. Uses *To Have and Have Not* to exemplify Hemingway's leftward movement, prompted largely by the Spanish Civil War and his desire to bolster his flagging critical reputation. Attributes both writers' easy transition away from leftist politics by the end of the 1930s to their essential apolitical nature.

"Hemingway, the Left, and Key West," by Dan Monroe, 91–103. Addresses criticism of Hemingway's failure to confront the national crisis of the Great Depression, defending the author by arguing that he engaged in social commentary in writings such as *To Have and Have Not.* Details Hemingway's negative view of the New Deal and its effect on Key West, making it a tourist hub. Explains Hemingway's shift from isolationism to interventionism during the Spanish Civil War.

"Harry and the Pirates: The Romance and Reality of Piracy in Hemingway's *To Have and Have Not*," by Susan F. Beegel, 107–28. Identifies traditions of historical and fictional portrayals of piracy as potential source material for *To Have and Have Not.* Discusses Hemingway's use of pirate motifs to critique capitalism and communism.

"Tropical Iceberg: Cuban Turmoil in the 1930s and Hemingway's *To Have and Have Not,*" by Paul Steve, 129–42. Manuscript study. Examines how the 1930s rebellion against Cuban dictator Gerardo Machado serves as background for *To Have and Have Not,* especially the unpublished fourth part, and contributes to the novel's themes of revolution and oppression. Concludes with a discussion of Hemingway's struggle to excise his personal political views from his writing.

"'The Poor Are Different from You and Me': Masculinity and Class in *To Have and Have Not,*" by Susan J. Wolfe, 158–71. Through a comparison to *The Sun Also Rises,* Wolfe considers the denigrating nature of class and masculinity in *To Have and Have Not,* which "attributes upper-class iniquities to the lack of masculine strength and resolve." Comments on Harry Morgan's demonstration of heroism and masculinity through his "marriage and commitment to his family."

"Hemingway, Faulkner, and Hawks: The Nexus of Creativity that Generated the Film *To Have and Have Not,*" by Mimi Reisel Gladstein, 172–86. Commentary on Howard Hawks's 1944 film adaptation of *To Have and Have Not.* Details alterations made to the novel to fit the big screen, adding to the collaborative nature of the final product. Argues that the film is an acceptable adaptation of the novel because much of Hemingway's theme, characterization, and narrative style is preserved.

"Reexamining the Origins of 'After the Storm,'" by Michael J. Crowley, 189–205. Composition history and manuscript study. Compares conflicting biographical accounts of when and where Hemingway first heard the source story from Bra Sanders, his Gulf Stream fishing guide. An examination of the manuscripts reveals the development of the story's narrative structure, demonstrating Hemingway's skillful fictionalization of the tale.

"Hemingway's Key West Band of Brothers: The World War I Veterans in 'Who Murdered the Vets?' and *To Have and Have Not,*" by James H. Meredith, 241–66. Provides a historical context for Hemingway's proletarian period beginning with his searing indictment of governmental indifference following the 1935 Key West hurricane in "Who Murdered the Vets?" Traces Hemingway's evolving depiction of soldiers from individuals to key types, detailing Hemingway's shift from personal portraits, such as that of *In Our Time's* traumatized Nick Adams, to the broader critique of social factors oppressing veterans found in the later *To Have and Have Not.* Concludes that Hemingway's evolving perspective away from the individual to the group experience paved the way for his successful "portrait of the Spanish irregulars who help Robert Jordan blow the bridge" in *For Whom the Bell Tolls.*

Donaldson, Scott. "The Last Great Cause: Hemingway's Spanish Civil War Writing." In *Fitzgerald and Hemingway: Works and Days.* New York: Columbia Univ. Press. 371–451.

The single new essay in a collection of previously published essays on Hemingway. Donaldson discusses Hemingway's time in Spain in 1937–38 and the various forms of writing stemming from it (e.g., war correspondence, drama, fiction). Focusing on the author's "leftward drift" and growing interest in the war, Donaldson asserts that Spain instilled in Hemingway an awareness of the importance of freedom and friendship, and concludes that "he did not abandon his conviction that the lost cause had been worth the effort." Comments on writings of the period, including "Who Murdered the Vets?" and *To Have and Have Not.*

Fleming, Robert E. "The Death of the Children in *Islands in the Stream.*" *North Dakota Quarterly* 76.1–2: 140–46.

Speculates on the reason behind Hudson's neglect of and failure to protect his children, attributing his aloof manner with his family to his inability to balance his artistry with his parenting.

Hemmingson, Michael. "*Esquire*'s Failure with Hemingway's 'Bimini.'" *Hemingway Review* 29.1: 140–44.

Examines correspondence between Mary Hemingway and *Esquire*'s fiction editor, Gordon Lish, on the 1970 publication of the "Bimini" excerpt of *Islands in the Stream.* Details Mary's disappointment with *Esquire*'s choice of cover photo and accompanying "Editor's Note."

Herlihy, Jeffrey. "'Eyes the Same Color as the Sea': Santiago's Expatriation from Spain and Ethnic Otherness in *The Old Man and the Sea.*" *Hemingway Review* 28.2: 25–44.

On Santiago's social condition as an expatriate in Cuba. Discusses his isolation from his Spanish community and negative treatment by his adopted community. Examines Santiago's attempts to assimilate into Cuban society along with the ways in which his foreignness affects his self-image.

Mort, Terry. *The Hemingway Patrols: Ernest Hemingway and His Hunt for U-boats.* New York: Scribner.

Biography focused on Hemingway's voluntary pursuit of German U-boats in the Gulf Stream in 1942–43. Relies on wartime documents, the *Pilar* log, personal correspondence, and other Hemingway papers to reconstruct Hemingway's larger-than-life efforts to go after German submarines in a small wooden fishing boat. Recounts Martha Gellhorn's skepticism, dismissing the danger and categorizing the patrols as merely adolescent parties with old drinking buddies. Details Hemingway's inclusion of his sons Patrick and Gregory on some of the missions. Reads these adventures as the embodiment of the "Hemingway hero," contending that they helped to shape his writing of *The Old Man and the Sea* and *Islands in the Stream.*

Seed, David. "Ernest Hemingway: The Observer's Visual Field." In *Cinematic Fictions.* Liverpool, UK: Liverpool Univ. Press. 68–85.

Traces the differing modes of visual representation in Hemingway's major fiction, including *The Old Man and the Sea* and *Islands in the Stream.* Analyzes Hemingway's cinematic technique through close readings of individual scenes, examining the author's experiments in perspective and careful sequencing of descriptive details through the gaze of an observer.

Shiflet, E. Stone, and James H. Meredith. "'If you don't like this town get out and stay out': Ernest Hemingway's Key West." In *Florida in the Popular Imagination: Essays on the Cultural Landscape of the Sunshine State.* Edited by Steve Glassman. Jefferson, NC: McFarland and Co. 147–58.

Biographical account of Hemingway's life in and ties to Key West, starting with his arrival in 1928. Chronicles both the factual and legendary stories of his life. Examines how Hemingway's legacy has affected Key West. Passing references to the *Esquire* articles, *To Have and Have Not,* and "Who Murdered the Vets?"

2010

Bak, John S. *Homo americanus: Ernest Hemingway, Tennessee Williams, and Queer Masculinities.* Madison, WI: Fairleigh Dickinson Univ. Press.

Influence study, examining the sociohistorical, sociopolitical, and literary connections between the two authors. Argues that Hemingway's posthumous novels, such as *Islands in the Stream,* more openly support Williams's efforts to challenge the cold war's sexual politics than earlier works, such as *The Sun Also Rises.*

Bennett, Eric. "Ernest Hemingway and the Discipline of Creative Writing, Or, Shark Liver Oil." *Modern Fiction Studies* 56.3: 544–67.

Traces Hemingway's influence on the evolution of creative writing instruction in an era in which his realistic brand of modernism stood in stark contrast to the New Humanists' abstract approach to literature. Claiming Hemingway's writing has influenced, often unconsciously, generations of postmodern writers, Bennett closes with an examination of the prose style and content of *The Old Man and the Sea,* along with commentary on the novella's usefulness for critics, teachers, and students.

Bouchard, Donald F. *Hemingway: So Far from Simple.* Amherst, MA: Prometheus Books.

Argues against those who find Hemingway's writing superficial and artless, showing how Hemingway's careful attention to style and lifelong concern with his career as a writer earned him the title of one of America's most important and influential authors. Draws on Hemingway's correspondence, *A Moveable Feast,* his statements about art, and the postmodernist writings of Foucault, Deleuze, and Said to trace Hemingway's evolving style in relation to changing times. Analyzes the major works chronologically, exploring Hemingway's shift away from modernism toward a gradually developing social and political awareness found in *To Have and Have Not.* Concludes with an analysis of *The Old Man and the Sea.*

Cirino, Mark. "An Evening at the Kennedy White House: Frederic March Performs Hemingway's *Islands in the Stream.*" *Hemingway Review* 29.2: 123–32.

Notes veteran actor Frederic March's 1962 reading of an excerpt (portion of the "At Sea" section) from Hemingway's then unpublished novel for a White House dinner honoring Nobel Prize winners.

——— and Mark P. Ott, eds. *Ernest Hemingway and the Geography of Memory.* Kent, OH: Kent State Univ. Press.

"Reclaimed Experience: Trauma Theory and Hemingway's Lost Paris Manuscripts," by Marc Seals, 18–27. Originally published in *Hemingway Review* 24.2 (Spring 2005): 62–72. Focusing on Hemingway's posthumous works, including *Islands in the Stream,* Seals examines how Hemingway attempted to heal the wounds of trauma he suffered over the 1922 loss of his manuscripts by repeatedly writing about the episode.

"Memory and the Sharks," by Sergio Perosa, 31–36. Previously published in Italian: "La memoria gli squali." In *Hemingway e Venzia.* Edited by Sergio Perosa. Florence, Italy: L.S. Olschki, 1988. Draws on Hemingway's correspondence and statements on writing to discuss his method of fictionalizing memory (balancing reality with imagination). Touches on *The Old Man and the Sea.*

"Lions on the Beach: Dream, Place, and Memory in *The Old Man and the Sea,*" by Larry Grimes, 57–66. Close reading of the lion imagery, demonstrating the connection between memory and physical geography. Argues for Hemingway's multicultural complexity by reading the Africa sections through the lens of Afro-Cuban religions.

Cray, Robert E., Jr. "Pilar Goes Sub Chasing." *WWII History* 9.4: 28–31.

Recounts Hemingway's 1942–43 adventures hunting German U-boats in the

Caribbean aboard the Pilar. Contends that the experience, while technically uneventful, served as the inspiration for *Islands in the Stream.*

Frederking, Lauretta Conklin, ed. *Hemingway on Politics and Rebellion.* New York: Routledge.

"The Rebel: Hemingway and the Struggle Against Politics," by Lauretta Conklin Frederking, 3–16. Analysis of Hemingway's political views evident in his writings, particularly in *To Have and Have Not.* Claims that Hemingway's belief that politics serve as a crucible for self-discovery was more important than his political ideology. By creating and reacting to conflict, characters confront themselves, leading to greater self-realization and actualization.

"Hemingway, Hopelessness, and Liberalism," by William Curtis, 50–72. Relying on Richard Rorty's theories of art and politics, Curtis argues that Hemingway's work exhibits a sense of hopelessness about the ability of politics to improve the human condition. Compares Hemingway's corpus to Jean Jacques Rousseau's philosophy of the noble savage, finding that while Rousseau is willing to move beyond the state of nature, Hemingway remains deeply cynical and pessimistic. Examining *To Have and Have Not* and other novels to demonstrate this political pessimism, Curtis concludes that "Liberals can read Hemingway as pointing out the dangers of hopelessness, and learn from his broken characters that hopelessness is something that must be recognized and politically attended to."

"Manly Assertion," by Harvey Mansfield, 91–103. Develops a theory of masculinity based on assertion rather than aggression, analyzing the presentation of manliness in *The Old Man and the Sea* and Homer's *Iliad.* In contrast to Achilles's political manifestation of manliness, Mansfield claims Santiago's manliness is rendered nonpolitical because the natural setting of the sea lacks social context.

"Hemingway, Religion, and Masculine Virtue," by Joseph Prud'homme, 104–29. Argues against the traditional reading of Hemingway as a nihilist and fair-weather Catholic, pointing to the strong Catholic sentiment running throughout *The Old Man and the Sea* and other texts as affirmation of Hemingway's devotion. Prud'homme characterizes the "Hemingway Catholic Hero" code and argues for its continued relevance to contemporary masculine values. Notes differences between Hemingway's depiction of Christ and portrayals found in Mel Gibson's film *The Passion of the Christ* and the Promise Keepers movement.

"'The Revolutionist,'" by David Winston Conklin, 151–70. On the rationality and motivation of the rebel. Compares macro and micro social theories of revolution to Hemingway's diverse treatment of the rebel hero in *The Old Man and the Sea* and other novels, revealing that Hemingway's heroes are truly ordinary individuals who are psychologically and emotionally transformed by their experiences. Conklin argues that Hemingway structures his heroes not as outcomes of ideology, but as individuals frustrated with conditions of inequality and oppression and thus driven to act.

"*To Have and Have Not:* Hemingway Through the Lens of Theodor Adorno," by Lauretta Conklin Frederking, 171–95. Noting both Adorno's and Hemingway's opposition to institutionalized power, Frederking relies on Adorno's political philosophy to read Harry Morgan as the embodiment of his concept of the rebel. Argues that Morgan exemplifies the liberated self, or rebel, through his autonomy and authentic engagement with his circumstances and the people he encounters. Contends that *To Have and Have Not* "provides insight into the relevance of the rebel who may fight without political intention but whose actions nonetheless carry political consequences."

Goodheart, Eugene, ed. *Critical Insights: Ernest Hemingway.* Pasadena, CA: Salem Press.

Guide to Hemingway's life and major works, geared toward students and general readers. Mostly previously published material.

"Cultural Imperialism, Afro-Cuban Religion, and Santiago's Failure in Hemingway's *The Old Man and the Sea,*" by Philip Melling, 283–305. Reprint from *Hemingway Review* 26.1 (2006).

Hasan, Rabiul. *Rediscovering Hemingway in Bangladesh and India, 1971–2006.* Lanham, MD: Univ. Press of America.

Surveys the teaching, reception, and influence of Hemingway's works in Bangladesh and India from 1971 to 2006, revealing the growing interest in Hemingway studies in the Indian subcontinent. Examines the cultural, social, and political factors influencing literary critics, academics, and the reading public. Opens with a brief overview of American and British criticism before moving into a survey of Indian and Bangladeshi criticism on Hemingway's short stories and novels and the challenges specific to teaching American literature in Bangladesh and India. Closes with an assessment of Hemingway's reputation and continued relevancy among academics, critics, students, and general readers, especially in the aftermath of September 11, 2001. Includes an examination of *The Old Man and the Sea.*

Huang, Liangguang. "Man is Invincible—About Hemingway's Humanism." *English Language Teaching* 3.2: 115–18.

Argues against interpreting *The Old Man and the Sea* as a Christian allegory in favor of a humanist reading celebrating the dignity, courage, and invincibility of humankind.

MacLean, John V. "Dealing with Loss: 'The Wanderer,' the Hemingway Hero, and *The Tempest.*" In *If You Teach It, They Will Read: Literature's Life Lessons for Today's Students.* New York: Rowman and Littlefield. 85–89.

Pedagogical approach, using *The Old Man and the Sea* to teach high school English students about the universality of loss.

Müller, Kurt. "The Change of Hemingway's Literary Style in the 1930s: A Response to Silvia Ammary." *Connotations: A Journal for Critical Debate* 20.2–3: 155–63.

Response to Ammary's claims that Hemingway's later self-reflexive work was ultimately a failure and stylistically dissimilar to his earlier texts. Müller argues that this stylistic difference, including shifts in length, wordiness, reflective quality, and theme, indicates Hemingway's artistic growth and response to the times. Includes an examination of *The Old Man and the Sea.* See Ammary's "The Road Not Taken in Hemingway's 'The Snows of Kilimanjaro.'" *Connotations* 18.1–3 (2008–09): 123–38.

Müller, Timo. "Hemingway: The Constructed Self." In *The Self as Object in Modernist Fiction: James, Joyce, Hemingway.* Würzburg, Germany: Konigshausen and Neumann. 221–76.

Studies the complex and variable mode of self-objectification in Hemingway's fiction, focusing on three main postures of "surrogate writers" found throughout his oeuvre: authenticity, simplicity, and independence. Analyzes the development of these postures, beginning with the successful *The Sun Also Rises,* and their subsequent modifications in later novels such as *To Have and Have Not.* Argues that in Hemingway's later works, the author revised his techniques to create greater distance between himself and his characters, ultimately resulting in his becoming one of the greatest writers of the modernist period.

Stoltzfus, Ben. *Hemingway and French Writers.* Kent, OH: Kent State Univ. Press.

Discusses the progression of Hemingway's major works, including *The Old Man and the Sea,* within the context of twentieth-century avant-garde Paris. Compares Hemingway's works with those of contemporary French novelists, such as Sartre, Camus, Montherlant and Gide, to reveal how each informs the other in their parallels experimentations with style, structure, and theme.

Wright, Chantal. "The Water under the Bridge: Tzveta Sofronieva's *Der Alte Mann, das Meer, die Frau.*" In *Shoreless Bridges: South East European Writing in Disaspora.* Edited by Elka Agoston-Nikolova. New York: Rodopi. 97–116.

Examines the Bulgarian poet's feminist retelling of *The Old Man and the Sea,* in which fishing is reduced to a hobby and Manolin is replaced by a woman.

2011

Bloom, Harold, ed. *Ernest Hemingway* (Bloom's Modern Critical Views). New York: Bloom's Literary Criticism.

Reader's companion of reprinted criticism on Hemingway's life and major works, including *The Old Man and the Sea.* Includes a bibliography and chronology of the author's life.

"Santiago and the Eternal Feminine: Gendering La Mar in *The Old Man and the Sea,*" by Susan F. Beegel, 109–34. Reprint from *Hemingway and Women: Female Critics and the Female Voice,* edited by Lawrence R. Broer and Gloria Holland (Tuscaloosa, AL: Univ. of Alabama Press, 2002).

"Cultural Imperialism, Afro-Cuban Religion, and Santiago's Failure in Hemingway's *The Old Man and the Sea,*" by Philip Melling, 157–74. Reprint from *Hemingway Review* 26.1 (Fall 2006).

Bluefarb, Sam. "The Essential Tragic Conservatism of Ernest Hemingway." *New English Review* July. http:/www.newenglishreview.org.

Defines Hemingway's apolitical conservatism by highlighting the dark vein of despair running throughout his work. Compares Hemingway's tragic vision with that of Spanish writer Miguel de Unamuno and further refines Hemingway's conservatism through a close biographical reading of his work, focusing specifically on *The Old Man and the Sea.*

Broer, Lawrence R. *Vonnegut and Hemingway: Writers at War.* Columbia, SC: Univ. of South Carolina Press.

Comparative study, arguing that "Vonnegut's life and work exist as a veritable palimpsest of Hemingway's." Broer examines their shared legacy of childhood trauma, disabling war experience, and depression and its impact on their writing, contending that despite Vonnegut's numerous attempts to exorcise Hemingway's ghost, his fictional self-creations mirrored the Hemingway hero's quest for wholeness and psychic balance. Closes with an examination of Hemingway's discovery of the transformative power of the buried feminine self in his later works, such as *The Old Man and the Sea* and *Islands in the Stream.*

Feldman, Andrew. "Leopoldina Rodríguez: Hemingway's Cuban Lover." *Hemingway Review* 31.1: 62–78.

Discusses the influence of Hemingway's longtime friend and possible lover on *The Old Man and the Sea* and *Islands in the Stream,* concluding that "Leo" Rodríguez was the inspiration for "Honest Lil" of *Islands.*

Hendrickson, Paul. *Hemingway's Boat: Everything He Loved in Life, and Lost, 1934–1961.* New York: Knopf.

Biography covering Hemingway's middle and final years, using unconventional methods (occasional first-person narration by the biographer, a structure based on the author's frequent returns to his beloved boat *Pilar*) and resources (the testimony of little-known acquaintances) to craft a new portrait, hailed by critics as both sympathetic and devastating. Scattered references throughout to *Islands in the Sea* and *The Old Man and the Sea.*

Herlihy, Jeffrey. *In Paris or Paname: Hemingway's Expatriate Nationalism.* New York: Rodopi.
Explores the function of place and cultural displacement in Hemingway's novels, including *The Old Man and the Sea.* Herlihy examines Hemingway's thematic preoccupation with foreign settings in relation to his protagonists' sense of identity, expatriate experience, and failed attempts at assimilation. Argues that the Hemingway hero, while longing for redefinition within a foreign culture, is unable to completely overcome his origins and thus fails to fully integrate into that foreign culture. Includes previously published material from the *Hemingway Review, European Journal of American Studies, North Dakota Quarterly,* and *Metamorphosis and Place* (2009).

Murray, Kathleen. "*To Have and Have Not:* An Adaptive System." In *True to the Spirit. Film Adaptation and the Question of Fidelity.* Edited by Colin MacCabe, Kathleen Murray, and Rick Warner. Oxford: Oxford Univ. Press. 91–113.
Murray examines the "flexible" model employed by director Howard Hawks in his 1944 film adaptation of *To Have and Have Not.* Argues that despite Hawks's dramatic reworking, the novel and film share deep connections in style and approach and concludes that the film can best be understood as the product of a series of systems (e.g., Warners picture, Hawks film, Faulkner screenplay) outside of the novel.

Nicholls, Peter. "Stein, Hemingway, and American Modernisms." In *The Cambridge History of the American Novel.* Edited by Leonard Cassuto. New York: Cambridge Univ. Press. 622–38.
Stylistic comparison of literary giants Hemingway and Stein, and their influence on the modernist movement. Comments on the sense of fatalism pervading Hemingway's longer works, such as *Islands in the Stream.*

Suàrez Galbàn, Eugenio. "Hemingway: Stories of the Last Good Land." In *The Last Good Land: Spain in American Literature.* New York: Rodopi. 199–223.
Examines the recurring theme of Spain as the last good land in Hemingway's stories written prior to and after the start of the Spanish Civil War, concluding that "if earlier Spain represented the more humane past, now it stands for the possible future that would save Europe and the world from the coming disaster of another and more brutal world war against the Fascist forces that were threatening them." Includes an analysis of "Nobody Ever Dies."

Yu, Yan. "The Call of the Wild: An Eco-critical Reading of *The Old Man and the Sea.*" *Canadian Social Science* 7.3: 167–75.

Relying on ecocritical theories, Yu examines Hemingway's ambivalent attitude toward nature and the novel's unsympathetic stance toward ecological consciousness reflected in Santiago's heroic image and "tough guy" spirit. Also discusses Santiago's use of and desire to conquer nature, along with his cruelty toward animals.

2012

Cirino, Mark. *Ernest Hemingway: Thought in Action.* Studies in American Thought and Culture Series. Madison, WI: Univ. of Wisconsin Press.
Identifying Hemingway as a psychological novelist, Cirino examines the role of consciousness within a range of texts, including *Islands in the Stream* and *The Old Man and the Sea.* Cirino focuses on the protagonists' internal struggles with present crises and past traumas to reveal the author's astute understanding of the modern mind's emotional and cognitive complexity, concluding that the "Hemingway hero is introspective enough to know his own impulse to think about things, which often leads to overthinking things; this tendency becomes the constant struggle that dominates the Hemingway text." Draws on the theories of Freud, James, Bergson, and others to explicate the function of consciousness. Includes previously published material from *The Hemingway Review, Papers on Language and Literature,* and *Ernest Hemingway and the Geography of Memory* (2010).

Claridge, Henry, ed. *Ernest Hemingway.* 4 vols. Critical Assessments of Major Writers Series. New York: Routledge.
Extensive four-volume collection of previously published essays, reviews, and other critical materials on Hemingway's life and work by renowned Hemingway scholars. Reviewers include contemporary authors and critics such as Gertrude Stein, F. Scott Fitzgerald, and Edmund Wilson. Chronological arrangement of materials allows readers to trace significant critical trends. Volume 3 is devoted to critical essays on the major works, including *The Old Man and the Sea* and *Islands in the Stream.*

Fruscione, Joseph. *Faulkner and Hemingway: Biography of a Literary Rivalry.* Columbus, OH: Ohio State Univ. Press.
Biographical and analytical study, examining Hemingway and Faulkner's complicated and contentious relationship of more than three decades. Fruscione demonstrates through their fiction, nonfiction, correspondence, and public statements how each informed and influenced the writing of the other and how their competitive rivalry simultaneously hindered and supported their literary efforts. Fruscione analyzes their corresponding writings decade by decade, arguing that their allusive works "form a kind of mod-

ernist intertext that traces a narrative of intense rivalry, joint psychological influence, riffing, and complementary authorial-masculine performance." Pairs *To Have and Have Not* with *Men at War.*

Gietschier, Steven P. "Slugging and Snubbing: Hugh Casey, Ernest Hemingway, and Jackie Robinson—a Baseball Mystery." *NINE: A Journal of Baseball History and Culture* 21.1: 12–46.

Detailed discussion of Hemingway's social interactions with members of the racially integrated Brooklyn Dodgers during the 1947 spring training session in Cuba. Attempts to set the record straight regarding Hemingway's alleged racial insensitivity. Also recaps Hemingway's lifelong love of baseball and includes a brief commentary on the pervasive use of baseball in *The Old Man and the Sea.*

Holcomb, Gary Edward, and Charles Scruggs, eds. *Hemingway and the Black Renaissance.* Columbus, OH: Ohio State Univ. Press.

"Looking for a Place to Land: Hemingway's Ghostly Presence in the Fiction of Richard Wright, James Baldwin, and Ralph Ellison," by Charles Scruggs, 55–77. Influence study, looking at how each author adapted Hemingway's existential theme of "a man alone" in his post-Harlem Renaissance writings. Scruggs focuses on their efforts to define their own independent places in American fiction through revision of Hemingway's themes of violence, loneliness, and search for refuge, found in texts such as *To Have and Have Not.*

"Knowing and Recombining: Ellison's Ways of Understanding Hemingway," by Joseph Fruscione, 78–119. On Hemingway's intellectual and stylistic influence on Ellison. Fruscione draws on biography, correspondence, and published materials to reconstruct Ellison's ambivalent attitude toward his "literary ancestor." Discusses Ellison's criticism of Hemingway's lack of racial awareness and moral exploration in *To Have and Have Not* and other works.

Hollenberg, Alexander. "The Spacious Foreground: Interpreting Simplicity and Ecocritical Ethics in *The Old Man and the Sea.*" *Hemingway Review* 31.2: 27–45.

Narratological examination of Hemingway's simply described natural settings to reveal how the author's foregrounding of nature creates a "parallel between the ethical challenges involved in mastering nature and those involved in mastering the otherness of the text through interpretation." Hollenberg focuses on Santiago's readings of the open and silent space that surrounds him, tracing the fisherman's gradual transition from an anthropocentric to a biocentric ethic.

James, Clive. "Style is the Man." *Atlantic Monthly* 309.4: 92–98.

Brief mention of American essayist Dwight Macdonald's disdain for *The Old Man and the Sea.*

Ng, Elaine Yin-ling. "The Translator's Style in Hemingway's *The Old Man and the Sea*." In *China and Its Others: Knowledge Transfer through Translation, 1829–2010*. Amsterdam: Rodopi. 165–88.

Linguistic analysis of Hai Guan's 1956 Chinese translation to reveal the work's historical context and propagandistic purpose. Ng discusses Guan's background and the social influence of China's Communist Party. Contends that images of Santiago as "an an unyielding hardened man persevering in a tough battle" were intended to inspire ordinary readers and arouse national consciousness.

Perrin, Thomas Gordon. "The Old Men and the 'Sea of Masscult': T. S. Eliot, Ernest Hemingway, and Middlebrow Aesthetics." *American Literature* 84.1: 151–74.

Perrin uses American essayist Dwight Macdonald's well-known critique of Hemingway's and Eliot's later works as middlebrow as the basis for his own examination of how *The Old Man and the Sea* (1952), in contrast to "The Undefeated" (1927), addresses the incoherencies of postwar modernist literature and thus reveals an opposing aesthetic philosophy. Perrin writes that *The Old Man and the Sea* "represents an author forced implicitly to acknowledge his middlebrow aesthetic because of an inability, despite his best efforts, to make his writing comprehensible in what had come to be accepted modernist terms."

2013

Feldman, Andrew. "Ernest Hemingway and Enrique Serpa: A Propitious Friendship." *Hemingway Review* 32.2: 58–76.

Details Hemingway's lengthy friendship with Cuban writer Enrique Serpa and the latter's influence on *To Have and Have Not* and *The Old Man and the Sea*. Feldman explores similarities in plot, character, theme, and prose style, focusing on Serpa's 1928 stories of Cuban fishermen, "The Marlin" and "Shark Fins," and his 1938 novel, *Contraband*. Concludes with a list of Serpa's books in Hemingway's Finca Vigía collection.

Meyers, Jeffrey. "The Swedish Thing." *Times Literary Supplement* 5745 (May 10): 14–15.

Delves into material in the Swedish Academy archive to shed light on the process that led to Hemingway's winning of the 1954 Nobel Prize. Includes commentary on Hemingway's candidacy, as well as on the deliberations of the Nobel committee. Brief reference to *The Old Man and the Sea*.

Moddelmog, Debra A., and Suzanne del Gizzo, eds. *Ernest Hemingway in Context*. Literature in Context Series. New York: Cambridge Univ. Press.

"Cinema and Adaptations," by Jill Jividen, 76–85. Claims that Hemingway's writing, despite his criticism of cinema, was influenced by film technique. Provides an overview of American filmmaking and film adaptations of Hemingway's works, including *To Have and Have Not* and *The Old Man and the Sea.* Concludes that "the movie industry has produced a visual legacy of a writer's works, but none of Hollywood's attempts to translate the writer to film has transcended the literature itself."

"Styles," by Milton A. Cohen, 109–18. Explores distinctions between Hemingway's early and later styles, correcting myths that the author wrote only in short, simple sentences and that his style never changed. Cohen examines texts such as *To Have and Have Not,* pointing to successful and failed experimentations with compound-complex structure, point of view, and narrative voice. Concludes with a brief discussion of Hemingway's immeasurable influence on Western prose.

"Posthumous Publications," by Robert W. Trogdon, 141–50. On problematic aspects of the posthumous materials published since 1964, criticizing those publications as unreliable representations of the author's intent. Trogdon reviews several works, including *Islands in the Stream,* noting extensive and intrusive editing resulting in excised plotlines and restructured content. Calls for more systematic plans for corrections and restorations of the texts.

"Fishing," by Mark P. Ott, 247–56. Argues that Hemingway's love of fishing, cultivated from his early years through the end of his life, had an indelible impact on his writing and personal ethics. Contends that fishing takes on various thematic roles over the course of his career and that his expertise in fishing the Gulf Stream made him intimately aware of the sociological and ecological problems of the area. "In the end," Ott concludes, "Hemingway reconciled the paradox of his pursuit of game with a very serious conservation ethic, resulting in a transformation in his creative work." References to *To Have and Have Not* and *The Old Man and the Sea.*

"Politics," by Robert E. Fleming, 287–96. Examines Hemingway's life in terms of his changing political views, arguing that "his political attitudes conformed to his times and experiences," rather than to any constant political philosophy. Draws on *To Have and Have Not.*

Stephens, Gregory, and Janice Cools. "'Out Too Far': Half-Fish, Beaten Men, and the Tenor of Masculine Grace in *The Old Man and the Sea.*" *Hemingway Review* 32.2: 77–94.

Draws on posthumanist theory to explore Santiago's heroic humility, the essential component of masculine grace in which one learns to live within boundaries. Analyzes Santiago's dependence on Manolin, respectful engagement with the feminized sea, and kinship with the natural world to show that one can maintain dignity and achieve a humbled state of grace while submitting to a worthy opponent.

Valdez, Charli G. "Racing *To Have and Have Not.*" In *Film and Literary Modernism.* Edited by Robert P. McParland. Newcastle upon Tyne, England: Cambridge Scholars. 123–30.

After recapping the critical debates over Hemingway's treatment of race in the novel, Valdez focuses on how Hemingway's use of racial epithets and construction of character translates in the film version. Valdez argues that while the film attempts to clean up the racism implicit in the novel, it only succeeds in "creatively and materially writing the black subject out of the narrative in its adaptation."

Works Cited

Donahue, Deidre. "Hemingway's Rise Purely Academic." *USA Today,* 30 Jun. 1994: D4+.

Hemingway

His Impact in the Cuban Press Today

NED QUEVEDO ARNAIZ

Hemingway's approach to Cuban topics in his narratives started with "After the Storm," through which he expresses his disapproval of the maritime authorities responsible for sinking the ship *Valbanera* in the Gulf Stream. After that, Hemingway drew on Cuba, a country he loved, as a great source of inspiration for his fictional work: notably *To Have and Have Not*, "Nobody Ever Dies," *The Old Man and the Sea*, and *Islands in the Stream*. Through all of these works, he expressed a sensitive and thoughtful concern about anything unfortunate that happened on the island; an attitude greatly appreciated by Cubans. We are proud that Hemingway made his home at Finca Vigía for so long.

Since he clearly valued Cuba, as we do, Cubans paid attention to him. His legend has become a part of the Cojímar wind and the atmosphere of Old Havana, and good feeling about him remains here. His influence on Cuban culture may be seen in the work of painters such as Carlos Piloto and Alexis Gelebert, musicians such as Lucia Huergo, dancers such as Laura Alonso and Roxana de los Rios, and writers such as Leonardo Padura, Marilyn Bobes, and Francisco López Sacha. His name has also been constantly referred to in Cuban newspapers and magazines because, more than his books, more than his sports records, more than the image of him cultivated for tourists in Havana, it is his simplicity and honesty as a man that inspires our respect and admiration. He is the one that everybody wants to give life to forever.

Hemingway's books have been widely read in Cuba, especially *The Old Man and the Sea*, *For Whom the Bell Tolls*, *A Farewell to Arms*, and the short stories gathered under the title *The Snows of Kilimanjaro*. However, many of his books are still unpublished in Cuba, a fact to be regretted, since most of us cannot read them. This fact also explains why it is Hemingway scholars, with access to most of his productive work, who have made the most exhaustive literary analyses of it, in papers presented at academic conferences held in Cuba.

Nevertheless, when I was asked to compile a list of the articles and books on Hemingway published in Cuba since the late twentieth century, I found, to my joy, that more than one thousand articles or essays on Hemingway and his work have been published here since 1970. I decided to start the list of references at 1970, because some earlier newspaper issues have been damaged by the passage of time and cannot be consulted. I have also selected only those works of popular journalism that analyze his literature in some way or that examine his Cuban settings or characters. Nevertheless, I hope the information I have left out can be added some day, to more fully reflect the range of our scholars' interest in Hemingway and his work.

Compiled Annotations

1970

Amare, Amaro. "Tres días de pericia, resistencia . . . y suerte [Three days of Skillfulness, Resistance . . . And Luck]." *Mar y Pesca* [*The Sea and Fishing*] Aug. 1970: 14–15. Magazine; organ of the National Fisheries Institute.
Deals with the Ernest Hemingway Tournament, and frequently refers to *The Old Man and the Sea.*

1971

Quiza, Ricardo. "Un nuevo campeón [A New Champion]." *Listos para Vencer* [*Ready to Win*] 25 May 1971: 3–7. Journal.

1973

Rego, Raúl. "A la caza del cazador [To Hunt the Hunter]." *Revolución y Cultura* [*Revolution and Culture*] Aug. 1973: 50–56. Organ of the National Fisheries Institute.
Full, detailed article about Hemingway's house, which eventually became a museum.

1974

Castro, José. "El baúl de los recuerdos [The Trunk of Memories]." *Proa y Puerto* [*Bow and Port*] Oct. 1974: 52–53. Organ of the Ministry of Merchant Navy and Ports.

Contains interviews of many fishermen who met Hemingway while fishing in the Gulf Stream.

Cruz, Mary. "Lo cubano en 'One Trip Across' [Cuba Reflected in 'One Trip Across']." *Anuario de Literatura y Lingüística* [*Literature and Linguistic Yearbook*] 1974: 101–29.

Analyzes story, especially the technical means used by Hemingway to achieve his desired effect with first-hand material that denotes how close he was to the Cuban atmosphere at that time. Explains why most of the symbols, thematic threads, settings, and secondary characters are Cuban. Even finds in the story the Ambos Mundos Hotel, the place where Hemingway was writing.

———. "Hemingway hasta el final [Hemingway Until the End]." *Bohemia* Jan. 1974: 8–13. Magazine.

Includes ideas that Mary Cruz was developing in her literary research on Hemingway. Her subsequent book, published some years later and including her own translation of "Poem to Miss Mary," is considered one of the most important contributions to Hemingway literary analysis in the island.

———. "Creto Gangá y Ernest Hemingway [Creto Gangá and Ernest Hemingway]." *La Gaceta de Cuba* [*Cuba Gazette*] July 1974: 26. Newspaper.

Compares Hemingway's works with those of Bartolomé Crespo Borbón. Borbón, a colorful writer of Spanish origin who lived in Cuba from 1811 to 1871, wrote works full of irony.

Masjuán, Miguel Ángel. "El hombre y la aguja [The Man and the Marlin]." *Bohemia* 24 May 1974: 36–37. Magazine.

Comments on the Hemingway Tournament, making reference to the American writer's *The Old Man and the Sea.*

1976

Fernández, Urbano. "Hemingway y el mar [Hemingway and the Sea]." *Cuba Internacional* [*Cuba International*] Sept. 1976: 74. Magazine.

Reference to one of Hemingway's passions is combined with discussion of his 1954 Nobel Prize acceptance speech.

Santovenia, Rodolfo. "Hemingway." *Mar y Pesca* [*The Sea and Fishing*] May 1976: 63. Magazine; organ of the National Fisheries Institute.

Includes an excerpt from *The Old Man and the Sea* describing Santiago's fight against the sharks and chronicles Hemingway's life, underlining his interest in sport.

1977

Hemingway, Mary. "Hemingway siempre estuvo a favor de la Revolución [Hemingway Was Always in Favor of the Revolution]." Interview by Luis Báez. *Mar y Pesca* [*The Sea and Fishing*] Sept. 1977: 68–69. Magazine; organ of the National Fisheries Institute.
Mary Hemingway, Ernest's last wife, discusses his opinions of previous presidents and his confidence in positive change in Cuba after 1959. Also provides her lasting impression of the encounter between Hemingway and Fidel Castro.

Recio, Renato. "¿Existió realmente Santiago, el pescador de 'El viejo y el Mar?' [Was Santiago, the Fisherman in *The Old Man and the Sea,* a Real Man?]." *Trabajadores* [*Workers*] 23 Dec. 1977: 8. Newspaper.
Explores the artistic and historical circumstances that influenced Hemingway's creation of the character Santiago.

1978

Fuentes, Norberto. "Nadie muere nunca [Nobody Ever Dies]." *Mar y Pesca* [*The Sea and Fishing*] June 1978: 3–4. Magazine; organ of the National Fisheries Institute.
Refers to an unpublished letter by Soviet reporter Román Karmén to Ernest Hemingway.

Fuentes Betancourt, Gregorio. "Una charla con Gregorio, el patrón de Hemingway [A Talk with Gregorio, Hemingway's Skipper]." Interview by Hubert Jerez Mariño. In *Bohemia.* 25 Aug. 1978: 4–6. Magazine.
Chronicles Hemingway Tournament and includes some quotations from Gregorio. The eighty-year-old skipper describes his first meeting with Hemingway. He also gives his version of the genesis of *The Old Man and the Sea.* They were approaching a boat in which an old man and a boy were trying to pull in a five-hundred-pound marlin, Gregorio recalled, when the old man said, "Yankis, get out of here." As they left, having deposited food near the old man's boat, they heard sharks mutilating the fish. The incident caught the attention of Papa, so Gregorio suggested the title to Hemingway.

Hernández Mendez, Mayra. "Ernest Hemingway: El Viejo y el mar [Ernest Hemingway: *The Old Man and the Sea*]." *Bohemia* 2 June 1978: 10–13. Magazine.
Includes short biography of Hemingway and literary analyses of his works. Hernández considers the homage paid to Cuban fishermen in *The Old Man and the Sea.* Also includes the story "Che ti dice la patria? [What Does the Fatherland Tell You?]."

Jerez Mariño, H. "Cuando el pez muerde el anzuelo [When the Fish Bites]." *Verde Olivo* [*Olive Green*] 28 May 1978: 44–47. Magazine of the Ministry of the Revolutionary Armed Forces; the name represents the color of Cuban soldiers' uniforms.

Journalistic article deals with the Sixteenth National Hemingway Tournament and the experiences of its third-place prize winners, the crew of *El Rayo* [*The Lightning*]. Attempts to draw parallels between the crew's experiences and the fishing scenes in *The Old Man and the Sea* and *Islands in the Stream.*

Mikoyan, Anastas. "Vale más ver una vez que escuchar cien veces [It's Worthier to See Once Than to Hear a Hundred Times]." Interview by Norberto Fuentes. *Revolución y Cultura* [*Revolution and Culture*] May 1978. Magazine.

Contains information Fuentes was gathering for his book on Hemingway and Cuba.

Morciego, Efraín. "Adios a las armas, reedición" [*A Farewell to Arms, Reissue*]. *Bohemia* 25 Aug. 1978: 29. Magazine.

Discusses the impact of Hemingway's novel on the Cuban reader.

Toural Camps, Eduardo. "Hemingway en el ruedo [Hemingway in the Arena]." *Revolución y Cultura* [*Revolution and Culture*] May 1978: 27–30. Magazine.

Refers to Hemingway's influence on short story and novel techniques during the twentieth century. Focuses on sources of information and the intensity Hemingway used for every action in his works. Uses *The Old Man and the Sea* as an example of clashing antagonistic values, out of which the individuality of old Santiago becomes a positive feature in the character, as a hyperbolic portrayal of man's fighting essence. Contains opinions about Hemingway taken from Enrique Lister's book *Nuestra Guerra* [*Our War*].

1979

Cruz, Mary. "Hemingway y la negación de la negación [Hemingway and the Refusal of Negation]." *La Gaceta de Cuba* [*Cuba Gazette*] Sept.–Oct. 1979: 3–5. Magazine.

Consists of a portion of what later became her book *Cuba and Hemingway on the Great Blue River,* published in 1981.

———. "Un cuento Cubano y revolucionario de Ernest Hemingway, veinte años antes y veinte años después [A Revolutionary and Cuban Story by Ernest Hemingway: Twenty Years Before and After]." *Casa de las Américas* [*Latin America House Magazine*] Sept–Oct. 1979: 126–33. Magazine.

A criticism of *Cosmopolitan Magazine*'s reprinting of "Nobody Ever Dies" in 1959, with an editorial note appended. Suggests that the effect was to soften Hemingway's political meaning in the story. Article contains Cruz's own analysis of the story, which later formed one of the chapters in her book *Cuba and Hemingway on the Great Blue River.*

1980

Quiza, Ricardo. "Ernest Hemingway." *Deporte Derecho del Pueblo* [*Sport, Right of the People*] Sept. 1980: 6–11. Journal.
Review of Ernest Hemingway International Marlin Fishing Tournament. Author recalls Papa's help in organizing the tournament and his approval to giving it his name.

1981

Cruz, Mary. "Cuba y Hemingway en el gran río azul [Cuba and Hemingway on the Great Blue River]." *Unión* [*Union*] Oct–Dec. 1981: 96–107. Magazine.
Keen analysis of Hemingway's fiction within contemporary literature. A detailed study concerning Cuban topics in Hemingway was fully developed in Cruz's book which has the same title.

———. "Nadie muere nunca" [Nobody Ever Dies]." *Trabajadores* [*Workers*] 2 July 1981: 2. Newspaper.
Brief comment about Hemingway's most outstanding narrative works, especially those about Cuba.

Expósito, Alejandro. "Hemingway en el golfo [Hemingway in the Gulf Stream]." *Control* Jan.–Feb. 1981: 49. Journal.
Fleeting commentary about Hemingway's new novel, *Islands in the Stream.*

Fuentes, Norberto. "De Buena Fuentes [From Lovely Fuentes]." Interview by Bernardo Marqués Ravelo. *Caiman Barbudo* [*The Bearded Cayman*] Mar. 1981: 28–29. Magazine.
Focuses on Fuentes's book, *Hemingway in Cuba.* Title contains a pun, *as fuentes* in Spanish means "sources of information."

———. "El Hemingway que esconden [A Hemingway Who Is Kept Censured]." *Bohemia* Sept. 1981: 40–43. Magazine.
Fuentes's criticism of two *New Masses*' articles, "Who Murdered the Vets" and "To the American Dead in Spain," which are almost forgotten because of Hemingway's sharp prose and denunciation. Fuentes's translations of both articles were published in the same issue.

García Márquez, Gabriel. "Mi Hemingway personal [My Personal Hemingway]." *Granma Resumen Semanal* [*Granma Weekly Review*] 13 Sept. 1981: 4. Newspaper; organ of the Central Committee of the Communist Party of Cuba.
Another Nobel Prize winner praises Hemingway's literary findings, which have influenced many later writers.

Marqués Ravelo, Bernardo. "Un pintor llamado Hemingway [A Painter Named Hemingway]." *Caiman Barbudo* [*The Bearded Cayman*] Apr. 1981: 30. Magazine.
Brief commentary on *Islands in the Stream.*

Otero, Lisandro. "Cuba en Hemingway [Cuba in Hemingway]." *Granma Resumen Semanal* [*Granma Weekly Review*] 12 July 1981: 4. Newspaper.
Journalistic work discussing Hemingway's admiration of Cuba and the Cuban Revolution and paying tribute to him on the tenth anniversary of his death. Same article published in May 1982 in *Cuba International.*

———. "Hemingway en cuerpo y letra [Hemingway in Letters and Soul]." *Revolución y Cultura* [*Revolution and Culture*] Dec. 1981: 54–60. Magazine.
Discusses Hemingway's training in journalism and the relationship between his journalistic works and Cuba. Points out the unusual style Hemingway used during his stay in China. Also refers to an article about Cuban fighters in "The Shot" in the April 1951 issue of *True Magazine,* which has not been published in Cuba.

Rodriguez Alemán, Mario. "Cuba y Hemingway en el gran Rio azul" ["Cuba and Hemingway on the Great Blue River"]. *Trabajudores* [*Workers*] 16 Dec. 1981: 4. Newspaper.
About the book of the same title, written by Mary Cruz.

Santos Caballero, Jorge. "Hemingway en boga: su novela Islas en el Golfo [Hemingway on Fashion: His Novel *Islands in the Stream*]." *Adelante* [*Go Forward*] 12 June 1981: 2. Newspaper.
Brief commentary on *Islands in the Stream.*

Santovenia, Rodolfo. "El Viejo y el mar [The Old Man and the Sea]." *Mar y Pesca* [*The Sea and Fishing*] Aug. 1981: 56–57. Magazine; organ of the National Fisheries Institute.
Deals with John Sturges's film, which was based on Hemingway's masterpiece.

1982

Bueno, Salvador. "Cuba y Hemingway en el Gran Río Azul [Cuba and Hemingway on the Great Blue River]." *Unión* [*Union*] Jan.–Mar. 1982: 170–72. Magazine.
Positive image of the writer introduces this commentary about Mary Cruz's book.

———. "En el Gran Río Azul [On the Great Blue River]." *Prisma.* May 1982: 41–42. Magazine.
Analyzes Cuba's presence in Hemingway's fiction and his reflection of it.

Campoamor, Fernando. "Hemingway y Cuba[Hemingway and Cuba]." *Trabajadores* [*Workers*] 3 Apr. 1982. Newspaper.
First article in a series by this Cuban friend of Ernest Hemingway. Features historical reference to Hemingway's ties to Cuba. Subsequent articles in the series were published weekly, on the same page, in following issues of *Trabajadores.* They are: "La casa del escritor [The House of a Writer]," 10 Apr. ; "Cojímar y el yate *Pilar* [Cojímar and Hemingway's *Pilar*]," 17Apr.; "La Habana

Vieja [The Old Havana]," 24 Apr. ; and "El Floridita [The Floridita]," 1 May. All reveal that it was no mistake that Papa had lived in Cuba for a long time, and that part of Cuba was reflected in Hemingway's narrative.

Cruz, Mary. "Cuba y Hemingway en el Gran Río Azul [Cuba and Hemingway on the Great Blue River]." Interview by Milagros Oliva. *Granma Resumen Semanal* [*Granma Weekly Review*] Oct. 1982: 7–8. Newspaper.
Friendly conversation to uncover Cruz's ideas on Hemingway's fiction, reflected in her book.

Fuentes, Norberto. "El ciudadano cubano Ernest Hemingway [The Cuban Citizen Ernest Hemingway]." *Granma Resumen Semanal* [*Granma Weekly Review*] Oct. 1982: 3–6. Newspaper.
Contains fragments of his book *Hemingway in Cuba*. The title is not hyperbole. Even though he said that he belonged just to Cojímar, Cubans regard Hemingway as a fellow Cuban, and hold him in their memory.

Fuentes Betancourt, Gregorio. "Entrevista [Interview]." Interview by Gilberto Dihigo. *Trabajadores* [*Workers*] 24 May 1982: 6. Newspaper.
Journalistic work deals with Gregorio's friendship with Hemingway, which they maintained until their deaths.

García Márquez, Gabriel. "Hemingway el nuestro [A Hemingway Who Is Ours]." *Bohemia* Dec. 1982: 12–17. Magazine.
Composed as the prologue to Norberto Fuentes's *Hemingway in Cuba*. Contains some photos of Hemingway in Finca Vigía and Cojimar, although they were eliminated in the book.

Hernández, Elena. "¿Hacia un nuevo mito? [Building a New Myth?]." *Nueva Gaceta* [*New Gazette*] Feb. 1982: 11. Magazine.
Criticizes Mary Cruz's critical work, *Cuba and Hemingway on the Great Blue River.*

Otero, Lisandro "Cuba en Hemingway" [Cuba in Hemingway]." *Cuba Internacional* [*Cuba International*] May 1982: 24–27. Magazine.
Discusses the fact that in August 1933, in a very dramatic moment of Cuba's social and political life, Pauline Hemingway witnessed a shooting on the street. Hemingway used this experience in *To Have and Have Not.* Also refers to Norberto Fuentes's book, then entitled Finca Vigía, and gives detailed description of Hemingway's and Fidel's mutual admiration.

Repilado, Ricardo. "Rescatando lo cubano en Hemingway [Rescuing Cuba in Hemingway's Works]." *Casa de las Américas* [*Latin America House Magazine*] Mar.–Apr. 1982: 159–63.
Deals with Cuban topics in Hemingway's fiction as they are seen in Cruz's *Cuba and Hemingway on the Great Blue River.* Praises Cruz's research method and admires Hemingway's reflections in his literature of the places he knew.

1984

Alvarez, Ismeldo. "Reseña de libros [Books Reviews]." *Revista de Literatura Cubana* [*Cuban Literature Magazine*] July 1983: 126–28.

Refers to Hemingway's Cuban fiction through analysis of Cruz's *Cuba and Hemingway on the Great Blue River.*

Caminada, Jaime. "Aquel soñador [That Dreamer]." *Deporte Derecho del Pueblo* [*Sport, Right of the People*] 30 May 1984: 19–24. Journal.

Shows the connection between the writer's life and his work, with special reference to the sports Hemingway practiced, such as hunting, boxing, and yachting. Also seeks to show Hemingway's sincere love for humanity. Journalist changed Gregorio's last name to Torres. Article reprinted in the magazine *Opina* [*View*] on 15 May 1987: 16–17.

Campoamor, Fernando. "Retrato de Hemingway [Hemingway Portrayed]" *Trabajadores* [*Workers*] Mar. 1984: 6. Newspaper.

Comments about pictures of Hemingway.

Castro Ruz, Fidel. "Hemingway nos ha acompañado en momentos cruciales [Hemingway Has Accompanied Us in Crucial Moments]." Interview by Norberto Fuentes. *Bohemia* 28 Sept. 1984: 14–19. Magazine.

Fidel declares his love at first sight of Hemingway's realistic narratives, acknowledges having read *The Old Man and the Sea* and other books, and admires Santiago's monologues and moral teaching in the story. The interview was included in Fuentes's *Hemingway in Cuba* and reprinted in *Granma Resumen Semanal* on 14 Oct. 1984: 7.

Diego, Eliseo Alberto. "*Hemingway en Cuba.* Un reportaje inagotable [*Hemingway in Cuba:* An Inexhaustible Report]." *Verde Olivo* [*Olive Green*] 6 Dec. 1984: 59. Magazine.

Commentary about *Hemingway in Cuba,* which Diego regards as a turning point in Cuban journalism and literature, since Fuentes discovered why Hemingway stayed in Cuba.

Fuentes, Norberto. "Hemingway: tanto de escritor como de hombre [Hemingway: He Has Much as a Writer and as a Man]." Interview by Rolando Pérez Betancourt. *Granma Resumen Semanal* [*Granma Weekly Review*] 30 Dec. 1984: 6. Newspaper.

Ideas of one man who has searched for the best of Hemingway.

———. "Hemingway en Cuba [*Hemingway in Cuba*]." *Revolución y Cultura* [*Revolution and Culture*] 1984: 14–21. Magazine.

Anticipates the launching of *Hemingway in Cuba,* presenting excerpts from his book to celebrate Hemingway's eighty-fifth birthday. The poem "The Man with the Golden Arm," presented here, was not included in Fuentes's book, nor were most of the photos used in this piece.

Nieto, Severo. "Su afición por los deportes [His Affection for Sports]." *Verde Olivo* [*Olive Green*] 10 May 1984: 50–51. Magazine.

Refers to the fact that Hemingway, a Nobel Prize winner, is one of the few writers who is remembered by means of a sports tournament. Sums up Hemingway's life and his stay in Cuba. Includes an anecdote showing Hemingway's certainty about Fidel Castro's destiny to make the Revolution, his refusal to believe reports that Castro had died in a battle, and his statement to that effect to Cuban journalist Luis Gómez Wangüermert.

1985

Aiguesvives, Eduardo. "Ernest Hemingway: acusioso y exigente lector [Ernest Hemingway: A Keen and Demanding Reader]." T*rabajadores* [*Workers*] 28 Feb. 1985: 2. Newspaper.

The way to approach reading Hemingway.

Bianchi, Ciro. "La Vigía de Hemingway [La Vigía of Hemingway]." *Cuba Internacional* [*Cuba International*] Dec. 1985: 50–55. Magazine.

Deals with Hemingway's house in San Francisco de Paula and gives details of objects in the rooms. Includes fragments from *To Have and Have Not,* the preface to *The Fifth Column,* the 1958 interview with George Plimpton, and quotations from G. García Marquez to support Hemingway's love for Cuba.

Castro Ruz, Fidel. "El mensaje de Hemingway [Hemingway Message]." Interview by Norberto Fuentes. *Cuba Internacional* [*Cuba International*] 1985: 28–31.

The idea that a man can be defeated but not destroyed was debated in the interview, which was included in Fuentes's *Hemingway in Cuba* and originally published in *Bohemia* on 28 Sept. 1984: 14–19 and in *Granma Resumen Semanal* on 14 Oct. 1984: 7.

Espinosa, Teodoro. "*Hemingway en Cuba* [*Hemingway in Cuba*]." *Casa de las Américas* [*Latin America House Magazine*] May–June 1985: 177–79.

Article about Norberto Fuentes's book with the same title.

Fuentes, Norberto. "Hemingway en Cuba [Hemingway in Cuba]." *Moncada* Jan. 1985: 26–29. Magazine; organ of the Interior Ministry of Cuba.

(The magazine was named for the Moncada Barracks in Santiago de Cuba attacked unsuccessfully by Fidel Castro and a group of rebels in 1953, seeking to overthrow Batista. This attack is generally regarded as the start of the Cuban Revolution.) Contains further excerpts from Fuentes's book on Hemingway.

Garrandés, Alberto. "Tras las huellas: Hemingway al desnudo [Searching for Footprints: Hemingway Uncovered]." *Revista Universidad de la Habana* [*Havana University Magazine*] Sept.–Dec. 1985: 243–45.

Positive criticism of *Hemingway in Cuba.*

1986

Alexeev, Alexandr. "Con Hemingway en Cuba [With Hemingway in Cuba]." *Bohemia* 29 Aug. 1986: 40–42. Magazine.

Former Soviet ambassador talks about Hemingway's stays in Cuba and his love of its revolution. Alexeev also discusses an invitation to Hemingway for hunting in Siberia and discredits reports that Mary Hemingway burned Ernest's letters at Finca Vigía.

Santos Moray, Mercedes. "El hombre de Finca Vigía [The Man at Finca Vigía]." *Trabajadores* [*Workers*] 3 July 1986: 6. Newspaper.

Discusses Hemingway's house.

This year saw publications about Hemingway's life and works by several well-known writers, including Fernando Campoamor, Mario Rodriguez Alemán, Romualdo Santos, Luis Sexto, and Mary Cruz.

1987

Guzmán, Mirtha, and Martha Delgado. "Aspectos significativos de la obra de Hemingway [Significant Items in Hemingway's Work]." *Varona* Jan.–June 1987: 119–32. Magazine from the Teacher's Training College Enrique José Varona in Havana.

Critical analysis of Hemingway's most important works: *The Sun Also Rises, A Farewell to Arms, For Whom the Bell Tolls, Islands in the Stream,* and *The Old Man of the Sea.* Considers whether these novels are socially engaged with reality or are concerned with essentially non-material and artistic issues. Also analyzes the stories "The Killers" and "Nobody Ever Dies," in support of the authors' hypothesis that Hemingway showed a highly moral intention in his works.

1988

Caminada, Jaime. "Nuestras aguas soleadas [Our Sunny Waters]." *Deporte Derecho del Pueblo.* [*Sport, Right of the People*] Sept. 1988: 10–12. Journal.

Discusses the Hemingway Tournament and the sea where Hemingway and his characters fished.

Fuentes, Gregorio. "El patrón del yate Pilar y compañero de pesca de Hemingway [The Pilar Skipper and Hemingway's Fishing Partner]." Interview by Julio San Martin. *Granma Resumen Semanal* [*Granma Weekly Review*] 26 June 1988: 3. Newspaper.

Gregorio reflects on the great team he and Hemingway made for fishing off Cuba.

Padura Fuentes, Leonardo. "No hay *Edén* para Hemingway [There Is No *Garden*

of Eden for Hemingway]." *Caiman Barbudo* [*The Bearded Cayman*]. June 1988: 24–27.
Analyzes Hemingway´s *Garden of Eden* as a novel and the social phenomena reflected.

1989

Fuentes, Norberto. "Nadie es una isla [Nobody Is an Island]." *Granma Resumen Semanal* [*Granma Weekly Review*] 30 Apr. 1989: 6. Newspaper.
Contains excerpts from Fuentes's book *Ernest Hemingway: Rediscovered,* which has not been published in Cuba, because Cuba lacked the material means to print books at that time, and because the author left the country.

1990

León Almeida, Ismael. "Cuarenta años de Torneos Hemingway [Forty Years of Hemingway Tournaments]." *Mar y Pesca* [*The Sea and Fishing*] May 1990: 10–15. Magazine; organ of the National Fisheries Institute.
Pays tribute to the Hemingway Tournament, which was named after him during his lifetime, an uncommon event on the island. Includes anecdotes about those sports events.

Masvidal Saavedra, Mario. "La iteración léxica como recurso estilístico y textual. Su uso en las obras de Hemingway [Lexical Interaction as a Textual and Stylistic Device: Its Uses in Hemingway's Works]." *Universidad de la Habana* [*Havana University*] Aug. 1990: 85–93. Magazine.
Stylistic analysis of Hemingway's most important works, including all those with Cuban topics.

Reytor Edilberto, Esmeralda Ávila y Oscar Atiénzar. "El Hemingway antifascista [Hemingway Antifascist]." *Adelante* [*Go Forward*] 9 May 1990: 2. Newspaper.
Analyzes Hemingway's participation in Spanish Civil War, his search for German submarines off Cuba, and his stay in Europe during World War II. Contains paragraph about *The Crook Factory,* Dan Simmons's fictionalized account of the counterespionage ring Hemingway set up in Cuba during that war.

1991

Valdés Pérez, Enrique. "El Museo Hemingway: el vivo espejo de su vida [Hemingway Museum: The Living Mirror of His Life]." *Bohemia* 6 Sept. 1991: 50–52. Magazine.
Interesting article about Hemingway's links with Cuban places. Contains important facts about his house, Finca Vigía, revealed by Gladys Rodriguez, former director of the Hemingway Museum. Among them is this quotation

from Carpentier's inaugural address at the museum: "Hemingway's house is going to be a mirror of his life. Everybody is going to see what surrounded Hemingway when thinking, writing, loving and living."

1997

Quevedo Arnaiz, Ned. "¿Quién asesinó a los veteranos? [Who Murdered the Vets?]." *Pedagogia* [*Pedagogy*] 97. Conference Memoirs. CD Rom.
Analyzes Hemingway's homonymous chronicle. Also refers to Hemingway's use of first-hand experience in *The Old Man and the Sea.*

1998

Bueno, Salvador. "Visitantes destacados: las estadías cubanas de Hemingway [Outstanding Visitors: The Cuban Stays of Hemingway]." *Bohemia* 6 Nov. 1998: 10–11. Magazine.
Refers to Hemingway's stays in Cuba and the reflection of those experiences in *To Have and Have Not* and *The Old Man and the Sea.*

García Arias, Nemis. "Hemingway: Struggle and Courage." *Newsletter* 4. 1–4 (Dec. 1998): 13. Sponsored by Cambridge Univ. Press. Journal; organ of the ALC-GELI (Cuban Linguists Association, Group of Specialists in English Language).
Asserts that Hemingway's characters are believable, the result of his vivid life experience, and that their struggles and courage illustrate Hemingway's ability, throughout his works, to employ apparently simple techniques to successfully attract the reader.

Masvidal Saavedra, Mario. "Del mito a la literature para entender la historia [From Myth to Literature to Understand History]." *Caiman Barbudo* [*The Bearded Cayman*] 30.280: 8–9. Magazine.
A study seeking to comprehend the relationship between Hemingway and history from a modernist point of view, as the North American writer witnesses certain events and reworks them in his literature through the use of ancient myths. Masvidal Saavedra uses semantic analysis to identify Odysseus in Harry Morgan and Prometheus in Enrique in *To Have and Have Not* and "Nobody Ever Dies" respectively.

Valle, Amir. "La otra mejilla o la cara equivocada de una promoción." [The Other Chick or the Wrong Face of Promotion]. *Caiman Barbudo* [*The Bearded Cayman*] 1997: 28–29. Magazine.
Exhaustive analysis of the last generation of Cuban writers, recognizing the influence of Hemingway and Malraux on the topic of war in the Cuban literature of the 1980s. This young author, together with two important writers, Eduardo Heras León and Francisco López Sacha, initiated *University*

for Everybody (academic lectures on television) with the course "Narrative Techniques."

1999

Arenal, Humberto. "El hombre y el mito [The Man and the Myth]." *Cuadernos del Sur* [*Journal of the South*] 15 July 1999: 47–48. A cultural supplement of the Spanish newspaper *Diario Córdoba* [*Cordova Daily*].
This famous play writer writes mostly about Hemingway's life. Remarks on coincidences between Enrique Serpa's *Smuggling* and *To Have and Have Not.* Observes that Carlos Montenegro's novel *Men Without Women* was published long before Hemingway's collection of short stories by the same name.

Ayala Rodriguez, Ida Maria. "La muerte en su obra [Death in His Works]." *Cuadernos del Sur* [*Journal of the South*] 15 July 1999: 44. A cultural supplement of the Spanish newspaper *Diario Córdoba* [*Cordova Daily*].
Argues that most post World War I writers, including Faulkner, Fitzgerald, and Hemingway, ran away from reality during the twenties, either physically or emotionally, to hide from frustration, disillusion, and mistrust, and asserts that it therefore was no coincidence that Hemingway depicted death in some form in everything he wrote. In her opinion, Hemingway's works continually restate the theme of man arising against all odds as voiced by Santiago in *The Old Man and the Sea:* "A man can be destroyed, but not defeated."

Benitez, Rafael. "Su Honda humanidad [His Deep Human Condition]." *Cuadernos del Sur* [*Journal of the South*] 15 July 1999: 59–64. A cultural supplement of the Spanish newspaper *Diario Córdoba* [*Cordova Daily*].
This late Cuban writer dedicates a long article to proving that Hemingway felt sincere solidarity with Cuban poor people, such as Leopoldina Rodriguez and Anselmo Hernández who, according to Benitez, were immortalized as Honest Lil and Santiago, in *Islands in the Stream* and *The Old Man and the Sea,* respectively. He also discusses certain other stories and the gossip that surrounds Hemingway's myth in Cuba.

Campos, Roberto. "Los golpes de "Papa [Papa's Blows]." *Cuadernos del Sur* [*Journal of the South*] 15 July 1999: 713. A cultural supplement of the Spanish newspaper *Diario Córdoba* [*Cordova Daily*].
Examines what he sees as the opportunist tendency of many biographers and journalists to discredit Hemingway as an ordinary man who just happened to win a touch of fame.

Cirules, Enrique. "El iceberg de Hemingway en la cayería de Romano [Hemingway's lceberg in Romano Keys]." *Casa de las Américas* [*Latin America House Magazine*] July–Sept. 1999: 35–44.
While perhaps overemphasizing Hemingway's affair with Jane Mason, Cir-

ules discusses other elements of Hemingway's legend. He confirms that Camagüey provided lodging for the American writer in Santa Martha, at the Grand Hotel and Colon Hotel in Camagüey, and at the Black Cat in Nuevitas, and also divulges true information on the German submarine that figured in *Islands in the Stream,* revealing that Hemingway had heard about the submarine when he navigated his yatch Pilar off the coast of Camagüey during World War II.

Del Río, Joel. "Al otro lado del esquema [The Other Side of the Frame]." *Juventud Rebelde* [*Rebellious Youth*] 7 Feb. 1999: 13. Newspaper.
Explains all the films based on Hemingway's novels and stories that were scheduled on Cuban television to remember Hemingway's centennial in Cuba.

Fournier, Carmen. "La mujer en sus cuentos [Woman in Hemingway's Stories]." *Cuadernos del Sur* [*Journal of the South*] 15 July 1999: 52–53. A cultural supplement of the Spanish newspaper *Diario Córdoba* [*Cordova Daily*].
This enthusiastic scholar approaches Hemingway's short stories from the perspective that the different behaviors given to his men and women characters may have sprung from Hemingway's sexual prejudices.

Hernández, Luis Rafael. "Cuba en el escritor [Cuba Inside the Writer]." *Cuadernos del Sur* [*Journal of the South*] 15 July 1999: 56–58. A cultural supplement of the Spanish newspaper *Diario Córdoba* [*Cordova Daily*].
Accurately compares Hemingway and the Cuban writer Enrique Serpa, as well as following all known traces of the origin of Santiago's story and concluding with a description of Hemingway's visible ties with Cuban culture.

León, Ismael. "Los peces de Mr. Hemingway [Mr. Hemingway's Fishes]." *Mar y Pesca* [*The Sea and Fishing*] June 1999: 15–17. Magazine; organ of the National Fisheries Institute.
Explores parallels between Hemingway's art of fishing and his life. Emphasizes Hemingway's contribution to ichthyology for the book *American Big Game Fishing in Cuba's Waters,* the Cuban national record he set in 1933, and his discovery of big-game fishing off the north coast of Cuba.

———. "Debilidad por la pesca [Weakness for Fishing]." *Cuadernos del Sur* [*Journal of the South*] 15 July 1999: 49–51. A cultural supplement of the Spanish newspaper *Diario Córdoba* [*Cordova Daily*].
Fragment of a bigger project León is developing on Hemingway and fishing. Contains many amazing details about trout and marlin taken from real life that Hemingway may have used in stories like "Big Two-Hearted River" or novels like *Islands in the Stream.*

Mesa, Raúl. "*El viejo y el mar* [*The Old Man and the Sea*]." *Cuadernos del Sur* [*Journal of the South*] 15 July 1999: 30–31. A cultural supplement of the Spanish newspaper *Diario Córdoba* [*Cordova Daily*].

What most strikes the sensibility of this university professor is the power of Hemingway's "non-human characters"—fish, sharks, and the sea—because they are very real, but not so easy to understand. Through polysemy he tries to discover and explain the variety of meanings in the different shapes of the natural creatures in the novel he regards as Hemingway's greatest.

Pérez, Armando Cristóbal. "Vida y trascendencia [Life and Transcendence]." *Cuadernos del Sur* [*Journal of the South*] 15 July 1999: 28–29. A cultural supplement of the Spanish newspaper *Diario Córdoba* [*Cordova Daily*].

Considers the Cuban reference as just a misunderstanding of the Cuban Revolution in the thirties. Acknowledges some coincidences among Hemingway's *To Have and Have Not,* Enrique Serpa's *The Trap,* and Alejo Carpentier's *The Pursuit.* Believes Hemingway's chief concern to be the exploration of the moral integrity of the individual, not his presence in society.

Plasencia, Azucena. "La habitación 511: Hemingway en el Hotel Ambos Mundos [Room 511: Hemingway in Ambos Mundos Hotel]." *Bohemia* 2 July 1999: 20–21. Magazine.

Discusses Hemingway's presence in this Havana hotel, and the fact that his room there, like Hemingway's house, has become a museum. Notes the celebration of Hemingway's one hundredth birthday by the siting of an academic conference there.

Quevedo Arnaiz, Ned. "El alma triangular de Hemingway." [Hemingway's Triangulate Soul]." *Videncia* [*Clairvoyance*] 1999: 65–68. A cultural magazine from Ciego de Avila.

Seeks to establish a Greek connection to Hemingway's life and its possible influence on his literature. Refers to symbols in *The Old Man and the Sea* that can be interpreted through numbers and geometric figures, as it was done in ancient times.

Quirantes, Carmen Zita. "El periodista en Cuba [The Journalist in Cuba]." *Cuadernos del Sur* [*Journal of the South*] 15 July 1999: 40. A cultural supplement of the Spanish newspaper *Diario Córdoba* [*Cordova Daily*].

Author points out that she has gathered in a bibliography most of the information about Hemingway published in Cuba. She also quotes Salvador Bueno's ideas about *The Old Man and the Sea:* "It's a book which has the characteristics of brevity and laconism and the concentrated force of his best stories, the living speech and the moderate and straight narration of facts."

Rodriguez, Gladys. "Un hombre cotidiano [An Everyday Man]." *Cuadernos del Sur* [*Journal of the South*] 15 July 1999: 65–67. A cultural supplement of the Spanish newspaper *Diario Córdoba* [*Cordova Daily*].

This former director of the Hemingway Museum shows how ordinary people intensively shared parts of their lives with Hemingway, who in return portrayed their way of living in his novels.

Sánchez Dotres, Mercedes. "Ernest Hemingway in the Territory of Camagüey." *Turespacio* [*Tourism*] July–Sept. 1999. In *Camagüey Magazine.*

Refers to Cirules's new publication about Hemingway, first known among his friends as *Hemingway's Iceberg in the Territory of Camagüey.* Points out most of the places that Hemingway visited there, according to Cirules.

Santos, Jorge. "Sentimiento y nostalgia [Feeling and Nostalgia]." *Cuadernos del Sur* [*Journal of the South*] 15 July 1999: 32–33. A cultural supplement of the Spanish newspaper *Diario Córdoba* [*Cordova Daily*].

This journalist demolishes the last stage of the literary division of Hemingway postulated by the Spanish critic José Barrio Marcos by using anthropological analysis to compare two of Hemingways novels from the fifties, *Across the River and into the Trees* and *The Old Man and the Sea.* Santos asserts that while *Across the River* was not artistically achieved, it anticipated the artistry of Hemingway's later masterpiece.

———. "Hemingway: entre la amistad, la guerra y la posteridad [Hemingway: Among Friendship, War and Posterity]." *Enfoque* [*Focus*] Apr.–June 1999: 34–39. A religious journal from Camagüey.

An exhaustive essay about Hemingway's leitmotif. Believes Hemingway's most affective friendship is in relation to common people. Argues that the most convincing feature of his narrative is the vigor of his main characters and asserts that Hemingway undertook each action himself before writing about it to let the reader live his emotions later through such fictional characters as Santiago.

Venegas, Guiomar. "El escritor en la television cubana [The Writer in Cuban Television]." *Cuadernos del Sur* [*Journal of the South*] 15 July 1999: 68–69. A cultural supplement of the Spanish newspaper *Diario Córdoba* [*Cordova Daily*].

Explains that while some of Hemingway's works were adapted for Cuban television, none of those programs reflected the Cuban topics. Also discusses the broadcasting of Cuban documentary films about Finca Vigía, the film version of *The Old Man and the Sea,* and a fictional program about Hemingway's ghost in Havana. The writer of the fictional program was Venegas herself.

Villar, Manuel. "Papa cumple cien años [Papa Is Going To Be One Hundred Years]." *Cuadernos del Sur* [*Journal of the South*] 15 July 1999: 55. A cultural supplement of the Spanish newspaper *Diario Córdoba* [*Cordova Daily*].

A brief analysis of Hemingway´s life. Cuba is seen as part of his legend.

2001

Peón, Carlos. "El viejo y el pincel [The Old Man and the Paintbrush]." *Antenas* [*Antennas*] Sept. 2001–Apr. 2002: 21–23. A cultural magazine from Camagüey.
Underlines an internet article that relates the discovery of some paintings signed by Hemingway. Peón believes that instead of imagining the works produced by his character Thomas Hudson in *Islands in the Stream,* Hemingway described some paintings by his friend Gatorno, a famous Cuban painter, to increase his legend in the island.

2002

Bianchi, Ciro. "Gregorio: El amigo de Hemingway [Gregorio: Hemingway's Friend]." *Juventud Rebelde* [*Rebellious Youth*] 20 Jan. 2002: 10. Newspaper.
Discusses the friendship of Hemingway and Gregorio, and underlines fact that Santiago was not inspired directly by Gregorio Fuentes, as Cuban journalists claimed after Hemingway's death.

———. "Hemingway, un ciudadano de Cojimar [Hemingway, a Cojimar Citizen]." *Juventud Rebelde* [*Rebellious Youth*] 27 Jan. 2002: 11. Newspaper.
Relates some interesting anecdotes about Hemingway, including his display of bad temper against the painters Massager and Juan David, the publication in *Bohemia* of *The Old Man and the Sea,* and a favor he owed to Cojímar fishermen.

2003

Bianchi Ross, Ciro. "La Habana de Hemingway [That Havana of Hemingway]." *La Jiribilla* [*The Jiribilla*] Nov. 2002. http://www.lajiribilla.cu/2002/n78_noviembre/1840_78.html. Online magazine.
Discusses the presence of Hemingway in Havana and his love for Cuba.

Cirules, Enrique. "The Pier Ernest Hemingway Knew." *La Jiribilla* [*The Jiribilla*] 2002. http://www.lajiribilla.cu/2002/n78_noviembre/1825_78.html. Online magazine.
Discusses Ernest Hemingway's presence in the north of Camaguey during World War II. Cirules refers mainly to some testimonies about Ernest Hemingway at the pier of San Fernando de Nuevitas.

Echavarría, Francisco. "¿Por qué un coloquio en Cuba sobre Hemingway? [Why a Hemingway Colloquium in Cuba?]." *La Jiribilla* [*The Jiribilla*] 2003. http://www.lajiribilla.cu/2003/n107_05/107_19.html. Online magazine.
Argues that Finca Vigía is the Mecca for Hemingwayans. Also discusses the importance of the Hemingway Museum now at Hemingway's home, its collection, and the colloquia that have been held there.

García Márquez, Gabriel. "Hemingway, el nuestro [Our Hemingway]." *La Jiribilla* [*The Jiribilla*] 2003. http://www.lajiribilla.cu/2003/n107_05/107_20.html. Online magazine.

Reprint of an essay written by Garcia Marquez for *Hemingway in Cuba,* by Norberto Fuentes.

Guerra, Alberto. "Finca Vigía [Lookout Farm]." *La Jiribilla* [*The Jiribilla*] 2002. http://www.lajiribilla.co.cu/2002/n78_noviembre/1842_78.html. Online magazine.

A short story about Hemingway and a young Cuban writer who wants to win the contest of short stories named after Hemingway. Written in May 1998, it was a prize winner for that year in the Ernest Hemingway Contest of Short Stories, and was first published in *Caimán Barbudo* [*The Bearded Cayman*] in 2000.

Heras León, Eduardo. "Nuestro, para todos los tiempos." [Ours Forever]." *La Jiribilla* [*The Jiribilla*] 2003. http://www.lajiribilla.cu/2003/n107_05/107_01.html. Online magazine.

Heras León recalls an encounter with Hemingway in the mid-1950s and its impact on his literary career and pays tribute to him at the closing ceremony in the Ninth International Colloquium in Havana.

2005

Núñez Jauma, Roberto "La colección fotográfica del Museo Hemingway [The Photograph Collection at Hemingway Museum]." *La Jiribilla* [*The Jiribilla*] 9–15 July 2005. Online magazine.

The Hemingway Museum contains a large and important collection of pictures taken by or about Hemingway, a collection that was Hemingway's treasure. It has been classified in three categories, according to the importance of the picture and whether or not Hemingway is present.

2009

Campoamor, Fernando G. "El Floridita de Hemingway [Hemingway's Floridita]." *La Jiribilla* [*The Jiribilla*] 27 June–3 July 2009. http://www.lajiribilla.cu/2009. Online magazine.

About the Floridita and Hemingway. Campoamor discusses Hemingway 's request for frozen double Daiquirís by Constante.

García Prieto, Miryorly. "Ernest Hemingway en el audiovisual cubano: entre el mito y la realidad [Ernest Hemingway in the Cuban Audiovisual: between Myth and Reality]." *La Jiribilla* [*The Jiribilla*] 27 June–3 July 2009. http://www.lajiribilla.cu/2009. Online magazine.

Here the author tries to demystify Hemingway, especially the persona of "macho man" that he represents for Cubans, by examining his destructive representation in Cuba's news media.

Montoto Pascual, Juan Manuel. "Tras los pasos de una leyenda [Following the Steps of a Legend]." *Juventud Rebelde* [*Rebellious Youth*] 14 Aug. 2009: 6. Newspaper.

This article discusses the paper presented by Andrew Feldman to the Twelfth International Hemingway Conference held in the Ambos Mundos Hotel, "Influence of Cuba in Ernest Hemingway's Narration, *The Old Man and the Sea.*"

Peón Casas, Carlos A. "Traducir a Hemingway [Translating Hemingway]." *La Jiribilla* [*The Jiribilla*] 27 June–3 July 2009. http://www.lajiribilla.cu/2009. Online magazine.

Discusses the way the Spanish translator Miguel Martínez-Lage translated Hemingway's dialogues in certain short stories, arguing that "I Guess Everything Reminds You of Something" and "Great News from the Mainland" are Cuban, as the setting is Havana. Peón Casas also asserts that the characters Mr. Wheeler and Stephen (Stevie) are Hemingway and one of his sons—probably Patrick with some characteristics from Gigi.

Pérez, Armando Cristóbal. "La amistad con Enrique Serpa: una primera impresión [Friendship with Enrique Serpa: a First Impression]." *La Jiribilla* [*The Jiribilla*] 27 June–3 July 2009. http://www.lajiribilla.cu/2009. Online magazine.

Analyzes books by Cuban writers, especially Enrique Serpa, in Hemingway's own collection in Finca Vigía.

Quevedo Arnaiz, Ned. "El desarrollo de la tragedia por oposición [The Development of Tragedy by Opposition]." *La Jiribilla* [*The Jiribilla*] 27 June–3 July 2009. http://www.lajiribilla.cu/2009. Online magazine.

Analyzes the ties to Greece found in Hemingway's best novel, *The Old Man and the Sea,* and the relation of his main character, Santiago, to Greek tragedy, a correspondence also revealed in Hemingway's own life.

Santos Caballero, Jorge. "El adiós a las armas que todos queremos [A Farewell to Arms that Everybody Likes]." *La Jiribilla* [*The Jiribilla*] 27 June–3 July 2009. http://www.lajiribilla.cu/2009. Online magazine.

Discusses the importance of analyzing the war to prevent war in the future.

2010

AIN. "Conmemoran encuentro entre Fidel y Hemingway." [Fidel and Hemingway meeting to be commemorated]." *Granma* [*Granma Daily*] 13 May 2010: 1. Newspaper.

Reports the celebrations commemorating the fiftieth anniversary of Hemingway's meeting with Fidel Castro on 15 May 1960, celebrations beginning in

Cojímar with an exposition of some photographs donated by the fishermen and some pictures of Hemingway.

Benítez Cereijo, Lourdes. "Conmemorarán medio siglo de encuentro entre Fidel y Hemingway [Fidel and Hemingway meeting will be commemorated]." *Juventud Rebelde* [*Rebellious Youth*] 29 Apr. 2010: 6. Newspaper.

Discusses the cultural program planned by the Hemingway Museum to commemorate the fiftieth anniversary of the meeting between Fidel Castro and Hemingway.

2011

Bianchi Ross, Ciro. "Otro día en Cayo Hueso [Another Day in Cayo Hueso]." *Juventud Rebelde* [*Rebellious Youth*] 5 Mar. 2011: 6. Newspaper.

A reference to Hemingway in Old Havana, while the writer discusses the development of life in this neighborhood in Havana.

Padura Fuentes, Leonardo. "Los misterios de Hemingway [Hemingway's Mysteries]." *Juventud Rebelde* [*Rebellious Youth*] 30 July 2011: 6. Newspaper.

Discusses mysteries concerning Ernest Hemingway's death and the role of the FBI in his final decision to commit suicide.

2013

Prensa Latina. "Estados Unidos digitaliza los recuerdos cubanos de Hemingway [USA Digitizes Hemingway's Cuban Memories]." *Granma* [*Granma Daily*] 7 May 2013. http://www.granma.cubasi.cu.

Reports that the Finca Vigía Foundation has been digitizing documents kept at Hemingway's home, among them, Hemingway's original acceptance speech, in Spanish, when he won the Pulitzer Prize.

———. "Abre hoy en Cuba Coloquio Internacional Ernest Hemingway [Ernest Hemingway International Conference Opens in Cuba]." *Granma* [*Granma Daily*] 20 June 2013.

Article concerning the international conference held in Hemingway Museum at Finca Vigía to commemorate the anniversary of Hemingway's first book.

Ruiz Worth, Andrés. "Aquí jamás estuvo Hemingway [Hemingway Was Never Here]." *Revista Sole* [*Sole Magazine*] 25 Apr. 2013 .

Describing Hemingway's presence in Havana, the reporter is surprised by a private restaurant owner who has a sign at the entrance denying Hemingway's presence in the place. "Durante los años treinta el escritor Ernest Hemingway pasó largas temporadas en el Hotel Ambos Mundos. Allí dejaría que el aire fresco de La Habana entrara por la ventana de su cuarto y le quitara la resaca de la noche anterior. Se embriagaría de pesca en el gran río y al atardecer, encerrado, escribiría libros, cuentos y artículos para diferentes revistas."

Hemingway's Books, Published in Cuba

1962: *The Old Man and the Sea.* Havana: Editora Nacional de Cuba.
1969: *For Whom the Bell Tolls.* Havana: Instituto del Libro. Ediciones Huracán.
1971: *The Sun Also Rises.* Havana: Instituto Cubano del Libro. Ediciones Huracán. (Prologue by Carlos Pujol. An essay about the process of creating the book.)
1975: *The Snows of Kilimanjaro.* Havana: Editorial Arte y Literatura. Ediciones Huracán. (Prologue by Felipe Cunill.) Short story collection.
1976: *The Old Man and the Sea.* Havana: Editorial Arte y Literatura. Ediciones Huracán.
1977: *A Farewell to Arms.* Havana: Editorial Arte y Literatura. Ediciones Huracán. (Prologue by Ricardo Viñalet.)
1980: *Islands in the Stream.* Havana: Editorial Arte y Literatura. Ediciones Huracán. (Prologue by Felipe Cunill.)
1980: *For Whom the Bell Tolls.* Havana: Editorial Arte y Literatura. Ediciones Huracán. (Prologue by Norberto Fuentes.)
1981: *Stories of Boxing.* Havana: Editorial Arte y Literatura. Ediciones Huracán. Volume II. Prologue by Omelio Ramos. A collection of chronicles and stories, two of which were written by Hemingway: "Fifty Grand" [110–41] and "The Battler" [141–52].
1984: *A War Correspondent Named Hemingway.* Havana: Editorial Arte y Literatura. Newspapers chronicle collection; written as introduction to *The School of Tough Guys: Lesson One,* by Norberto Fuentes.
2002: *The Old Man and the Sea.* Havana: Instituto Cubano del libro, Ediciones Especiales. Taken from 1976 edition of the novel; published in form of a tabloid and as introduction, "Un viejo, el mar, un pez y Hemingway [An Old Man, the Sea, a Fish and Hemingway]" by Enrique Cirules.

Books about Hemingway, Published in Cuba

1981: Cruz, Mary. *Cuba y Hemingway en el gran río azul* [*Cuba and Hemingway on the Great Blue River*]. Havana: Ediciones Unión. Ciudad de la Habana. A book of literary analysis dealing with nearly everything Hemingway wrote about Cuba. The writer, a very skillful critic, has devoted a series of chapters, each a literary essay, to a variety of topics, dealing with Hemingway's life and work in Cuba. She reveals how close his works were to Cuban reality, and identifies the modifications made to real places, people, and the background environment and events portrayed in his fiction. The editorial note written by Miguel Barnet follows the same pattern.

1984: Fuentes, Norberto. *Hemingway en Cuba* [*Hemingway in Cuba*]. Havana: Editorial Letras Cubanas.

One of the most accurate compilations of a range of testimonials and documents related to Hemingway's life and work in Cuba, including where he stayed and what he wrote. The introduction to this book was written by Nobel Prize Winner Gabriel García Márquez.

1995: Prado Laballós, José. *Tras las huellas de Hemingway en La Habana* [*Searching Hemingway's Footprints in Havana*]. Havana: Publicigraf.

A summary of some ideas developed by Norberto Fuentes in his book about Hemingway's presence in Havana. Its contribution is to show how much people in Cuba still love Hemingway, the Bronze God of Literature. There is some confusion when the book deals with areas outside the capital city. Romano Key, which Hemingway described in Islands in the Stream, retains its natural beauty, even though it is now connected to the mainland by a road of rocks and gravel across the sea. Coco Key, near Romano, is likewise connected to the mainland by a similar road, but the tourist facilities have been constructed in the midst of the key's wildlife.

1999: Cirules, Enrique. *Hemingway en la cayera de Romano* [*Hemingway in Romano Keys*]. Havana: Editorial José Marti.

Cirules, the writer who knows best all the keys and channels displayed in the coral reef north of Camagüey, has written passionately about a place almost forgotten in Hemingway's biographies. It was the setting of the third chapter of *Islands in the Stream* and also the site where Hemingway fought his sea war against the antifascists in 1942 and 1943.

2000: Silveyra, Jesús M. *Gregorio y Hemingway* [*Gregorio and Hemingway*]. Havana: Editorial Arte y Literatura.

A fictional account, based on an interview with Gregorio Fuentes, whose aged brain (he was then more than one hundred years old) added a great deal of fantasy to his facts. The Argentinean writer was attracted by Gregorio's stories, which the old man told with the assistance of an entourage of Cuban friends.

2002: Cirules, Enrique. *El Hemingway de Cuba* [*Hemingway of Cuba*]. CD-ROM produced by CITMATEL.

A CD-ROM based on Cirules's book. Includes some pictures and videos about Hemingway's life in Cuba.

Santos Caballero, Jorge. *En la otra esquina del ring* [*On the Other Corner of the Boxing Ring*]. Las Tunas: Editorial Sanlope.
A compilation of Santos's papers presented at Hemingway conferences in Camagüey and Havana. The topics include Cuba, Hemingway's, journalism and his literature on Cuban topics.

2009: Mariño Rodríguez, Osmar. *La Habana de Hemingway y Campoamor* [*Havana of Hemingway and Campoamor*]. Havana: Ediciones Extramuros.
Full anecdotes concerning the experiences in Havana of both writers, contemporaries who are linked in Cuba's literary and cultural memory. Mariño relates Hemingway's handing over of his Nobel Prize in Literature to Campoamor.

2011: García Prieto, Miryorly. *El mito Hemingway en el audiovisual cubano* [*The Hemingway Myth in Cuban Audiovisual Material*]. Havana: Ediciones ICAIC.
Discusses all the videos and films about Hemingway created by Cubans, who have enlarged Hemingway's myth in the island through their use of Hemingway as a character or reference in many audiovisual materials to hide their own bias about the author or to support Cuban social phenomena.

Conferences on Hemingway, in Cuba

1986, July: First National Colloquium, at Finca Vigía, Havana

1989: Symposium, Santiago de Cuba

1994, Dec. 8–10: Second National Colloquium, at Finca Vigía, Havana
Important Papers:
"From the Great Blue River to San Francisco de Paula," by Elisa Pérez
"Different Editions of the Novel *The Old Man and the Sea*," by Melba Rosa García
"Fishing Environment in Ernest Hemingway's Prose," by Ismael León
"Notes for a Study of Hemingway's Photograph Collection," by Roberto Nuñez Jauma

1995, July 16–21: First International Hemingway Colloquium, in The Old Man and the Sea Hotel at Marina Hemingway, Havana
Important Papers:
"Man and Nature in Hemingway," by Miguel Mejides
"The Writer's Artistic Sensibility," by Elisa Pérez
"The Magnetized Condition in Hemingway's Prose," by Francisco López Sacha
"Hemingway and Pablo de la Torriente Braw," by Ned Quevedo Arnaiz
"Crystallization of Hemingway's Style," by Eduardo Hera León

"Historical Panorama of Cuba Pseudorepublic in Ernest Hemingway," by Romelia Santana
"Hemingway in the Mind," by Enrique Cirules

1996, Sept. 23–26: International Ernest Hemingway Conference: The Journalism of Tough Guys, Havana
Important Papers:
"Hemingway in Cuban Press," by Carmen Zita Quirantes and lleana Ortega
"Hemingway: The Iceberg in *Islands in the Stream,*" by Enrique Cirules
"Tourism and History: *Islands in the Stream,*" by Esmeralda Avila
"From Journalism to Cuban TV," by Geomar Venegas

1996, Oct. 25–27: Third National Hemingway Colloquium, Havana
Important Papers:
"Culinary Preferences in Hemingway's Works," by Elisa Pérez
"The Key which Hemingway Called Paraiso," by Rafael Azcuy
"Hemingway in *The Old Man and the Sea:* A Teaching Experience," by Carmen Fournier
"Cuban Ngyc Ngay and Hemingway," by Jorge Santos
"*To Have and Have Not:* The Discovery of Transcendence," by Armando Cristobal Pérez
"Ernest Hemingway: From the Myth to Literature to Understand History," by Mario Masvidal Saavedra

1997, July 19–23: Second International Hemingway Colloquium, Havana
Important Papers:
"*To Have and Have Not:* The Discovery of Transcendence," by Armando Cristobal Pérez
"Ernest Hemingway: From the Myth to Literature to Understand History," by Mario Masvidal Saavedra
"Hemingway's Triangulate Soul," by Ned Quevedo Arnaiz
"Sixtieth Anniversary of the Publication of *To Have and Have Not,*" by Enrique Cirules
"Photos for an Archive: Evaluation of Hemingway Collection," by Roberto Nuñez Jauma
"Mr. Hemingway, Whom I Haven't Met," by Jorge Santos
"Afrocuban Elements Portrayed in *The Old Man and the Sea* and *Islands in the Stream,*" by Maria Caridad Valdés

1998, Apr. 31–May 3: Symposium: Hemingway Discovers Havana, Havana
Important Papers:
"Pablo de la Torriente and Hemingway: Influences and Overlapping," by Ned Quevedo Arnaiz

"Hemingway Off Cuba," by Ismael León
"Hemingway and Cuba: The Man and the Place," by Jorge Santos
"Cuban Context in *To Have and Have Not,*" by Armando Cristobal Pérez
"Antillanidad in *The Old Man and the Sea,*" by Teresa Buronate
"Hemingway in Jaimanitas," by Mario Masvidal

1998, Sept. 21–24: Academic Conference: Hemingway Discovers Havana, Havana
Important Papers:
"Spain in Cuba," by Mario Masvidal
"The Cuban Hemingway: The Modelo Brewery, a Forgotten Place," by Roberto Campos
"Hemingway in José Antonio Portuondo: A Vision of the Fifties," by Armando Cristobal Pérez
"In Hemingway: The Intellectual and Sportsman in Love with Cuba," by Ned Quevedo Arnaiz
"*The Old Man and the Sea:* Fact or Polysemy?" by Raúl Mesa

1998, Oct. 23–25: Fourth National Hemingway Colloquium, Camagüey
Important Papers:
"Sister Places: Cojimar and San Francisco de Paula," by Ernesto García Gutiérrez
"Hemingway 'Cubano Sato,'" by Giomar Venegas
"*Pilar* and Its Boat *Tin Kid,*" by Ismael León
"The Good and the Bad in Hemingway's Stories," by Modesta Correoso
"Ernest Hemingway, One of the Twentieth Century's Top Persons," by Carmen Zita Quirantes and Ileana Ortega
"Ernest Hemingway, a Twentieth Century Man," by Luis E. Colás

1999, June 7–11: Hemingway on the Great Blue River Conference, Havana
Important Papers:
"A Woman in a Story in Cuban Context," by Carmen Fournier
"*The Old Man and the Sea,* the Birth Perspective," by Ned Quevedo Arnaiz
"Intertextuality in Hemingway," by Armando Cristobal Pérez
"Feeling and Nostalgia to Reach *The Old Man and the Sea,*" by Jorge Santos

1999, Oct. 10–15: Third International Hemingway Colloquium, Havana
Important Papers:
"Hemingway in Contemporary Literature," by Enrique Cirules
"The Included Cuba in *To Have and Have Not,*" by Romelia Santana and Blanca Marrero
"Ernest Hemingway in the Cuban Radio," by Yolanda Portuondo
"Analysis of an Important Document," by Gladys Rodriguez

"Genesis of Hemingway's Library in Finca Vigía," by Frank Echevarria
"Hemingway the Fisherman and the Fiftieth Anniversary of his Tournament," by Ismael León
"The Cuban Music Collection in Finca Vigía," by Maria Caridad Valdés
2000, Oct. 13–15: National Conference Hemingway in the Year 2000, Camagüey
Important Papers:
"Modernity in Hemingway Narrative," by Angela Casanova, Grisel Llera, and Midiala Villar
"Hemingway Legacy," by Mircia Fernández, Maribel García, Marlén Bonet, Niurka Garcia, and Illeana Ferrero
"The Other Hemingway," by Mario Masvidal
"Hemingway, a Man on Foot," by Luis E. Colás
2001, Nov. 23–25: Hemingway and the Avant Garde Literature Conference, Camagüey
Important Papers:
"The Old Man and the Paint Brush and Cuba," by Carlos Peón
"Hemingway, Finca Vigía and Cuba," by Evelio González
"Hemingway in the Cuban Press," by Carmen Zita Quirantes
"*The Old Man and the Sea:* Heritage in Cuban Culture," by Ned Quevedo Arnaiz
"Ernest Hemingway: Myth and Fact," by Enrique Cirules
"Some Notes about Hemingway's Binnacle Notebook," by Alberto Issac Perojo
2003, May 19–21: Ninth International Hemingway Colloquium, Havana
Important Papers:
"Hemingway's Bells in Cuban Television ," by Geomar Venegas Delgado
"As Time Goes By," by Mario Masvidal Saavedra
"Why a Hemingway Colloquium in Cuba?" by Francisco Echavarría
2005, May 23–25: Tenth International Hemingway Colloquium, Havana
Important Papers:
"Hemingway," by Lisandro Otero
"Maracas, Mojitos and Women: Papa's Lost Paradise in Havana," by Mario Masvidal Saavedra
"*For Whom the Bell Tolls,* Hemingway's Documentary Novel," by Ned Quevedo Arnaiz
"Cuban television interviews Hemingway for his Nobel Prize," by Geomar Venegas Delgado
"The Spanish Civil War in Ernest Hemingway's Stories: Some Spanish Retellings and the Cuban one," by Carlos Peón Casas
"The Other Look at the Cuban Hemingway," by Armando Cristobal Pérez

2007, May 23–26: Eleventh International Hemingway Colloquium, Havana
2009, June 18–21: Twelfth International Hemingway Colloquium, Havana
Important Papers:
"Translating Hemingway," by Carlos Peón Casas
"Friendship with Enrique Serpa: a First Impression ," by Armando Cristobal Pérez
"The Development of Tragedy by Opposition" by Ned Quevedo Arnaiz
"*A Farewell to Arms* that Everybody Likes" by Jorge Santos Caballero
2013, June 20–23: Fourteenth International Hemingway Colloquium, Havana

Hemingway and Cuba

A Chronology

Plain Face = events in Cuban life
Bold Face = events in Hemingway's life

1886 Slavery is abolished in Cuba.

1895–98 José Martí leads a second war of independence.

Sinking of the USS *Maine;* United States declares war on Spain, February 15, 1898.

Battle of Kettle Hill/San Juan Heights, involving Theodore Roosevelt's Rough Riders, fought July 1, 1898.

1898–1902 Under Brig. Gen.Leonard Wood as military governor, U.S. occupies Cuba.

1901 U.S. Congress passes the Platt Amendment (formally abrogated in 1934)

1902 Brig. Gen. Wood's "whites only" immigration policy reinforces that pattern of immigration after 1898, prompting immigration mostly from Galicia, Asturias, and Canary Islands.

Tomás Estrada Palma is elected first president of the independent Republic of Cuba, 20 May 1902.

U.S. Marines leave Cuba.

1906 In the August War, 24,000 rebels, many black, stage an insurrection.

In September, 2,000 U.S. Marines land in Havana at request of President Palma under the terms of the Platt Amendment.

1907 Evaristo Estenoz establishes the Independent Party of Color.

1912 Estenoz leads a revolt in which 3,000 blacks die; Estenoz is killed on June 12 and his body is laid out in Moncada barracks, Santiago.

U.S. Marines return to Cuba.

1913–1921 Under presidency of Mario Menocal y Deop, Cuba experiences economic growth and great expansion of sugar plantations.

1916 The pope declares the Virgin of Cobre to be the patron saint of Cuba.

1917 Liberals revolt in a rebellion known as "La Chambelona" but are defeated; U.S. Marines return to Cuba to protect sugar plantations.

1921 Sugar market crashes; National Bank closes.

U.S. Marines once again return to Cuba.

1924 Gerado Machado y Morales of the Liberals wins election and establishes an authoritarian dictatorship, with support from the U.S. ambassador, Bert Crowder

1925 In August, the Communist Party is formed.

1928 Hemingway first experiences Havana as he transfers to a boat headed for Key West; he passes through Havana again during European trips in 1930 and 1931.

1929 Julio Antonio Mella, student activist and founding member of Cuba's Communist Party, is assassinated in Mexico on Machado's orders.

1930 In September, Directorio Estudiantil reemerges as a secret organization engaged in a violent, terrorist campaign against Machado.

Nicholas Guillen publishes *Motivos de Son,* a collection of poetry that places the Afrocubanismo movement in the foreground of Cuban arts; this movement, which energized Cuban art during the 1920s and 1930s, focused on negritude, on a poetic mestizaje or creole, and was admired by Hemingway.

1931 **Hemingway, returning from Europe to Key West (via Havana), meets Jane Mason on Ile de France.**

In March, Hemingway meets Gregorio Fuentes while fishing in the Gulf from Key West.

1932 **Between April and June, Joe Russell and Carlos Gutiérrez introduce Hemingway to marlin fishing from Havana; Hemingway stays at Hotel Ambos Mundos, spending time with Jane Mason.**

In September, the radical right issues its ABC Manifesto-Programme, an anti-black reform program based on Italy's fascist program of 1919.

1933 Economic hardship prompts a general strike in August and a revolution against Machado.

In early February, Hemingway begins To Have and Have Not.

On May 24, 1933, Jane Mason wrecks a car in which John and Patrick Hemingway are passengers; Jane Mason is hospitalized in Havana. She leaves for New York in July and wears a back brace for a year.

A short-lived semifascist ABC interim government, led by Céspedes, forms, only to be ousted by a coup staged by lower-level military officers; led by a mulatto typist, Fulgencio Bastista Zaldívar, they form a provisional revolutionary government and are joined by Estudiantil to form a student-soldier government that produces the "Proclamation to the People of Cuba."

Hemingway publishes his first nonfiction piece on fishing from Cuba, "Marlin Off the Morro: A Cuban Letter," which appears in the autumn issue of *Esquire*.

1934 Batista emerges as the arbiter of political power in Cuba, operating behind the scenes until 1940. Island under increasing military control; term *gangsterismo* coined; machine-gun shootings occur.

In April, Hemingway publishes first short story set in Cuba, "One Trip Across," in *Cosmopolitan;* it is later revised as first chapter of *To Have and Have Not.*

On May 6, 1934, Enrique Serpa publishes the short story "The Aguja," about an old fisherman, his grandson, and a great fish, in *Carteles.*

In May, Hemingway takes possession of new fishing boat, *Pilar.*

On May 29, 1934, Platt Amendment removed from Cuban constitution and a new treaty is signed with the United States.

On July 18, 1934, Hemingway begins a month-long marlin fishing expedition and scientific study of marlin, with Charles Cadwalader and Henry W. Fowler of the Academy of Natural Sciences of Philadelphia, setting off from Havana on *Pilar.* Reporter Richard Armstrong serves as photographer; Grant and Jane Mason often on board. Returns to Key West in early October.

1936 **In February, Hemingway publishes a story set in Cuba, "The**

Tradesman Returns," in *Esquire;* a revised version later becomes the second part of To Have and Have Not.

On April 14, 1936, Hemingway takes *Pilar* to Havana, returning to Key West on May 27.

In October, at Hemingway's request, reporter Richard Armstrong sends a picture and a thirteen-page letter detailing activities of a revolutionary group in Havana. Hemingway uses this material in *To Have and Have Not.*

In December, Hemingway meets Martha Gellhorn at Sloppy Joe's, Key West.

1937 In mid-October, while Hemingway is in Madrid, *To Have and Have Not* is published; much Cuban material is removed from published edition.

1938 Cuban novelist Enrique Serpa publishes *Contrabando.* Many parallels with *To Have and Have Not.*

1939 In February, Hemingway goes to Havana for a month. Begins *For Whom the Bell Tolls.* Writes two chapters.

In March, Hemingway publishes "Nobody Ever Dies," a short story set in Cuba, in *Cosmopolitan.*

In April, he publishes a nonfiction piece in *Esquire,* "On the Blue Water," with comments about an old Cuban fisherman; also in April, he returns to Cuba with Patrick on *Pilar,* and meets Martha.

In May, Martha rents Finca Vigía and Ernest moves in with her.

In mid-August, Hemingway leaves for Sun Valley, Idaho, returning to Finca on December 27 via Key West.

In late December 1939, at the Finca, Hemingway works steadily and hard on a novel.

1940 New constitution is approved in Cuba. Batista is elected president of Cuba.

World War II boosts Cuba's sugar economy; Cuba enjoys relative stability during Batista's 1940–44 term of office.

On August 26, Hemingway posts *For Whom The Bell Tolls* to Scribner.

In early September, he leaves Cuba for Sun Valley, returning to Cuba in late December.

1941 In late January, Hemingway begins Far East (China) trip, returning in May.

In late September, Hemingway leaves Sun Valley.

In December, he learns about bombing of Pearl Harbor on road trip back to Key West/Havana.

1942–43 In May 1942, Hemingway gains approval for counterintelligence operation ("Crook Factory") in Cuba. *Pilar* patrols through the summer.

In November, he turns counterintelligence operation over to Gustavo Duran; various antisubmarine patrols, long and short, are conducted through July 1943.

From late September though December, Hemingway stays alone in Cuba.

1944 In February, Hemingway ends *Pilar* patrols.

In April, he leaves Cuba on assignment as a war correspondent.

In May, he meets Mary Welsh in London.

In June, Grau San Martín is elected to succeed Batista as president, taking office in October; government moves to the right.

1945 In March, Hemingway returns to Cuba from the war.

In May, Mary joins Hemingway at the Finca.

In June, Mary is hospitalized from auto accident.

Between October and December, Hemingway, in Cuba, works on his Bimini novel, begun before the war.

1946 From January through mid-August, Hemingway, depressed, works in Cuba, continuing with the Bimini novel and beginning *The Garden of Eden*.

On March 23, Hemingway marries Mary Welsh in Havana.

In mid-August, he leaves Cuba for Ketchum, Idaho, saving Mary's life (endangered by complications from ectopic pregnancy) en route.

1947 In January, Hemingway returns to Cuba and resumes work on *The Garden of Eden*.

In April, Patrick visits and becomes very ill.

In June, Hemingway receives the Bronze Star at the U.S. Embassy in Havana. On June 17, Max Perkins dies.

In early August, Hemingway is implicated in a Cuban-based plot against the Dominican Republic.

In September, he leaves for Sun Valley, via Walloon Lake, Michigan. Mary stays behind to care for Patrick (still convalescing) and has the tower built at the Finca.

1948 In February, Hemingway returns to Cuba, where Malcolm Cowley interviews him for *Life* magazine.

In June, in an atmosphere of much corruption, violence, and

polarization, Carlos Prío Socarrás is elected to succeed Grau.
In August, Hemingway's lawyer, Maurice Speizer, dies.
In September, Hemingway leaves Cuba to travel to Italy with Mary. In December, he meets Adrianna Ivancich near Venice. He does not return to Cuba until late May 1949.

1949 In May, Hemingway works on *Across the River* on return trip to United States by boat; he arrives at the Finca in Cuba on May 27 and continues to work on *Across the River,* steadily and with excitement, through November.
In November, Hemingway indulges in bad boy episode with the whore Xenophopia during Mary's absence. On November 16, he flies to New York en route to Europe.
Lillian Ross interviews him before he sails on the *Ile de France.*

1950 In early April, Hemingway returns to Cuba.
In early June, he finishes *Across the River;* he has a concussion on *Pilar.*
In September, *Across the River and Into the Trees* published, but Hemingway is deeply depressed, even suicidal.
On October 28, Adrianna Ivancich and her mother, Dora, arrive at the Finca.
In December, Hemingway finishes the Bimini book, naming it *The Island and the Stream.* On December, he begins three intense weeks of work on *The Old Sea When Absent.*

1951 Early in the year, Hemingway works on *The Old Man and the Sea.*
On January 19, Adrianna returns to Italy.
By mid-February *The Old Man and the Sea* is nearing completion.
Between March and May, Hemingway works on *Islands,* claiming he is "finished" in May.
On June 18, Grace Hall Hemingway (Ernest's mother) dies; bells toll in San Francisco de Paulo.
On October 1, Pauline Hemingway dies.
In December, Hemingway stays in Cuba over the Christmas holidays.

1952 On February 11, Charles Scribner dies.
On March 10, Batista stages a successful military coup and returns to office.
In April, Hemingway begins "The Last Good Summer."
Life agrees to publish *The Old Man and the Sea.*

On September 1, *Life* publishes *The Old Man and the Sea,* selling more than 5 million copies in forty-eight hours.

On September 8, a trade edition of *The Old Man and the Sea* is published. On September 23, Hemingway receives a Medal of Honor from the Cuban Tourist Institute. During September, he catches twenty-nine marlin.

1953 On May 4, *The Old Man and the Sea* is awarded the Pulitzer Prize.

On June 14, Hemingway leaves Cuba for Spain and Africa, returning June 1954.

In July, Hemingway is awarded Cuba's highest civilian honor, the Order of Carlos Manuel de Céspedes, which is conferred by Batista the following year in July.

On July 26, Fidel Castro leads an assault on the Moncada barracks, an unsuccessful revolt against the Batista regime.

1954 On January 23 and 24, Hemingway survives two plane crashes in Africa.

In June, Hemingway returns to Cuba.

On July 21, Batista confers the Order of Carlos Manuel de Céspedes on Hemingway

On October 28, Hemingway is awarded the Nobel Prize in literature.

1955 Hemingway works on his "African" book most of the year; African "fantasies" are enacted at the Finca.

In April and May, Hemingway embarks on a fishing interlude with Mary.

In September, marlin fishing off Cuba for *The Old Man and the Sea* film.

On November 17, Hemingway receives the Order of San Cristóbal from the Batista government.

On Novermber 20, Hemingway suffers serious illness that keeps him in bed for sixty days.

1956 In February, Hemingway puts away the 856-page manuscript of his African novel and devotes himself to *The Old Man and the Sea* project.

Late April and early May, Hemingway leaves Havana to film marlin fishing off the coast of Peru for *The Old Man and the Sea.*

Between late May and September, Hemingway, in Cuba, works on World War II short stories.

In September, Hemingway leaves Havana for Europe, where

he meets Antonio Ordónez. His Africa visit is canceled by Suez Crisis.

He finds his 1920s notebooks and papers at the Ritz in Paris. He experiences serious health problems while abroad.

On December 2, Granma lands in eastern Cuba from Mexico and Castro takes to the Sierra Maestra mountains where, aided by Ernesto "Che" Guevara, he wages a guerrilla war.

1957 **In March, Hemingway returns to Cuba from Europe in poor health. He works and recovers steadily at the Finca.**

In August, Batista soldiers looking for rebels enter Finca and kill Hemingway's dog Machakos.

In September, Hemingway takes a short holiday in New York and then returns to Havana.

Between fall 1957 and summer 1958, Hemingway works on his Paris sketches and the *Garden* manuscript at the Finca.

Amidst political chaos and violence in Cuba, Hemingway dumps a cache of weapons in the ocean. In Cuba's revolutionary turmoil, Hemingway's position is difficult; he is a rich American with a leftist record on Spain.

1958 The United States withdraws military aid to Batista.

In October, Hemingway leaves Havana for Idaho, where he rents, then buys, a home in Ketchum.

1959 On January 1, Castro leads a nine-thousand-strong guerrilla army into Havana, forcing Batista to flee. Castro becomes prime minister; his brother, Raul, becomes his deputy; and Guevara becomes third in command.

On March 29 (Easter Sunday), Hemingway arrives in Havana from Idaho, where he prepares notes (now at the JFK Library) to brief Castro before his upcoming visit to United States.

In early May, Hemingway leaves Havana to follow bullfights in Spain.

On November 4, Hemingway returns to Havana from Spain where he is greeted by a big airport reception. He kisses the hem of a Cuban flag and calls himself a true Cuban.

1960 All U.S. businesses in Cuba are nationalized without compensation; the United States breaks off diplomatic relations with Havana.

In January, Hemingway returns from Idaho to Havana, where he works on a bullfight article for *Life* magazine.

On May 15, Hemingway fishing contest is won by Fidel Castro. Mary says Ernest told her that, in a brief conversation between Ernest and Fidel after the contest, Castro stated that he used *Bells* to plan revolutionary activities. On May 28, Hemingway finishes his bullfight article, having written 120,000 words for a 10,000-word assignment

On July 25, Hemingway boards a ferry for Key West, leaving Cuba for the last time.

1961 On April 17, the United States sponsors an abortive invasion by Cuban exiles at the Bay of Pigs; Castro proclaims Cuba a communist state and begins an alliance with the Soviet Union.

On July 2, Hemingway commits suicide at his home in Ketchum, Idaho.

Contributors

Emma Archer is Assistant Director of the American Language Institute at Indiana University of Pennsylvania. She received a master's degree in TESOL from American University in Washington, D.C., and a bachelor's degree in Spanish and English from Bethany College in West Virginia.

Lawrence R. Broer is a Professor Emeritus of English at the University of South Florida and the author or editor of nine books, including *Hemingway's Spanish Tragedy* (1973), *Sanity Plea: Schizophrenia in the Novels of Kurt Vonnegut* (1989), *Hemingway and Women: Female Critics and the Female Voice* (2002), and *Vonnegut and Hemingway: Writers at War* (2011).

Mary Cruz (Camagüey, 1920–2013) has written definitive historical and literary works, such as *Camagüey, biografía de una provincia* (1955), *El Mayor* (1973), *Sab* (1973), *Creto Gangá* (1974), *Cuba y Hemingway en el gran río azul* (1981), and *El hombre Martí* (2007). Her award-winning novels include *Los últimos cuatro días* (1988), *Colombo de Terrarrubra* (1994), *Niña Tula* (1998), and *Tula* (2001).

Joseph M. DeFalco is Emeritus Professor of English at Marquette University. He is the author of *Theme of Individuation in the Short Stories of Ernest Hemingway* (1961; rpt. 2011), *The Hero in Hemingway's Short Stories* (1963; 1968), and *Collected Poems of Christopher Pearse Cranch* (1971; 1986), and has written various scholarly articles on Hemingway, Frost, Poe, Cooper, and Whitman.

Albert J. DeFazio III is editor of *Dear Papa, Dear Hotch: The Correspondence of Ernest Hemingway and A. E. Hotchner* (2005) and associate editor of *The Letters of Ernest Hemingway,* Vol. 1 (2011). He also has contributed essays to several collections, notably "Contemporary Reviews" (in *Ernest Hemingway in Context,* ed.

Debra Moddelmog and Suzanne del Gizzo [2012]), "Skillful Teaching of *The Sun Also Rises* in the Secondary Schools" (in *Teaching* The Sun Also Rises, ed. Peter L. Hays [2012]), and "Bibliographic Essay: The Contours of Fitzgerald's Second Act" (in *A Historical Guide to F. Scott Fitzgerald,* ed. Kirk Curnutt [2004]).

William E. Deibler is retired after more than fifty years as a writer, editor, and journalist, the last thirty at the *Pittsburgh Post-Gazette.* He was a U.S. Air Force correspondent during the Korean War and an Associated Press correspondent before joining the *Post-Gazette,* where he served as legislative correspondent, city editor, managing editor, and senior editor. He has participated in literary conferences and written extensively about Ernest Hemingway.

Mary Delpino, daughter of Mary Cruz, has been a teacher of English as a second language for more than forty years. She has also worked as a translator.

Alma DeRojas is Director of Writing and Editorial Services for University Advancement at Florida International University (FIU) in Miami. She received her Master of Arts in Latin American and Caribbean Studies in 2004 from FIU, where she previously served as a coordinator at the Cuban Research Institute for three years.

Larry Grimes is Emeritus Professor of English in the Perry and Aleese Gresham Chair in Humanities at Bethany College. He is the author of *The Religious Design of Hemingway's Early Fiction* (1985). His essays and reviews have appeared in several anthologies and journals, including the *Hemingway Review, Modern Fiction Studies,* and *Studies in Short Fiction.*

The late **Keneth Kinnamon**, formerly the Ethel Pumphrey Stephens Professor of English at the University of Arkansas, was perhaps best-known as a distinguished scholar of African American literature and a passionate champion of civil rights. His many publications include books on Richard Wright and James Baldwin and articles on Ernest Hemingway.

Kelli A. Larson is Professor of English at the University of St. Thomas in St. Paul, Minnesota, and current bibliographer for the *Hemingway Review.* In addition to publishing articles on a variety of American writers, including Hemingway, Nella Larsen, and Ambrose Bierce, she is the author of *Guide to the Poetry of William Carlos Williams* (1995) and *Ernest Hemingway: A Reference Guide* (1990; rpt. 1992).

David B. Martens was hired at the *State Journal* in Lansing as a Michigan State University student. He later worked as a journalist at the *Detroit Free Press,* the *Los Angeles Times,* and Times Mirror cable television. He was publisher of the *Advertiser-Tribune* in Ohio and of the *York Daily Record* in Pennsylvania. He is now publisher of the *York Dispatch.*

Scott O. McClintock is an Associate Professor of Arts and Humanities at National University. His research interests include the literatures of the Americas, antiterror discourse critique, the Indian novel in English, and cold war cultural studies. He has published articles on these topics in several journals, including *South Asian Review, Comparative Literature Studies, Revista Iberoamericana,* and *Clio.*

Yoichiro Miyamoto is Professor of American Literature and Cultural Studies at the University of Tsukuba, Japan. His publications in Japan include *The Twilight of the Modern: Deconstruction of Imperialist Cultures and Construction of Postmodernism in the American 1930s* (2002). He is currently working on a book on American cold war cultural politics.

Kim Moreland is Professor of English at George Washington University. Her book, *The Medievalist Impulse in American Literature,* includes an extensive chapter entitled "Ernest Hemingway: Knighthood in Our Time." Her most recent article is "Hemingway and Women at the Front: Blowing Up Bridges in *The Fifth Column, For Whom the Bell Tolls,* and Other Works," in *The Mailer Review,* 5.1 (2011): 370–406. She has published many other articles on Hemingway and has presented many papers at Hemingway conferences.

Charlene M. Murphy retired in 2003 as Professor of English at Massachusetts Bay Community College, where she taught composition, American literature, and a special course on Hemingway. She has presented papers at several Hemingway conferences and has published in the *Hemingway Review.* She is now preparing a contribution for an edited collection on Hemingway and the natural world.

James Nagel is retired from his position as Eidson Distinguished Professor of American Literature at the University of Georgia and president of the Society for the Study of the American Short Story. Among his twenty-two books are *Stephen Crane and Literary Impressionism* (1980); *Hemingway in Love and War* (1989), which was made into a Hollywood film starring Sandra Bullock; *Ernest Hemingway: The Oak Park Legacy* (1996); *The Contemporary American Short-Story Cycle* (2001); *Anthology of the American Short Story* (2008); *A Companion to the American Short Story,* edited with Alfred Bendixen (2010); and, most recently, *Race and Culture in the Stories of New Orleans.* He has been a Fulbright Professor as well as a Rockefeller Fellow.

Yuri Paporov served as a cultural attache to the Soviet embassy in Mexico City in the 1950s and as a correspondent for Novosti in Havana in the early 1960s.

In testimony before a House Subcommittee in 1975, he was listed as a KGB agent. He is the author of ten books, including *Hemingway na kube,* originally published in Moscow in 1979 and later expanded and translated into Spanish as *Hemingway en Cuba* in 1993, the source of his essay here.

Ann Putnam teaches Creative Writing, American Literature, and Gender Studies at the University of Puget Sound. She has published short fiction, personal essays, and literary criticism in such anthologies as *Hemingway and Women, Hemingway in Context,* and *Hemingway and the Natural World.* Her recently completed novel, *Cuban Quartermoon,* came out of six trips to Cuba as part of the Cuban International Hemingway Colloquium. Her latest publication is the memoir *Full Moon at Noontide: A Daughter's Last Goodbye.*

Ned Quevedo Arnaiz (Ned Quividas) is Professor of English Linguistics and Methodology of Scientific Research at Camagüey University, Cuba, and author of several articles based on his research in linguistics analysis, literature analysis, and communication comparison between English and Spanish. He participated in the illiteracy campaign in Nicaragua. He is also a guest professor at the Universidad Estatal del Sur de Manabi, Ecuador.

Gladys Rodriguez Ferrero served as Director of the Museo Ernest Hemingway from 1980 through 1997. An expert on the life and work of Ernest Hemingway in Cuba, she serves as coordinator of the Agreement for the Preservation of the Documentary Heritage of the American writer Ernest Hemingway in Cuba, and is a Consultant Scholar for the International Consulting Scholar Group, working with the Editorial Project for the Complete Letters of Ernest Hemingway. She is a founder of Cuba's National Hemingway Colloquium (taking part in 1986, 1994, and 1996) and of the International Ernest Hemingway Colloquium, in which she has participated since its beginning in 1995, and serves as President of the Hemingway Chair of the José Marti International Institute of Journalism.

Jorge Santos Caballero is a critic, journalist, curator of fine art expositions and university professor. Devoted to the study of the works of Ernest Hemingway and Raúl Roa García, he holds a masters degree in Latin America and has written four books and several essays published in national and foreign journals and magazines. As a journalist, he also covers up-to-the-minute Cuban social and political events.

H. R. Stoneback is Distinguished Professor of English at SUNY-New Paltz. He has published, as author or editor, thirty books of literary criticism and poetry, as well as some two hundred articles on Hemingway and others. Recent books include *Reading Hemingway's* The Sun Also Rises (2007), *Hemingway's Paris: Our Paris?* (2010), and *Voices of Women Singing* (2011).

Bickford Sylvester, Emeritus Professor of English at the University of British Columbia, has organized conferences and published widely on the work of Ernest Hemingway. He has served on the board of the Hemingway Foundation and on the editorial board of the *Hemingway Review.* He is preparing a manuscript on *The Old Man and the Sea* for the Kent State University Press's *Reading Hemingway* series.

Index